Democratization by Elections

Democratization by Elections

A New Mode of Transition

Edited by
Staffan I. Lindberg

The Johns Hopkins University Press
Baltimore

Printed in the United States of America on acid-free paper
9 8 7 6 5 4 3 2 1

The Johns Hopkins University Press
2715 North Charles Street
Baltimore, Maryland 21218-4363
www.press.jhu.edu

Library of Congress Cataloging-in-Publication Data

Democratization by elections : a new mode of transition / edited by
Staffan I. Lindberg.
p. cm.
Includes bibliographical references and index.
ISBN-13: 978-0-8018-9318-6 (hardcover : alk. paper)
ISBN-10: 0-8018-9318-6 (hardcover : alk. paper)
ISBN-13: 978-0-8018-9319-3 (pbk. : alk. paper)
ISBN-10: 0-8018-9319-4 (pbk. : alk. paper)
1. Elections. 2. Democratization. 3. Comparative government. I. Lindberg,
Staffan I., 1969–
JF1001.D465 2009
321.8—dc22 2008046463

A catalog record for this book is available from the British Library.

The Johns Hopkins University Press uses environmentally friendly book materials, including recycled text paper that is composed of at least 30 percent post-consumer waste, whenever possible. All of our book papers are acid-free, and our jackets and covers are printed on paper with recycled content.

Contents

Figures

Tables

Foreword

This volume—which collects a groundbreaking set of empirical essays by a number of the best scholars in comparative politics today—comes at a timely and possibly historic moment in the course of global democratic change. Since 1974, the world has been swept by an unprecedented wave of transitions to democracy, nearly 100 in all. As Staffan I. Lindberg notes in his introduction and several authors explain in their chapters, many of these transitions have been forged in the crucible of the electoral process. Lindberg showed in his earlier seminal work on sub-Saharan Africa that even when elections left a lot to be desired in terms of freedom and fairness, the process of repeated, competitive elections tended to generate momentum for greater democratization (Lindberg 2006a, 2006c). This has been true both in providing a procedural means to achieve a breakthrough to genuine democracy, with opposition victories or at least improved quality of elections, and in the deepening of democracy with respect to political rights and civil liberties over time.

Lindberg's finding, that even deficient elections were worth holding and engaging because they could advance real democratic change, brought the debate about elections and democracy full circle, in a sense. In the early days of the third wave—for example, during the administration of Ronald Reagan—U.S. policy was criticized for an overemphasis on elections as the litmus test of democracy. Terry Karl and other political science critics exposed what they saw as a "fallacy of electoralism," stressing that (even multiparty) elections do not equal democracy, and that many of the regimes in Central America and elsewhere that were being accepted and praised as democracies were in fact hybrid regimes (Karl 1986, 1995). Yet, in Central America and beyond, elections gradually became increasingly competitive and fair, and during the 1980s, El Salvador gradually transformed from what Steven Levitsky and Lucan Way (2002b) call a "competitive authoritarian regime" to at least an electoral democracy (though in many ways still an illiberal one).

Beginning with the presidential snap election in the Philippines in early 1986, a new model of democratic transition began to emerge. An authoritarian regime like that of Ferdinand Marcos in the Philippines would hold a contested election figuring it could win it, or if necessary rig it. Of course, autocrats prepare to do the latter and have elaborate systems in place for intimidation, fraud, and control, leaving nothing to chance. But one should not underestimate the extent to which dictators like Marcos, General Augusto Pinochet in Chile, and Slobodan Milosevic in Serbia delude themselves into believing the fawning reports from their intelligence agencies that the people are behind them. What was significant about the Philippines as a model is that it was the first case in which a substantial domestic election monitoring effort successfully demonstrated fraud, mobilized nonviolent resistance against it, and helped to bring down the dictatorship and implement the real results of the election.

This model—using the space of contested elections and partial civic pluralism in a competitive authoritarian regime to mobilize for a breakthrough to democracy—has been a common mode of democratic transition during the second (post–cold war) phase of the third wave (Ackerman and Karatnycky 2005; Ackerman and DuVall 2000). It resulted in the peaceful transfers of power and transitions to democracy in Ghana, Senegal, and Mexico in 2000, and most recently in the Maldives in 2008, where the long-ruling parties in competitive authoritarian regimes lost elections and simply left power. It also produced the "color revolutions" that reversed electoral fraud and brought the election winners to power in Serbia (2000), Ukraine (2004), and Georgia (2003). More generally, as Bunce and Wolchik show in their chapter, the post-Communist world has most often and clearly hosted a distinctive "electoral model" of democratic transition, in which regimes become vulnerable through prior citizen defection, and then oppositions mobilize a new, "energizing" electoral strategy, evoking greater optimism about the chances for change and igniting much more widespread participation in the campaign and the voting.

Yet, it is important that we not get too carried away with the model of democratization through elections, which seems bound by time, geographic space, and structural conditions, and which is also clearly shaped by the relative skill, strength, and tactics of the regime and the opposition, as Andreas Schedler also shows in Chapter 7. In fact, it is a tribute to the editor that he has welcomed debate on his findings and arguments and included in this volume a number of essays that question or challenge them. Indeed, in his concluding chapter Lindberg himself notes that under certain circumstances, "repeated elections can also play a role in autocratization." As Ellen Lust-Okar notes in her essay, the model of democratization through elections has simply not traveled to the Arab world. After decades of formally contested elections in such authoritarian Arab regimes as Morocco, Jordan, Egypt, and Yemen, the Arab world still remains deeply stuck in what Daniel Brumberg (2003) has called "the trap of liberalized autocracy." These regimes fall short in various ways of the greater pluralism (and thus scope for electoral breakthrough) that one finds in more competitive authoritarian regimes—a context which Roessler and Howard in their chapter and Brownlee in his effectively identify as a key condition for democratization through elections. In Africa as well there are, as Lise Rakner and Nicolas van de Walle note in their chapter, quite a number of regimes, like Cameroon and Ethiopia for example, where the repeated holding of competitive elections has not moved the country closer to democracy, but where overbearing presidencies and numerous other factors keep oppositions weak and democracy at bay. And if we travel back a bit in time in Latin America, as Hartlyn and McCoy help us do here, we see authoritarian regimes persisting for a long time even in the midst of regular, contested elections.

There are also regimes that are rated as democracies by organizations like Freedom House but do not meet a more stringent test of electoral democracy, like that applied by Levitsky and Way. Moreover, as Rakner and van de Walle note, the strength of opposition parties seems to be a critical (if rather obvious) factor in enabling competitive elections to serve as a vehicle for democratization, and the remaining autocracies of Africa are plagued with chronically weak oppositions (and clever and ruthless presidential regimes that have kept them weak, while perpetuating authoritarian legacies).

This raises another challenge to the model, one which reintroduces the variable of historical time. Democratic transitions do not take place in a vacuum of time and space. They are influenced by what has gone before, particularly in neighboring countries (as much literature shows, diffusion is most powerful within regions). Democratic movements have drawn inspiration, organizational assistance, strategies, and tactics from successful democratic movements in neighboring countries, and even at times very distant ones. But recently, authoritarian regimes, panicked by the specter of more "color revolutions" diffusing to their own countries, have also learned lessons. They have noted the conditions and techniques that result in democratization through elections. They have realized (if they did not already know inductively) that granting too much political space for opposition mobilization and independent media is very risky, and they have tightened it rather ruthlessly. They have learned that election monitoring efforts and parallel vote tabulations work to document electoral fraud and show the real results, and they have frustrated and disabled such efforts. They have seen international flows of technical and material assistance to democratic parties, civic organizations, media, and election monitoring efforts result in empowered democratic movements, and they have sought to shut down and even criminalize these flows of assistance.[1] As a result of this authoritarian learning—and no doubt also the structurally less propitious conditions in many of these countries—contested elections have not produced democratic breakthroughs in recent years in post-Soviet countries like Russia, Belarus, Armenia, and Azerbaijan, nor in African countries like Zimbabwe, Ethiopia, and Equatorial Guinea.[2] Neither have they done so in Cambodia, where repeated elections since the end of violent conflict have instead coincided with the entrenchment of a more hegemonic form of authoritarian rule.

There are two other sobering aspects to the current moment. First, we are seeing a number of cases of alternation back and forth between authoritarianism and democracy, in countries like Pakistan, Bangladesh, and Thailand, with no clear prospect of consolidation or path to democratic improvement. In these cases, elections do not seem to play a clear role in moving democracy forward, only in making it possible. And in fact, elections also expose cleavages in society that can become polarized in the electoral process. This is not an argument against elections, but it is certainly a cautionary note about the institutional design and timing of them. One thing we learn from the literature on postconflict democracy building is that ill-timed (premature) elections and elections that make use of ill-considered institutional designs (which, for example, do not generate incentives to transcend identity divisions and commit to the democratic game) can actually deepen or renew violent conflict and even help to derail a possible democratic transition (Diamond 2006; Dobbins et al. 2007).

Finally there is the recent slump or even rollback of democracy globally. As competitive elections have proceeded in many countries around the world, the quality of governance in administrations produced by those elections has stagnated or deteriorated in a great many of the emerging democracies and near-democracies of the third wave. As a result, democracy has become more fragile, as many citizens become disillusioned. Sooner or later, a context of pervasive corruption, rank opportunism, and shallow commitment to the rule of law tends to degrade the electoral process as well, resulting in a loss of democracy in such countries as Nigeria, Venezuela, the Philippines, and Nicaragua in recent years. In fact, it is somewhat alarming to note that of the 25 breakdowns or reversals of democracy that have taken place from the beginning of the third wave in 1974 through the end of 2008, 17 of them (about two-thirds) have occurred in the past decade (beginning with the Pakistan coup in October 1999). In addition, Freedom House has noted a downward trend in levels of freedom in the past two or three years (Diamond 2008a, 2008b; Puddington 2008). If democracy is faltering in the presence of competitive elections, what is left of the theory that the repeated holding of contested elections improves the prospects for democracy?

In fact, key elements of the argument or model do survive. Whatever has happened since does not erase the historical facts: In the past two decades or so, many countries have moved to democracy, either gradually or fairly suddenly, with the process of contested elections playing a critical role. If the model of democratic breakthrough via an election in a competitive authoritarian regime has largely played itself out, it is not yet fully exhausted—as the small but revealing case of the Maldives has revealed in 2008. Nor can we rule out the possibility that at some future moment of regime decay and vulnerability, a contested election will become the pivot point for another major transition to democracy, even in a country as big and significant as Egypt or Iran. Theory, experience, common sense—and the empirical evidence in this book—all tell us that where the political terrain is most pluralistic and the opposition has best mobilized its strength, the model of democratization by elections is most promising. We can therefore look to Malaysia as one of the likeliest near-term prospects to experience a democratic transition by essentially electoral means, and Venezuela as a good prospect to return to democracy via these means.

I would offer two other conclusions, stimulated by the rich and diverse collection of excellent empirical analyses in this book. First, if the degree of pluralism in society, the strength of the opposition, and the ability to mobilize in and monitor elections all matter for the possibility of contested elections serving as an instrument of democratization, then we cannot forget the role of the international community. International assistance can make a difference in several respects: by pressing hybrid authoritarian regimes to open up more political and civic space and to allow more professional and independent electoral administration; by assisting that electoral administration technically to conduct better, fairer elections; by strengthening the capacity of political parties in ways that will help to strengthen the competitive ability of democratic opposition forces (and even perhaps gently encourage their coalescence in the electoral struggle); and by supporting domestic election monitoring efforts with financial and technical assistance and the presence of international observers as well. And if Pippa Norris is correct in her finding here that electoral system design also plays a key role in outcomes, then international actors can (and sometimes do) usefully advise on that as well.

Second, if—as I believe—the most urgent challenge for democracy in the world is to consolidate the new democracies that have come into being, then we cannot forget the electoral dimension. While it remains emphatically true that "elections do not equal democracy"—that there is much more to having democracy and making it work than free, fair, and truly competitive elections—it is also the case that institutionalizing free and fair elections, with rigorous and effective electoral administration, is a crucial aspect of democracy. And over time, it will have a tonic effect on the governance problem. If elections are rigorously free and fair, preempting or correcting most fraud and manipulation, then they provide the voters with a crucial instrument of accountability, to reward good performance and punish bad.

Over time, this crucial means of vertical accountability helps to generate incentives for elected officials to govern more honestly and responsibly, and it may also shore up support for democracy among citizenries that recognize the ability of democracy to bring political accountability and change (Bratton 2008). This is not the end of the story of what needs to be done to sustain and consolidate democracy, but it is a good beginning.

Larry Diamond

Preface

This volume offers a fresh way of thinking about elections as a new "mode of transition." It deliberately makes reference to the literature stemming from Guillermo O'Donnell and Philippe Schmitter's *Transitions* project of the 1980s. Since then, elections have been used merely as indicators of the end of a transition to democracy or as indicators of the level of democracy as a proxy for democratic consolidation if and when there is an alternation in power as a result of elections (the famous "turnover" test). In this volume, we find something new. Elections are not only indicators but also a *mode* of transition themselves, whereby electoral processes and incentives under certain conditions play causal roles in furthering democratization. However paradoxical it may seem, we argue that elections are not only an undeniable constitutive part of democracy, but their practice can also in itself foster democratization.

The insights and conclusions presented here have come together through multiple cooperative research endeavors over the last few years. Inspired by Andreas Schedler's work, particularly his 2002 article "The Nested Game of Democratization by Elections," my own book *Democracy and Elections in*

Africa came out in 2006. In the same year, Marc M. Howard and Philip G. Roessler's article "Liberalizing Electoral Outcomes in Competitive Authoritarian Regimes" appeared, as did Valerie Bunce and Sharon Wolchik's on post-Communist countries, "Favorable Conditions and Electoral Revolutions." In slightly different ways, we all made the same argument: Elections are much more than indicators; they are arenas, processes, institutional incentives, and opportunity structures causing democratization. Soon thereafter Axel Hadenius and Jan Teorell's article "Authoritarian Regimes: Stability, Change, and Pathways to Democracy, 1972–2003" added further to this argument. Meanwhile, Ellen Lust-Okar's very important articles offered contradictory evidence from the Middle East region, Jason Brownlee's book *Authoritarianism in an Age of Democratization* argued that elections in fact do not matter, and Terry Karl's earlier warning of the "fallacy of electoralism" got reignited attention. The debate was on.

At the African Studies Association's 2006 annual meeting in San Francisco, Larry Diamond from Stanford University, Joel Barkan from University of Iowa, Stephen Ndegwa from the World Bank, Carrie Manning from Georgia State University, and I held a roundtable session, "The Role of Elections in Democratization." Over 150 persons attended the panel session and encouraged us to continue wrestling with this topic. At the American Political Science Association's 2007 annual meeting in Chicago, two panels grappled with the subject. The panels included Andreas Schedler from CIDE/Mexico; Jonathan Hartlyn from the University of North Carolina–Chapel Hill; Jennifer McCoy from Georgia State University; Philip G. Roessler, then at Stanford University; Marc M. Howard from Georgetown University; Ellen Lust-Okar from Yale University; Axel Hadenius and Jan Teorell from Lund University in Sweden; Bryon Moraski from the University of Florida; and Gerardo Munck from the University of Southern California. Together we agreed that we had a joint research agenda in the making that deserved further exploration and collaborative expression.

To that end Larry Diamond and Marc F. Plattner facilitated obtaining a grant from the International Forum for Democratic Studies at the National Endowment for Democracy and have continued to give moral as well as substantial support to the project. The University of Florida through the International Center, Office of Research and Grants, the College of Liberal Arts and Sciences, the Department of Political Science, the Center for European Studies, Center for African Studies, and the Center for Latin America Studies also contributed financially. With that backing, I convened a workshop entitled "Democratization by Elections?" at the University of Florida from November 30 to December 2, 2007. Additional scholars who joined us were Kjetil Tronvoll from Oslo University in Norway, Lars Svasand from Bergen University in Norway, Pippa Norris from Harvard University, Diego Abente Brun from the International Forum for Democratic Studies, and Leslie Anderson, Lawrence Dodd, Goran Hyden, Philip Williams, and Benjamin Smith from University of Florida. For two and a half days, we scrutinized and debated intensely new and reworked papers. The conference deliberations formed the basis for the present volume.

In addition to the many scholars who have developed this project, I want to thank the excellent graduate students who helped organize the 2007 workshop, in particular Steve Lichty, Robert Scharr, Levy Odera, and Patricia Mupeta, led by the ever-present and dedicated Dominic Lisanti. Throughout this period, and not the least during the conference, I have had the continuous and unwavering support of Winifred Pankani.

I would like to offer final thanks to Larry Diamond for his continued support; to the anonymous reviewers for the Johns Hopkins University Press; to Ann Wainscott for excellent editorial assistance; to Carolyn Moser for very professional and sensitive copy-editing; and to all the contributing authors, whose engagement, critical views, and relentless work have made this book possible. We all believe this book makes an important and lasting statement on "democratization by elections" as a new mode of transition.

Staffan I. Lindberg
Gainesville, Florida

Democratization by Elections

Democratization by Elections

A New Mode of Transition?

Staffan I. Lindberg

In the opening of their 1978 seminal volume *The Breakdown of Democratic Regimes*, Juan J. Linz and Alfred Stepan wrote: "High priority for further work . . . should now be given to the analysis of the conditions that lead to the breakdown of authoritarian regimes, to the process of transition from authoritarian to democratic regimes" (Linz and Stepan 1978, ix–x). Indeed, they did not know at the time how right they were. The number of "free" (to use Freedom House terminology) democratic countries around the time their work was published was about 40, and the corresponding number is over 90 today. Many more nations that have not yet made a full democratic transition have seen substantial improvement in the characteristics we typically associate with democracy such as political rights, civil liberties, the rule of law, growth of a civil society, and strengthening of independent state bodies. Some countries have admittedly stalled, while others have even slid back into unequivocal authoritarianism. But as noted by many observers over the last decade or so, a distinguishing feature of the present period is that less-than-democratic regimes typically hold elections that at least on paper are multiparty and competitive.

This empirical phenomenon surely contributed to the broad category of "semi-democracy" used in the 1970s and 1980s, giving way to an increasing number of "democracies with adjectives" in the 1990s (Collier and Levitsky 1997). The established categories of political regimes—totalitarian, authoritarian, semi-democratic, and democratic—could no longer capture empirical realities in a meaningful way. Was it only a matter of adjusting the descriptive categories, however? Was it only that the spectrum of regimes spanning the space from authoritarian to semi-democratic regimes had become more differentiated, exposing partially new types such as nondemocratic, half-democratic, or "hybrid" regimes? Or did this change also indicate that the processes of authoritarian breakdown and democratic transition, respectively, had taken on a new dynamic where the old transition paradigm of prior regime types, hard- and soft-liners, and types of elite pacts were no longer defining for the "mode of transition"? Was the world witnessing the emergence of a new "mode" of democratic transition in the last decade of the twentieth century, a *democratization by elections* whereby authoritarian regimes sometimes break down, sometimes morph into new forms of electoral authoritarian types, and sometimes become gradually transformed into an electoral democracy? This is what this book is about.

"Democratization by election" is one possible explanation for the phenomena discussed here; stalled transition and reproduction of stable competitive authoritarianism and the gradual erosion into hegemonic electoral autocracy are others. All the chapters in this volume focus on interrogating the idea of an electoral mode of transition as a new empirical phenomenon in need of a theory. In the end, we also provide two building blocks for such a theory in Chapter 12 and Chapter 13, respectively. This represents the first collective effort at expressing the causal properties of a theory of democratization by elections as a new mode of transition.

A Changing Landscape

It is now, in 2009, almost 20 years since the most recent political transformation of Eastern Europe, Africa, and Asia started. Southern Europe and Latin America had taken the lead in what became known as the "third wave" of democratization, starting in Spain and Portugal in the mid-1970s. Those political changes—they were mostly political—were documented and analyzed in the *Transitions* project led by Guillermo O'Donnell and Philippe

Schmitter, giving rise to a whole new literature on "transitology," the study of regime transitions as highly contextual and indeterminate processes in which elites' idiosyncratic calculations carried the day. Larry J. Diamond, Juan J. Linz, and Seymour M. Lipset's far-reaching project *Democracy in Developing Countries* (1988), although putting more emphasis on structural aspects, largely supported the development of country-specific explanations building on process-tracing, mostly qualitative studies in contrast to the much more structural and quantitative bent of earlier approaches. Juan J. Linz and Alfred C. Stepan's large project *Problems of Democratic Transition and Consolidation: Southern Europe, South America, and Post-Communist Europe* (1996) entrenched the genuine tradition of regime studies but also advertised some of the differences on the "new" transitions that had taken place in Eastern Europe. In their wake, cross-national studies incorporating structural, institutional, and behavioral aspects have resurfaced, contributing to the methodological and substantial pluralism in the study of comparative democratization we see today.

The empirical landscape changed in several ways with the events following the fall of the Berlin Wall on November 12, 1989. A wide range of countries—eventually encompassing 27 states in the former Eastern bloc, almost 50 African nations, and more than 15 Asian countries—started to change. The sheer magnitude of this shift was in itself a watershed; from fewer than 50 in the early 1980s, 123 nations are presently "electoral" democracies, meaning they live up to a minimum definition of "polyarchic" democracy (Dahl 1971). Academically, the collapse of the Soviet empire along with the end of the cold war left scholars with increasing numbers of countries to study as cases of regime breakdown and transition. In Africa, Senegal's controlled democracy became increasingly unrestrained, while Madagascar's electoral regime has, from its inception in 1982, morphed into a real multiparty regime; and many more countries turned from socialist or military autocracies toward more democratic dispensations. Of sub-Saharan Africa's 48 countries (from 1993, when Eritrea became independent), over 20 can now be considered relatively democratic by a minimum standard definition, while another 20 or so (from Nigeria to Chad and Zimbabwe) are electoral authoritarian in various guises, and 5 countries remain closed authoritarian (Angola, Ivory Coast, Eritrea, Somalia, and Swaziland). Many of these newcomers to political transitions also faced another problem that was most pronounced in the former socialist "second" world but that in many ways pertained also to countries in Africa and Asia: the simultaneous transformation of not only the political system but also the economic system, from a highly regulated, state-planned and -controlled economy to a market- and capitalist-based one. These countries ventured into the unknown by attempting something that had never been done. In Eastern Europe and Eurasia, the former Soviet republics and satellite countries were thrown into turmoil, and transitions sometimes led forward and sometimes led backwards to increasingly authoritarian regimes.

With the help of particularly intensive international democracy assistance, the attraction of European Union membership, and more capable civil societies, the East European countries have largely fared well, becoming both successful capitalist economies and relatively democratic in two waves of "electoral revolutions" (see, e.g., Bunce and Wolchik 2006a; see also their contribution to this volume). Many of the former Soviet republics have made much less progress. Countries like Russia have regressed considerably, at least in political terms. While some countries are making great economic advances, the same cannot be said of attempts at political reform in Asia. While political transformation is under way some places, even if uneven and erratic, as in South Korea, Taiwan, and Thailand, it is being boldly resisted in China and Vietnam at the one end of the political spectrum and in Singapore on the other.

On the Role of Elections

Defined by the southern European and Latin American experiences, for a long time almost the entire literature on democratization was built on the O'Donnell and Schmitter (1986) approach to transitions as an indeterminate process of elite pacting and on the Linz and Stepan (e.g., 1996) emphasis on prior regime types and social mobilization. Both posited "founding" elections as the hallmark of a successfully completed process of disposing of an old authoritarian regime and installing a new democratic dispensation. According to the standard wisdom of the transitions literature, elections had little to do with the transition process except as indicators of its successful completion. This kind of approach was also adopted by many other leading scholars, such as Diamond (1996), Diamond and Plattner (1999), Günther, Diamandouros, and Puhle (1995), and Valenzuela (1992). The influential volume by Linz and Stepan (1996) even uses the date of the first election as the day when the transition process ended, and Bratton and van de Walle (1997, 195) adopted this approach in their analysis of Africa's post–cold war democratic experiments. Aspects like number of elections, voter turnout, competitiveness, and turnovers were used to analyze the degree or process of democratization (e.g., Barkan 2000, Herbst 2001; van de Walle 2001); the level or quality of democracy (e.g., Altman and Linán 2002; Foweraker and Landman 2002; Vanhanen 1997); or the consolidation of democracy (e.g., Diamond 1999; Fomunyoh 2001; Huntington 1991). Most of the existing cross-national measures of democracy also give empirical preference to election-related indicators (e.g., Polity IV; Freedom House surveys; Przeworski et al. 2000).

Assuming, then, that a democratic regime had been installed, scholars proceeded to the issue of democratic regime survival. With this came the upsurge of studies based on the democratic "consolidation" concept (Munck 2001a). Originally identified by O'Donnell (1992) as the prevention of an erosion or slow death of democracy—*democradura*[1]—this new area of democratic studies sought answers to the vital issue of when democracies could be said to have survived the threats of democratic breakdown. By and large, consolidation came to be depicted as the only game in town, focusing on attitudes and behavior in Linz's (1990) classic formulation, yet little care was taken to conserve the integrity of the concept. The original analytical meaning of "regime stabilization" was stretched and redefined to cover a panoply of problems straddling young democracies (Schedler 1998).[2] In none of the uses of the term in the literature, however, did elections play a part other than to signify the genesis or completion of consolidation. At best, elections were indicators of consolidation, as in Huntington's (1991) use of two alternations in power after successful completion of first elections—the "two-turnover test."

The inescapable conclusion is that neither the dominant theories of democratization nor those depicting consolidation of democracy have furthered elections as a causal factor in the democratization process. The insights from the earlier literature debating the meaning and role of elections in nondemocratic regimes in Latin America and Africa (e.g., Hermet, Rose, and Rouquié 1978) seemed forgotten. Gradually, a number of us who worked to disentangle the causal processes of regime breakdown and democratic transitions in Asia, post-Communist countries, and Africa started to question the wisdom of this approach. Perhaps Terry Karl's warning about the electoral fallacy—that elections do not a democracy make (Karl 1990; see also Karl 2000)—gave us one of the first leads, to be followed up by Carothers (1997, 2002a, 2002b), who cautioned about the over-reliance on elections as the most important venue for donors' democracy support. While Karl's point was to warn us against assuming that a country is democratic just because it holds what looks like reasonable multiparty elections, her observation made something else obvious: if competitive elections and democracy can be separated both conceptually and empirically, there is the possibility of a causal relationship between the two. As indicated above, it was not an entirely new agenda, but one that had been forgotten for quite some time.

It is of course impossible to conceive of representative democracy without elections (see, e.g., Clark 2000; Powell 1982, 2000; Zakaria 1997). As a core institution of representative democracy, elections are supposedly the only means of deciding who holds legislative or executive power. Yet, the widespread and often dramatic breakdowns of authoritarian regimes since 1989, leading to a mixture of sometimes barely democratic but more often "hybrid" regimes, made the obvious impossible to ignore. Multiparty elections that are sometimes even meaningfully competitive take place in undemocratic countries as well, and elections, *pace* the political system writ large, can be characterized by varying degrees of democratic features ranging from zero to a theoretical maximum. Elections can fill many functions, however, both in democratic and undemocratic systems (e.g., Powell 2000; Schedler 2006). Besides the obvious façade elections meant for international display only, multiparty elections can have important internal reproductive functions for regimes, such as enhancing legitimacy (e.g., Bayart 1978; Schmitter 1978), splitting the opposition into factions (e.g., Linz 1978), strengthening party organization and patronage structures (e.g., Hyden and Leys 1972), bringing opposition into the open for identification and targeting (e.g., Way 2006), and buying time for a later exit (e.g., Hermet 1978). That said, disappointments during a particularly bad experience with electoral practices—inflated voters' registries, political violence during the campaign and polling day, outright fraudulent voting and collation of votes, and intimidation of voters and political opponents—may stimulate activism in society even more than free elections (e.g., van de Walle 2002, 2006). Therefore, the positive effects of holding repetitive elections are not necessarily restricted to free and fair elections, at least not in the early stages of democratization. As the "mode of transition" expression implies, these and other strategies may fail and can also lead to unintended consequences as they interact with strategies and actions employed by opposition parties and third-party actors such as the courts.

A mode of transition, as defined by O'Donnell and Schmitter (1986), is a process that is to some extent indeterminate and dependent on the configuration of actors and institutions. This leads us back to Dahl's original and still very relevant formulation of democratization, as the outcome of increasing the costs of repression while decreasing the cost of toleration (1971). The formal rights and liberties that come with a multiparty electoral regime provide at least leverage for raising the cost of repression. Any form of popular mobilization and opposition party organization acts in similar ways. A little increase in media freedom and independence of bodies such as the judiciary, electoral commissions, and national commissions of human rights provides possible avenues for positive, if gradual, change. Elections can be manipulated, yes, but manipulation typically comes at a cost in decreased legitimacy that should function to lower the cost of toleration. Expectations probably play a vital role in elections becoming instruments of democratization, to paraphrase Powell (2000). The higher the expectations for more democratic freedom among the general public and opposition leaders, the higher the costs of repression. If the repetition of elections can create such pressures and incentives, they become what Rustow (1970) envisaged as institutions that can "trick, lure, even cajole" leaders to act in democratic ways that gradually institutionalize democracy and instill democratic beliefs in younger generations. It is not, however, a one-way street, nor is it inevitable, as the many examples of persistent electoral authoritarian regimes show.

Thus emerges the central focus of this volume. What, exactly, is the relationship between repetitive multiparty elections held in various types of regimes from hegemonic authoritarian systems to electoral democracies, and democratization? Are more elections always good for democratization, or do "flawed" elections in elected authoritarian regimes cause hybrid regimes to become more institutionalized rather than to move further toward democracy? Similarly, do institutions such as electoral management bodies, voter education organizations, parliaments, members of parliament, old parties, and other participating institutions learn and adapt to become "pro-democratic" and promote further democratization, or do they become entrenched and locked in by incentives for reproducing less than democratic practices? Can institutions, as Rustow (1970) once hoped, create democrats by setting incentives, locking actors in, learning, and adaptation?

Our work is part of a growing research agenda with much earlier precedents than is often remembered. Hyden and Leys (1972), Barkan and Okumu

(1979), Hermet (1974), and Wiatr (1962) were among the first to study the function and consequences of non- and semi-competitive elections in authoritarian regimes. In 1976, Guy Hermet, Richard Rose, Alain Rouquié, and Juan J. Linz brought together some of the best scholars in the field at the time to examine "the ballots most frequently held in the world today"; the result was the underappreciated book *Elections without Choice* (Hermet et al. 1978). Their investigation of electoral authoritarianism (although they did not use that label) found both negative and positive effects of elections "without choice." Schmitter's contribution on Portugal, for example, shows how elections served the rapid transition to democracy in the mid-1970s, while Linz's work on Germany, Italy, and Spain in interwar Europe demonstrated how elections in a polarized context contributed to the breakdown of the regimes. Delineating the principal lessons, Hermet (1978, 13–17) emphasized, in particular, socialization and learning processes under noncompetitive elections, leading to expectations and pressures from both elites and citizens that eventually become hard for rulers to control. Seligson and Booth's study of six nations in Central America (1995, 269–71) found that an opening up of the political space for citizens to associate more freely allowed people to mobilize and pursue their interests; over a few electoral cycles the initial mistrust between actors diminished among elites in the six countries. Similarly, Eisenstadt's (2004) detailed study of the protracted Mexican transition made the case that the repetition of elections made further gains possible by motioning actors to use electoral processes as the main platform available for challenging the ruling regime. Barkan (2000) concluded that the preparations for and holding of elections often gave rise to increased room to maneuver for actors even when elections were flawed. On the more theoretical side, Schedler's work on electoral routes to democracy (2002b) was concerned with the "nested two-level games" involving strategic dilemmas of actors in the context of structural ambivalence during transitions.

This theme and focal interest has been developed by a new literature emerging out of the landscape of almost universal electoralism of the late twentieth century, defined best, perhaps, by Schedler's edited volume *Electoral Authoritarianism: The Dynamics of Unfree Competition* (2006a). In this book, a rich set of studies centered on "unfree" elections as Tsebelian-inspired nested games involving principally citizens, opposition parties, and rulers. Focusing exclusively on the hybrid form of regime labeled electoral authoritarian regimes, it contributed greatly to our understanding of how the new world of "democratization by elections" may be possible or impossible in the current phase of history. The focus of that volume, however, was on the logic and mechanisms of electoral authoritarianism. There was a need to take the next step and focus exclusively on the causal relationship between competitive elections and transitions across the full range of regimes.

We have thus gathered in this volume a wide range of global and regional studies that in various ways evaluate the central hypothesis that in simplistic terms can be stated as follows: *The more elections, the more democratic the regime and society in general.* Building on the works cited above, and on Schedler's (2002b) insights, we can state a slightly more sophisticated version of this hypothesis: *De jure competitive elections provide a set of institutions, rights, and processes stacking up incentives and costs in ways that tend to further democratization.* The chapters in this volume interrogate this overall hypothesis using original datasets and present findings never published before.

Several subsidiary questions arise immediately. Do elections fill different roles in different types of electoral regimes, and if so, in which type(s) do they have positive versus negative effects on democratization? Is it better to start as soon as possible with elections, or is a more gradual, incremental process in which a new constitution and elections come later more likely to lead to a successful democratization? What happens when regimes hold flawed elections, manipulate institutions, and try to control electoral processes? The intuitive answer is perhaps that such practices are bad news for democracy and lead to electoral authoritarianism or worse. But can it also be that such practices provoke reactions and even stronger pressure for democratization, provide learning opportunities for pro-democratic actors, and reduce the leverage for future actions by the incumbents? Is there a causal relationship between repetition of elections and active, pro-democratic citizenship? Do "good" elections lead to more active and supportive citizens, or is it "better" that some flawed elections and manipulated institutions "provoke" strong reactions? A crucial part of the recent scholarly debate, which has also reverberated in policy circles, pertains to the value of elections at early stages of regime change, perhaps especially in postconflict societies.

Another aspect we interrogate concerns the role of expectations in the game over the cost of repression and the benefits of toleration. As with social phenomena like revolutions, can elections and electoral institutions further democratization in society in what we may call a self-fulfilling diffusion process? There is evidence in the institutionalist literature that strategies of individuals are mutually dependent on expectations of how other individuals will behave in ways that lead to self-fulfilling expectations. When the number of individuals is large and relations are impersonal, institutions play an even greater role in structuring such expectations and making them plausible. Are elections and such institutions structuring expectations and choices for entire nations of eligible citizens to the extent of in some sense "causing" future developments? Do elections play a crucial role in setting up a self-fulfilling prophecy because they can produce a critical mass of citizens believing that elites—from the military to political leaders—will act democratically and allow democratic rules to stay in place? And if so, when does this occur?

Expectations and incentives also affect the actions of political leaders. For example, when members of an autocratic regime are elected members of parliament (MPs) in competitive elections, they gain new interests and stakes. Power distribution within the party or ruling group changes in the new institutional setting of elections—even if these are not free and fair—and an MP with a strong electoral base builds his or her own base. Strong electoral support decreases the incumbent party's need to subvert electoral processes to stay in power; and the incumbent MP's incentive is now to retain the electoral game, even if the election is tainted by some irregularities, to secure his or her seat. When an independent electoral commission is formed, the commission's staff gradually find their future careers and status becoming linked intrinsically to preserving and upholding the rules of the game. To the extent that such a body does in fact have some autonomy, it has the possibility of inducing pro-democratic behavior among actors.

A third aspect of our overall hypothesis pertains to how parties behave during democratization and whether what they do matters. Is it important, for example, for opposition parties to unite, and do repetitions of elections teach them how and when to do this? Is solving such collective action problems one of the ways elections function to cause "better" or "more" democracy? Also, with the establishment of electoral rules and regulations, law adjudication and enforcement authorities are given a formal role in the protection of political rights. Does this create incentives for military, police, and security agencies as well as courts to advance their status, individual careers, and prominence on pro-democratic actions? Do elections and electoral institutions create a pay-off structure with costs and benefits where being anti-democratic is no longer necessarily the default option? The defense of the competition of ideas, the right of association, and the protection of property rights as well as legitimate procedures for hearing and adjudication in the social sphere are possible venues for asserting a new standard.

The overall hypothesis that we investigate in this volume thus consists of a number of suggestions of various, often interrelated, causal mechanisms. Hypothesizing a relationship between independent and dependent factors ought to be framed by a theory of causal mechanism to avoid unabashed empiricism.[3] The chapters of this volume engage not only in an extensive empirical analysis with global reach but also provide building blocks for a coherent theory of elections as a mode of transition. The final two chapters then synthesize and reformulate the combined theoretical insights in a statement of a theory of democratization by elections as a mode of transition.

Democratization—How Do We See It?

We are bound to pay closer attention to the concepts of democracy and democratization—the latter being the unified dependent variable of this collaborative exercise. How do we see it? It seems to us that the definition of democracy for empirical research is no longer that much of an contested issue. The baseline used in this volume is the mainstream definition descending from Joseph Schumpeter (1947, 269) and elaborated by Robert Dahl (1971, 3) in his concept of "polyarchy." Democracy requires not only extensive political competition and participation but also enforcement of political rights and civil liberties. Dahl's formulation has been further expanded by scholars like O'Donnell and Schmitter, Linz and Stepan, and Diamond in three ways to guarantee that the definition allows only fully "liberal" democracies to be called democracies. Under this extended definition a true democracy must have

1. an absence of "reserved domains" of power for the military or other political forces that are not accountable to the electorate;
2. established and effective mechanisms for "horizontal accountability" of officeholders to one another, constraining executive power and protecting the rule of law; and
3. extensive provisions for political and civil pluralism, as well as for individual and group freedoms.

The authors in this volume emphasize various aspects of this understanding of democracy to slightly different degrees, but there are no significant differences between us in terms of what democracy is, and is not. Generally speaking, we see democratization as a gradual process whereby a regime becomes increasingly democratic.[4] The study of such processes requires graded measures that can capture not only the divide between democracies and nondemocracies but also differences in degrees of democratic qualities among less-than-full democratic political systems as well as differences between minimally democratic electoral democracies and fully democratic liberal democracies. This reasoning translates into viewing democracy as an attribute of the political system.[5] An essentially different view is to approach democracy as an object in itself (Collier and Mahon 1993; Coppedge 2005; Munck 2001a; Sartori 1984; Schedler 2001a), which brings up the controversy between those who view democracy as a matter of difference in kind or degree (cf. Collier and Adcock 1999).[6] Scholars like Alvarez et al. (1996), Cheibub et al. (1996), Geddes (1999b), Huntington (1991, 11–12), and Linz (1975, 184–85) rather vigorously argue in favor of a dichotomous approach. Other scholars like Dahl in his formulation of polyarchy (1971, 2, 8; 1989, 316–17), and later Bollen and Jackman (1989, 612–18), Coppedge and Reinicke (1990), and Diamond (1996, 53; 1997; 2002), posit that democracy is always a matter of degree, with most countries along a continuum between full democracy and complete nondemocracy. We find ourselves largely in the latter camp. Democratization, thus, consists of processes that move any political regime closer toward this state of "expanded polyarchy."

At this point we need to display the full spectrum of possibilities of political regime transitions that this book interrogates, starting with the question of the general direction of change. Much of the focus in this book, and in others in our genre, is on what we label "democratization," meaning moving toward democracy. We should recognize that the process can be reversed and backtrack as well—as often happens in the real world. There is a special literature on the breakdown of democratic regimes, of course (e.g., Linz and Stepan's classic from 1978), but the phenomenon is more general than that. "Autocratization" *pace* democratization, can be fruitfully thought of as any move away from democracy.[7] This has important implications. For one, we should not expect either of the two generic directions of regime transitions to be teleological or given. For another, there are multiple pathways and outcomes of both democratization and autocratization. A move from a fully lib-

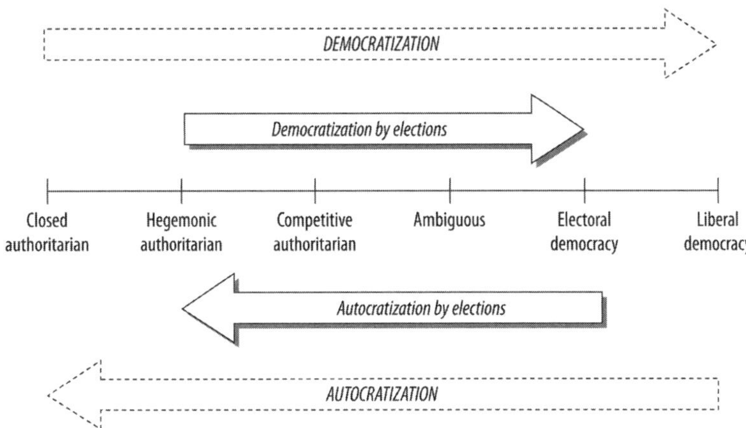

Figure I.1. Elections as a mode of transition: democratization and autocratization

eral democracy to the more limited version of electoral democracy is a very different path and outcome of autocratization than a change from electoral democracy to a hegemonic authoritarian regime. The reverse is also true with regards to democratization. Finally, we have a third alternative and that is regime reproduction when a regime successfully reproduces itself from time t to time $t + 1$. Figures I.1 and I.2 illustrate this reasoning.[8]

As is illustrated in Figure I.1, any move toward the right end of the spectrum is one pathway of transition toward (though not necessarily *to*) democracy. The same is true for the reverse process of autocratization, which in Figure I.1 runs from right to left. Elections as a mode of transition can be a factor both in democratization and in autocratization but do not play much of a role at either end of the spectrum. The shaded arrows indicate where on the continuum one would expect the role of elections to be higher. Many of the chapters in this volume testify to various ways in which elections have become a causal factor in democratization, but examples from Zimbabwe, Ethiopia, Russia, and perhaps Venezuela show how the interaction of ruling regimes and opposition in repeated elections can also play a role in autocratization. Finally, as evidenced most prominently by Ellen Lust-Okar's chapter, electoral authoritarian regimes that have managed to establish hegemony (by virtue of natural resource wealth or other means) can utilize electoral processes in regime reproduction. In the Middle East, many governing parties have turned the electoral game into what seems to be an equilibrium of competitive clientelism stacking up powerful incentives against collective action by the opposition. A key in their strategy has been making sure that the collective third principal actor—the voters—pressurize elected members for clientelistic goods that in turn make legislators easy prey for co-optation by the government.

This helps to explain the findings by Roessler and Howard in the fourth chapter. Many hegemonic electoral authoritarian regimes have proven relatively stable. Repetitive elections in such regimes are successful strategies for regime reproduction. Similarly, toward the other end of the spectrum, electoral democracies are also relatively stable; electoral processes and rights help to reproduce the limited democracy in these countries but do not contribute to the next type of transition to a liberal democracy. Most of the "action" in terms of transitions, where elections play a much greater role, is in the muddled middle in the transitions between competitive electoral authoritarian regimes, the ambiguous category, and electoral democracies.

Multiple Pathways of Democratization and Autocratization

This brings us to the next point. Most of the literature on both democratization and the breakdown of democratic regimes conceptualizes the key issue as a matter of *a* transition, or *a* regime breakdown. Reality is much messier than our models: most regimes do not make just one transition but several. There are many theoretical possibilities in terms of paths of transition (understood as going from one type of regime to another), as Figure I.2 illustrates. A closed authoritarian regime can move to either of the two electoral authoritarian regimes (hegemonic or competitive), to an ambiguous regime in the gray zone, or to one of two types of democracy, thus making five direct transitional paths; hegemonic authoritarian regimes have four possibilities; and so on. Using this very restricted typology, there are thus a total of 15 direct transitional paths of democratization.

To take just one example, Ghana became a closed authoritarian regime on December 31, 1981, when Jerry J. Rawlings and his approximately 30 compatriots staged his second military coup. In 1987 and 1988, one of the key figures in the Provincial National Defense Council (PNDC), Justice D. F. Annan led the process of starting competitive (but nonparty) local elections for district assemblies, which in effect became a transition to a hegemonic authoritarian regime.[9] In 1992, a new constitution was adopted, and national multiparty elections were held. Although the opposition eventually decided

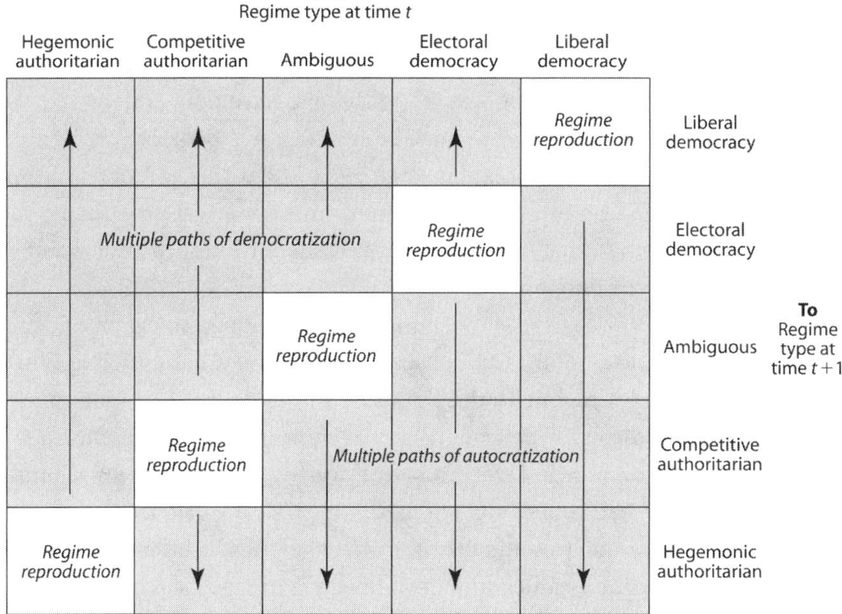

Figure I.2. Elections and regimes: multiple paths and outcomes

to boycott the legislative elections, it was clear that Ghana had transitioned to a competitive electoral authoritarian regime. Second elections were held in 1996 after a series of electoral reforms and significant expansion of civil liberties and media freedom. These elections were largely acceptable, the opposition won a significant one-third of the seats in parliament, but there were still a number of questions with regard to the "real" democratic qualities of the regime. The situation in Ghana was thus a prime example of the ambiguous category for a few years. With the elections in 2000 that led to a win for the opposition in both legislative and presidential elections, it was clear that Ghana had transitioned again, this time to an electoral democracy. By the time of the fourth successive elections in 2004, it was generally recognized that the expansion of civil liberties had gone as far as to merit the designation of Ghana as a liberal democracy.

Ghana's recent political history thus displays a "best-case" scenario in which a series of five transitions from one type of regime to another eventually led to a liberal democracy. The observant reader has already realized that there are then innumerable possible combinations of pathways whereby a country can move forward, backward, and forward again, be stalled for a number of years, and so on, and that the outcome of such paths of transition varies. There is no easy way to depict these many possibilities, but Figure I.2 illustrates them in a schematic way. Note that we have deliberately omitted the closed authoritarian regime type. The focus in this book is on elections as a mode of transition, and it is therefore self-evident that elections cannot be a mode of transition from closed regimes. In the interest of reducing the complexity somewhat, that category is not included. Even so, a large number of possible paths and outcomes remain.

At any given point in time (t), a country has one of the modal types of regime at the top of the figure. At a subsequent time ($t + 1$), the regime is any of the modal types of regime to the right side in the figure. This (sometimes temporary) outcome can either be the same regime type (reproduction), the result of a transition *toward* democracy, or the effect of a move *toward* autocracy. Each shaded cell represents one path, or process of transition, that in some ways is different from the others. Adding to the complexity, we know that the type of regime can change several times in steps, such as the best-case scenario in Ghana, progressively toward democracy, can move in a back and forth manner, or can backtrack along one of the possible paths of autocratization. In order to track a country's process, one has to take every outcome on the right-hand side, put it at the top of the figure, and start over.

Dahl (1971) concluded his study by positing that countries with unfavorable conditions are unlikely to transform into *stable* polyarchies in the near future. This prediction has been borne out for more than 30 years now. At the same time, the present volume examines a blind spot in Dahl's and many others' reasoning. While repetitive elections are the mechanism we know to work best to translate self-government into reasonable government in a modern state, if elections also in and of themselves further the spread and depth of fundamental democratic freedoms, it seems that they are no small or insignificant thing to note.

Organization of the Book

The following chapters are grouped in two main sections—Part I, which presents a debate on the democratizing power of elections, and Part II, which examines in more detail why elections sometimes lead to democratization and at other times underlie authoritarian regimes. Based on this collaborative effort, the final section of the book, Part III, develops a theory of democratization by elections.

The chapters in Part I debate the overall question about a general pattern of democratization by elections as a new mode of transition and after careful empirical analysis arrive at somewhat contradictory answers: "yes," "no," and "sometimes." The overall hypothesis of the project, that *multiparty elections provide a set of institutions, rights, and processes stacking up incentives and costs in ways that tend to further democratization,* based on my 2006 book, *Democracy and Elections in Africa*, is here interrogated in several ways. In the first chapter, I revisit the analysis of the 48 sub-Saharan African countries and find that the results previously reported remain robust. Despite great variation in structural preconditions and types and configurations of elites and reformists, the repetition of elections tends to lead to greater democratic qualities. About two-thirds of these countries have followed a path whereby civil liberties expand as a result of an uninterrupted series of consecutive elections. This provides strong evidence of the institutional effects of constraining and enabling certain types of behavior. The more elections, the more democratic a country becomes in Africa. The policy implications are obvious: Support for holding elections as soon as possible is a very important policy, but it must be continued over several electoral cycles. The current trend in Africa, where international actors often scale down pressure for elections after the first or second election, is a dangerous path.

In Chapter 2, Jennifer McCoy and Jonathan Hartlyn analyze the effects of elections in Latin America's 18 countries. Their finding that in at least two-thirds of the cases in Latin America countries have not followed such an "electoralist path" seems to fit the original mode of transition thesis formulated by O'Donnell and Schmitter in 1986. Rulers and reformers negotiated pacts and regime changes *before* elections were held. For many countries in Latin America there is actually a negative relationship between holding many elections and democratization—pointing to the successful use of elections to uphold, rather than break down, authoritarian regimes in the cold war era. McCoy and Hartlyn's analysis thus provides a cautionary note to policymakers: The role and function of elections is not unequivocally positive or "democratizing." Chapters 1 and 2 thus set the stage for a more conclusive debate on if, where, when. how, and why elections can have democratizing effects or not.

In Chapter 3 Jan Teorell and Axel Hadenius take the analysis to the most general level by using the widest possible scope geographically and temporally, controlling for a host of other factors and drawing on cross-sectional time-series data at best covering a global sample of 193 countries from 1919 to 2004. Two versions of the main hypothesis are tested. The first maintains that the holding of an election would yield democratizing gains more or less immediately. The second version instead holds that the historical experience with a prolonged series of elections would in the end yield a democratizing effect. They find support for both proposals, but for the most part the evidence that elections *universally* further democratization is relatively weak; it does not further democratization in all countries, at all times, and the average effect is therefore relatively small. When and where do elections matter then?

In the fourth chapter, Philip Roessler and Marc Howard make two principal contributions. First, they consolidate the emerging consensus on the principal categories of autocratic and democratic regime types and their operationalization. Roessler and Howard then map out the changes in regime types over the past 20 years using GPS technology. They find that the "action" is mostly in the middle: electoral processes in *competitive* authoritarian regimes tend to lead to electoral democracy, but this is less often the case in *hegemonic* electoral authoritarian regimes. At the other end of the scale, in *electoral democracies* elections do not improve upon democracy beyond the narrow electoral democracy. Thus, their findings can explain the weak findings in Teorell and Hadenius's study, and also the regional inquiries: Latin American countries have a for long time been "too democratic" for the democratization-by-elections mode of transition, and the countries in the Middle East "too autocratic," while many African and post-Communist countries seem to be right in the middle of more competitive electoral authoritarian regimes.

In Chapter 5 Jason Brownlee tests the robustness of the argument that the level of competition in elections under authoritarianism is the key feature, using a different methodological approach. His study adds to the value of the volume in several ways. He shows by descriptive analysis that if we look at the breakdown of all authoritarian regime (and he lists them), most of them lead *not to democracy* but to another authoritarian regime. Yet, he shows that autocratic regimes holding somewhat competitive elections before the breakdown are dramatically more likely to become electoral democracies.

In the final chapter of Part I, Pippa Norris makes a convincing argument that there is also variation between electoral systems in terms of the effects of elections on democratization. It is not only the level of competition but also the type of electoral institutions that matters. Proportional representation and other measures associated with Lijphart's plead for power-sharing approaches are associated with a greater degree of democratization in a series of elections—showing another way in which democratization by election varies spatially. It is a mode of transition influenced not only by actors and strategic interactions but also by adjacent electoral institutions.

In short, the chapters in the first part of the book reveal that while there is no universal phenomenon of democratization by elections, there is a clear pattern, especially in the post–cold war era, with countries whose authoritarian regimes allow for some amount of competition following an "electoral mode" of transition and achieving gradual democratization as a result. This raises an important question: Why do some countries become competitive rather than hegemonic authoritarian regimes?

Part II addresses this question by interrogating the electoral mode of transition as an indeterminate process, just as was done with the original formulation of modes of transitions. Looking closer at the causal processes involved, the chapters in this section start to lay bare the factors, calculations, and actions that cause elections sometimes to advance democratization, and sometimes prevent it. In other words, this section goes into the logic and mechanisms of elections as a mode of (non)transition.

In Chapter 7 Andreas Schedler takes as the focal point the strategic dilemmas facing rulers and opposition in choosing strategies in the situation of uncertainty that characterizes electoral authoritarianism. He thereby speaks directly to Brownlee's and Roessler and Howard's chapters but also to others in Part I which found that more competitive authoritarian regimes are strongly related to democratization after a regime breakdown. Going back in the chain of causation and analyzing the sources of increasing competition, cognizant of the fact that democratization must involve decreasing margins of victory and eventually turnover, Schedler finds that electoral manipulation by incumbents most often does not have an impact on competition, but that participation by the opposition—and in particular protests—are "magical" in making elections become tools of democratization.

This is a theme in terms of causal mechanisms that is followed up by Lise Rakner and Nicolas van de Walle in Chapter 8, which shows the importance of successful monopolization strategies by incumbents and failing strategies by the opposition in explaining why in many of Africa's presidential regimes, democratization by elections has stalled and not led to full transition to electoral democracies. Analyzing Africa's presidential regimes these authors document the means that incumbent rulers use, often successfully, to co-opt and disunite opposition political forces. These tactics seems to be more useful (to rulers) in more hegemonic regimes than in more competitive settings, a finding that again relates both to Schedler's findings and to those of several chapters in Part I.

In Chapter 9 Ellen Lust-Okar takes a closer look at hegemonic regimes in the Middle East and North Africa. Her analysis evidences an extreme form of the tactics discussed by Schedler, Bunce and Wolchick, and Rakner and van de Walle. These hegemonic regimes, with lots of resources (oil revenues) for patronage, have managed to give elections a particular function. What Lust-Okar labels "competitive clientelism" is a way to undermine the ability of potentially serious contenders to build power bases and compete with the ruling elites. By allowing relatively competitive elections based on patronage, these regimes ensure that all who run for legislative office ruin themselves and then need the regime's favors to recoup, fulfill promises to the electorate, fulfill social responsibilities, and get reelected. This tactic allows voters to have real power to select candidates and makes candidates compete among themselves for regime favors (thus preventing collective action), since the newly elected officials are pressured by the electorate for as much patronage as possible.

In Chapter 10 Valerie Bunce and Sharon Wolchik analyze a set of critical electoral episodes in a number of post-Communist countries in Eastern Europe and Eurasia. Providing a wealth of statistical and qualitative data, they show how the vulnerability of incumbent governments in combination with the opposition's use of a full-fledged "electoral model"—crucially including mass protests prepared well in advance of elections—have played a determining role in the success or failure in unseating electoral authoritarian regimes in former Communist countries. With great empirical detail, they also show how inspirational "lessons learned" were diffused from one country to another.

In Chapter 11, Bryon Moraski elucidates a crucial but until now unnoticed institutional factor that can be determining in whether or not a relatively well-mobilized opposition succeeds in making elections become democratizing. In his intense case-study comparison of Georgia and Armenia, we see how the success of the opposition in challenging incumbents in a hegemonic regime can depend crucially on institutional complexity and a multitude of possibilities in the "line of attack" on the regime. His analysis of the judiciary in election conflicts suggests that when the opposition has many entry points and can challenge the ruling elite on several fronts simultaneously, the strategic interaction game quickly becomes too complex for the ruling elite to handle and control. This is not only an important conclusion regarding causal mechanisms but also a lesson for constitution builders and institutionalists in democratization.

Part III of this book consists of two chapters. In Chapter 12 Andreas Schedler presents a new and more sophisticated theoretical model of the strategic dilemmas facing both rulers and opposition in less-than-democratic regimes. Building on his earlier work (e.g., Schedler 2002b, 2006a, 2006b), he details the fundamental principles of the two-level game of regime and elections and shows how the two parties' actions shape and change costs and benefits in their future interaction.

The final chapter is more than a summation. It focuses on a theory-building exercise in which I seek to build on and extend the proven usefulness of O'Donnell and Schmitter's mode-of-transition model to include perhaps the most significant feature of the last few decades: holding a series of elections *before* a transition to democracy takes place. Building on Dahl's (1971) theory of polyarchy, insights from Tsebelis (1990) about the logic of multilevel games with varying outcomes, Schedler's theoretical model in the previous chapter, and the key theoretical and empirical insights gathered in this volume by a series of leading scholars in the field, this final chapter provides a theoretical synthesis in a theory of elections as a mode of transition.

PART I / The Democratizing Power of Elections

A Debate

This first part of the volume spells out theoretical expectations and empirically interrogates the relationship between elections and democratization across the world. The six chapters build to a large extent on quantitative explorations, some of which are more advanced than others but are all backed up with large amounts of qualitative case knowledge by the authors. As suggested by the Introduction, some authors find limited or very little evidence of a democratizing power of elections; others find substantial and convincing patterns in the data. There is regional variation: Latin America seems to display much less, if any, evidence of an independent value of holding competitive elections, whereas we see the opposite in Africa and in many post-Communist countries. There is also temporal variation, and the end of the cold war seems to have been a watershed. The chapters differ in terms of methodological choices, unit of analysis (country, country-year, regime type, or election), and indicators for independent and dependent variables. Nevertheless, these chapters paint a relatively consistent picture of a new pattern where elections have emerged as a new mode of democratic transition. That these alternative approaches produce similar substantive findings strengthens our confidence that democratization by election has become a new mode of transition.

CHAPTER ONE

The Power of Elections in Africa Revisited

Staffan I. Lindberg

When the "third wave" of democratization hit the African continent, there was an outburst of optimistic scholarship voicing hopes for a "second liberation" (e.g., Ayittey 1992; Hyden and Bratton 1992) that soon turned into sour commentaries on the lack of "real" change (e.g., Carothers 1997; Joseph 1998). Luckily, we seem to have moved on from that unproductive and sometimes highly emotional debate. The picture is in reality mixed, with some countries moving ahead and becoming more free (e.g., Ghana) while others drag their feet (e.g., Angola) or regress (e.g., Zimbabwe). The picture is also mixed within countries as certain civil liberties such as freedom of association are successfully upheld while others such as equality under the law are not. In the political realm, elections can be free and fair while media coverage remains highly biased and political opponents are jailed after the elections to quell opposition. Unevenness and ambiguity characterize most countries' histories as well as cross-national developments.

The first 5 to 10 years of this period also saw a heated debate on the relative importance of international versus domestic factors as forces of change. Again, that "dialogue of the deaf" (Chabal 1998) has largely given way to a more productive acknowledgment that international actors and factors played, and continue to play, a larger role in some countries than in others, with their importance also varying over time. Our most important job as scholars is to try to measure and weight such variance without reaching conclusions based on impressionistic or partial data for the sake of winning arguments.

After 30 years of scholarship on Africa reporting mainly "bad news" that fed into a view of African "exceptionalism," the reinvigoration of research on African politics from the 1990s onwards has been refreshing. Not only is it a relief to be able to report on more positive findings such as clean elections, alternations in power, populations supportive of democracy, the end of civil wars, the failure of attempts to subvert democratization processes, and the like, but this new outlook has also brought renewed interest in Africa among young scholars and students, promising a wealth of comparative studies.

Africa is becoming part of the "normal" world again, a place where issues and theories that have been worked on in other areas can now also be studied. Without any pretense of doing justice to all contributions or being representative, new research on democracy in Africa published in the past few years includes the following: executive, judicial, and electoral systems, and consociationalism (Lemarchand 2007; Lindberg 2005; Taylor 2006; von Doepp 2006); women and politics (Bauer and Britton 2006; Hassim 2006; Lindberg 2004a; Tripp 2000; Yoon and Bunwaree 2006); capitalism, development, and democracy (Ayers 2006; Burgess 2004; Gazibo 2005; Koeble and LiPuma 2006); war, corruption, clientelism, and democracy (Blake and Martin 2006; Ellis 2006; Lyons 2005; Roeder and Rothchild 2005; Sandbakken 2006); various features and effects of party systems (Bogaards 2004; Erdman 2004; Hyden 2005; Ishiyama and Quinn 2006; Kuenzi and Lambright 2001, 2005; LeBas 2006; Lindberg 2007; Manning 2005; Morrison 2006); voter and citizen attitudes (a host of Afrobarometer working papers and journal articles following them, at www.afrobarometer.org; Kagwanja 2006; Lindberg and Morrison 2005, 2008; Moehler 2006); ethnicity, culture and religion, and democracy (Green 2006; Hagmann 2006; Paden 2005; Pitcher 2006; Posner 2005; Soares 2006); and general studies of democratization (Bauer and Taylor 2005; Gibson 2002; Sandbrook 2005; Villalón and Von Doepp 2005). Some efforts to understand issues like party systems have suffered from methodological problems undermining findings (Mozaffar and Scarritt 2005), but that is to be expected when new ground is being broken.

We are thus in a very dynamic period of academic research on Africa, and as always, scholars differ in their conclusions on where countries are heading, whether things are getting better or worse, and to what extent the developments we see fit various theories. This is as it should be; debates and contrasting perspectives only further the cause of better analysis by forcing us to sharpen our tools and theories and improve the quality of our data and the stringency of our analyses. Africa is a large continent, not only geographically but in numbers too. About a quarter of all the world's nations are found on the continent, and it accordingly has produced a wide variety in terms of political institutions and outcomes. Deciphering where Africa is heading is therefore a delicate task for anyone, and the wealth of approaches used in single or comparative case studies make this even harder. As we all know, when countries are studied on different factors, or even the same on the same factors but measured and weighted in various fashions, comparisons are inherently fraught with difficulties. There is thus a continuous need to take stock and attempt to measure comparatively how all these countries are developing in this new era of—supposedly—democratic elections. Table 1.1 lists the African countries by their different stages on the election spectrum and how they are evaluated in provision of "on-the-ground" protection of political rights, according to Freedom House.

In *Democracy and Elections in Africa* (Lindberg 2006a), I refuted a number of then-established hypotheses, finding no general negative trend either in the frequency or the quality of African elections. Rather, the inception of multiparty elections usually initiates liberalization, and repeated electoral activities create incentives for political actors, fostering the expansion and deepening of democratic values. In addition to improving the democratic qualities of political regimes, a sequence of elections tends to expand and solidify de facto civil liberties in society. Controlling for other standard factors of democratization I sought to demonstrate that the impact of repetitive elections, even if "imported," is consistent in Africa's diverse contexts, making the case that electoral processes are an important causal factor in the development of democracy and thus extending Rustow's (1970) theory that democratic behavior produces democratic values.

This chapter revisits the issue of democratization by elections in sub-Saharan Africa: Do multiparty elections change incentives, such as the increase in the costs of repression, as argued by Dahl (1971), to become a main factor of democratization? Can elections and institutions that provide

Table 1.1 Number of successive elections held and Freedom House political rights (PR) score, January 2007

No elections	PR	1st elections	PR	2nd elections	PR	3rd elections	PR	4th or later	PR
Angola	6	Burundi	4	Comoros	3	Burkina F.	5	Benin	2
Ivory Coast	7	CAR	5	Lesotho	2	Cameroon	6	Botswana	2
Eritrea	5	DRC	5	Niger	3	Chad	6	Cape Verde	1
Somalia	7	Guinea Biss	4	Nigeria	4	Djibouti	5	Gabon	6
Swaziland	7	Liberia	3	Sudan	7	Eq. Guinea	7	Ghana	1
		Mauritania	5			Ethiopia	5	Madagascar	4
		Rwanda	6			Gambia	5	Mali	2
		RoC	6			Guinea	6	Mauritius	1
		Sierra Leone	4			Kenya	3	Namibia	2
						Malawi	4	Senegal	2
						Mozambique	3	Seychelles	3
						São Tomé	2	Togo	6
						South Africa	2	Zambia	3
						Tanzania	4	Zimbabwe	7
						Uganda	5		
Mean PR	6.4		4.7		3.8		4.6		3.0

iterated two-level games trick, lure, and cajole leaders into behaving more democratically and even into becoming democrats, as Rustow (1970) once theorized? Is it true that we first need democratic institutions inducing democratic behavior before we get leaders who are democrats at heart?

Revisiting Elections in Africa

The book *Democracy and Elections in Africa* covered a period from 1989 to June 30, 2003, with total of 232 cases. What has changed, if anything, after three and a half years and the addition of 50 new elections? Looking first at the number of elections, and the number of countries holding *de jure* multiparty elections, not very much, as Figure 1.1 shows. The characteristic wave-like pattern of elections that I depicted in *Democracy* continues as predicted with a slight upward trend indicating a continuously positive development. This is even more pronounced when we look, as in Figure 1.2, at the share of elections that have been free and fair.[1]

When I concluded the *Democracy* study, the average percentage of elections deemed free and fair seemed to have leveled out, displaying a more or

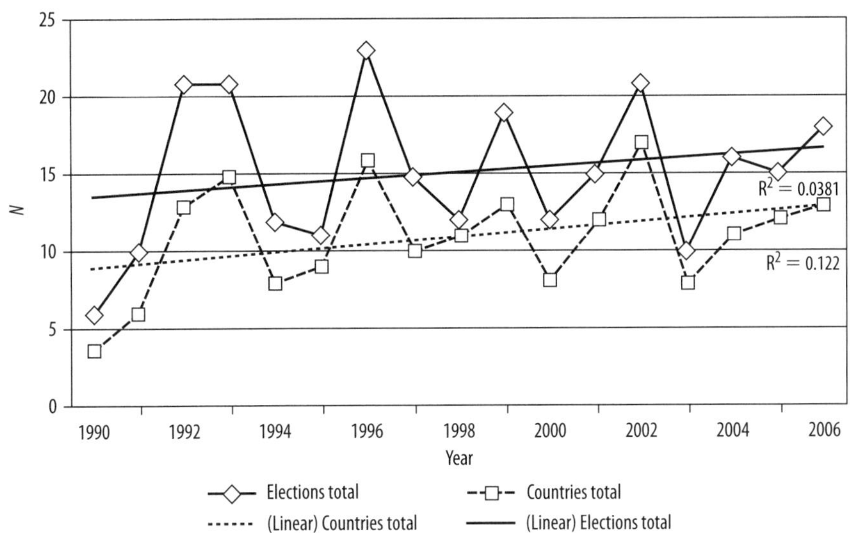

Figure 1.1. Number of elections and number of countries with multiparty elections, Africa, 1989–2006

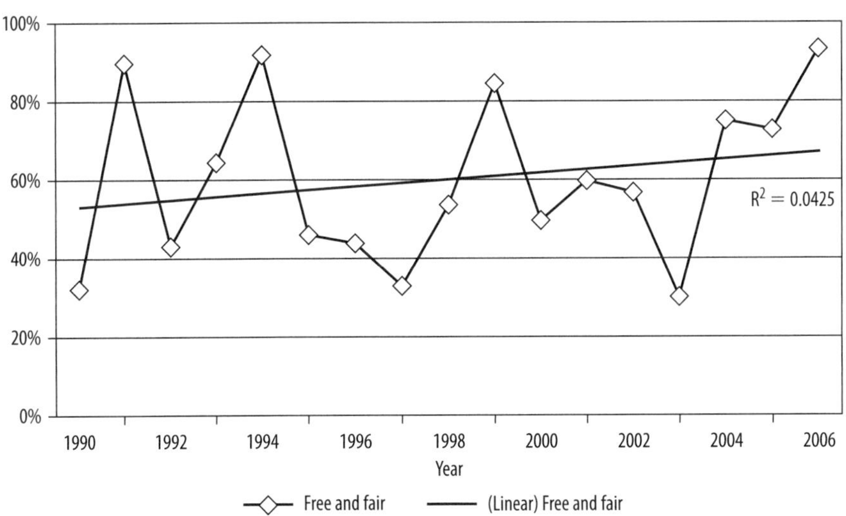

Figure 1.2. Percentage of free and fair elections, Africa, 1989–2006

Table 1.2 Democratic participation in first, second, third, and later elections

Indicator	Type of election	No. of poll: 1st	2nd	3rd	4th+	All	*p**: No. of poll	Free & fair
Voter turnout	Free & fair	68%	67%	62%	67%	67%	.304	6.403
	Std.	18.4	17.9	13.3	16.0	17.0	(.822)	(.012)
	N	67	36	32	31	166		
	Flawed	61%	62%	64%	55%	61%		
	Std.	.196	.167	.161	.066	.175		
	N	46	34	20	5	105		
Opposition participation	Free & fair	90%	94%	97%	97%	94%	3.396	.536
	N	61	34	32	31	158	(.001)	(.000)
	Flawed	34%	55%	60%	60%	47%		
	N	17	21	12	3	53		
Autocrats gone	Free & fair	7%	14%	24%	50%	20%	.375	4.112
	N	5	5	8	16	34	(.000)	(.000)
	Flawed	2%	8%	30%	60%	12%		
	N	1	3	6	3	13		
Free & fair *N*		68	36	34	32	170		
Flawed *N*		50	38	21	5	114		
Total *N*		118	74	55	37	284		

* Spearman's correlation values and significance for ordinal variables, and ANOVA F-values and significance for the interval variable.

less constant pattern. There were ups and downs, but over time nothing much changed. Today we see that free and fair elections are becoming increasingly common and that 2003 was a particularly bad year for democratic elections in Africa. Since then things have improved significantly again, and the data presented in the two figures combined tell us that overall, more countries are holding elections, with an increasing share of elections achieving a minimum standard of democratic fairness. This first cut thus seems to corroborate my earlier findings that as countries in Africa hold more elections, the quality of those elections improve. But what do the more detailed indicators for the three dimensions of democratic quality—participation, competition, and legitimacy[2]—say about this pattern?

Stagnant Popular but Increasing Elite Participation

Voter turnout simply does not change much as countries move from first and "founding" elections to second and third and so on. Among free and fair elections this is actually reassuring rather than disappointing: People in African states continue to put a high value on the act of political participation despite often disappointing performances by elected representatives. The Afrobarometer studies report that in many countries after the third round of elections citizens are increasingly dissatisfied both with leaders' performances in terms of policy output and the "supply of democracy" (e.g., Bratton and Cho 2006), yet, apparently, they continue to go to the polls to cast their votes. In other words, this finding tallies well with the Afrobarometer findings that people in most countries (with the notable exception of Nigeria) show a continuing high support for democracy, in most cases a much higher level of support than in Latin America and even Western Europe.

It is only in the case of flawed elections that we see a general drop in popular participation, as Table 1.2 shows: the level of participation is down to 55% on average in fourth and later elections. Again, this seems reasonable. If you have participated in more than three flawed elections without any real effect, disillusion starts to set in, and staying at home (or at work) is a more attractive option. This is further evidenced by the statistically significant differences between participation in free and fair elections and flawed ones. People know a flawed process when they see one.

Opposition parties do not give up as easily. It is encouraging to see that elite participation now comes very close to 100% in third, fourth, and later free and fair elections. The strategic boycotting by opposition parties that are trying to win public relations points for denouncing the electoral process when they stand no chance of winning the vote is waning, and that is a good sign. Third elections seem to be a break-off point when party elites start realizing that playing foul does not pay off in the long run.

Parties operating in electoral autocracies are also choosing to participate more and more as countries move from first to second and subsequent elections. This also seems to be a positive trend, given the findings about the "democratizing" effects (Schedler 2002b) and "liberalizing outcomes" (Howard and Roessler 2006) of elections in general, the "electoral route" to democracy (Hadenius and Teorell 2007), the power of "electoral revolutions" (Bunce and Wolchik 2007c), the learning and mobilization dynamics of repetitive elections (Anderson and Dodd 2005, Barkan 2000, Eisenstadt 2004), and the association between opposition participation in flawed elections and later transformation to electoral democracy (Lindberg 2006c). Finally, the "old guard" in the form of leaders previously holding senior government positions in authoritarian regimes is gradually but steadily retiring, leaving room for a new generation to take over. All in all, the indicators on participation seem to reaffirm the findings reported in *Democracy and Elections in Africa*.

Increasing Competition for Executive Office but Not for Legislative Seats

Democracy and Elections in Africa found that free and fair elections for executive office are increasingly becoming highly competitive affairs, especially with fourth elections, but that electoral systems, historical cleavages, and band-wagoning behind winning candidates make legislative outcomes very much different. As Table 1.3 indicates, legislative opposition groups continue to be very weak, thus raising questions about the functioning of checks and balances in what continue to be mostly presidential systems across the continent.

On the other hand, the frequency of alternations in power is steady at about a third of all elections, and in a fifth of all third and later elections. This somewhat reduces the concern about strong legislative majorities: So long as power rotates at some sort of regular basis, legislative dominance shifts from one set of hands to another much like it usually does in a country like Britain. This is not the case in all countries (yet). South Africa, Mozambique, Tanzania, and Namibia for example, all have stable one-party-dominant systems even though they are (at least electoral) democracies. Only a few countries have experienced more than one peaceful alternation in executive office in a series of elections uninterrupted by coups and similar events: Benin (3), Cape Verde (2), Madagascar (3), Mali (2), and Mauritius (3). The list of countries with at least one turnover is much longer, and this fact may be construed by an optimistic observer as perhaps setting a precedent for leaders in Africa in how to handle electoral defeats. To a more pessimistic observer, a legitimate question still remains as to whether ruling elites in countries like Tanzania, Mozambique, Guinea Bissau, Lesotho, Niger, and Zambia will actually agree to step down if and when electoral defeat becomes reality. Only time will tell.

Tenuous and Shallow but Improving Legitimacy

On the indicators for electoral legitimacy—losers' acceptance of results, the peacefulness of the process, and survival of the electoral regime—the picture is even more clearly positive in terms of the direction things are mov-

Table 1.3 Democratic competition in first, second, third, and later elections

Indicator	Type of election	No. of poll 1st	2nd	3rd	4th+	All	p* No. of poll	Free & fair
Winner's % of votes	Free & fair	52%	62%	61%	47%	56%	3.836	10.001
	Std.	18.6	15.7	14.8	8.4	16.8	(.012)	(.002)
	N	30	16	15	9	70		
	Flawed	64%	74%	60%	56%	66%		
	Std.	21.7	17.9	19.8	6.1	20.2		
	N	23	17	10	2	52		
Largest party's % of seats	Free & fair	57%	64%	64%	65%	62%	2.058	8.696
	Std.	21.6	21.0	18.7	16.1	19.8	(.108)	(.004)
	N	38	20	18	23	99		
	Flawed	66%	77%	72%	75%	71%		
	Std.	21.4	.19.3	21	20.3	20.6		
	N	24	20	10	3	57		
2nd party's % of seats	Free & fair	20%	20%	20%	22%	21%	1.186	6.036
	Std.	10.1	12.8	14.7	13.2	12.2	(.317)	(.015)
	N	37	20	18	23	98		
	Flawed	17%	13%	14%	22%	15%		
	Std.	13.8	11.6	11.3	.18.5	12.8		
	N	24	20	10	3	57		
Turnover of power	Free & fair	46%	11%	21%	22%	29%	–2.297	.406
	N	31	4	7	7	49	(.022)	(.000)
	Flawed	8%	0%	0%	20%	4%		
	N	4			1	5		
Free & fair *N*		68	36	34	32	170		
Flawed *N*		50	38	21	5	114		
Total *N*		118	74	55	37	284		

* Spearman's correlation except for means where ANOVA F-values are used.

ing, yet on two of the three the level of "democraticness" is also lower than on the previous two dimensions.

The detailed data in Table 1.4 indicate that as losers accept the outcome of elections more readily, the percentage of peaceful electoral processes increases, and that breakdowns of the electoral regime become less and less frequent as countries hold more elections. The average levels have increased compared with what I found in *Democracy and Elections in Africa,* and that is a positive. The levels are still lower than we would hope, with losers' acceptance at less than two-thirds for fourth and subsequent free and fair elections

Table 1.4 Democratic legitimacy in first, second, third, and later elections

Indicator	Type of election	No. of poll 1st	2nd	3rd	4th+	All	*p** No. of poll	Free & fair
Losers accept	Free & fair	47%	47%	58%	66%	53%	2.991	.646
	N	32	17	19	21	89	(.003)	(.000)
	Flawed	2%	3%	0%	0%	2%		
	N	1	1			2		
Peaceful process	Free & fair	25%	50%	49%	53%	40%	4.017	.321
	N	17	18	16	17	68	(.000)	(.000)
	Flawed	6%	11%	20%	0%	10%		
	N	3	4	4		11		
Regime survival	Free & fair	74%	89%	91%	100%	85%	4.307	.048
	N	50	32	30	32	144	(.000)	(.471)
	Flawed	80%	90%	95%	100%	87%		
	N	40	34	19	5	98		
Free & fair *N*		68	36	34	32	170		
Flawed *N*		50	38	21	5	114		
Total *N*		118	74	55	37	284		

* Spearman's correlation.

and violence still plaguing the election processes in about half of these elections.

It should be noted, however, that the coding standards are pretty high. These figures include only cases where losers are reported to have accepted the election results immediately (and not a few days or weeks later, after contesting them in court) and cases that are completely void of reports of election-related violence. Yet, it still seems that in the eyes of crucial elites the legitimacy of electoral procedures still remains slightly tenuous even if it is improving. Finally, the trend reported earlier—that electoral regimes do not break down after three or four electoral cycles—continues, and this supports the overall conclusion from *Democracy* that the repetition of elections leads to improving not only democratic qualities but also regime stability.

Constraining and Cajoling Political Leaders

Almost all countries in Africa have presidential systems with separate elections for the legislature and the executive. Presidents in African states tend also to have dominating powers conferred upon them by both constitutional design and traditional, or informal, norms and rules of behavior. It is therefore easy to argue that the elections for president are the more important elections to study, since the office of the president is the great prize, and with the patronage powers of the officeholder, legislatures can be bought off if not lured to comply with the wishes of the executive.

Can we see any evidence, then, of an impact of iterated electoral games under a set of new institutions and incentives on leaders' behavior in Africa's presidential systems? Does the behavior of leaders in Africa seem to conform with Rustow's hypothesis that once democratic institutions are in place, democratic behavior will follow, which will in turn foster democrats?

Figure 1.3 depicts three trends in the behavior of leaders in and around presidential elections. We can see that presidential elections are increasingly becoming free and fair just like all other elections, indicating that the power of leaders to undermine democratic behavior is increasingly constrained. Assuming that political leaders in Africa (and we could assume much the same about any political leaders in the world) would prefer to be able to manipulate elections in their own favor in order to stay in power, these trends seem to indicate that the cost of repression, in Dahl's terms, has indeed gone up significantly.

We get the same message from the other two indicators. After the relatively high level of turnout in the first elections, which resulted from unexpected turmoil in many countries and the miscalculations of incumbent autocrats who thought they could win by "preemptive" elections, the percentage of presidential elections leading to alternations in power went down significantly in the second and third elections. With the fourth and later elections, however, this figure has risen again and significantly so, to the extent of actually being higher than for the "exceptional" first elections. Perhaps this is also reflective of the trend of the third indicator: The old guard—individuals who were presidents and ministers in former authoritarian regimes—are leaving the electoral arena in increasing numbers. One could of course make the opposite inference—that old elites are now few and far between because of the number of alternations in power—and it is true that one can find examples of such a sequence. The more common pattern in Africa, however, has been that the old guard leaves because of old age or other misfortunes, and then the nature of the electoral game changes in favor of new opposition parties and their leaders.

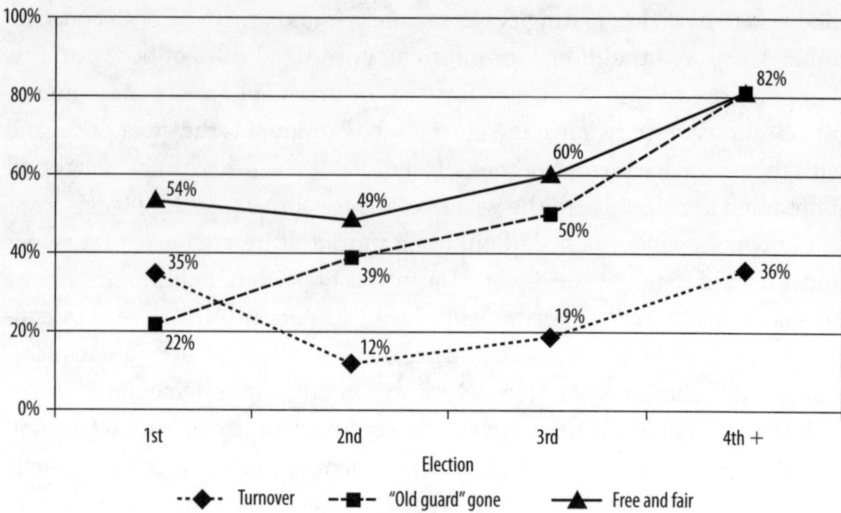

Figure 1.3. Indicators of constraints on rulers in Africa's presidential elections

Figure 1.4 depicts the continent-wide cumulative effect of this trend. This is something that I find has gone relatively unnoticed so far. The two lines represent the cumulative percentage of African countries that have experienced at least one alternation in power by the ballot box. The first line includes the first (founding) elections, and by that measure more than half of all countries holding elections have seen their president lose an election, accept defeat, and leave office peacefully. This is indeed a major shift in the cognitive and representational history of Africa. Even if we exclude first elections following Huntington's (1991) advice that these are nonroutine events immediately following the breakdown of an authoritarian regime that should not be given the same significance as later elections, the second line indicates that about one-third of countries have still experienced an alternation in the presidential office.

It seems fair to conclude that these tentative indicators do indeed provide supporting evidence that Dahl and Rustow were right. We need democratic institutions and rights that can stack up incentives and costs in ways that increase the cost of repression while facilitating and rewarding democratic behavior among both incumbents and opposition leaders. We cannot say anything about the kind of experiential learning and socialization especially implied by Rustow, but recently I conducted an investigation with Devra Moehler and we found significant effects (Moehler and Lindberg 2007, 2009).

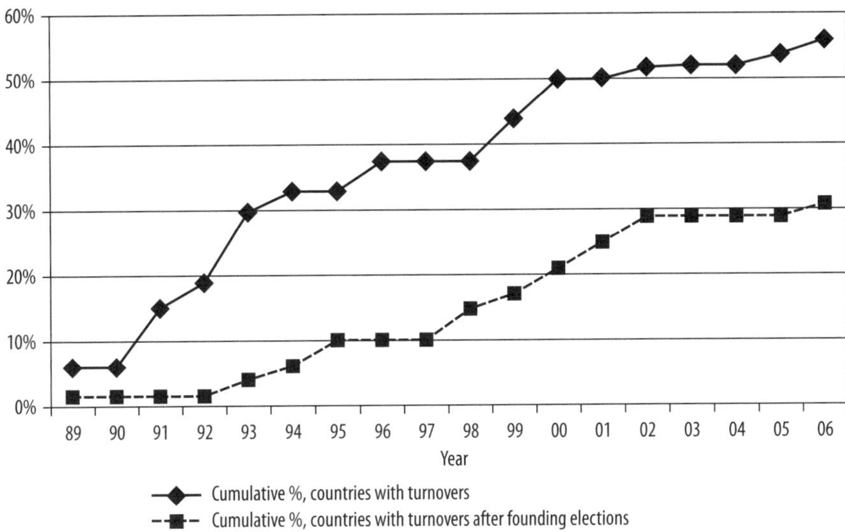

Figure 1.4. Cumulative percentages of countries in Africa with turnovers

Analyzing all available survey data from the Afrobarometer's three rounds with data on elections in these countries, we found that electoral turnovers lead to significant changes in people's perceptions of the legitimacy of state institutions. Winners and losers in the electoral game then come closer to shared perceptions of the legitimacy of state institutions, the functioning of democracy, and the behavior of their leaders. To the extent that these results prove robust in the longer run, we have evidence that repetitions of elections that eventually (in many cases at least) lead to alternations in power indeed create democrats.

Democratization by Elections Revisited

Another major finding in *Democracy* was that repetitive elections also improve and spread democracy outside of the electoral arena as measured by Freedom House's civil liberties ratings. It was shown not only that civil liberties improved with the holding of successive elections, but also that such improvements tended to come as a result of holding elections, while periods before and in between elections were generally not associated with any improvements. Table 1.5 shows the first step in revisiting these findings, and again the evidence corroborates earlier results.

Table 1.5 Civil liberties development over electoral periods

	1st period		2nd period		3rd period		4th+ period	
	Pre-election	1st election effects	Non-election	2nd election effects	Non-election	3rd election effects	Non-election	4th+ election effects
Mean change	.17	.83	–.07	.26	.06	.12	.00	–.09
Mean ranking	5.37	4.27	4.34	3.83	3.81	3.19	3.11	3.19
Total *N*	70	70	60	61	30	30	21	21

Inspecting the data, it is evident that the deviating figure for fourth and later elections is still driven by Zimbabwe. Zimbabwe is a deviant case in many respects; for one, it is the country that most obviously goes against the general trend—thus far, the more elections held in Zimbabwe, the worse they get. Overall, elections are significantly related to and actually seem to cause improvements in civil liberties, thus providing renewed support for the kind of causal mechanisms laid out in *Democracy and Elections in Africa* as well as in other publications (e.g., Lindberg 2006b). This pattern of democratization by elections still holds true for a majority of countries in Africa, as reported before. Gradually and unevenly but surely, countries tend to move from obvious electoral authoritarianism, to an ambiguous gray zone, to electoral and in some cases liberal democracy. Yet, we need to still ask ourselves, How important is the holding of elections compared with other well-known factors in democratization?

Explaining the Level of Civil Liberties

In the final part of the *Democracy* project, I looked into the question: To what extent can the *level* of democratic qualities in society in any one country also be explained by the number of elections held? In other words, can repetitive elections—still regardless of their quality—explain not only *if* and *when* positive changes occur but also *how far* countries have come in their democratization? The dependent variable continues to be civil liberties, now using the value from 2007 (in effect measuring the situation in 2006). However, since Freedom House also presents both an aggregate total score for the four dimensions of civil liberties (individual rights, associational rights, the rule of law, and freedom of expression and belief), as well as the component scores for each of the individual dimensions, we can now for the first time assess the constituent parts of the civil liberties rating. Thus, we have six dependent variables rather than one, in effect an important improvement in the specification of the dependent variable.

In order to ensure comparability, I use the same indicators as in *Democracy* for intervening and other variables in order to make the findings comparable. International influences of the dependency-type argument (cf. Hadenius 1992)—that a higher rate of economic reliance on the more developed states in terms of trade and capital investments affects democratization negatively—was corroborated recently by Li and Reuveny (2003). If countries in Africa are affected by economic ties to a world economy dominated by countries insisting on both elections and expansion of civil liberties, we could have been misled by a spurious relationship. The proxy for relative involvement in the world economy is the net sum of exports and imports as share of GDP—from 1990 in order to ensure sufficient delay between the independent and dependent variables. Second, we check for reliance on foreign aid and political conditionalities as instruments for pressuring authoritarian regimes into the fold of both holding elections and improving the level of democracy. Two alternative indicators are used to measure this aspect: total official development assistance (ODA) as a share of GDP from 1989 to 1993 and Bratton and van de Walle's (1997) count of structural adjustment programs (SAPs) from 1980 to 1990, which they argued was a better indicator of de facto donor influence. A variation on the economic ties thesis is the resource-curse argument that the presence of easily accessible and concentrated natural resources exerts a negative influence of the spread of democracy. The value of fuel exports as percentage of merchandise exports is used to control for this factor.

The modernization hypothesis originally formulated by Lipset (1959), as the more well-to-do a nation is, the more democratic it is likely to be, and corroborated by many studies (e.g., Buckhardt and Lewis-Beck 1994; Gasiorowski and Power 1998; Londregan and Poole 1996) is assessed using both the Human Development Index (HDI) from 1992, and, in model 2, the alternative indicator [log]GDP/c/ppp from 2003. Przeworski and associates (2000, 137), however, claim that economic conditions developed under nondemocracy cannot be used to predict the emergence of democracy, but that democracies are much more likely to survive under prosperity. In order to assess this possible confounding effect we include average annual growth from 1990 to 2000 to indicate regime performance.

Another robust finding has been the consistently negative impact of Islam found both in Lipset's early article (1959) and in later additions such as Ross (2001). To assess the importance of this variable the share of the population that adheres to Islam is employed. Another related issue is ethno-linguistic fractionalization, where the soundness of various measures has been hotly contested (e.g., Chandra 2004; Mozaffar, Scarritt, and Galaich 2003; Posner 2004; Scarritt and Mozaffar 1999). Regardless of the outcome of that debate, a high level of fractionalization has been thought to impede democratization by infusing the polity with too high stakes because of fierce competition among more traditionally based societies. The ethnic heterogeneity index from Ellingsen (2000) is used.

Finally, in the aftermath of the revolutionary changes in Eastern Europe and Africa after 1989, Lipset (1994) tested the influence of popular mobilization on democratization. In Africa, this became the perhaps most renowned finding from Bratton and van de Walle's (1997) study: that popular protests were one of the key driving forces in the introduction of democracy on the continent. While this finding has been questioned in a replication using the original data set (Lindberg 2002), it is still influential in the literature and therefore merits closer scrutiny; thus, it is included using Bratton and van de Walle's own measure of the number of politically motivated protests between 1985 and 1994.

Empirical Results

This selection of independent variables is used in Tables 1.6–1.8 to present the new results from what was in the *Democracy and Elections in Africa* models 1, 4, and 5 only. Here, I include for each model regressions on six variants of the civil liberties indicator: the ordinary rating 1 through 7, the additive aggregate score for all four constitutive indicators, and individual scores for each of the four dimensions. It should be noted that the analysis here does not attempt to develop a full model that can be used to explain the level of democratization; instead, the purpose is only to explore the possible placement of a range of factors as intervening factors or as sources of a spurious relationship. As long as the control variables do not eradicate the significance of elections' statistical relationship to the level of civil liberties (CL), the result is positive, indicating support for the argument of the "power of elections" thesis.

All the values reported in Tables 1.6–1.8 are *t*-statistics and unstandardized beta coefficients to facilitate interpretation of the results. Bratton and van de Walle's measure of the number of popular protests was dropped after running the first model, since this measure showed no significance whatsoever but had the liability of reducing the size of the sample significantly.

The results are strongly supportive of the power of elections thesis. In fact, the adjusted R-square in models 1 and 4 is increased by about half and double, respectively (from 19% to 27.4% and from 16.4% to 35.0% explained variance), when regressed on the normal CL ratings. In both cases, the number of elections held is, as before, the only predictor with statistical significance. In model 5 (Table 1.8) the results are virtually unchanged except that official development assistance (ODA) loses its significance compared with the earlier results. In short, holding an increasing number of elections is by far the most important causal factor in increasing and spreading respect for civil liberties in Africa. This result is also corroborated further by regressions on the noncompressed scale of additive scores on all four indicators for civil liberties ranging from 4 to 60. Increasing the variance on the dependent variable (making it, in effect, harder to explain) actually *increases* the explained variance in all three models, most significantly so in model 4, from 35% to 43% explained variance. The more we add precision to the measure of civil liberties, the better the number of elections predict its values.

But which civil liberties, more precisely? Freedom House has a checklist of 14 civil liberties arranged along four dimensions covering everything from individual rights, rule of law, associational rights, and freedom of expression and belief. One criticism has always been that we do not know how much each one of these dimensions weigh in each country score and how they then compare cross-nationally. For each model, regressions were run using the original scores on each of these four dimensions as dependent variable, one after the other. The results are generally consistent with the results reported above (elections are the most important predictor across the board). Looking at the differences over the four dimensions we find that elections by far predict individual rights and rule of law better than anything else and that international pressures through aid conditionalities primarily affect the rule of law positively. These results support the thrust of the causal mechanisms that were discussed in *Democracy*.

Table 1.6 The power of elections and possible confounding factors, model 1

Variable	Indicators	DV: Freedom House civil liberties, Jan. 2007[a]					
		CL 1–7	CL 4–56	Individual rights	Rule of law	Associational rights	Expression & belief
Elections	Number of successive repetitive elections as of Dec. 31, 2006	–.563***	4.409***	1.184***	1.348***	.824**	1.053**
		(–3.370)	(3.328)	(4.261)	(3.195)	(2.336)	(2.640)
Oil export	Fuel exports as % of merchandise exports, c. 1990	–.003107	.01524	.001125	.0007363	.005145	.008233
		(–.324)	(.200)	(.071)	(.030)	(.254)	(.360)
International influence	ODA share of GDP, 1989	–.01149	.137	.01864	.04784	.0334	.03748
		(–.733)	(1.104)	(.714)	(1.208)	(1.009)	(1.001)
	Number of SAPs, 1980–90	–.03266	.03866	.03637	.02573	.01084	.003915
		(–.498)	(.074)	(.334)	(.155)	(.078)	(–.219)
Modernization	HDI 1992	.00035	.004355	.000594	.001539	.002718	–.000496
		(.156)	(.243)	(.158)	(.269)	(.569)	(–.092)
Regime performance	Average GDP growth, 1990–2000	–.118	.534	.193	.107	.0489	.185
		(–.848)	(.484)	(.834)	(.304)	(.166)	(.558)
Religion	Moslem share of population, c. 1985	.007553	–.06261	–.0198	–.00187	–.01895	–.02198
		(.962)	(–1.005)	(–1.516)	(–.094)	(–1.143)	(–1.173)
Ethnicity	Ethnic fractionalization index, c. 1990	.01633	–.09739	–.03174	–.04637	.003091	–.02237
		(1.339)	(–1.007)	(–1.565)	(–1.506)	(–1.007)	(–.769)
Popular mobilization	Number of popular protests, 1985–94	.01722	–.142	–.4342	–.06588	–.02909	–.003915
		(.508)	(–.530)	(–.771)	(–.770)	(–.407)	(–.048)
	Constant	4.292***	23,900**	5.885**	5.34	3.451	9.224***
		(3.066)	(2.153)	(2.528)	(1.511)	(1.168)	(2.761)
	Adjusted R^2	.274	.289	.462	.277	.132	.150
	p	.031	.025	.001	.030	.162	.136
	N	37	37	37	37	37	37

Abbreviations: DV = dependent variable, CL = civil liberties, ODA = official development assistance, SAP = structural adjustment programs, HDI = Human Development Index

[a] The top numbers in each cell are unstandardized beta coefficients; the second number, in parenthesis, is the *t* statistic.

*p < .10 **p < .05 ***p < .01

Table 1.7 The power of elections and possible confounding factors, model 4

		DV: Freedom House civil liberties, Jan. 2007[a]					
Variable	Indicators	CL 1–7	CL 4–56	Individual rights	Rule of law	Associational rights	Expression & belief
Elections	Number of successive repetitive elections as of Dec. 31, 2006	–.415***	3.764***	.881***	1.151***	.791***	.941***
		(–3.495)	(4.082)	(4.293)	(3.962)	(3.244)	(3.357)
Oil export	Fuel exports as % of merchandise exports, c. 1990	–.000562	.01714	–.00189	–.00252	.008886	.01267
		(–.070)	(.276)	(–.137)	(–.129)	(.541)	(.671)
International influence	ODA share of GDP, 1989	–.01816	.206*	.03732	.06928*	.04517	.05469
		(–1.217)	(1.782)	(1.448)	(1.898)	(1.474)	(1.552)
	Number of SAPs, 1980–90	–.01036	.09756	.01992	.004385	.04641	.02684
		(–.215)	(.261)	(.239)	(.037)	(.469)	(.236)
Modernization	GDP/c/ppp 2003 (log)	–.300	5.522	1.349	1.801	1.228	1.145
		(–.464)	(1.101)	(1.209)	(1.139)	(.925)	(.750)
Regime performance	Average GDP growth, 1990–2000	–.08436	.136	.09635	.04442	–.03118	.02624
		(–.665)	(.138)	(.440)	(.143)	(–.120)	(.088)
Religion	Moslem share of population, c. 1985	.006736	–.0500	–.01551	–.002166	–.01988	–.01244
		(1.124)	(–1.075)	(–1.499)	(–.148)	(–1.615)	(–.879)
Ethnicity	Ethnic fractionalization index, c. 1990	.009819	–.07344	–.01887	–.03758	.00063	–.01762
		(.933)	(–.957)	(–1.105)	(–1.554)	(.031)	(–.755)
	Constant	5.632**	4.785	.957	–.743	.159	4.412
		(2.297)	(.251)	(.226)	(–.124)	(.032)	(.762)
	Adjusted R^2	.350	.430	.502	.444	.288	.283
	p	.004	.001	.000	.000	.012	.013
	N	41	41	41	41	41	41

Abbreviations: DV = dependent variable, CL = civil liberties, ODA = official development assistance, SAP = structural adjustment programs, HDI = Human Development Index

[a] The top numbers in each cell are unstandardized beta coefficients; the second number, in parenthesis, is the *t* statistic.

$^*p < .10$ $^{**}p < .05$ $^{***}p < .01$

Table 1.8 The power of elections and possible confounding factors, model 5

Variable	Indicators	DV: Freedom House civil liberties, Jan. 2007[a]					
		CL 1–7	CL 4–56	Individual rights	Rule of law	Associational rights	Expression & belief
Elections	Number of successive repetitive elections as of Dec. 31, 2006	–.392***	3.402***	.820***	1.062***	.708***	.813***
		(–3.930)	(4.074)	(4.160)	(4.117)	(3.372)	(3.448)
International influence	ODA share of GDP, 1989	–.01377	.121	.02260	.04472*	.02127	.03273
		(–1.568)	(1.650)	(1.302)	(1.968)	(1.150)	(1.577)
	Constant	5.372***	18.343***	3.938***	2.846***	4.261***	7.298***
		(14.086)	(5.745)	(5.228)	(2.885)	(5.307)	(8.098)
	Adjusted R^2	.256	.272	.270	.288	.188	.210
	p	.001	.000	.000	.000	.004	.002
	N	46	46	46	46	46	46

Abbreviations: DV = dependent variable, CL = civil liberties, ODA = official development assistance, SAP = structural adjustment programs, HDI = Human Development Index

[a] The top numbers in each cell are unstandardized beta coefficients; the second number, in parenthesis, is the *t* statistic.

$*p < .10$ $**p < .05$ $***p < .01$.

Conclusion

Nearly 20 years of political change in Africa have spurred a new generation of scholarship promising a much-needed turn away from African exceptionalism and overdependency on case study narratives. Strictly speaking, the problem is not that too many case studies and narratives with a heavy reliance on historical and ethnographic data have been carried out; it is that too few comparative case studies, survey projects, and large-*N* efforts have been done. Presently, a more appropriate balance is emerging. It is also commendable that a new generation of scholars is making successful strides to integrate African politics into mainstream comparative politics in two ways: first, by increasing usage and testing of standard comparative theories in the context of African data, and secondly, by bringing theoretical insights based on the study of Africa to the knowledge of non-Africanists by publishing more and more in general political science journals and contributing to testing these hypotheses on empirical cases outside of Africa.

My own limited efforts have often been to try to lay a foundation for such cross-pollination. The *Democracy* project was in large part—or became—a "basic research" venture collecting some very basic data on national elections and democracy in Africa's 48 states, and analyzing some basic features of those elections in order to weed out existing unfounded misconceptions and hypotheses and put some things straight, so to speak. In the course of doing that work, I happened to find evidence for what I had long suspected: that elections are a powerful force for political change. They are sometimes the ignition that sparks other processes, sometimes arenas for forces of positive change, sometimes constituting actors and their interests, sometimes events with their own dynamics and processes that tend to cause direct improvements in a country's level of political freedom and civil rights.

The statistical evidence speaks clearly in corroborating this hypothesis, and the inspection and analysis of case narratives and illustrations—although excluded from this chapter because of space constraints—also supports the overall findings. Yet, I am more than acutely aware that these are still preliminary conclusions, or "tentative" if one prefers the terminology O'Donnell and Schmitter once used in their *Transitions* project. Empirical reality has a way of providing constant surprises and new twists and turns, making our job as scholars both harder and more interesting. Just to mention one example: China remains a socialist republic and continues its aggressive investment and involvement policy in Africa. We might find that China could tip the balance of forces disfavoring the power that elections and other factors have, effectuating a number of reversals in the near future. Yet, I am a little more confident about my thesis today than I was when I finished the *Democracy* study, for two reasons. One is that, as reported above, revisiting the results of that study with the additional data from three and a half years and some 50 more elections, I find that the results are much the same and, if anything, stronger than before.

The other reason is that similar findings have emerged from both global and regional studies carried out by other scholars. Although those studies and mine are not directly comparable, since we use different indicators and analytical approaches, they point in the same direction. Howard and Roessler (2006) in their global study of electoral autocracies found strong support for what they label the "liberalizing effects of elections." In recent contributions Bunce and Wolchik (e.g., 2007c) termed the transitions in Eastern Europe and the former Soviet republics "electoral revolutions," while Hadenius and Teorell (2007) in their global study of democratization find that most successful transitions go "the electoral route" of successively more free and fair elections, eventually bringing them to a democratic dispensation. Schedler was the first to use the label "democratization by elections" (Schedler 2002b), and the chapters in this volume represent a collaborative effort in extension of his work.

Where does this leave us? There is no doubt in my mind that Africa has gradually become more politically and economically free over the past almost 20 years and that apart from analyzing the most important causes, this new landscape of institutions, norms, actors, and actions have important effects as well. It seems to me that there is much work to be done. Almost every day I find myself reading (usually flicking through to be honest) one or two articles on American, European, Eastern European, Asian, or Latin American politics and thinking, "Hmm, we should really do a similar study in Africa and see what that tells us." Resources and time are, as always, limited, but no one need hesitate to study African politics today; it is important, challenging, and dynamic. Last but not least, there are loads of intriguing empirical data out there and a heap of hypotheses waiting to be tested, refined, and elaborated. It should be a fun period ahead.

CHAPTER TWO

The Relative Powerlessness of Elections in Latin America

Jennifer L. McCoy and Jonathan Hartlyn

There is a growing literature examining the fact that in the recent era many countries have not followed a pattern of unmistakable, rapid transition from authoritarian to democratic rule with subsequent consolidation of a sustainable democratic regime. Some scholars have opted to focus on the emergence of competitive authoritarian regimes, not all of which transform to democracies, as evidenced by Roessler and Howard's contribution to this volume (see also Levitsky and Way 2002b; Schedler 2006a). Others focus more hopefully on the potential democratizing impact of repeated, even if imperfect, elections as a mode of transition; this focus is seen in the current volume in the chapters by Lindberg, Brownlee, and Bunce and Wolchik.

There is considerable evidence that simply holding elections under authoritarianism does not necessarily foster democratization, and we review this issue again for Latin America. Some scholars have noted that in a number of contemporary authoritarian regimes, incumbents take part in scheduled multiparty elections, which they seek to distort sufficiently to their advantage to win while simultaneously projecting the appearance of permitting enough competition to gain legitimacy from the exercise. At times, a surprising incumbent loss can occur, triggering a democratic transition. As Schedler (2002b and in this volume) argues, with Mexico as a prime empirical referent, in these regimes there is a simultaneous, interactive process of both electoral competition (though the opposition may ultimately boycott and thus choose not to compete) as well as a "metagame" of electoral reform, which unfolds simultaneously and interactively. Although he acknowledges that the game can "end" prior to democratization for several reasons, his main argument is that if the process of elections continues, the "inner logic of the game pulls it away from authoritarianism," creating a self-subversive spiral, rather than a self-enforcing equilibrium. Repeated elections thus undermine the institutional and electoral bases of the authoritarian incumbents (Schedler 2002b, 111; see also his Chapter 7 in this volume).

Lindberg's review in the previous chapter of the recent electoral history of countries in Africa leads him to argue that in Africa, when an uninterrupted sequence of multiparty elections has taken place (regardless of their initial or overall quality), it has led to democratic advances in terms of expanded civil liberties (though he does not seek to explain why first elections are embarked upon to begin with). This leads him, in turn, to reject a "transitions" argument for that region—in other words, that prior liberalizing and democratic advances lead to the holding of a "founding" election and the successful installation of a manifestly democratic regime. Instead, he argues that in Africa most transitions to democracy have taken place over several electoral cycles and that it has been during these electoral cycles that civil liberties have expanded the most. In this view, the more uninterrupted, successive elections are held, the more democratic a nation becomes; and there are reasons to be optimistic about hybrid regimes that hold elections because over time these types of regimes are likely to advance democratization (Lindberg 2006c, 140, 144–46; Lindberg 2006a; see also his chapters in this volume).

Most definitions of democracy embraced by scholars who form part of this debate highlight competitive elections as a necessary (though, except for the most minimalist definitions, not sufficient) element for political democracy. Thus, how to examine the validity of the electoralist argument is not always clear. It is almost tautological to note that consolidating democracy is not possible without practicing democracy, which inevitably means the holding of successive competitive elections. Yet, what about elections under authoritarian regimes? Do successive elections of any type under authoritarianism tend to lead over time to higher-quality electoral processes and to democracy? A broad argument at its simplest and most direct can be derived from a perspective that "*the more successive elections, the more democratic a nation becomes*" (Lindberg 2006c, 149; italics in original).[1]

Beyond defining democracy in terms of the quality of elections, we can look at additional elements of democracy to determine whether elections contribute to them. For many scholars, including Lindberg, greater democracy implies improvements in civil liberties, separate from competitive electoral processes, improvements that can lead to other forms of participation and freedom beyond elections. But in both analytical and empirical terms, it is difficult to distinguish the concept of competitive electoral processes from the civil liberties of freedom of speech, movement, and association, which are all also a vital part of competitive elections.[2] As other scholars have noted, an expanded definition of democracy would encompass additional dimensions such as accountability, separation of powers, rule of law, inclusiveness, responsiveness, the capacity of elected officials to govern, and other types of human and even social and economic rights (Mainwaring, Brinks, and Pérez-Liñán 2002; Morlino 2004; O'Donnell, Cullell, and Iazzetta 2004; UNDP 2004). If repeated elections contributed to improvements in these dimensions—in other words, to what we might term the quality of democracy—that would be a powerful finding indeed in support of an electoralist argument.

Notwithstanding the definitional and measurement challenges just noted, it is appropriate to ask if a broad electoralist argument holds in other world regions, such as Latin America, since the suggested potential causal mechanisms through which elections help generate democratization are general. We do this in the first section below. We show that quite clearly successive elections have frequently not led to political democracy, understood as electoral democracy (honest, competitive elections with basic civil liberties). Indeed, in Latin America during the cold war period there is no relationship between the number of elections a country has held and its democratic experience. Holding unfree elections was common under authoritarianism; these elections were sometimes totally uncontested, and on other occasions had some "permitted" contestation which sometimes led to unpleasant surprises for the authoritarian incumbents, necessitating their "fixing" the results through subsequent fraud or nullification. For some of these authoritarian governments, holding elections may have been an effective way for them to prolong their stay in power, even as the holding of competitive elections of course remained a defining feature of democracies in the region, as elsewhere. We also find that the standard transition argument largely does hold for many Latin American countries in this most current third wave of democratization—in many of the cases of democratic restoration and in some of the other cases, with civil liberties improving particularly around the time of a pivotal transitional election rather than over several electoral cycles.

There is a narrower reading of the electoralist argument, focused on a subset of contemporary authoritarian regimes in which incumbents (parties or individual leaders) involve themselves in elections with opposition participation for the purpose of external and/or internal legitimation (thus excluding cases of political redemocratization without incumbent participation and implicitly "smuggling in" international contextual pressures). These elections give opposition forces some potential room for maneuver as incumbents seek to balance credibility with control. This pattern is evident in a subset of Latin American countries, typically ones that have had limited prior democratic experiences, rather than ones that are "restoring" democracy which had succumbed to military government. In some countries, then, pursuing this electoral path may be the best available option for a democratic opposition, even if it means a potentially protracted transition to democracy. Whether this represents a true electoral mode of transition—one in which repeated electoral processes arguably have had a causal impact over time—cannot necessarily be assumed, but needs to be examined. Finally, according to some versions of the electoralist argument, repeated elections are also expected to produce continuous improvement in the quality of democracy. Here, the Latin American record is not encouraging, pointing rather to the powerlessness of elections. The improvement of political democracy, once established, demands much more than the continuous holding of elections.

Elections and Democracy in Latin America Post-1945

Republican institutions and presidential democracy were introduced to Spanish America following independence in the early nineteenth century and similarly in Brazil after it abolished the empire in 1889. For most countries, these represented more an aspiration than a practiced reality, as the adoption of new constitutions over the subsequent decades sometimes reflected an authoritarian leader's effort to legitimate or extend his rule. Yet, by the end of the nineteenth century, liberal constitutional doctrine, though not of course its application, was largely triumphant across the region. Similarly, elections in the region have also been common, even if they have not always been regular occurrences, much less free and fair. Universal suffrage and the secret ballot came unevenly to the region beginning in the first half of the twentieth century, with sometimes considerable variance between law and practice. The last countries to remove formal legal suffrage restrictions were Ecuador and Peru in their transitions to democracy in the late 1970s. Broadly speaking, the countries in Latin America that have had the most overall success with democracy in the second half of the twentieth century and into the twenty-first also had early elite democracies, with the exception of Venezuela (Diamond, Hartlyn, and Linz 1999; Hartlyn and Valenzuela 1994). Yet, even countries without these democratic periods had frequent electoral experiences. Thus, in contemporary Latin America there are no political systems for which electoral processes to determine top leadership positions would be novel experiences; elections in this period have not been *introduced.* If they have not been held continuously (whether manipulated or not), they may have been banned for a period, but then in all cases over the past several decades (except for Cuba) eventually they have been *reintroduced.*

It might still be the case, however, that the democratic experiences of countries in the region are associated with electoral processes. If so, this would be a powerful confirmation of the electoralist argument stated in its simplest and boldest form: countries whose governments, of whatever nature, hold successive elections have more extensive histories of democracy than those which do not, for if elections are held under authoritarian regimes, successive elections gradually push them to democracy. If this is true, then there should be a positive relationship in the region between the number of electoral processes held in a country and its overall experience with democracy.

The data collected in Table 2.1 examine this question. In that table, we provide information on the total number of elections held and the overall record on democratization for 18 Latin American countries from 1945 until each country's first "third-wave" transition from authoritarianism.[3] Three countries in the region—Colombia, Costa Rica, and Venezuela—did not succumb to authoritarian rule in the 1970s; the table provides information on the total number of elections in these countries until 1978, when transition processes commence in the region. As the data in the table indicate, there is no simple relationship between elections and democracy. A correlation

Table 2.1 Latin America, 1945 to third wave transition election: relationship between total number of executive and legislative elections and extent of democratization

Country	Transition year	Extent of democratization	No. of elections, 1945–transition	No. of elections in which incumbent won by		Democracy score, 1945–transition[a]	Mean no. of elections, top and bottom 4 countries
				90% or more	60% or more		
Paraguay	1989	Semi-democratic	24	17	24	0	
Mexico	1988	Semi-democratic	21	5	18	0	
El Salvador	1984	Semi-democratic	20	8	13	0	
Nicaragua	1984	Semi-democratic	11	4	11	0	19
Honduras	1982	Semi-democratic	8	2	2	7	
Dominican Republic	1978	Democratic	14	6	8	8	
Guatemala	1986	Semi-democratic	22	0	2	9	
Bolivia	1982	Democratic	18	2	10	9	
Argentina	1983	Democratic	14	0	4	17	
Peru	1980	Democratic	10	2	4	19	
Panama	1990	Semi-democratic	22	0	4	23	
Ecuador	1979	Democratic	15	0	0	30	
Brazil	1985	Democratic	15	0	2	34	
Colombia	[1978]	n.a.	20	3	7	28	
Venezuela	[1978]	n.a.	10	0	2	43	
Costa Rica	[1978]	n.a.	16	0	3	52	
Uruguay	1985	Democratic	16	0	0	56	
Chile	1990	Democratic	15	0	0	56	14
Total *N*			291	49	114		
Average			17			22	
Correlations elections / democracy score				–.53	–.60		

Sources: Electoral data from Nohlen 2005; democracy scores from Mainwaring, Brinks, and Pérez-Liñán 2002 (sum of annual democracy scores from 1945 to date of transition).

Coding rules for elections: Presidential and legislative elections each count separately even if on same day; presidential second round counted; partial legislative elections and elections for vice-president only counted as 0.5 elections; constitutional assemblies and referenda not counted (unless to elect president); upper and lower legislative elections counted jointly as 1 if held in the same year.

[a] Key to democracy scores: authoritarian = 0; semi-democracy = 1; democracy = 2.

between the number of executive and legislative elections a country held and its democracy score is actually slightly negative (though not statistically significant).[4] Countries that were authoritarian over the entire period from 1945 until their year of transition also held elections frequently. In fact, the four countries with a democracy score of 0 over this time period held an average of 19 elections, somewhat more than the four countries with the highest democracy scores, which held an average of 14 elections. In sum, the data in this table provide little support for a direct electoralist argument: there is no relationship between holding frequent elections and democracy in Latin America over this time period.

Two major factors appear to play a role in explaining the absence of a causal link. The most important is that many authoritarian regimes held undemocratic elections regularly for decades, without making any progress toward democracy. As Table 2.1 also indicates, the countries with the lowest democracy scores are also typically those whose regimes most frequently held elections in which the incumbent or incumbent party received an oversized majority, indicating one-party elections or something very close to that. In Table 2.1, we show results for when incumbents receive 90% or more of the vote in elections ($r = -.53$ for correlation between democracy score and these number of elections), and for when they receive over 60% of the vote ($r = -.60$ for correlation between democracy score and these number of elections). In the region, most of these elections were held in six countries: in the neopatrimonial or sultanistic regimes of Alfredo Stroessner in Paraguay and the Somozas in Nicaragua (both based in part on a preexisting party), and of Rafael Trujillo and then Joaquín Balaguer in the Dominican Republic; in El Salvador, with a military-dominated party; in Mexico, with the PRI dominance; and in Bolivia, which was dominated by a revolutionary party in the 1950s and early 1960s until it succumbed to military rule.[5] Second, in many countries in the region where democratic elections led to undesirable results for the military or elite groups, military coups or other actions interrupted their democratic rule. Thus, elections in this period sometimes led to the breakdown of democracy, even when in some cases these interruptions were short-lived and were followed quickly by renewed elections (cf. Drake and Silva 1986).

A narrower version of the electoralist argument, which excludes periods in a country's history when uncompetitive elections were held, may yet find support. Here, the argument refers to elections in which the incumbent permits at least some measure of competition, even if still in contrived, unfair conditions, unleashing repeated elections that gradually expand civil liberties and lead to greater freedom and democratization.

Yet, it is difficult to understand the decision in these countries to move beyond uncompetitive elections without considering the changing international context that increasingly made noncompetitive elections unviable. The international context often meant that elections in such countries, rather than being isolated domestic events, were influenced significantly by international pressure. In the period between 1945 and the late 1970s, the electoral dynamic was largely manageable by authoritarian leaders in the region. During this cold war period, the United States sometimes actively supported, and rarely opposed, military coups against democratically elected governments and maintained close relations with friendly tyrants who carried out openly fraudulent elections. But international norms and pressures began to evolve in the late 1970s in the region, with the shift toward a more vigorous human rights policy under President Jimmy Carter (1977–80). By his second term in office, President Ronald Reagan was also largely explaining his policy toward Latin America in the language of the promotion of democracy and support for competitive elections (Carothers 1991).

This trend became even more evident in Latin America in the more globalized post–cold war era of the 1990s. The transition wave in Latin America was initiated with the 1978 elections in the Dominican Republic, where pressure from the United States and other international actors played an important role in forcing a reluctant incumbent government to permit more open elections and then acknowledge its defeat at the polls. Domestic dynamics were also important in this case, as the opposition party purposefully moderated its policies and sought accommodation with the United States and conservative interests in the country leading up to the election. And international influence played an important direct role in several subsequent electoral processes as well. In other countries in the region, less vulnerable to U.S. leverage, domestic dynamics may have played a more significant role in initiating and sustaining transitions; one author describes the U.S. role in South American democratic transitions as primarily "applause" (Carothers 1991).

Nevertheless, it is clear that international and U.S. pressures for political democratization (understood particularly and narrowly in terms of elections) became increasingly important in the region after the 1970s in ways that simply were not true in the immediate post–World War II era. Thus, effects that may appear to be due to domestic dynamics of electoralism, may in fact be (or may have been, to the extent they are less present today) supported by or even principally a consequence of an international context that inhibits certain actions by incumbents and provides support to democratic opponents. As Levitsky and Way (2006) argue, Latin America has experienced this kind of democratizing electoralist pressure in the contemporary era through increasing levels of international linkages, with the smaller, more vulnerable states in the region also typically experiencing direct international leverage (see also Mainwaring and Pérez-Liñán 2005).

In the Latin American context, there was a polarized debate around the question of elections and democratization during the 1980s focused particularly on Central America. Some scholars accused U.S. policymakers of promoting an "electoralist" fallacy that "simply holding a technically clean election would establish or secure democratic rule" (Booth 1995, 16). They decried U.S.-sponsored elections in El Salvador as "demonstration elections" (Herman and Brodhead 1984) intended primarily to provide legitimacy for continued U.S. military aid and diplomatic support (as previously had taken place in countries ranging from Vietnam to the Dominican Republic). Yet, as political processes unfolded in El Salvador and Nicaragua, scholars debated the extent to which and the ways in which electoral processes helped foster processes of democratization. Scholars noted that in other countries, elections imposed by the United States for its own purposes still had important consequences within those countries that needed to be examined (cf. Hartlyn 1998). In a 2000 review of electoralism, Terry Karl noted that scholars concur that the introduction of elections into a country "will almost always have significant political meaning," as contending political forces must adapt their strategies and as some actors are strengthened and others weakened. However, the overall effect is not always positive; sometimes elections can impede democratization (when "undesirable" results motivate a military coup) or even have unintended consequences, such as "igniting or perpetuating civil war" (Karl 2000, 95). At the same time, the scholarly focus on "democratization by elections" was the subject of various analyses of politics in Brazil (e.g., Lamounier 1989; Soares 1986) and gained particular strength in studies of Mexico, as the authoritarian PRI incumbent gradually ceded power in a "protracted transition" (Eisenstadt 2004; Schedler 2002).

Let us thus turn next to the narrower electoralist argument in the more favorable international context for electoralism and political democracy of the last several decades. The fifteen countries of the region involved in the wave of transitions between 1978 and 1990 can be placed in two broad groups.[6] One group consists of those countries whose transitions can be considered restorational in the sense that these political systems were restoring civilian democratic rule that had existed in the not too distant past in their countries. This group includes countries with relatively more extensive past democratic histories (Brazil, Chile, and Uruguay) and those with less extensive past democratic histories (Argentina, Bolivia, Ecuador, and Peru). To the extent that past democratic history matters for current democratic success, overall the countries in the restorational group are more likely to achieve democratization through a rapid transition than through gradual liberalization involving successive elections. They should also do better in the current period than countries in the nonrestorational group.

The second group consists of countries for whom this democratic transition was in some significant sense foundational or in which democracy took place via gradual democratic reform. Several of these countries had extremely limited experience historically with political democracy, and thus these transitions involved founding, rather than restoring, democracy. In these countries, democratic transitions emerged from autocratic regimes with patrimonial or prolonged oligarchical systems and where revolution, civil war, assassination, or other forms of violence played a central role in undermining the previous regime. In other cases, democracy advanced through democratizing reform by the gradual extension of democratic principles and procedures in the context of civilian authoritarian regimes functioning with dominant parties, or with dominant individuals who relied at least to some extent on a political party vehicle. In some cases, a combination of these two processes was involved. While there is potential overlap across these subgroupings, especially as one turns from static categorization to analysis of processes over time, the first subgroup, with founding elections, includes the Central American countries of El Salvador, Guatemala, Nicaragua, and, with some qualifications, Honduras. In the second subgroup, countries with gradual democratic reform, we find Mexico and, more ambiguously, the Dominican Republic, Panama, and Paraguay (cf. Garretón et al. 2003).[7] It is particularly in this latter group that we would expect to find an electoral mode of transition, one in which successive elections played an important role in liberalization and democratization.

Table 2.2 Civil liberty scores for initial electoral and nonelectoral periods in Latin America and change over the period 1978–2004

	Change in score				Mean civil liberty score (2001–4)	Absolute change from 1st election to ave. 2001–4 score
Types of transition	1st-period pre-election	1st election	2nd-period pre-election	2nd election		
Restored democracies (*N* = 7)	1.16	1.29	0.72	0.03	8.09	0.95
Foundational democracies (*N* = 4)	0.12	1.55	0.30	0.59	6.78	1.25
Gradual democratic reform (*N* = 4)	0.35	1.07	−0.86	−0.21	8.21	1.07

Source: Freedom House; authors' calculations.

Note: Freedom House civil liberty scores are reversed and rescaled such that 10 = high and 1 = low. For complete country-by-country data, see Table 2A.1.

The first election scored was either the first de jure competitive election for president that was not boycotted by all major opposition forces, or the first election to a Constituent Assembly (see Table 2A.2). In Brazil, 1985 was selected because it was the date of an indirect presidential election in the legislature elected in 1982; in Chile, 1988 was selected as the date because of the plebiscite determining whether or not General Pinochet's term as president would be extended. Nonelectoral periods were years with no elections. When elections were held in concurrent years, civil liberty scores were averaged for those years and they were treated as a single electoral period. The first period pre-election compares average scores in the three years prior to the first election with the score four years prior.

In Table 2.2, we examine some of the narrower electoralist arguments. Lindberg finds that in Africa civil liberty scores improve gradually over time and especially during electoral periods as successive *de jure* (but variably and often not de facto) competitive elections are held, and he contrasts this to a transitions argument in which prior democratic advances and liberalizing reforms produce a founding election for regimes which thus quickly emerge as political democracies. For reasons of replication, we rely here on Freedom House data, even while acknowledging that it has been criticized for having a "cold war" bias (favoring pro-U.S. over anti-U.S. ruling elites) and because recent improvements in data collection and scoring also mean that comparison over time can be complicated (Munck and Verkuilen 2002). We find that average civil liberty scores under authoritarian regimes in Latin America are considerably higher than in Africa: average civil liberty scores associated with Africa's first free and fair elections were only 5.0 compared with Latin America's average civil liberty scores for the first transitional election of 7.0 (with the Freedom House scores reversed, so that higher is better, and rescaled to 10).

In Table 2.2 we examine whether a transitions or an electoralist pattern is observable across the three broad types of democratizing experiences previously identified (we also provide the complete country-by-country data in Table 2A.1 in the appendix to this chapter). Columns provide the change in civil liberty scores for the first two electoral cycles; large increases in the first cycle of election would provide support for a transitions over an electoralist pattern. The last two columns provide each country's average civil liberty score for the most recent period (2001–4) and then compare this with the score when the first election took place: a large positive change in the score would provide evidence that a gradual electoralist pattern is evident.

The scores are not distinguishable across the three categories (certainly not in any statistical sense). We do find that the largest increases in civil liberty scores are in the period leading up to and during the first election in the restorational cases (by 2.45 out of 10) and that subsequent improvements are modest (0.95 over the rest of the period). Yet, for the other two groups, there is also considerable improvement around the first key election and more modest subsequent improvements. For the four countries we consider foundational, the improvement around the first election is also evident; these countries end the period with considerably lower average civil liberty scores, as one might expect given their more limited past democratic experience. The four cases of gradual democratic reform do show somewhat less of a boost in their civil liberty scores around the first election than the other two groups and a comparable subsequent increase over the time period as compared with the other groups. A review of country-by-country results for 11 election cycles (Table 2A.1) does not indicate any differences in electoral versus nonelectoral effect, contrary to what Lindberg observes in Africa. Overall, then, the results in this table tend to reinforce a transitional argument built around an initial key election (an argument which, indeed, was derived in part from the Latin American experience), rather than one based on a logic of liberalization over successive elections.

We also examined an expanded definition of freedoms to include not only civil liberties but also basic human rights (freedom from physical abuse and arbitrary detention by the state). None of our quantitative tests examining the impact of electoral versus nonelectoral periods on civil liberties and human rights over more extended periods of time in the region, considering all country cases together, attain statistical significance, even without controlling for other variables. This was the case for civil liberties whether we used the Freedom House measure or a modified form of CIRI's Empowerment Index, and for human rights was also borne out by CIRI's Physical Integrity Index and the Political Terror Scales.[8] Regionwide, there is little evidence that successive elections have fostered liberalization and democratization in the contemporary period.

In turn, the results country by country in Table 2A.1, buttressed by qualitative analysis, do point to some exceptions to this general finding for Latin America. Not surprisingly, this is particularly true for the cases of gradual democratic reform. The pattern for civil liberty scores is most congruent with an electoralist logic in Mexico and, to some extent, in Panama.

That we find the phenomenon of an improvement in civil liberty scores surrounding the key transitional electoral process in so many of the country cases, and across all types of transition cases, indicates that elections are always part of the story but not necessarily always a causal part of the story. In a number of Latin American cases—most clearly Mexico over the 1980s and 1990s—repeated electoral processes arguably had a causal impact over time. However, in several Central American cases, although there were uninterrupted sequences of elections, these were not the central causal factor fostering democratization. More important was the successful negotiation of critical prior agreements or peace pacts between contending parties in civil wars. The electoral calendar played an important role in terms of the timing and sequence of the extension of rights and helped provide a crucial channel for conflict through an alternative means to violence; elections also helped to generate political parties and party organizations, and in this way can also be considered to have played a complementary role (Montgomery 1995).

The causal role of elections in democratic transitions in South American cases has also varied widely. In Argentina, the military made an independent decision to withdraw in a context of economic crisis and after the Falkland/Malvinas humiliation, leading to a classic "transitions" process, as improving conditions for civil and political rights preceded the 1983 elections that ushered the military out of power. In the case of Chile, the 1988 plebiscite on extending General Augusto Pinochet's rule for another lengthy term served as a single critical electoral moment rather than as part of an extended series of elections encouraging a process of democratization. In other cases, fraudulent victories by incumbents mobilized domestic and international forces, most dramatically in the case of the U.S. invasion of Panama overthrowing General Manuel Noriega in Panama in 1989, but also in the case of Alberto Fujimori, who was forced to resign in Peru in 2000 shortly after his reelection (Conaghan 2005; Scranton 1998). In some cases, as in Brazil and Uruguay under their military governments, unexpected electoral defeats of incumbents almost certainly encouraged the moderate opposition to continue to press for a democratic transition (Cardoso 2006; Gillespie and Gonzalez 1989). In the Dominican Republic, the existence of an electoral calendar established a crucial framework within which the democratic opposition could concentrate its efforts, ultimately leading to success in 1978, but there is little evidence of gradual improvements in rights over repeated electoral processes (Hartlyn 1998).

In sum, in Latin America during this most recent third wave of democratization, there have been multiple paths to democracy, and elections have played varied roles in them. The gradual electoralist path is only one such possible route, and one that played a limited role in the region. The next section examines whether there is a longer-term positive association between repeated electoral cycles and improved liberties and human rights in the "post-transition" period.

Elections and the Quality of Democracy

Do repetitive electoral cycles contribute to, or are they at least associated with, an improvement in the quality of democracy in terms of expanded protection of rights and freedoms? To examine this question, we look at trends in several different measures of civil liberties, citizen empowerment, and human rights over time. We have seen from the analysis presented above and the country data in Table 2A.1 that in Latin America there is no discernible improvement in civil liberties, as measured by Freedom House, during election years as compared to nonelection years. These results call into question for Latin America the hypothesis that successive election campaigns, rather than broader sociopolitical processes with impacts across electoral and nonelectoral periods, could be the key mechanism for improving liberties by opening up the media and reinforcing rights of association and movement.

Now we consider longer-term trends in the quality of democracy measured in terms of civil liberties, citizen empowerment, and human rights since the transitions.[9]

We begin this analysis with the first relatively competitive presidential election in each country during the third wave (beginning in 1978) or the Constituent Assembly election leading to the presidential election; that is, we consider those elections in which some credible alternative candidates participated, even if not all the potential opposition participated and even if the results were nullified or reversed. These elections are presented in Table 2A.2. We examine whether we can discern a relationship between repeated competitive elections and changes in civil and human rights scores over time in these countries. We already know that when all countries in the region are considered together, there is no statistically significant relationship between repeated elections and expanded rights and liberties during the third wave. Here, we look at the experiences of individual countries within the transition-type groups to see if any discernible patterns emerge, adding a fourth group for the long-term democracies that did not experience an interruption during the time period under analysis (Colombia, Costa Rica, and Venezuela). We then speculate on other factors that may have helped or hindered their democratic experience.

We find a complicated story, with few discernible patterns. Table 2.3 presents the country experiences, identifying the electoral period in which the first substantial boost in rights occurred, the nature of the change in rights scores since the transition (volatile or stagnant), and the direction of change in rights scores from the first transitional election to 2004. Using a slightly stricter standard than in our earlier discussion, we identify "first boosts" and also positive change over time as those instances in which at least one of our three scores showed a minimum 1.85 points increase in value (of their normalized scores on a 1–10 scale, with 10 the best).

The data for the first transition type, restored democracies, do show that the first (and generally only) boost in human rights, empowerment, and civil liberties occurred around the transitional election in all of these countries except Ecuador (which finally experienced a boost in score prior to the third election). This would confirm the notion that these countries were restoring democracies, and presumably rights and liberties, in a rapid fashion after the withdrawal of the military authoritarian governments. (Lack of comparable data prior to the 1960s' military authoritarian wave prevents a direct confir-

Table 2.3 Elections and changes in civil liberties and human rights

Transition type	Electoral period of 1st boost[a]	Change over subsequent elections	Change from 1st election to 2004[b]	Explanation of late-occurring "1st boosts"
Restored democracy				
Argentina	1st	Volatile	Mixed	
Bolivia	1st pre	Volatile	Positive	
Brazil	1st	Volatile	Neutral	
Chile	1st pre, 1st	Volatile	Positive	
Ecuador	3rd pre	Volatile	Neutral	
Peru	1st pre	Volatile	Mixed	
Uruguay	1st, 2nd pre	Volatile	Positive	
Long-term democracy				
Colombia		Volatile	Negative	
Costa Rica		Stagnant	Negative	
Venezuela		Volatile	Negative	
Founding election				
El Salvador	5th pre	Volatile	Positive	1992 peace accords
Guatemala	1st, 4th pre	Volatile	Mixed	1996 peace accords
Honduras	2nd pre	Stagnant	Mixed	
Nicaragua	1st, 2nd	Volatile	Positive	
Gradual transitions				
Dominican Republic	6th pre	Stagnant	Negative	1995 (negotiated election)
Mexico	2nd, 5th pre	Volatile	Mixed	1985, 1993 (unclear)
Panama	3rd pre, 3rd	Volatile	Mixed	1989 U.S. invasion
Paraguay	1st	Volatile	Negative	

Note: Changes in civil liberties and human rights as measured by Freedom House civil liberties scale from 1972 and CIRI human rights data from 1980 (physical integrity index and empowerment index).

[a] Electoral periods begin with first post-1978 transitional election, identified in Table 2A.1. Boost is defined as a minimum 1.85 points increase in value for at least one variable (Freedom House civil liberties scale, CIRI empowerment index, or CIRI physical integrity).

[b] Positive = value change of at least 1.85 in one or more variables and all the same sign
Neutral = value changes between –1.85 and 1.85 for all three variables
Mixed = mixture of positive and negative impacts with at least one value change > 1.85
Negative = value change of –1.85 in one or more variables and all the same sign

mation of this presumption.) Perhaps more interesting is that none of these countries showed a consistently improving pattern of rights and liberties scores; instead, they were all volatile. And while over the longer term, none of them deteriorated markedly in liberties and rights, only three of the seven (Bolivia, Chile, and Uruguay) showed a positive change beyond the first election. Improvements in rights and liberties in the others were either neutral or a mix of some progress and some regression. Thus, this finding does *not* lend support to the thesis that repeated elections in electoral democracies will over time improve the quality of democracy with a significant expansion of rights. Instead, the finding indicates a potential ceiling or threshold effect in which these Latin American democracies achieved a certain level of civil liberties, citizen empowerment, and human rights protections with the return of electoral democracies, but have not been able to improve significantly beyond that initial boost.

Our findings for the second grouping of countries, long-term democracies, are more alarming. Colombia, Costa Rica, and Venezuela each have had continuous democracies since 1958. In this study, we examined changes in their civil liberties, citizen empowerment, and human rights scores since 1978, during the third wave period in which the rest of the continent was restoring or installing democracy. Not only do we fail to see a steady improvement in rights and liberties with continuous electoral democracy, but we actually see in all of these countries a *deterioration* in these scores. Costa Rica still retained fairly high scores (with an average of 8.69 out of 10 possible for the three scores between 2001 and 2004), but Venezuela and Colombia declined to an average of 5.23 and 4.48, respectively. This surely indicates that other explanations are needed to understand the limits of Latin American democracies' capacity to protect basic rights and liberties, a point to which we return in the conclusions.

The next transition type, founding elections in Central America, shows the most diversity in terms of relationship with civil liberties, citizen empowerment, and human rights. Three of these countries were undergoing civil wars in the 1980s and undertook founding elections only after negotiated peace settlements, although they also conducted elections during their civil wars without the participation of all sectors of society. We start coding elections for El Salvador and Guatemala in 1982 and 1984, respectively. El Salvador held Constituent Assembly elections in 1982; these led to competitive presidential elections in 1984 and regime change from nondemocratic to semi-democratic. Guatemala's 1984 Constituent Assembly elections led to competitive presidential elections in 1985 and regime change from non-democratic to semi-democratic. Nevertheless, the first elections in which all major sectors, including the left, participated occurred only *after* negotiated accords (in 1994 for El Salvador and 1999 for Guatemala), leading to democratic ratings those same years (Mainwaring, Brinks, and Pérez-Liñán 2002). Concomitantly, we see major boosts in their human rights scores—especially in physical integrity—in the period immediately following the peace accords and leading up to the founding election. (Guatemala also experienced an earlier boost in civil liberties and empowerment scores during the first recorded election period in 1984–85, though its physical integrity scores declined in those years.)

Nicaragua's dictator was overthrown by an armed revolutionary force in 1979, and the country held its first election in 1984 in the midst of a U.S.-sponsored counterrevolutionary civil war, though it was boycotted by some of the opposition parties. Physical integrity rights improved temporarily during those elections, but then deteriorated as the contra war dragged on. Yet, in this case what was important was not a series of successive elections. Rather, once the Sandinistas became convinced they could not win a military victory over the contras (and in the midst of an economic embargo by the United States), they came to view the holding of credible elections as the key mechanism that would help generate a cease-fire and facilitate a negotiated end to the war. As an incentive for the United States to end its support to the contras, the Sandinistas moved up the date for the elections by several months and, with considerable international mediation, successfully negotiated a series of guarantees with opposition forces in order to ensure their participation (Carter Center 1990; Ramirez 1999, esp. 272–75 and 149 on the contrasting logic of the 1984 elections). The 1990 elections thus became the "founding" elections in that all parties participated and the civil war ended, though renewed fighting threatened the election itself in part of the country. Civil liberties and empowerment showed a big boost with the 1990 elections, while physical integrity scores improved only after those elections and a final negotiated end to the fighting and repatriation of the contras.

In all three of these Central American cases, then, elections became a vehicle for the peaceful selection of leaders only after internationally mediated peace accords ended civil wars. The prior elections held during the civil wars did not themselves lead to democratization and indeed were criticized by some as "demonstration elections" to uphold a military-backed autocratic regime (or a revolutionary regime in the case of Nicaragua). Honduras is somewhat different in that it did not experience an armed insurgency and civil war, but it was involved in its neighbors' wars as it sheltered the contras in particular. Its Constituent Assembly election and founding election in 1980 and 1981 marked the transition from a military regime to a semi-democratic one, with concomitant improvement in rights scores, particularly physical integrity.

Only two of the founding election cases improved the quality of their democracy across the board in terms of rights and liberties—El Salvador and Nicaragua—though these scores were volatile. Guatemala and Honduras had mixed records. In all cases, physical integrity improved markedly compared with the first election measured, but in Guatemala and Honduras, empowerment and civil liberties remained stagnant or eroded.

The final transition type, gradual reform transitions under hegemonic party rule, would be expected to most closely fit the electoralist effect Lindberg found in Africa. Nevertheless, we do not find this to be the case for the four countries in this subgrouping: Mexico, the Dominican Republic, Panama, and Paraguay. Mexico is the quintessential gradual democratizer over a series of elections, yet an examination of civil liberties, empowerment, and human rights scores does not support the argument that increased electoral competition leads to improvements in the quality of democracy. Civil liberties are rated as either stagnant until they jump with the 2000 elections (Freedom House) or as showing peaks at every election year followed by valleys (with the exception of the 1994 presidential elections, when they bottom out) in the CIRI empowerment index. Curiously, the empowerment index declines during the most competitive election years in Mexico's history (2000 and 2003), while Freedom House's civil liberties scores jump then. Physical integrity scores are somewhat volatile over the period, with an overall slight decline. The data are contradictory: Freedom House's more aggregated scores show an improvement beginning in 2000, while the two disaggregated CIRI scores both show some erosion since the first scored elections in 1982. Thus, we see no sustained improvements in either civil liberties or human rights from 1982 to the present to go along with increased electoral competition. We also note that the absolute physical integrity scores are much lower than the empowerment and civil liberties scores, highlighting Mexico's continued problems with crime and security, including involving state forces.

In the Dominican Republic, strongman Joaquín Balaguer dominated politics until 1996 but did allow competitive elections in 1978, which he acknowledged losing after considerable domestic and international pressure. (He was in office from 1966 to 1978 and from 1986 to 1996.) Nevertheless, we see no impact on civil liberties with that election; the empowerment index shows a gradual climb, to peak in 1985 and then fall a bit thereafter (when Balaguer returned to power), with further deterioration in more recent years. Likewise, human rights show no improvement as a result of repeated electoral cycles and instead show some deterioration in the period 1978–2004. Two election cycles that also correlate with temporary drops in the CIRI scores are 1990 and 1994; both of these were contentious elections with allegations of fraud, and the latter resulted in a negotiated shortened term for Balaguer, followed by new elections from which he was barred two years later. Thus, this protracted transition also fails to improve civil liberties and even results in a decline in human rights.

Paraguay is the only country in Latin America (other than Cuba) that had yet to rate a "democracy" ranking by Mainwaring, Brinks, and Pérez-Liñán during the time period of this study through 2004. It had one of the longest-running hegemonic parties in the world until the April 2008 elections, when opposition leader Fernando Lugo defeated the incumbent party candidate for president. We thus consider its transition as partially a "democratic reformer" gradual transition (from nondemocracy to semi-democracy) under the Colorado Party, and partially a founding election after the coup against Stroessner in 1989. We see a major boost in rights and freedoms during the 1989 elections and again leading up to the 1993 elections. While civil liberties and citizen empowerment are essentially sustained through our final scores in 2004, physical integrity scores, somewhat surprisingly, deteriorated after the founding election.

Panama's third-wave transition begins with elections occurring under the strongman rule of General Manuel Noriega in 1984 and 1989 (the first elections in two decades). The 1984 election was widely viewed by Noriega opponents as manipulated, as its outcome was a narrow victory for Noriega's favored candidate under questionable circumstances. These elections led to an initial drop in civil liberties and human rights scores until after the fraudulent and nullified elections of 1989 and the U.S. invasion in 1990 removed Noriega and installed the presumed victors in office. A large boost in rights and freedoms occurred after the U.S. invasion and was essentially sustained through our final scores in 2004. Through external armed intervention, then, Panama shifted to semi-democratic status in 1990 and democratic status in 1994, and was able to sustain its improved democracy (both in civil liberties and in human rights) thereafter.

Assessing the Electoralist Argument regarding Deepening Democracy

In only one-fourth of the Latin American countries we examined (5 of 18) is there a pattern of association between repeated electoral cycles and the deepening of democracy (in terms of improved civil liberties and human rights) after the first transitional elections from nondemocracies. A closer look at these five countries—Bolivia, Chile, Uruguay, El Salvador, and Nicaragua—shows that the electoralist argument does not appear to weigh equally in explaining their relative improvements in civil liberties and human rights. In two cases (Uruguay and Chile), the restoration, after a military interruption, of the strongest democratic legacies in Latin America made it much easier to also restore and improve civil liberties, citizen empowerment, and human rights. The most significant boosts in rights came directly preceding, during, and immediately after the first election cycle, supporting a transitional argument. Some continued improvement, particularly in physical integrity, occurred, and these two countries have the highest absolute scores across the board.

Bolivia had prior experience only with semi-democracy, and its initial transition in 1979–80 was troubled, with elections interspersed with coups for two years. Civil liberties improved several years before the transitional elections but, along with human rights, plummeted during the first unstable years. Liberties and rights were soon recovered and sustained at moderate levels, though further political instability since 2002 had some negative effect. In the other two cases (El Salvador and Nicaragua), both absent any prior democratic history, international factors helped to improve liberties and rights only after negotiated peace, whether the end of external support to both the military and guerrillas and the subsequent peace accords in El Salvador, or the negotiated cease-fire, elections, and end to U.S. support for the contras in Nicaragua.

A second pattern also involving five countries is that of a clear deterioration in rights and liberties scores. This is particularly surprising, in light of the electoralist argument, in that these are either long-standing democracies in which we would hope to see a continuously improving quality of democracy, or countries with gradual transitions best fitting the electoralist argument. Perhaps the most worrisome is the deterioration of rights and liberties in the three countries with continuous democracies since 1958—Costa Rica, Colombia, and Venezuela. Costa Rica has experienced a slight decline but remains near the top of Latin American scores in absolute terms. On the other hand, Venezuela and Colombia have suffered substantial declines since 1978 and now have some of the lowest scores in the region. This experience belies the expectation that repeated elections may help to improve other rights and indicates the need to look at other factors. Colombia's long-running, multifaceted internal war and extensive human rights violations linked to state security forces and their allies most likely explain its low human rights scores from the onset of measurement in 1980s. Civil liberties, though generally in the mid-range, show erosion after 1988. In Venezuela, concomitant with declining oil prices in the 1980s and growing political unrest in the 1990s, we see slowly eroding civil liberties and empowerment after 1988. Human rights scores showed a serious decline in the protest-filled 1990s, followed by an uptick, and then volatility with the political conflict of 2002–4.

The other two countries with a negative trend are the Dominican Republic and Paraguay, although these declines are less serious than in Colombia and Venezuela. Still, it is notable that two of the countries with protracted, gradual transitions have failed to maintain or improve gains in rights and freedoms relative to the first elections. In both cases, physical integrity is the lowest of the three scores in recent years (though still in the mid-range), indicating continued problems with security and abuse by state security forces.

The remaining eight countries show either little movement (a neutral result) or a mixed result with improvement in one dimension and deterioration in another. This is the case for four of the restored democracies, indicating an ability to restore rights in the context of the transition but an inability to deepen democracy in these dimensions. The contextual factors are obviously key to understanding these patterns. In Peru, the Shining Path guerrilla movement and hyperinflation ushered in the electoral authoritarian rule of Alberto Fujimori in the 1990s, and the concomitant erosion of rights; in Ecuador weak political institutions contributed to severe political instability, protests, and stagnation in rights and freedoms; in Argentina, a history of hyperinflation contributed to Carlos Menem's hyperpresidentialism and the concomitant restriction of rights in the 1990s, followed by financial collapse and political instability in 2001; in Brazil, continued problems with crime and personal security are associated with relatively lower and eroding physical integrity scores. The mixed results for two founding election cases (Guatemala and Honduras) and two gradual transition cases (Panama and Mexico) also indicate an uneven ability to sustain and improve rights' gains early on in the transition.

This third grouping of countries, then, demonstrates a clear association between transitional elections and an improvement in civil liberties and human rights in the short term, but also the difficulty in sustaining these rights in the long term. This pattern is reflected in Latin America's general success in providing political rights to elect and remove leaders in the third wave while remaining stymied in providing consistent civil rights and minimally acceptable social rights to all citizens. The 2004 United Nations Development Program report on the state of democracy in the region, along with numerous scholars, have pointed out the inability of Latin American states to provide widespread equal rights to their citizens. Our analysis confirms the problem and points to the complicating factors of drugs, guerilla insurgencies, and financial collapse inhibiting the ability of the state to protect human rights. Low human rights scores cannot be attributed solely to illegal nonstate actors, for our measures focus on state policies and abuse. However, the response of the state to severe security challenges probably leads to restrictions in civil liberties and the abuse of human rights in the most serious cases. Likewise, severe financial collapse has contributed to political instability, which may in turn spur governments to crack down on civil liberties or human rights.

Such complicating factors as armed nonstate actors and financial collapse could be mitigating the electoralist impact in the post-transition phase. In a few cases international actions helped to overcome strong internal obstacles and spurred improved rights and freedoms in the wake of negotiated peace agreements. In these cases, the elections following the peace agreements were not the first elections, but they were pivotal, since they generally involved all political sectors for the first time and served as a mechanism for the peaceful selection of leaders instead of armed conflict. They also occurred in the context of significantly improved rights and freedoms.

Overall, the logic of electoral calculation does not appear to have contributed to improvements in other democratic rights in the first 25 years of the transition. After two and a half decades, we may be witnessing a change, though, as excluded citizens in many of the countries in the second two groups use the ballot box to bring in new governments promising to improve their rights. Whether these electoral processes and their outcomes will produce a deepening of democratic rights, or be manipulated so as to erode them, remains to be seen.

Conclusions

Our principal conclusion based on this review of the evidence for Latin America is that electoralist arguments must be qualified, for three reasons. First, they provide incomplete explanations, analytically, for the causes of democratization. The apparent power of electoralism appears to be dependent on a "period effect." The role of international actors in persuading incumbents to enter what might be termed "riskier" electoral processes (i.e., elections that are more truly competitive with uncertain outcomes) can change across time periods; international influence is also not constant across regions or countries even in the same time period. Thus, these international factors should be incorporated into any general model as a key prior variable (which can also change over time), even as it is then appropriate to trace how the subsequent electoralist logic plays out. Arguably in Latin America, there are country cases where direct international involvement may have played a less significant role in the decision of incumbents to embark upon and sustain an electoralist path. Here, the reluctance of incumbents to engage in increasingly risky elections and the commitment of democratic forces to the "dual game" of elections and electoral reform is important, but it forms only a part of the set of factors which (in Dahl's well-known phrase) enhance the odds of authoritarian acceptance of exit from power because they lower the costs of tolerating the opposition and increase the costs of suppressing opponents steadily over time (Dahl 1971, 15–16).

Second, electoralist arguments must be qualified because electoral processes are blunt, and sometimes ineffective, instruments in terms of their ability to promote or deepen democratization. Our review of Latin American countries over the recent past indicates little relationship between electoral processes and democratic deepening; indeed, the manipulation of electoral processes has in some cases played an important role in undermining democracy. In fact, the Latin American cases demonstrate a relative powerlessness of elections to improve the quality of democracy once the minimal threshold of electoral democracy has been reached, which is similar to what Roessler and Howard find in their cross-regional analysis for this volume.

For these reasons, in our view any blanket policy advice about the "power of elections" should be avoided. Elections alone are insufficient to move countries to liberal democracy. While elections are obviously necessary to maintain electoral democracy, other socioeconomic and political-institutional factors need to be addressed to improve the quality of democracy.

Third, Latin America's far more extensive prior experience with democracy and its higher initial average levels of civil liberties across both restorational and even non-restorational cases compared with Africa may also help explain the differential relevance of the electoralist argument in the two regions. The average civil liberty scores associated with Africa's first free and fair elections were only 4.4, compared with Latin America's average scores at the time of transitional elections from some sort of authoritarianism of 2.9 (Freedom House scores, where higher is worse). A similar pattern holds when comparing more recent civil liberty scores for the two regions; in Africa average scores in 2003 were 3.97, whereas Latin America's were 2.67. That elections were not a first-time experience during the third-wave transitions in Latin America contrasts with Africa and may help explain the differing relationship between elections and greater liberties.

Appendix

Tables 2A.1 and 2A.2 follow on pages 72–76.

Table 2A.1 Change in civil liberties, empowerment, and physical integrity scores by election period (mean change in scores, 1975–2004)

	1st data year[a]	1st PPE	1st PE	2nd PPE	2nd PE	3rd PPE	3rd PE	4th PPE	4th PE	5th PPE	5th PE
Restored democracies											
ARG											
Phys Int	1983		3.33	0.00	1.11	1.11	–2.22	0.00	1.11	–3.33	2.22
Emplnd	1983		2.22	–2.22	2.22	1.11	–1.11	1.11	0.00	0.00	–1.11
FHCL	1983	0.95	1.90	1.43	0.00	1.43	0.00	0.00	–1.43	–1.43	0.00
BOL											
Phys Int	1985				1.11	1.48	1.85	–1.11	0.00	0.00	1.11
Emplnd	1985				–1.11	0.00	2.22	0.00	0.00	–0.37	–0.74
FHCL	1979	1.90	–0.48	1.43	0.00	0.00	0.00	0.00	0.00	–0.47	0.47
BRA											
Phys Int	1985	0.37	0.74	–0.56	–1.11	–0.19	0.74	–0.74	–1.48	1.11	1.11
Emplnd	1985	0.00	2.22	–0.56	0.56	0.00	–1.11	.37	0.74	–0.37	0.37
FHCL	1985	0.48	0.95	–0.71	0.00	–1.19	–0.96	0.00	0.00	0.96	0.47
CHL											
Phys Int	1988	1.85	0.37	1.11	–1.81	2.55	–0.05	–2.92	1.67	0.56	1.94
Emplnd	1988	1.48	2.41	0.93	–1.01	1.01	0.42	0.00	0.00	0.00	0.00
FHCL	1988	0.48	2.38	1.43	0.00	0.00	0.00	0.00	0.00	0.00	0.00
ECU											
Phys Int	1984				–0.74	–2.22	0.00	0.00	1.11	2.22	–2.22
Emplnd	1984				–1.48	2.22	0.00	–2.22	2.22	0.00	–2.22
FHCL	1978	0.00	1.43	1.43	–1.43	0.00	0.00	1.43	0.00	0.00	0.00
PER											
Phys Int	1985						–1.08	–0.64	0.64	1.11	–1.11
Emplnd	1985						0.00	–0.83	–1.39	0.00	0.00
FHCL	1978	2.86	0.00	0.00	1.43	0.00	0.00	–0.71	–0.72	–1.42	0.00
URY											
Phys Int	1984		–0.37	3.61	–0.28	–0.28	0.28	–1.11	1.11	0.28	–1.39
Emplnd	1984		0.74	2.50	0.83	–0.83	–1.39	1.67	0.56	–1.94	–0.28
FHCL	1984	1.43	2.86	0.00	0.18	–0.18	0.00	0.00	0.00	1.43	0.00
Long-term democracies											
COL											
Phys Int	1982							–1.93	0.76	1.17	–3.33
Emplnd	1982					1.11	0.00	0.00	–1.67	0.56	–0.63
FHCL	1978	–1.43	0.00	0.00	0.00	0.00	0.00	–0.95	–0.48	0.00	0.00
CRI											
Phys Int	1982					–0.37	0.37	0.00	0.00	–1.11	0.00
Emplnd	1982					–0.37	0.37	–0.37	–0.74	–1.85	0.74
FHCL	1978	0.00	0.00	0.00	0.00	0.00	0.00	0.00	0.00	–0.48	–0.95
VEN											
Phys Int	1983					–2.22	1.11	–3.33	–1.11	0.56	2.41
Emplnd	1983					0.56	0.56	–2.50	0.28	0.00	1.11
FHCL	1978	0.00	0.00	0.00	0.00	0.00	–1.43	0.00	0.00	0.00	–1.43

6th PPE	6th PE	7th PPE	7th PE	8th PPE	8th PE	9th PPE	9th PE	10th PPE	10th PE	11th PPE	Final score (ave. last 3 yrs)	Absolute change[b]
0.00	−0.37	−0.74	0.00	−2.22	1.11	−1.11	0.00	1.11	1.11	−1.11	5.93	−1.85
−1.11	0.00	1.11	0.00	0.00	−1.11	1.11	−1.11	2.22	0.00	−1.11	9.63	0.74
0.00	0.00	0.00	0.00	0.00	0.00	1.43	−1.43	0.00	1.43	0.00	8.10	0.96
−1.67	1.67	−2.22									7.41	1.85[c]
0.00	−1.11	0.00									6.67	0.00[c]
0.00	0.00	0.00									7.14	1.43
0.00											5.56	−1.11
−1.11											8.15	−0.74
0.00											7.14	−1.43
1.02											8.52	4.07
−1.16											7.41	0.19
1.43											10.00	2.86
1.11	−2.22	1.11	2.22	−1.11	−0.37	−0.37	0.74	−1.11			5.93	−0.74[c]
0.00	1.11	−2.22	1.11	1.11	−0.37	−1.48	−0.37	0.56			7.04	−0.74[c]
−1.43	0.00	0.00	0.00	0.00	−0.48	0.48	0.00	0.00			7.14	0.00
0.56	1.67	−0.28	0.83	−0.56							4.44	2.22[c]
−0.56	−0.56	1.94	0.83	−2.41							5.93	−2.96[c]
0.71	0.71	0.36	1.07	0.00							7.14	1.43
											8.52	2.96
											7.78	1.11
											10.00	1.43
	0.00	0.81	1.52	−2.33							1.78	−2.67[c]
0.26	0.37	0.00	−1.11	−1.11							5.93	−1.85[c]
0.00	0.00	0.00	0.00	0.00							5.71	−1.43
0.00	0.00	−0.37	0.37	0.00							8.89	−1.11[c]
1.11	0.00	0.37	−0.37	−1.11							8.15	−1.85[c]
0.00	0.00	−2.86	2.86	0.71							9.05	−0.95
−0.19											4.81	−2.96[c]
−3.33											5.19	−3.70[c]
−0.36											5.71	−2.86

continued

Table 2A.1 continued

	1st data year[a]	1st PPE	1st PE	2nd PPE	2nd PE	3rd PPE	3rd PE	4th PPE	4th PE	5th PPE	5th PE
Founding elec. nonrestorat.											
SLV											
Phys Int	1982			0.00	0.61	1.72	−1.72	0.61	0.00	4.44	1.11
Emplnd	1982			0.00	1.11	1.11	0.56	−2.78	1.11	0.56	1.67
FHCL	1982	0.48	−0.47	0.00	1.42	0.71	−0.71	0.00	0.00	1.43	0.00
GTM											
Phys Int	1984		−0.81	2.70	−1.48	1.85	−0.74	2.22	0.00	−0.74	1.85
Emplnd	1984		2.59	0.28	−0.28	0.00	0.00	2.22	−1.11	0.37	−2.59
FHCL	1984	0.00	3.57	0.71	−1.43	−1.42	0.00	1.43	0.00	0.00	0.00
HND											
Phys Int	1985			2.97	1.48	−1.11	0.00	0.37	0.74	0.74	0.37
Emplnd	1985			1.11	0.00	−0.37	0.37	−1.48	−0.74	1.85	−0.74
FHCL	1980	0.00	0.00	0.00	0.00	0.00	0.00	0.00	0.00	0.00	0.00
NIC											
Phys Int	1984		2.30	−1.80	0.69	2.67	0.67	0.28	−0.28	0.00	
Emplnd	1984		−1.48	−0.91	6.47	−1.11	0.00	0.83	−0.83	0.00	
FHCL	1984	0.00	0.00	0.00	2.85	−1.43	1.43	0.00	0.00	0.00	
Gradual democratic reform											
DOM											
Phys Int	1982					0.74	−0.74	1.11	−2.22	−0.37	−2.96
Emplnd	1982					0.37	−0.37	0.00	−2.22	1.48	−1.48
FHCL	1978	−0.48	0.47	−0.95	0.95	−1.43	0.00	0.00	0.00	0.00	0.00
MEX											
Phys Int	1982			−2.22	−1.11	1.11	1.11	−2.83	0.61	2.22	−2.22
Emplnd	1982			−2.22	2.22	−1.11	1.11	−1.67	−0.56	−1.11	−1.11
FHCL	1982	0.00	0.00	0.00	0.00	0.00	1.43	−0.71	−0.72	0.72	−0.72
PAN											
Phys Int	1984		−0.37	−0.28	−4.17	3.33	2.22	−1.11	1.11	0.56	−0.56
Emplnd	1984		−1.11	−1.11	−4.44	5.56	0.00	−1.67	0.56	0.83	0.28
FHCL	1984	0.48	0.95	−2.50	−1.78	5.71	0.00	−1.43	0.00	0.00	1.43
PRY											
Phys Int	1989	0.00	3.33	−3.33	1.11	2.22	−3.33	3.06	−3.06	1.11	−1.11
Emplnd	1989	1.33	4.44	−1.11	−2.22	4.44	0.00	−1.67	2.78	−1.11	0.00
FHCL	1989	1.43	2.85	0.00	0.00	0.00	0.00	0.00	0.00	−2.85	2.85
Ave. for Latin America											
Phys Int		4.64	5.20	5.07	5.51	6.17	5.93	5.48	5.52	6.11	6.28
Emplnd		4.07	7.28	7.18	7.87	8.69	8.78	8.28	8.22	8.16	7.79
FHCL		6.11	7.02	7.15	7.27	7.39	7.38	7.33	7.14	7.02	7.14

Note: Physical integrity scores come from CIRI human rights scores, normalized to a 1–10 scale, with 10 being the best. The Empowerment Index is a modified form of the CIRI human rights score that omits political participation, normalized to a 1–10 scale, with 10 being the best. The FHCL is the Freedom House civil liberties score, normalized to a 1–10 scale and reversed so that 10 is the best.

6th PPE	6th PE	7th PPE	7th PE	8th PPE	8th PE	9th PPE	9th PE	10th PPE	10th PE	11th PPE	Final score (ave. last 3 yrs)	Absolute change[b]
0.56	0.56	−1.11	−0.56	1.11	−1.67						7.04	6.04
−0.56	0.56	1.11	−0.56	−0.56	−1.11						8.15	2.59
0.00	0.00	0.00	0.00	0.00	0.00						7.14	2.85
0.00											6.30	5.30
1.11											6.67	0.00
0.00											5.71	−0.71
−1.48	1.48	−1.11									6.67	4.45[c]
0.74	−0.74	−2.22									6.67	−2.19[c]
0.00	0.00	0.00									7.14	0.00
											6.67	2.22
											7.78	4.44
											7.14	2.86
2.22	0.00	0.00	−2.22	2.22	0.00	0.00	1.11	−1.11	0.00		5.93	−1.85[c]
2.22	0.00	0.00	0.00	−1.11	0.00	0.00	0.00	−2.22	0.00		6.30	−2.59[c]
0.00	0.00	0.00	0.00	0.00	1.43	0.00	0.00	0.00	0.00		8.57	0.00
0.56	0.56	1.11	−1.11	0.00	1.11	0.00					4.07	−1.48
1.67	1.67	−0.56	−1.67	1.11	−1.11	1.11					7.41	−2.59
0.72	−0.72	0.00	1.43	0.72	0.71	0.00					8.57	2.86
1.11	0.00										9.26	2.59
0.00	−1.11										7.04	−0.74
0.00	0.00										8.57	1.43
0.56	1.67	−1.11									6.67	−2.22
−1.11	−1.11	0.00									7.04	−0.74
0.00	0.00	0.00									7.14	0.00
6.13	6.44	5.86	5.80	5.33	5.70	5.09	5.93	5.56	6.11	5.56		
7.67	7.87	7.94	8.19	7.69	7.70	7.87	7.41	7.59	7.78	8.89		
7.03	7.02	6.66	7.14	7.32	7.62	8.21	7.62	7.62	8.57	8.57		

Abbreviations: PPE = period pre-election, PE = period election

[a] First election year that data were available.

[b] Absolute change from first election.

[c] Compares to election year other than first one noted due to missing data.

Table 2A.2 Latin America: first de jure competitive election selected

Transition type	Election year
Restorational cases	
No incumbent in elections	
Argentina	1983
Bolivia	1979
Ecuador	1978
Peru	1978
Uruguay	1985
Incumbent in elections	
Brazil	1985
Chile	1988
Panama	1984
Foundational and/or reform cases	
Direct incumbent involvement	
Dominican Republic	1978
El Salvador	1982
Guatemala	1984
Mexico	1982
Nicaragua	1984
Paraguay	1989
Indirect incumbent involvement	
Honduras	1980

CHAPTER THREE

Elections as Levers of Democratization

A Global Inquiry

Jan Teorell and Axel Hadenius

The core question posed in this volume is: Do elections promote democracy? To be sure, political democracy, as we know it, is primarily institutionalized through the holding of repetitive and competitive elections. This is not a claim we are questioning. Rather, we are probing the proposition that the holding of elections in itself spurs the development of greater democracy in other respects in a country. As presented in other chapters in this book, there are actually two versions of this proposition. One focuses on distinct and separate elections, arguing that they work as events that trigger a process of democratization that goes beyond the quality of these elections in themselves (see the chapters by Schedler, Bunce and Wolchik, and Moraski, for example). The other version holds that democracy evolves as a result of a long series of repetitive elections stretched over time (investigated by, for example, Lindberg, McCoy and Hartlyn, and Brownlee). Whereas the first argument puts primacy on the current effects of single elections, the second stresses the cumulative experience of multiple elections. Both are versions of the argument that elections constitute a unique mode of democratic transition, an argument that is systematically analyzed for the first time in the present volume. In this chapter, we analyze the broadest possible scope, using a global sample of 193 countries from 1919 to 2004 to test these claims.

To minimize the risk of an overlap between measures of elections and their consequences for democracy, we apply two strategies to measure current election effects. The first is to employ a *temporal lag*, whereby democratic effects are measured at a point in time after the election. We use two different lags: a one-year lag (which implies that we are looking at effects in the following year) and a monthly lag (i.e., effects during the election year but measured at least one month after the election). The second strategy is to use a *nonelectoral measure* of democracy, namely, the Freedom House civil liberty scores. To make this measure really waterproof, we control for political rights scores (also from Freedom House). However, as it could be argued that this control is too rigorous, we also run analyses without it. We find the most noteworthy effects from multiparty elections (noncompetitive elections thus have little import), when—employing the first strategy—a monthly lag within the election year is applied, and when—using the second strategy—civil rights are accounted for without control for political rights.

To examine the cumulative experience of elections, we start by reckoning the total historical *stock* of elections country by country from 1919 onwards. Because the democratic payoff of elections may decrease with the number and frequency of elections, we also calculate the *square root* of the total number of elections and an *annual depreciation rate*. We find that that there is indeed also a cumulative electoral effect. But not all elections are equally important. Only multiparty elections count; and really democratic elections count the most. Furthermore, we find that the way elections are accounted for actually matters. We notice the most prominent effect when the square root variable is applied. This implies that the number of elections is important. But it also implies that the relative importance of each new election is declining.

In the analysis that follows, we first review the recent literature on the subject of elections as causes of democratization. We then present our data and estimation strategy, followed by the results for current and historical election experiences. We conclude by discussing the implications of our findings.

The Democratizing Power of Elections Hypothesis

Until recently, consideration of the role played by political institutions has been surprisingly absent in theoretical approaches to explaining democratization (Snyder and Mahoney 1999). A small but growing body of literature focusing on elections as institutions has begun to change this picture, however. Of seminal importance in this regard is the work by Bratton and van de Walle (1997). Arguing in favor of a "politico-institutional" approach, they put a premium on two institutional features in explaining democratization in sub-Saharan Africa during the 1990s: the extent of political competition and the degree of political participation during the previous authoritarian regime. Most notably for the present purposes, they found that the sheer number of elections held since independence—regardless of the freedom and fairness of these elections—helped explain transition outcomes to a significant degree. The explanation for this finding, according to the authors, would be that even rigged or noncompetitive elections, by providing opportunities for political participation, make people better prepared for the experience with real democracy.

On a more theoretical note, Schedler (2002b) portrays the logic of ambivalent elections in authoritarian regimes as unstable two-level games that tend to set countries on paths toward democratization. The uncertainty created by acceding voting rights to citizens with unknown preferences, the possible manipulation of election results by incumbent autocrats, and the coordination problems faced by evolving opposition parties—all these tend to create a "self-subversive" spiral that either leads to the shutting down of the electoral arena or, if the game is repeated, to a progressive movement away from authoritarianism: "Even if democratic progress is not inevitable, the inner logic of the game pulls it away from authoritarianism." Schedler (2002b, 111) approvingly cites Barkan's (2000) analogy with "the mouse nibbling at the proverbial piece of cheese. After a period of time, the piece, in this case the authoritarian state, is no more."

A critical feature of Schedler's (2002b) argument is that only *multiparty* elections generate the ambivalence that over time may defeat an electoral autocracy. In contrast to the view of Bratton and van de Walle, then, Schedler argues that some room must be provided for opposition participation in the electoral contest in order for elections to have a potentially democratizing effect. This theme has recently been developed further by Lindberg (2006a), who sketches an institutional learning theory of societal democratization, in which people's repetitive experience with *de jure* competitive and inclusive elections pay off for democracy in the nonelectoral arena (even if these elections turn out to be *de facto* neither free nor fair). Both individuals and voluntary associations bring to other spheres of society the resources, skills, and norms they have learned in the electoral arena. Moreover, elections may result in a stronger sense for the rule of law within the judicial sphere and an enlarged taste for informational freedom by the mass media (Lindberg 2006a, 111–16). In sum, Lindberg's overall hypothesis may be summarized as "the longer an uninterrupted series of elections a country has, the more its society will become imbued with democratic qualities" (2006a, 99).

Upon closer scrutiny, this democratizing power of elections hypothesis may be interpreted in (at least) two ways. The mouse-nibbling metaphor suggests that each time an election is held, some more or less immediate real gains are made in the level of democracy. If there is any cumulative effect of repetitive elections over time, according to this view, then that is simply the sum of a series of smaller gains that each occur in the wake of a single election. Another way to interpret the same theory, however, would be to say that what is gained at each successive election is an increased *potential* for democratization. As more people learn through election experiences, as new organizations form, as more democratic values are imbued in society and so on, the larger the probability for a democratic breakthrough. According to this second view the effect of elections on democratization is not captured by the metaphor of mouse nibbling, but rather by that of a pressure chamber. Cumulative experiences with elections imply that the pressure for democratization rises—even though no actual gains in the level of democracy are made at each successive election. The pressure may be rising although the chamber itself is not expanding. If the theory is right, however, one day the chamber would explode—that is, one day the pressure for democratization results in a real democratic breakthrough.

The pressure chamber version of the theory comes closest to Eisenstadt's (2004) story of the protracted transition to democracy in Mexico. According to Eisenstadt, the groundwork for the 2000 watershed presidential election, where the opposition finally ousted the hegemonic Party of the Institutional Revolution (PRI), had been laid in the series of postelection struggles throughout the 1990s. What eventually matters for democratization is a process that "transpires behind the curtain before democracy's opening act, and is thus not visible to observers focusing instead on democracy's debut" (2004, 2, 24). Although Eisenstadt's metaphor is different, the idea is the same: elections matter, not as a single-shot event but as a cumulative experience over time.

We will term the first interpretation of this theory ("mouse nibbling") the *current* effect of elections hypothesis, and the other interpretation ("pressure chamber") the *cumulative* effect of elections. Either one of the two interpretations may imply that elections of all sorts matter (as Bratton and van de Walle 1997 suggest), or that only nominally competitive elections have a democratizing effect (as Schedler 2002b and Lindberg 2006a would have it). But perhaps even more is required from elections in order for them to have a democratizing effect. Perhaps in the end only free and fair elections are what matters. Interpreted in the current elections sense, this proposition would of course be purely tautological: surely the freedom and fairness of an election matter immediately for the state of democracy in a country. But in the historical sense this proposition becomes more interesting: that the more prolonged previous experience with *democratic* elections an authoritarian country has, the larger the probability for a democratic comeback, or for the upholding of democracy once installed.

As a matter of fact, quite a few arguments on the importance of democratic legacies for the prospect of democratization have been made in the literature, although none of them refers directly to the importance of elections in themselves. Huntington (1991, 44) points out that in the early phase of the third wave of democratization (from around 1974 to 1990), "an excellent predictor . . . of whether a country with an authoritarian government would become democratic was whether it had been democratic." Similarly, Skaaning finds that the best predictor of the state of civil liberties in Latin America and Eastern Europe in the 1990s was the "liberal-bureaucratic legacy" of the country, that is, their "former experiences with liberal regimes and a vibrant civil society" as well as "the state's traditions for formal-rational bureaucratic rectitude" (2006, 14). Persson and Tabellini (2007) find in a large sample of countries covering 150 years that both transitions to democracy and democratic survival are promoted by longer historical experiences with democracy. According to Hadenius (2001, 86), this effect could be attributed to political learning through prolonged exposure to pluralistic institutions. Over time people in more democratic contexts develop political abilities and resources (in a broad sense). Under authoritarianism these assets may be preserved to some degree and can be revitalized when the system opens up. From this perspective, accordingly, an early introduction of pluralist institutions is generally preferable. Even if the experiment fails, an investment has been made which could later pay off. The longer the democratic practice has continued—and the less distant in time it is, one could thus presume—the more likely is such a delayed return.

This historical learning theory could be interpreted as another "pressure chamber" hypothesis, suggesting that authoritarian rule will in the end give way to democracy in the presence of a strong democratic historical legacy. The slight difference concerns what kind of legacy matters: the holding of any kind of elections, of at least nominally competitive elections, or—as this last theoretical argument would have it—of fully free and fair elections.

Not all scholars agree on the democratizing power of elections. Carothers (2002b), for one, dispels the notion—according to him widely held in the U.S. foreign policy community—"that in attempted transitions to democracy, elections will not just be a foundation stone but a key generator over time of further democratic reforms." Against this view Carothers argued that even "reasonably regular, genuine elections" in many transitional countries have generated no political participation beyond voting and only shallow government accountability, and have done precious little "to stimulate the renovation or development of political parties" (Carothers 2002b, 8, 15). Along similar lines some case study comparativists have raised doubts about any democratizing results from holding elections. Brownlee (2007a, 9–10), for example, holds that "authoritarian elections tend to reveal political trends rather than propel them," that elections are "symptoms, not causes." He instead argues that what made authoritarian regimes crumble in Iran and the Philippines, as opposed to Egypt and Malaysia, was the ruling party's coalition management. Lust-Okar (2006a), in an intriguing case study of electoral politics in Jordan, argues that the primary role for elections in this country has been to organize the distribution of patronage and government spoils, not to act as an arena for struggles over regime change. Her conclusion is a direct challenge to supporters of the democratizing power of elections hypothesis: "Indeed, the logic of authoritarian elections should lead us to question the value of pressing for, and applauding, the introduction of elections in authoritarian regimes . . . Such elections are more likely to help sustain the authoritarian regime than they are to promote democracy" (Lust-Okar 2006a, 468; see also in her contribution to this volume).

Data and Research Design

In order to examine the proposition that elections spur democratization, we have put together a large cross-sectional time-series dataset, covering just about every country of the world (193 nations in all) from 1919 to 2002. Although some data sources would have allowed an even longer time-series component, we estimated that the net gains of using data before 1919 did not outweigh the labor costs. In 1919 there were only some 60–70 independent nations in the world, and this figure would of course have fallen had we ventured even further back in time. In terms of country coverage, then, there is relatively little to gain from using information from the nineteenth or early twentieth century. Even more importantly, as a result of the First World War many borders (particularly in Europe) were redrawn as old empires fell and new nations emerged. As a consequence the pre-1919 historical experiences of the set of independent nations present in the world today are cumbersome to assemble and assess.

Our dependent variable is the "rate of democratization," measured as annual change in a set of graded measures of democracy, all converted to range from 0 (no democracy) to 10 (full democracy): the Revised Combined Polity Score (Marshall and Jaggers 2005), the Freedom House (2006) civil liberties ratings, and the average Freedom House (combining both the political rights and civil liberties ratings) and Polity scores. All these measures have their strengths and drawbacks (Munck and Verkuilen 2002), and we have argued elsewhere that the best response to this situation is to average the Freedom House and Polity measures (Hadenius and Teorell 2005a). This combined average score will thus be our favored measure of democracy,[1] together with the Freedom House civil liberties ratings, which we—following Lindberg (2006a)—will employ in order to approximate a nonelectoral measure of democracy (more on this below). As a robustness check we will also make use of a unique feature of the Polity data: variables that for years of large changes in the Polity score record the month in which the prior regime ended and the month in which the subsequent regime started.

The choice of both the combined average Freedom House / Polity measure and the Freedom House civil liberties rating implies that we will concentrate on explaining democratization in the world from 1972 onward, that is, the so-called third wave of democratization (Huntington 1991). There is also another reason for this choice, namely, that it is only for this latter period that we have systematic data on determinants of democratization other than elections (to be used as controls). When constructing measures for the historical experience of elections and democracy, however, we will be able to draw on data all the way back to 1919.

That we rely on graded measures of democracy, and hence of democratic change, is critical to our inquiry. We are not trying to predict the demise of autocracies (as a nominal category) and their replacement by a "democratic" alternative; nor will we explain the demise or survival of that alternative. What we purport to do is to test the extent to which elections may lead to *gradual* democratic reforms—be they small or large. In other words, some of the regime changes we try to predict may be very limited, such as lifting a minor ban on newspapers or reluctantly increasing the ruling elite's tolerance toward the organization of opposition groups. Other changes may, however, be of larger consequence, such as the opening of the executive for electoral contestation or the establishment of an autonomous and impartial electoral commission. We believe this way of specifying our dependent variable is more in keeping with theoretical expectations. What these propositions on the democratizing power of elections predict are regime changes of various sorts, including minor shifts in the rules of the game, and *not only* the ways in which these regimes extricate themselves and hand over power to "qualitatively democratic" institutions.

Information on the holding of elections has been extracted primarily from two data sources: Banks (2002) and the 2004 version of the Database on Political Institutions (Beck et al. 2001; Keefer 2005). Although these two sources are, of course, overlapping to a great extent, they each have their own unique features. Banks's election data provide the longest time coverage—all the way back to our starting year, 1919—but these data only cover parliamentary elections (and elections to constituent assemblies). The DPI distinguishes between executive and legislative elections and records the month of the election, a feature we will make use of, but only covers the time period from 1975 onward. For the purpose of this chapter, then, we will be using the DPI in order to test the current effects of elections and Banks to test the historical effects.[2]

A key feature of these election variables is that they simply record the holding of an election in any country in any given year, regardless of the "quality" of that election. These election records thus include single-party elections allowing no freedom of choice. In order to also assess whether an election allowed multiparty competition, we have proceeded in two ways. For the "current effect" models, where the time period is from 1972 onward, a multiparty election is defined as one held under a "limited multiparty system" or "democracy," according to the data on types of authoritarian regimes reported in Hadenius and Teorell (2007). In the "cumulative effect" models, which measure the cumulative experience of multiparty elections going back to 1919, we have been forced to use a proxy, namely, whether the winning party or candidate received less than 100% of the votes according to Vanhanen's (2005) indicator of the degree of competition. This is thus an ex post facto measure of multiparty competition and must, as such, be deemed inferior to the first measure, which allows an election to be classified as multiparty "ex ante"—that is, even if the opposition in the end boycotted the elections or the winner received all the votes by rigging the ballot. For overlapping observations, however, these two indicators correlate very strongly (r = .94), which we interpret to mean that the historical proxy variable works as intended.

In order to assess the importance of historical experiences with elections, we will try several alternative measures. The most straightforward test just adds the number of elections held in a country since 1919 (or independence). This is thus simply a measure of the "stock" of elections accumulated throughout the history of a country. We produce one such stock variable for all elections held and one for the number of multiparty elections held.[3] Since there might be a decreasing marginal effect from holding another election, we also test this variable with a different functional form by taking its square root (implying that the number of elections needs to be quadrupled in order to achieve the same effect as a doubling of the simple additive stock variable). Using this measure we assume that an additional election adds less democratic stimulus than the former. Moreover, we have applied weights in order to take into account the distance in time from the present to the historical experience of elections. Although various such time-weighted versions could be constructed, we have tried only one, with a 5% annual depreciation rate. What this means is that if an election, for example, is held in country *X* at time *t*, the addition of that election to the accumulated stock of elections is only 0.95 at time $t + 1$, 0.95^2 at $t + 2$, 0.95^3 at $t + 3$ and so on. More generally, following Persson and Tabellini (2007, 21), the time-weighted cumulative number of elections at time *t* is computed according to the following formula:

$$(1-\delta)\sum_{\tau=0}^{t-t_0} elec_{t-\tau} \cdot \delta^{\tau}, \tag{3.1}$$

where *elec* is a dichotomous indicator of whether an election was held (1) or not (0) for each year of observation, δ = 0.95 (the annual depreciation rate), and *t* is the year of independence or 1919, whichever comes last. What this time-weighted cumulative stock variable does is essentially to discount the importance of the more distant path in favor of a country's more recent electoral history.

Although these three versions of the cumulative stock variables (three each for the count of all elections and the count of all multiparty elections) are highly interrelated (correlations lie in the range of .90 and above), there are important but nuanced differences among them. The most important difference between the square root and the untransformed version is of course to depreciate the importance of very long series of elections. By 1973, for example, the United States had held 24 congressional elections since 1919, which is four times more than the stock of 6 parliamentary elections in Spain for that same year. In terms of differences in the square root of these numbers, however, the United States had a stock of elections only twice as large as that of Spain (about 4.90 vs. 2.45). The most important implication of the time-weighted version, moreover, is that the stock of cumulative elections is depreciated in nonelection years. This difference plays out most importantly during long spells of the absence of elections. Thus, all six elections that entered Spain's stock in 1973 had been held in the 1920s and 1930s, before the advent of the Franco autocracy. By contrast, Bangladesh too had had six parliamentary elections by 1973 (taking into account all elections held during the period in which Bangladesh belonged to Pakistan), but these had been held more recently (in the period since 1955). In terms of the (square root of the) time-weighted stock of elections, this implies a much larger number for Bangladesh (2.09) than for Spain (0.77).

To be able to test the importance of having a long experience with relatively "democratic" elections, we must also somehow take the "quality" of an election into account. In order to accomplish this for the long time series of elections going back to 1919, and in order to maximize country coverage, we rely on the Vanhanen (2005) measure of democracy. We then assume that the level of democracy awarded to a country in an election year is a suitable proxy for the quality of that election. This assumption might, of course, prove wrong in certain cases, where, for example, other events unraveling in the wake of an election take precedence in the final democracy assessment for that country. Lacking any better alternatives, however, this proxy is the best we can accomplish. We thus construct a measure of the "effective" number of cumulative "democratic" elections in a country at time *t* by applying the following formula:

$$\sum_{\tau=t_0}^{t} \frac{elec_\tau \cdot dem_\tau}{10}, \tag{3.2}$$

where dem_τ is the Vanhanen measure of democracy (scored from 0 to 10) for time τ.[4] In other words, this procedure weighs the importance of each election according to the level of democracy of the country for that year. (For example, if an election is held in a country with a Vanhanen score of 8, according to this measure only 0.8 "effective democratic elections" have been held this year.) As with the simple stock variable taking no regard of the quality of an election, this cumulative stock measure will also be tested using a different functional form (the square root) and with a time weight applied (again using a 5% annual depreciation rate).

A potentially serious missing data problem with all these historical stock variables concerns countries that gained independence only after 1919. Since most data sources start coding a country in or around the year of independence, we usually lack information about the holding of elections, or the level of democracy, in the years under external rule. For certain types of external rule, what might be called "contiguous empires," this problem could be ameliorated by assuming that data for the "empire" also applies to all constituent contiguous "countries" (Gerring, Thacker, and Alfaro 2005, 15). Data for Estonia, for example, which are missing from the time of the Soviet occupation around 1941 until Estonia regained independence in 1991, could be rather safely filled in with data from the USSR.[5] A larger problem arises with former noncontiguous overseas colonies, since such colonies cannot, as a rule, be assumed to have been governed in the same way as their colonizing country. With data for former colonies more or less entirely missing, we instead have to assume that their colonial period generated no electoral or democratic legacy at all. Although we are aware that this assumption is probably wrong in some cases, such as in colonial India and Algeria, we simply see no way in which this problem may be solved systematically for all relevant cases.

With continuous dependent variables, our estimation strategy will be to use ordinary least squares (OLS) regression with lagged dependent variables in order to correct for temporal autocorrelation. Although the general methodological advice with cross-sectional time-series data is to also correct for panel heteroskedasticity and spatial autocorrelation through panel-corrected standard errors (Beck and Katz 1995, 1996), preliminary testing shows that when we concentrate on the estimates for the *current* election variables, taking these additional error sources into account makes no or very little difference to the estimates of error variances. The simple explanation for this is that there is not much cross-country variability in the holding of elections, nor is there much correlation in the holding of elections across countries for any single year. Elections are a common phenomenon in all countries, regardless of regime type, whereas the election cycle is very country-specific. Hence, to save estimation time we simply report ordinary OLS standard errors for the tests of the current effects hypothesis. Because of the varying years of independence for overseas colonies, however, the *cumulative* number of elections varies to a great extent across countries. This of course applies even more strongly if the competitiveness or democratic quality of these elections is also taken into account. Hence, for the cumulative effects analyses we must take the spatial part of the error structure into account.

Although the lagged dependent variable(s), apart from mopping up the autocorrelation, also take a certain form of reversed causation into account, there is another serious threat to any sensible estimate of the democratization power of elections that needs to be accounted for: the threat of tautology. We argued above that it seems reasonable to assume that the measure of democracy for a given country in election years also measures to some extent the democratic quality of that election. This assumption of course most strongly applies to the more "electoral" measures of democracy—those that rely on indicators most closely related to the electoral process—such as Polity and Freedom House political rights ratings. That a measure of democracy also captures the quality of an election is a property we are able to take advantage of in our construction of historical variables tapping into the experience of democratic elections. When we use any of these measures as our dependent variable in regressions with elections as the independent variable, however, that particular feature is turned into a direct disadvantage. We would then be trying to estimate the "effect" of the very elections that already have been incorporated into the measurement of the dependent variable—a close to tautological exercise.

To avoid tautology, we will employ two strategies in the assessment of current election effects. The first is to create a temporal lag between the election and democracy variables. We are then able to estimate any consequences for democratization that *in time* go beyond the holding of an election itself. We will first apply the simplest lag that still maximizes the chances of observing an election effect—namely, the *one-year lag*—but since even the one-year lag could be argued to be too long, we will also make use of the monthly dating of elections in the DPI and of regime changes in the Polity data. By excluding elections held in the same month or after the beginning of a "new regime" (i.e., when a shift of 1.5 or more in the Polity score on a 0–10 scale occurs), or elections held in the same month as the end of the "old regime," we approximate a monthly lag applied *within* the election year.

The second strategy is based on Lindberg (2006a), who primarily looks at current elections (without applying a lag) but endeavors to avoid the tautology problem by using a nonelectoral measure of democracy: the Freedom House civil liberties ratings. Since this particular measure of democracy (at least on paper) does not take the quality of elections as such into account, there should be less risk of tautology. It is still the case, however, that the civil liberties rankings mostly change together with the political rights scores (Coppedge, Alvarez, and Maldonado 2008). The correlation between annual changes in the two rankings is .51 in election years. In order to ascertain that only changes in the civil liberties are picked up, we will therefore control for the changes in political rights. Since this control might appear too rigorous, we will also present results without it.

As with any other causal proposition, the democratizing power of elections must of course be tested *ceteris paribus* to the greatest extent possible. In other words, we must be able to assess whether the holding of an election (or an extended experience with elections) is merely correlated with changes in the level of democracy, or if that association also holds when other characteristics of the case in question are taken into account. We will therefore expose the electoral proposition to a host of substantial control variables that also vary within countries and/or over time. The controls comprise a wide range of hypothesized determinants of democratization, including colonial background, religious composition, societal fractionalization, country size, modernization, resource wealth, international dependence, diffusion effects, regional organizations, and popular mobilization (for details, see Teorell and Hadenius 2007).

Hence, it is a matter of a demanding test. What we are probing is the extent to which the holding of elections has a democratizing import—on top of a number of other factors which have proved to play a significant role. It should be noted that this is the most rigorous examination so far of the electoral proposition, as it is based on global data, including a long historical record, and is accomplished, moreover, controlling for a broad set of competing explanatory factors.

Democratization and Current Experiences of Elections

We start our exploration by looking at the democratizing effects of current elections. Tables 3.1 and 3.2 employ the first testing strategy outlined above—that is, by using lags in the election variable—whereas Tables 3.3 and 3.4 employ the second strategy, using a nonelectoral measure of democracy. In Table 3.1 we use our preferred measure of democracy, the average Freedom House and Polity scores, and a combined indicator of both legislative and executive elections. As indicated in both model 1, with no controls, and model 2, with controls added, there is a significant and positive change in the degree of democracy occurring in election years. After the year they are being held, however, these elections in general appear to have no democratizing effect.[6] This picture changes slightly when noncompetitive elections are excluded in models 3 and 4. The lagged election effect is now stronger but is rendered marginally significant under controls. Moreover, it turns out that both the magnitude and the (marginal) significance of the lagged multiparty election effects now rely on only two cases: the elections held in Uruguay in 1984 and those in Paraguay in 1988. If these two extremely influential outliers are excluded, the estimated effect is almost halved and rendered completely insignificant (coef = .041, se = .036, p = .257).

Neither of these countries serves well as a paradigmatic case for the power of elections hypothesis. The elections of November 1984 in Uruguay had been agreed upon by the Naval Club Pact of August that same year and did not produce any stunning results or other departures from the road toward democracy specified in that same agreement (Gillespie 1986, 192–93). In 1988 in Paraguay, the Colorado Party under President Alfredo Stroessner managed

Table 3.1 Democratizing effects of parliamentary and executive elections: Freedom House and Polity measures, one-year lags

Variable	Model 1	Model 2	Model 3	Model 4
Any election at time *t*	.311***	.287***		
	(.034)	(.033)		
Any election at time *t* – 1	.035	.032		
	(.034)	(.034)		
Multiparty election at time *t*			.407***	.375***
			(.036)	(.036)
Multiparty election at time *t* – 1			.077**	.063*
			(.037)	(.037)
Control variables	No	Yes	No	Yes
Adjusted R^2	.056	.095	.070	.107

Note: Entries are unstandardized regression coefficients, with OLS standard errors within parentheses. Either parliamentary or executive elections are counted (the source is DPI), with multiparty elections defined by the limited multiparty/democratic regimes of Hadenius and Teorell (2007). The dependent variable is yearly change in the mean FH/Polity measure of democracy (scored 0–10). In all models, two one-year lags of the dependent variable are entered to purge the standard errors from serial autocorrelation. In models with control variables the following factors, lagged one year (where appropriate), are included: British, French, Spanish, Portuguese, and Belgian/Italian/Dutch colonial background; the proportion of Protestants, Orthodox Christians, Christians of other denomination, Buddhists, Hindus, Muslims, nonreligious and of other denomination; ethno-linguistic and religious fractionalization; the log of the country area; a composite index of socioeconomic modernization; oil and minerals; trade and capital flows; democratic diffusion at the level of neighboring states, within regions, and globally; membership in democratic regional organizations; growth and inflation; demonstrations, strikes, and riots.

Model 1: any election, no controls; Model 2: any election, controls; Model 3: multiparty election, no controls; Model 4: multiparty election, controls

No. of observations = 2771; no. of countries = 145; time period covered = 1976–2002

$*p < .10$ $**p < .05$ $***p < .01$

to win yet another rigged election, which on the face of it appears distantly related to the coup that overthrew Stroessner the following year and led (after another election) to the substantial liberalization of the political regime under Andres Rodríguez (Powers 1992). Whatever the exact interpretation of these two cases, the fact remains that the already weakly significant lagged effect of multiparty elections under controls is not robust, since it hinges on these two particular observations. With the combined Freedom House and Polity measure of democracy, there thus seems to be no democratizing effect of elections over the one-year time horizon.

But perhaps the one-year lag is too long. In Table 3.2 we decrease the lag length by taking advantage of the possibility of dating both election months

Table 3.2 Democratizing effects of parliamentary and executive elections: Polity measures, within-year lags

Variable	Model 1	Model 2	Model 3	Model 4
Any election, within-year lagged at time *t*	.091**	.078*		
	(.043)	(.043)		
Multiparty election, within-year lagged at time *t*			.187***	.161***
			(.047)	(.046)
Control variables	No	Yes	No	Yes
Adjusted R^2	.030	.070	.035	.073

Note: Entries are unstandardized regression coefficients, with OLS standard errors within parentheses. The dependent variable is yearly change in the mean Polity measure of democracy (scored 0–10). The within-year lag is approximated by excluding elections held in the same month or after the beginning of a "new regime" (i.e., when a shift of 1.5 or more in the Polity score occurs), or elections held in the same month as the end of the "old regime." For other details, see note to Table 3.1.

Model 1: any election, no controls; Model 2: any election, controls; Model 3: multiparty election, no controls; Model 4: multiparty election, controls

No. of observations = 2618; no. of countries = 135; time period covered = 1975–2002

$^{*}p < .10$ $^{**}p < .05$ $^{***}p < .01$

in the DPI data and the month of substantial (≥1.5) changes in the scores of the Polity data. As shown in models 1 and 2, the effects are strengthened by applying this shorter time lag, since even the measure that counts all elections (including noncompetitive ones) has a marginally significant impact on democratization.[7] The strongest showing for the power of elections hypothesis, however, again appears when we restrict our attention to competitive elections. Even after controls (in model 4), a multiparty election on average appears to increase the Polity score of 0.161 in the year it is held. This effect is both statistically significant and robust to the exclusion of some relatively extremely influential outliers.[8]

We may thus conclude that by deploying the first testing strategy for current elections, the one where lags are used, we find support for the power of elections hypothesis when multiparty elections are considered over a time span shorter than a year. But with a one-year lag, or if noncompetitive elections are also included, the support for this hypothesis is fragile at best.

In Table 3.3 we turn to the second testing strategy, which employs a nonelectoral measure of democracy. As argued above, the best available such measure for our purposes appears to be the civil rights ratings issued by Freedom House (scaled from 0 to 10, where 0 means no respect for civil liberties,

Table 3.3 Democratizing effects of parliamentary and executive elections: Freedom House civil liberties rating, controlling for political rights

Variable	Model 1	Model 2	Model 3	Model 4
Any election at time *t*	−.012	−.028		
	(.034)	(.034)		
Any election at time *t* – 1	.045	.036		
	(.034)	(.033)		
Multiparty election at time *t*			.041	.022
			(.037)	(.036)
Multiparty election at time *t* – 1			.077**	.065*
			(.036)	(.036)
Change in FH's political rights scale	.354***	.343***	.350***	.339***
	(.014)	(.014)	(.014)	(.014)
Control variables	No	Yes	No	Yes
Adjusted R^2	.208	.243	.209	.244

Note: Entries are unstandardized regression coefficients, with OLS standard errors within parentheses. The dependent variable is yearly change in Freedom House's civil liberties rating (scored 0–10). In all models, a one-year lag of the dependent variable is entered in order to purge standard errors from serial autocorrelation. For other details, see note to Table 3.1

Model 1: any election, no controls; Model 2: any election, controls; Model 3: multiparty election, no controls; Model 4: multiparty election, controls

No. of observations = 2772; no. of countries = 145; time period covered = 1976–2002

$*p < .10$ $**p < .05$ $***p < .01$

10 the opposite). In order to restrict our attention even more exclusively to the nonelectoral changes in this measure, we also include throughout Table 3.3 a control for the yearly change in Freedom House's political rights ratings. We again make use of the DPI measure of elections, both at time *t* and at time *t* – 1. Since there is now less risk of tautology, measures at both times may be interpreted as support for the electoral proposition.

In models 1 and 2 we start by including all kinds of elections, again generating nonsignificant results (although, notably, these results also apply for election years). When we restrict attention to nominally multiparty elections in model 3, there is a small but significant effect of the lagged election variable (although not for the unlagged version). This effect is, however, rendered only marginally significant under controls in model 4. Moreover, it now hinges on the inclusion (or not) of two extremely influential outliers.[9] Accordingly, the result lacks a desirable degree of robustness.

Yet, it could be argued that we eliminate too much of the substantial overtime variation in civil liberties by controlling for the simultaneous change in political rights. As the two variables are strongly correlated, the one obviously has a propensity of washing out the other. For this reason, we repeat in Table 3.4 the setup from Table 3.3, except that we exclude this particular control. This lowering of the security provisions has two implications. The first is a slight increase in the lagged effect of elections, particularly of the multiparty type. In model 4, this lagged effect holds even in the presence of controls, but it is again completely dependent on two influential cases: Paraguay in 1989 and Panama in 1990. We have already commented upon the negligible effect of the 1988 election in Paraguay, but Panama is a more complicated case. Whereas the elections which Manuel Noriega lost were held in May, the newly installed democratic regime came about as the result of the U.S. invasion in December, with most bans on civil rights being raised only in 1990 (Pérez 1995, 132–35). Although the downfall of the authoritarian regime was not directly attributable to elections, elections might still be argued to have had an indirect effect: since the elections were "stolen" (Thompson and Kuntz 2006), they may have precipitated later events that led to the downfall of the Noriega government. If we include Panama, the remaining effect is only marginally significant (coef = .077; se = .040; p = .053) and thus hinges on the interpretation of a single influential outlier.[10]

The second and more important change resulting from our more permissive test in Table 3.4 is therefore a considerable improvement in the within-election-year effect. As can be seen in models 1 and 2, this simultaneous effect of elections holds even when noncompetitive elections are counted and when control variables are included. The most pertinent effect again is for multiparty elections, which holds true with the inclusion of controls (model 4). As compared with the lagged effect, moreover, the effect on civil liberties in election years does not hinge on any particular influential outliers. Even when a few relatively extreme outliers are deleted (India in 1977, Grenada in 1984, and Paraguay in 1989), the effect is positive and statistically significant.

Whether we choose to believe that this effect is causal is then a judgment call that depends on how we interpret Freedom House's measurement process. If we accept the assumption that the civil liberties ratings are arrived at without taking the quality of the electoral process into account for any given election year, we may interpret this as a truly democratizing effect of elections. If, however, we are more inclined to believe that the extent to which civil liberties are upheld during an election year cannot be assessed without

Table 3.4 Democratizing effects of parliamentary and executive elections: Freedom House civil liberties rating, not controlling for political rights

Variable	Model 1	Model 2	Model 3	Model 4
Any election at time t	.133***	.109***		
	(.037)	(.037)		
Any election at time $t-1$	.058	.047		
	(.037)	(.037)		
Multiparty election at time t			.211***	.184***
			(.040)	(.039)
Multiparty election at time $t-1$			.102**	.088**
			(.040)	(.040)
Control variables	No	Yes	No	Yes
Adjusted R^2	.026	.073	.031	.078

Note: Entries are unstandardized regression coefficients, with OLS standard errors within parentheses. For other details, see note to Table 3.3.

Model 1: any election, no controls; Model 2: any election, controls; Model 3: multiparty election, no controls; Model 4: multiparty election, controls

No. of observations = 2772; no. of countries = 145; time period covered = 1976–2002

*$p < .10$ **$p < .05$ ***$p < .01$

at least in part evaluating the electoral process itself (as would most likely be the case for associational and organizational rights), then the more conservative result from Table 3.3 should be our preferred conclusion—in other words, that there is a small and nonrobust effect on civil liberties occurring in the year following elections. Taking also into consideration the positive result from Table 3.2, where multiparty elections were found to have an effect on the within-year horizon, we have a slight preference for the first interpretation. Current elections appear to have some democratizing potential, but this potential is marred with uncertainty and only applies in the brief wake of an election or in the nonelectoral arena of democracy.

Democratization and the Cumulative Experience of Elections

We now turn to our tests of the "pressure chamber" version of the power of elections hypothesis. To begin with, there are a series of negative results which we for space-conserving reasons have decided not to show. The first concerns the cumulative measure that takes all elections, competitive or not, into account. In no instance have we found any significant impact of this variable, regardless of functional form and time weights. The second, slightly more positive result, concerns the mean Freedom House / Polity score. With this as our dependent variable, we find a positive and statistically significant effect of both the cumulative number of multiparty elections and the effective number of cumulative democratic elections. This effect, however, is not robust to the exclusion of influential outliers.

Let us instead turn to Table 3.5, where Freedom House's civil liberties ratings are again used as our dependent variable. As indicated in model 1, the number of parliamentary multiparty elections held in a country since 1919 exerts a positive and significant effect on the prospects for democratization, even when the current election year effect is taken into account. Although model 2 shows this effect is not robust to the inclusion of substantial control variables, it turns out that functional form is of critical importance. If we take the square root of the cumulative stock in model 3, which decreases the marginal impact of each additional election, the effect is strengthened and again statistically significant—despite the presence of controls, including the change in the political rights rating. The average marginal effect of 0.061 implies that it would take roughly 269 multiparty elections to raise the civil liberties rating by 1 point (on the 0–10 scale), indicating that we should not expect any dramatic improvements as a result of electoral legacies. The effect is statistically significant, however, and not an artifact of any extremely influential outliers. When we make use of both the square root functional form and the time weights in model 4, the effect is still positive and significant, but somewhat weaker. Interestingly, this implies that elections held in the distant past are as important as those held more recently.

Turning to the "effective" number of cumulative "democratic" elections measure in Table 3.6, we see a similar but stronger pattern. The mean marginal effect of the square root measure in model 3 is now 0.153, indicating that it would take an historical stock of 43 fully democratic elections to notch up the civil liberties ratings one point. This is again not a very strong effect in substantial terms, but it is significant at conventional levels, and robust to the exclusion of a number of extremely influential outliers.[11] As was the case for the cumulative number of multiparty elections, the time-weighted version fares somewhat worse. What matters is thus the full stock of historical experience with democratic elections, regardless of the time passed.

In sum, we find support for the notion that democratization is furthered

Table 3.5 Democratizing effects of the cumulative number of multiparty elections: Freedom House civil liberties rating

Variable	Model 1	Model 2	Model 3	Model 4
Cumulative no. of multiparty elections at time $t-1$	.015*** (.004)	.006 (.004)	.061*** (.022)	.054** (.023)
Parliamentary election at time t	–.040 (.033)	–.052 (.033)	–.050 (.033)	–.053 (.033)
Change in FH's political rights scale	.342*** (.018)	.333*** (.018)	.333*** (.018)	.333*** (.018)
Control variables	No	Yes	Yes	Yes
Square root of elections	No	No	Yes	Yes
Time-weighted elections	No	No	No	Yes
Adjusted R^2	.208	.234	.235	.234

Note: All multiparty parliamentary elections since 1919 are counted (from Banks 2002, using Vanhanen's [2005] indicator of competition > 0 as the criterion for multiparty elections). The dependent variable is yearly change in the Freedom House civil liberties rating (scored 0–10). In all models, a one-year lag of the dependent variable is entered in order to purge standard errors from serial autocorrelation. For other details, see note to Table 3.1.

Model 1: no controls; Model 2: controls; Model 3: controls, square root; Model 4: controls, square root, and time-weighted

No. of observations = 2939; no. of countries = 151; time period covered = 1974–2002

$^*p < .10$ $^{**}p < .05$ $^{***}p < .01$

by a historical legacy of elections. Not just any elections matter, however, and some dimensions of democratization are more easily affected than others. The elections must be of the multiparty or, even stronger, more democratic kind. Moreover, we only find a robust impact on the extent of civil liberties protection. When the more electoral aspects of democracy themselves are taken into consideration, the cumulative experience of elections has a weak and nonrobust impact. Finally, it should be noted that the effect of an electoral legacy on civil liberties is not strong. This implies that electoral pressure may eventually make the democratic "pressure chamber" expand, but hardly explode. More precisely, upon closer scrutiny we find that the primary cumulative effect of elections is to hinder downturns in already relatively democratic countries, not to spur upturns in authoritarian ones. In other words, what electoral pressure does is to help keep the democratic chamber from contracting.[12] Hence, more than being a stepping-stone, elections serve as a backbone of democracy. This finding supports the idea that elections at a minimum can facilitate democratization by giving more time and room for

Table 3.6 Democratizing effects of the cumulative number of democratic elections: Freedom House civil liberties rating

Variable	Model 1	Model 2	Model 3	Model 4
Cumulative no. of democratic elections at time $t - 1$	.056***	.022	.153***	.127**
	(.013)	(.016)	(.055)	(.058)
Parliamentary election at time t	−.035	−.051	−.048	−.052
	(.033)	(.033)	(.033)	(.033)
Change in FH's political rights scale	.343***	.333***	.334***	.333***
	(.018)	(.018)	(.018)	(.018)
Control variables	No	Yes	Yes	Yes
Square root of elections	No	No	Yes	Yes
Time-weighted elections	No	No	No	Yes
Adjusted R^2	.208	.234	.236	.235

Note: All parliamentary elections since 1919 are counted (from Banks 2002), weighted by the level of democracy at election year (according to Vanhanen's [2005] index of democracy, scored 0–1). The dependent variable is yearly change in the Freedom House civil liberties rating (scored 0–10). In all models, a one-year lag of the dependent variable is entered in order to purge standard errors from serial autocorrelation. For other details, see note to Table 3.1.

Model 1: no controls; Model 2: controls; Model 3: controls, square root; Model 4: controls, square root, and time-weighted

No. of observations = 2939; no. of countries = 151; time period covered = 1974–2002

*$p < .10$ **$p < .05$ ***$p < .01$

the types of causal processes discussed by Schedler, Rakner and van de Walle, and Morski, among others, in the second part of this book.

Conclusion

In this chapter we have scrutinized the hypothesis that elections have a democratizing effect. Two version of this proposition have been tested. One maintains that the holding of an election tends to yield democratizing gains more or less immediately, either in the time period shortly after the election or for the nonelectoral aspects of democracy. The second version holds that the historical experience with a prolonged series of elections in the end tends to yield a democratizing effect. In our empirical testing, where a broad set of demanding control variables was applied, we have found significant support for both propositions—at least for certain ways of measuring the effects in question.

As for the short-run (current) effects of elections, we can establish that such effects are indeed at play. Using the composite, but mainly electoral, measure of democracy provided by Polity, we find weak but still notable democratizing effects during the same year, in the immediate aftermath of elections. Such effects stem most plainly from plural (multiparty) elections. However, in the following years no robust effects could be observed. Hence, the democratizing effect of elections tends to kick in soon and then fade away.

Using another measure, the Freedom House civil liberties score, we could also register significant and robust effects, again mostly from multiparty elections—but only when political rights were not simultaneously controlled for. The substantial implication of this finding could certainly be disputed. It could be argued that relying only on civil liberty measures is too easy an approach, as these are correlated with political rights scores that contain the electoral components, the effects of which we aim to explore. On the other hand it could be said that because of this correlation, the inclusion of a control for political rights would in all probability wash out any effect on civil liberties. As we see it, there is no obvious way out of this dilemma. Basically, it has to do with the degree of independence—in the way codings are actually made—between the two Freedom House measures.

Turning to the other proposition, regarding long-term (cumulative) effects, we find evidence of a decreasing marginal utility of elections. Thus, the total number of elections counts, but to a diminishing degree. Furthermore, we conclude that this positive impact is largely from multiparty, and especially fairly democratic, elections, and that the impact is mostly upon the nonelectoral aspects of democracy (i.e., civil liberties). In a separate test, we tried to find out more precisely the nature of this effect. Does a prolonged history of multiparty or democratic elections spur democratic upturns as well as hinder democratic downturns? The answer is that the latter effect predominates. Countries that can rely on a substantial record of elections have a democratic advantage (though, as we saw, to a gradually diminishing degree), as they are more immune to democracy-challenging forces. In regard to their causal implications—serving as a backbone rather than as a stepping-stone of democracy—elections in their cumulative effect resemble another prominent promoting factor, socioeconomic modernization (Teorell and Hadenius 2007).

Thus, overall we find substantial support for the view taken by the "optimists"—for example, Huntington and, in this volume, Lindberg, Roessler and Howard, Schedler, and Bunce and Wolchik—who claim that the holding of elections, and fairly democratic elections in particular, have positive democratic side effects. Instead of being just a token of some kind of democratic achievement, as "pessimists" such as Carothers have claimed, the holding of elections has a cumulative although not very substantial consequence for democracy's future. And there is even, according to our findings, evidence of a short-term effect. Current elections have a democratizing potential, but this potential applies only briefly in the wake of an election or, perhaps, in nonelectoral arenas such as civil liberties.

Joining the optimist party, we would maintain that supporting the holding of elections, and preferably truly pluralistic and democratic elections, is indeed a desirable activity on the part of both domestic and international actors. Elections appear to set the stage for a process of democratic learning, a finding also reported by Brownlee in this book. Therefore, it is advantageous to introduce elections as soon as possible, and to make them ongoing and eventually more pluralistic. The project may derail, but nevertheless it will pay off, both in the short and the long run. Having said this, the effects that we register are not very large in substantial terms. No democratizing miracles should thus be expected from the electoral experience.

CHAPTER FOUR

Post–Cold War Political Regimes

When Do Elections Matter?

Philip G. Roessler and Marc M. Howard

The third wave of democratization and the end of the cold war significantly altered the map of political regimes around the world. The collapse of the Soviet Union was the death knell for most Communist governments, which were forced to open their political systems and introduce economic reforms. Other non-Communist dictators lost foreign patronage and found themselves vulnerable to domestic protest and international pressure. Multiparty elections were held in many African countries for the first time since the decade after independence.

At first, political science scholarship treated the end of the cold war as initiating a political process in which these authoritarian regimes were in transition to democracies. Much research focused on explaining the sequence by which this democratization process would take place. But as many "transitions" stalled and the resulting regimes proved surprisingly durable, other scholars recognized the need to understand the regimes as they existed, rather than understanding the extent to which they fell short of a set of standards and criteria that were probably unrealistic in the first place. New studies began to focus on the emergence of these "hybrid regimes" (Karl 1995), which defied simple classification as democratic or authoritarian because they contained elements of both regime types (Diamond 2002). The work of Levitsky and Way (2002b) and Schedler (2002a) made important advancements in this burgeoning field by introducing the concepts of competitive and electoral authoritarianism, respectively.

Building on these conceptualizations, a new and growing research program has emerged. Empirical studies have focused on the effect of external factors on changes in and the persistence of competitive authoritarian regimes (Levitsky and Way 2005), the determinants of liberalizing electoral outcomes within competitive authoritarian regimes (Howard and Roessler 2006), the conditions leading to mass political protest before and after elections in electoral authoritarian regimes (Schedler 2006b), and the democratizing power of elections (Lindberg 2006a).

While this research program has produced a variety of rich and valuable conceptualizations of nondemocratic regimes, there has been less progress on how to operationalize them by measuring and scoring a global set of political regimes consistent with the systematized concepts of competitive and electoral authoritarianism (Munck and Snyder 2004). Operationalization is important because it helps us to refine and check the validity of our systematized concepts (Adcock and Collier 2001). Moreover, it allows us to compare regime types systematically across a global sample, bridging artificial regional divisions that scholars tend to impose (Bunce 2003).

This chapter has two key objectives: to contribute a clear and precise operationalization of post–cold war political regimes and to analyze empirically which regimes are more susceptible to elections as a mode of democratic transition. The first objective should provide a useful basis for examining and comparing the relative impact of elections on democratic processes within different regime types. Based on the degree of contestation and participation for the selection of the executive, we distinguish between five different regime types—closed authoritarianism, hegemonic authoritarianism, competitive authoritarianism, electoral democracy, and liberal democracy—and develop a measurement scheme to score countries as belonging to one of these five regime types in any given year.

Applying these criteria to all countries (with populations greater than 500,000) between 1987 and 2006 reveals several important empirical trends. First, we find that as democratic regimes around the world have surged, backsliding into authoritarianism has been surprisingly rare, occurring only 24 times out of a possible 1,454 country-years during the time period of study. Second, hegemonic authoritarian regimes have more than doubled since 1987 and emerged as the modal authoritarian regime type in 2005 (representing 38% of the world's authoritarian regimes). This trend may reflect a calculation by some authoritarian incumbents that significant electoral competition is too risky; others may have allowed minimal contestation as a nod to external donors demanding some liberalization. Interestingly, incumbents in hegemonic regimes rarely abandon multicandidate elections once they adopt the procedure—though contestation is so circumscribed in these elections that these incumbents almost never lose. Competitive authoritarian regimes tend to be the most volatile regime type; more than half of the elections in these regimes either lead to a crackdown in contestation and opposition boycotts or, more frequently, a relatively free and fair election and opposition victory.

Looking at geographic trends, we find that immediately after the end of the cold war, democratic transitions occurred disproportionately in Eastern Europe, but since then they have been quite diffuse. With the exception of North America and Europe, each region of the world has experienced at least one democratic transition since 1995.[1] During this time period, the greatest number of democratic transitions (10) have occurred in Africa, though the region has also experienced the most incidences (16) of competitive authoritarian regimes backsliding to other types of authoritarian regimes or collapsing altogether.

Regarding the paper's second objective, our analysis suggests an important temporal distinction between the period at the end of the cold war (1987–94) and the last 12 years. For democratic transitions triggered by the end of the cold war, the type of authoritarian regime appears not to matter. In contrast, since 1995 democratic transitions have been significantly more likely to occur in competitive authoritarian regimes—usually as a result of elections—than in hegemonic or closed authoritarian regimes. This finding underscores the changing nature of democratization over the last 20 years and speaks to the central question of this volume: How, if at all, do elections matter for democratization?

We find that in the late 1980s and early 1990s many democratic transitions resulted from the sudden and severe weakening of authoritarian regimes and the rewriting of the rules of the game to allow for greater participation and competition in the selection of the executive, culminating in the holding of a "founding election." In the past decade, in contrast, the dominant mode of transition has been via electoral processes in competitive authoritarian governments—that is, a subset of authoritarian regimes that allow a considerable degree of electoral contestation (as measured by the preceding election). Electoral processes provide an opportunity for opposition parties to coordinate their antigovernment activities and unify behind a single candidate or form a single coalition, which increase the costs for the incumbent to use force and fraud to stay in power. Our previous research has found opposition coalitions and incumbent turnover to be the key factors that drive liberalizing electoral outcomes in competitive authoritarian states (Howard and Roessler 2006). Bunce and Wolchik (Chapter 10, below) point to how opposition groups, often in conjunction with civil society groups, have skillfully applied a variety of techniques, including protest, voter-mobilization campaigns, dissemination of public opinion polls, and election monitoring—collectively referred to as the "electoral model"—to galvanize the public to resist incumbents' efforts to steal the election and help to usher in liberalizing change.

While the data indicate that elections in competitive authoritarianism provide an arena for possible post–cold war democratization, the data also suggest the limitations of elections as levers of liberalization. (See Teorell and Hadenius in Chapter 3 of this volume for a systematic treatment of this subject.) First, electoral processes in competitive authoritarian states can also lead to backsliding, as incumbents—perhaps learning from prior elections as well as from the fate of their less repressive colleagues (see Bunce and Wolchik in Chapter 10 below)—institute more restrictive rules and harsher practices against the opposition to avoid the risk of defeat. The effect is that contestation becomes severely circumscribed and the government tilts in a more hegemonic direction.

Second, the data suggest that elections in hegemonic authoritarian regimes and electoral democracies have little effect on greater liberalization. Though rulers in hegemonic authoritarian regimes commit to continuous elections, albeit with significantly longer interim periods, on average this does not lead to political liberalization. The mean Freedom House civil liberties score in these countries is slightly *worse* in the years after they have held more than one consecutive election than in the year they made the transition to hegemonic authoritarianism (usually from closed authoritarianism) after the end of the cold war.[2] Moreover, these hegemonic regimes tend to be some of the most stable of all authoritarian regimes, underscoring the central point of Lust-Okar (Chapter 9), who argues that elections can reinforce authoritarianism if incumbents use them as an instrument to manage dissent and deepen their societal control. On the democratic side, consistent with Hartlyn and McCoy's analysis of Latin America (Chapter 2, above), in a global sample we see little evidence to suggest that holding successive elections in electoral democracies results in a change to liberal democracy.

In the sections that follow, we begin by conceptualizing post–third wave political regimes, disaggregating them, and developing a coding scheme to operationalize these types and score all countries between 1987 and 2006. We then document and analyze trends in regime type frequency, proportion, and change over this time period. We also examine regional variation in regime types by means of world maps created with geographic information systems (GIS) software. We then analyze various trends in democratic transitions and regime volatility, highlighting important differences between the regime types.

Conceptualizing and Operationalizing Political Regimes

The starting point of our measurement typology is the background concept of political regimes—the rules and procedures that determine how national, executive leaders are chosen. This concept covers all political systems, whether democratic or authoritarian. To disaggregate the broader concept of regimes into more systematized types, we distinguish them based on the degree to which the rules adopted to select authoritative national leaders allow for contestation and participation in selection of a government (Dahl 1971). These rules are (1) whether selection is through national elections or through lineage, party decree, or military orders; (2) whether there are national elections for an executive, whether the rules and procedures allow for contestation; (3) whether the elections are free and fair or fraudulent; and (4) whether the regime is based on the rule of law and "political and civic pluralism," or whether the rights and liberties of some individual and groups are still violated (Diamond 1999, 8–13).

Figure 4.1 presents a tree diagram that illustrates the key distinctions between the five different types of regimes in the world today. The four main

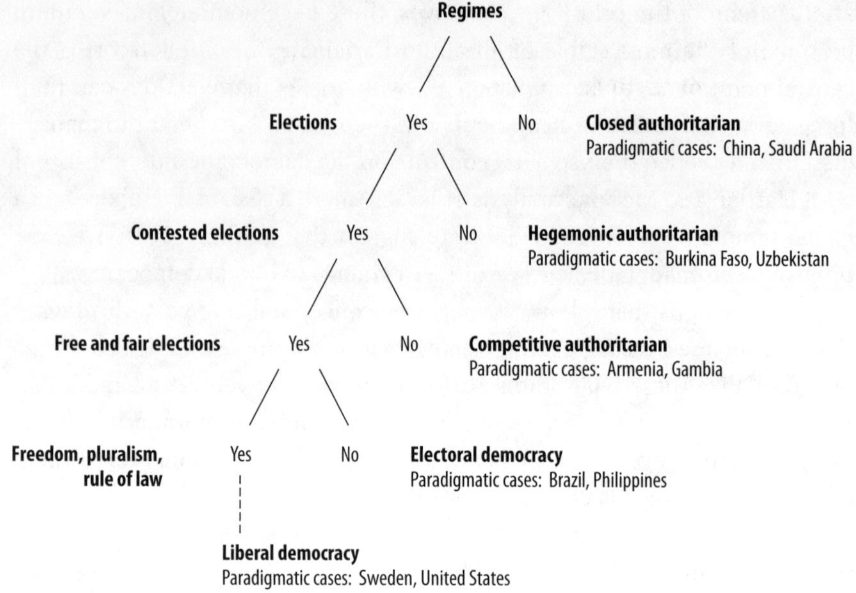

Figure 4.1. Disaggregation of political regimes by various dimensions of democracy

factors that distinguish regimes are listed on the left of the figure, and the regime types are listed on the right. Employing these rules, we identify five global regime types: closed authoritarianism, hegemonic authoritarianism, competitive authoritarianism, electoral democracy, and liberal democracy.

Two important caveats are necessary regarding this figure. First, it is intended to depict a typology, not a linear or teleological progression from one regime to the next. The last decade has shown that, contrary to the "democratizing bias" (Levitsky and Way 2002b, 51) of much of the earlier democratization literature, these regime types can be stable and enduring, or can even revert to a more consolidated form of authoritarianism. Second, our conceptualization scheme revolves around the institution of national elections because no better objective and parsimonious metric of contestation and participation exists. But we are also conscious of the "fallacy of electoralism" (Karl 1995) and the pitfalls of focusing on the significance of elections at the expense of other important attributes of democracy. Indeed, democracy involves much more than just elections. Robust civil society, effective and independent legislatures and judiciaries, and a civilianized military are just three of the many factors that are necessary for a consolidated democracy (Linz and Stepan 1996). At the same time, however, democracy cannot be less than free and fair elections. Until a country's selection of national leaders occurs consistently through a public, competitive, and free and fair process, the deepening of democracy will remain elusive.

Regime Types

Building on the work of Schumpeter (1942), Dahl (1971), Diamond (1999), and others, we distinguish regimes based on the degree of contestation and participation in the selection of national leaders. *Closed authoritarian* regimes are those in which the selection of a country's leaders is the responsibility of a small group of elites from the ruling family, the army, or a political party; the citizenry is constitutionally excluded from participating in the selection. Thus, there are no multicandidate national elections; there may be referendums or plebiscites, but no elections that allow for contestation between the incumbent and another candidate. To enforce their monopoly on executive recruitment, the elites ban opposition political parties, rely heavily on repression to maintain political control, and squash free media and civil society.

Distinct from closed systems are *electoral* authoritarian regimes (see Schedler 2002a; 2006a)—those in which the executive recruitment process does allow for regular national elections, where there is a choice in candidates (if rival candidates choose to participate rather than boycott), and in which a substantial segment of the citizenry is able to participate, but in which the integrity of the process is fundamentally violated by the incumbent administration's application of rules, procedures, and practices that tilt the playing field in its favor to try to guarantee political survival. Important variation exists among electoral authoritarian regimes, however, depending upon the degree to which the playing field favors the incumbent and infringes upon the opposition's opportunity to contest the election. The cases of Egypt in 2005 and Ethiopia in 2005 are illustrative. In Egypt electoral participation was restricted to a limited number of opposition parties licensed by the Political Parties Committee, which is controlled by the ruling party, while independent candidates were required to collect signatures from 5% of the country's elected officials (again, almost all of whom belonged to the ruling political party) (Freedom House 2006). These and other restrictions, such as a ban on religious parties and the barring of international monitors, ensured that most opposition parties were excluded and that the incumbent, Hosni

Mubarak, easily won reelection. In contrast, in Ethiopia the main opposition parties were allowed to participate in the electoral process, hold political rallies, and have access to the media. Despite a more open electoral process, the opposition's ability to compete fairly was hindered by irregularities, fraud, and lack of transparency in the counting of votes, all of which contributed to the ruling party's electoral victory (European Union 2005). To capture the differences in contestation highlighted by the Egyptian and Ethiopian cases, we distinguish between two types of electoral authoritarian regimes—hegemonic and competitive.

In *hegemonic* authoritarian regimes the restrictions on opposition parties and their political activities, bias in state-owned media coverage, and other forms of repression so severely circumscribe contestation that the incumbent candidate or party does not face the possibility of losing (Munck 2006, 33), often leading to a de facto one-party state.[3] Thus, hegemonic authoritarian regimes absolutely violate Bunce's maxim on the central elements of democracy (2001, 45): "freedom, uncertain results, and certain procedures." In hegemonic authoritarian regimes, the dominance of the political system by the incumbent and the ruling party ensures that there is never any uncertainty in the outcome of national elections; the incumbent nearly always prevails. Though elections are rendered meaningless in the selection of the executive as the outcome is a foregone conclusion, they are not irrelevant; elections, particularly legislative ones, often serve as a key instrument employed by rulers to manage society nonviolently and consolidate political control (Gandhi and Przeworski 2006; Lust-Okar, this volume).

Competitive authoritarian systems, on the other hand, permit a substantively higher degree of contestation, leading to greater uncertainty in the outcome of the elections between the ruling party and a legal and legitimate opposition, which usually chooses to participate, rather than to boycott the election. But the incumbent government still uses fraud, repression, and other illiberal means "to create an uneven playing field between government and opposition" (Levitsky and Way 2002b, 53) to try to ensure that it ultimately prevails in the electoral contest—even though it sometimes loses (Howard and Roessler 2006; see the appendix to this chapter).

Democracies can be distinguished from the broader set of electoral authoritarian regimes by "the freedom, fairness, inclusiveness, and meaningfulness of elections" (Diamond 2002, 28). At one end of the democratic spectrum are *electoral democracies,* which permit a competitive process for the selection of the executive that is held under genuinely free and fair conditions. Even if the outcomes of elections in electoral democracies are occasionally one-sided, and even if there are sporadic violations of civil liberties, there is a much more level playing field between the incumbent and the opposition. Finally, *liberal democracies* go a step beyond: they are strictly bound by the state's constitution and the rule of law, with horizontal accountability among officeholders, protection of pluralism and freedoms, and the lack of "reserved domains of power for the military or other actors not accountable to the electorate" (Diamond 1999, 10).

Having defined and explained our relatively abstract typology of regime types, we still need to show how they can best be measured empirically in the real world. There are two ways whereby one can identify how countries should be classified. One is to select cases on the basis of the "I know it when I see it" formula, namely, by analyzing countries independently and determining which ones fit the overall definition. The other is to establish criteria derived from the coding of other data sources and "let the chips fall where they may." Both are plausible and defensible strategies. We have chosen the latter, thereby avoiding the temptation to select cases based on our subjective judgments, and instead applying a common, precise, and systematic set of criteria based on existing indices. Any classification system is, of course, arbitrary, but by applying these criteria consistently, we aim to contribute a more objective measurement of these regime types—while recognizing that no such measurement is perfect and that there may still be some disagreement about the inclusion or exclusion of individual cases.[4]

Operationalization

To disaggregate political regimes into the five mutually exclusive types conceptualized in the previous section, we employ the criteria illustrated in Figure 4.1. Our primary sources for the coding distinctions are the two most commonly used indices of regimes, Freedom House (various years) and Polity (various years).[5] By using a combination of these two indices—both of which are imperfect, of course—we are able to have a firmer, more reliable basis on which to make our regime type determinations.

We code countries as closed authoritarian when there are no multicandidate national elections for the direct or indirect selection of the executive.[6] Also included in this classification are regimes with referenda for the president or unopposed "elections" in which rival candidates or parties are formally banned, since the citizenry is given no choice in the selection of the executive and its participation is inconsequential.[7]

As long as a regime does not allow multicandidate national elections for the selection of the executive, it maintains a closed authoritarian score for each country-year. If there is a change in the rules and procedures by which the executive is selected between 1987 and 2006 (i.e., if direct multicandidate presidential elections are introduced), then the closed authoritarian regime is reclassified based on whether the new rules allow for contestation, a free and fair electoral process, and the protection of the rule of law and other freedoms.[8]

The other four regime types do hold national executive elections, of course, albeit in quite different ways. In our operationalization, we first distinguish between countries on either side of what we consider the "democratic threshold," or the minimal requirements to be considered an electoral democracy. Countries with either a Freedom House political rights score of 2 or better *or* a Polity score of 6 or higher are coded as minimally democratic.[9] Conversely, countries that have *both* Freedom House scores of 3 or worse *and* Polity scores of 5 or lower are considered electoral authoritarian.[10]

Within the category of electoral authoritarianism, we distinguish between hegemonic and competitive authoritarianism based on the degree of contestation—i.e., the degree to which rules and practices allow for the possibility of incumbent defeat (Munck 2006). Comparing and distinguishing between regimes on the basis of contestation is tricky, however. The rules and practices incumbents employ to manipulate elections, constrain the opposition, and try to guarantee reelection are rarely transparent and vary widely across countries (Schedler 2006a, 7–10). Thus, there exist few objective and analogous indicators that allow us to capture precisely the integrity of the electoral process or the degree to which the rules and practices allow each participant an equal possibility of electoral victory.

To differentiate between competitive and hegemonic regimes, we use the outcome of the previous election as the distinguishing criterion.[11] If the winning party or candidate received more than 70% of the popular vote or 70% of the seats in parliament in the previous election, we code the regime as hegemonic. [12] A country keeps its categorization as a hegemonic government until the next election unless there is a significant change in the rules and procedures for selecting the executive prior to the next election.[13] If the winning party or candidate received less than 70% of the popular vote or of the parliamentary seats, the regime is coded as competitive.[14]

While an electoral percentage threshold has been criticized for conflating contestation with competitiveness (Munck 2006, 34), we believe that it captures the degree of contestation fairly well, since many authoritarian incumbents who gain 70% or better benefit from a boycott by one or more of the major opposition parties.[15] A boycott by the opposition suggests that the regime's electoral rules were so restrictive, and its practices so repressive, that the opposition forces calculated that they had little or no chance at all of winning. By contrast, in elections in which the incumbent received less than 70%, there was often broader participation by the opposition party members, who calculated that though the playing field was tilted against them, they still had a chance of electoral victory.[16] In other words, this rule partially captures the opposition's own calculations about the integrity of the electoral process, and the opposition is probably the best judge of whether the electoral process offers the possibility of non-incumbent electoral victory.

We broadly distinguish democratic regimes from authoritarian ones on the basis of countries' passing the democratic threshold described above—i.e., a Freedom House political rights score ≤ 2 or a Polity score ≥ 6. And we differentiate between the two types of democracies by coding countries that receive a score of both 10 on Polity and 1 on Freedom House political rights as liberal democracies, with the others being classified as electoral democracies.

Table 4.1 summarizes the coding rules employed to operationalize political regimes. (See the appendix to this chapter for various tests to check the validity of the measurement scheme.)

Global Trends in Regime Types, 1987–2006

Our universe of cases includes all political regimes in countries with populations over 500,000. It begins in the year 1987 (or the year of the country's independence) and extends until 2006. Our unit of analysis is the type of political regime in any given country-year. Applying the coding rules from Table 4.1, Figure 4.2 maps out the frequency and pattern of regime types over this 20-year span. As the figure shows, there has been a striking increase in democracies as a proportion of total regimes (a nearly 25% gain from 1987

Table 4.1 Operationalizing political regimes

Regime type	Measurement criteria
Closed authoritarianism	No multicandidate national elections for selection of executive
Hegemonic authoritarianism	FH ≥ 3 *and* Polity < 5 *and* winner received ≥ 70% of the vote or seats in previous election
Competitive authoritarianism	FH ≥ 3 *and* Polity < 5 *and* winner received < 70% of the vote or seats in previous election
Electoral democracy	FH < 2 *or* Polity ≥ 6
Liberal democracy	FH = 1 *and* Polity = 10

to 2006). This shift (in which the proportion of democratic regimes in the world reached 50% for the first time in history in 2000) is a consequence not only of the third wave of democratization and the end of the cold war, but also of a steady increase in democratic regimes between 1999 and 2006. Most of the increase in democratic regimes, however, has been due to a rise in electoral democracies, which have increased in frequency by almost 150% (from 25 to 62) between 1987 and 2006 and represent the modal regime type in the world from 1992 onward. In contrast, liberal democracies have not kept pace; the increase in these regimes since the end of the cold war has been less than 15%.

As with democratic regimes, there have been important changes in the trajectories of different types of authoritarian regimes. As illustrated in Figures 4.2 and 4.3, the number of closed authoritarian regimes declined precipitously between 1987 and 2006. Most of the drop in closed authoritarian regimes was due to the end of the cold war and the collapse of the Soviet Union. But the downtrend continued between 1998 and 2005, with a slight uptick in 2006. In contrast to closed authoritarian regimes, hegemonic authoritarian regimes rebounded after the end of the cold war, more than doubling since 1992, and actually becoming the modal authoritarian regime type by 2005. Competitive authoritarian regimes have experienced greater volatility. This type surged after the end of the cold war as incumbents of closed or hegemonic authoritarian regimes, facing tremendous international and domestic pressures, were forced to open their political systems. Multiparty elections were held to appease international donors and domestic opposition, but the autocratic incumbents frequently employed force and fraud to try to guarantee their political survival (Joseph 1997; Levitsky and Way

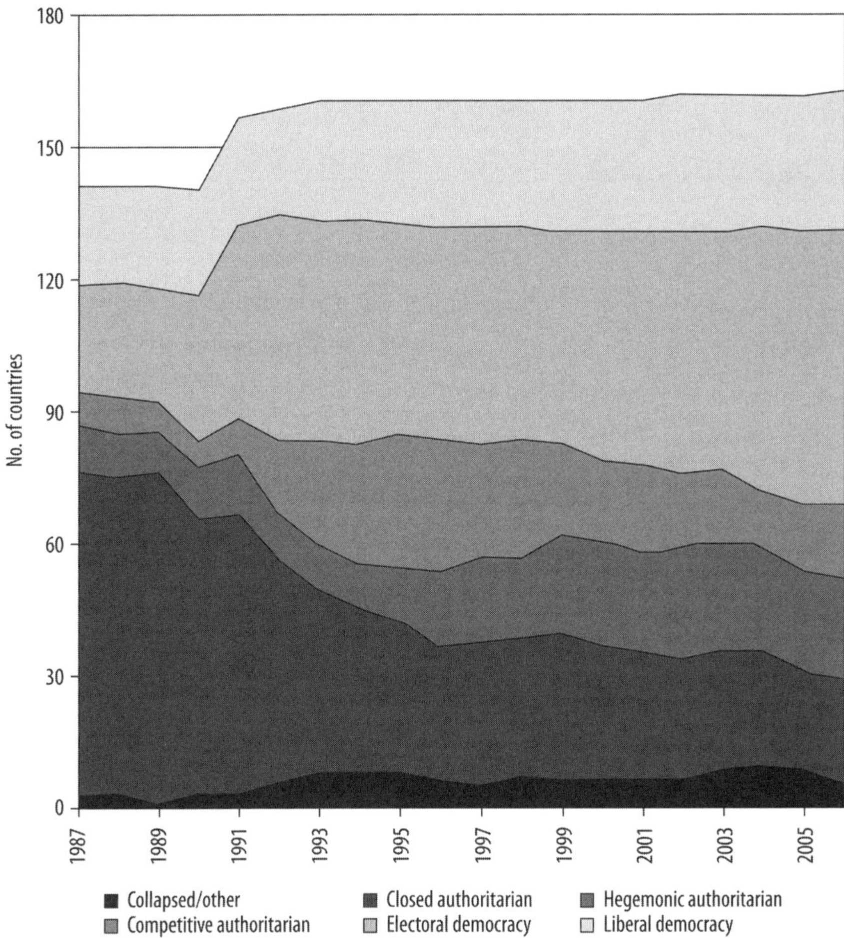

Figure 4.2. Frequency of regime types, 1987–2006

2002b). Thus, by 1995 there were more competitive authoritarian regimes than liberal democracies. But over the next 10 years the number of competitive authoritarian regimes declined sharply, from 19% of all regimes in 1995 to less than 10% in 2004 though slightly rebounding in 2005 and 2006.

The data presented in Figures 4.2 and 4.3 show the overall numbers and proportions of each regime type, but not their geographical location. The next three figures are world maps that illustrate the regime types of each country in the world with a population greater than 500,000 at three different time periods: 1987, 1996, and 2006.

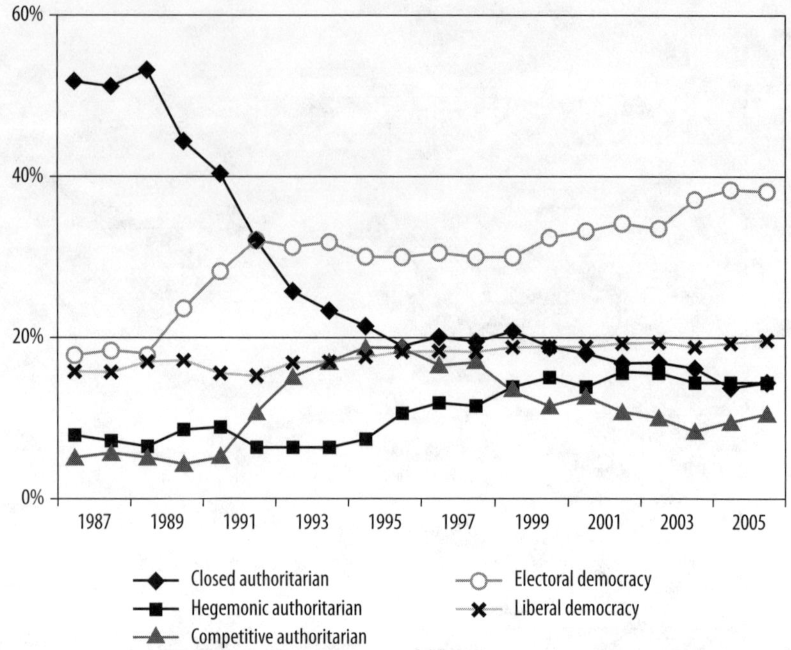

Figure 4.3. Proportion of regime types, 1987–2006

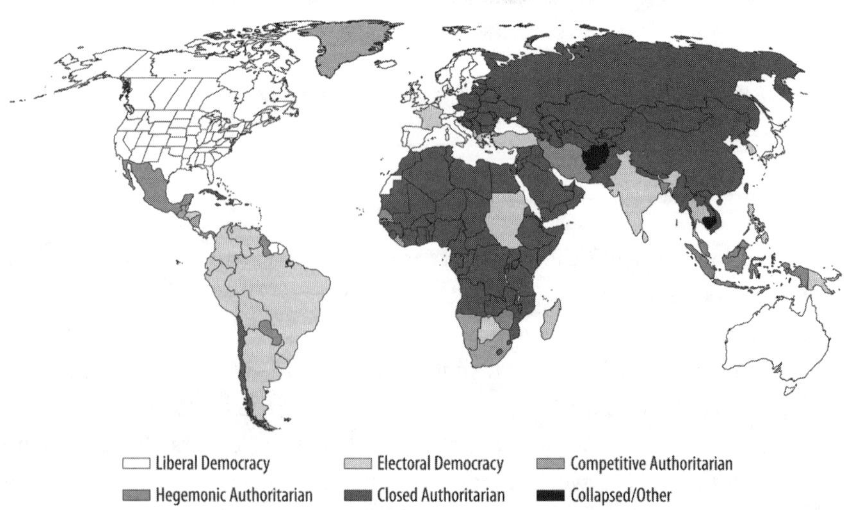

Figure 4.4. Global distribution of political regime types, 1987

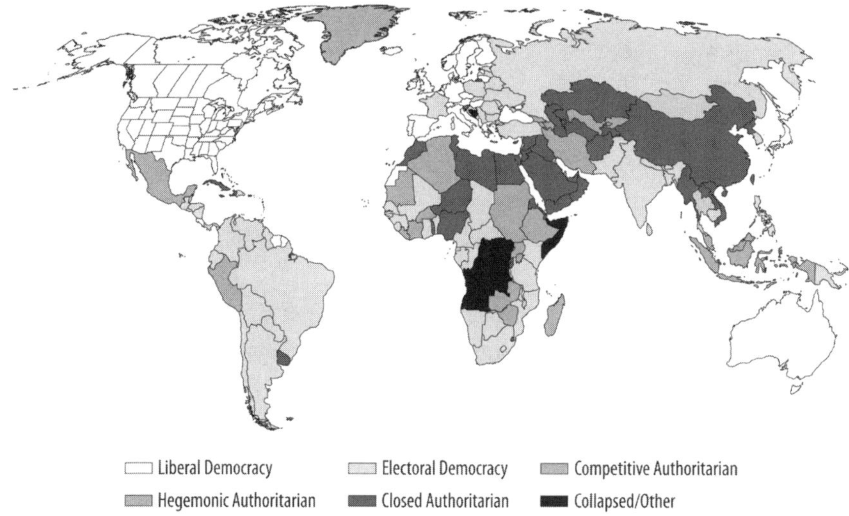

Figure 4.5. Global distribution of political regime types, 1996

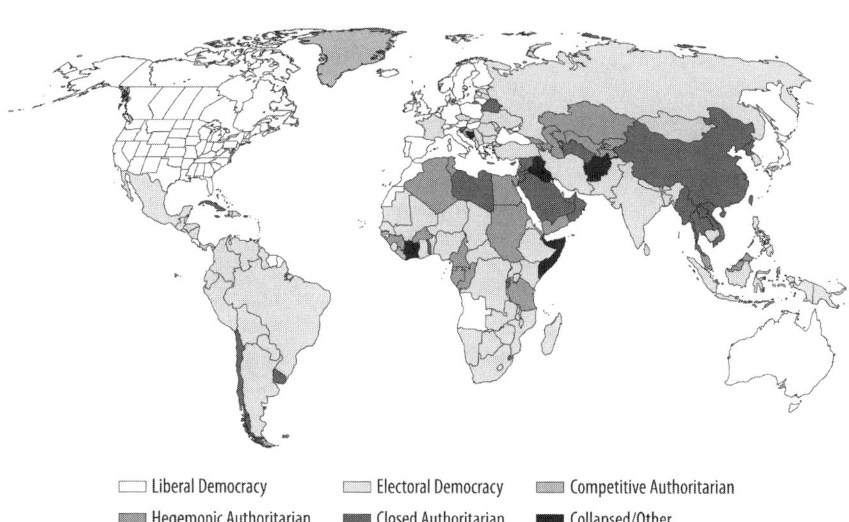

Figure 4.6. Global distribution of political regime types, 2006

Our starting point, 1987, reflects regime types at the very end of the cold war. Figure 4.4 shows that North America, much of Western Europe, Japan, and Australia could be considered liberal democracies in 1987. Most of the countries in Latin America were electoral democracies, along with South Asia and East Asia, and the rest of Western Europe (along with Turkey). The Soviet bloc was still closed authoritarian, and most countries in Africa were either closed or hegemonic authoritarian as well.

After the collapse of Communism in Eastern Europe and the Soviet Union, along with the concomitant end of the cold war and the ideological divisions throughout many other parts of the world, many closed regimes begin to open up. By the early 1990s, many of the countries in Eastern Europe had become electoral democracies, Russia was competitive authoritarian, and other parts of the former Soviet Union had become primarily competitive or hegemonic authoritarian. In sub-Saharan Africa, after early founding elections in Benin and Zambia and independence for Namibia, these countries joined Botswana as electoral democracies, while most of the continent remained closed or hegemonic authoritarian.

By 1996, as shown on Figure 4.5, there was a clear drop in the number of closed systems. Because of additional founding elections, many countries in Africa began to open up. Some in which the incumbents were voted out of power (e.g., Malawi, Mali, Niger, and Madagascar) became electoral democracies. In others (e.g., Kenya, Cameroon, Gabon, and Senegal), the incumbents used force and fraud to win highly contested elections. At the same time, the former Soviet Union opened up further, but a group of former Soviet republics (Azerbaijan, Georgia, Uzbekistan, and Kyrgyzstan) became hegemonic authoritarian. Within the Western hemisphere, Peru and Mexico still stood out as competitive authoritarian regimes, while Castro's government in Cuba remained the lone closed authoritarian regime.

The trends and patterns solidified in the 2000s. Central Asia remained an authoritarian bloc. Africa began to distinguish itself as the region with the most diversity: roughly one-fourth of the states were closed or collapsed regimes; one-fourth were hegemonic; one-fourth competitive; and one-fourth electoral democracies. With the transition in Mexico, mainland North America became all democratic for the first time in its history.

By 2006, as displayed on Figure 4.6, all of the Americas with the exception of Cuba, Haiti, and Venezuela were either electoral or liberal democracies. But only Chile and Uruguay moved from electoral to liberal, indicating that there is very little movement between those two types of democracy. The democratizing trend in Africa continued as electoral democracies increased by 70% between 2000 and 2006 (from 11 to 18), though more than 60% of the countries remained authoritarian or collapsed. Of the 23 countries in the world that remained closed systems, 70% of them were concentrated in either Asia (Bhutan, Burma, China, Laos, Nepal, North Korea, Turkmenistan, and Vietnam) or the Middle East and North Africa (Bahrain, Jordan, Kuwait, Libya, Morocco, Oman, Qatar, Saudi Arabia, Syria, and the United Arab Emirates).

This whirlwind tour across time and space shows us that the post–cold war process of democratization around the world was certainly not uniform or straightforward. And while there are clear regional patterns, one can also find considerable diversity within many regions.

Analysis

Variation in Democratic Transitions

As has been well-documented, the most striking change in regime types between 1987 and 2006 is the complete reversal in the number of authoritarian and democratic regimes. In 1987 there were 91 authoritarian regimes; by 2006, 94 democracies can be counted. Figures 4.4 through 4.6 suggest that, while in the immediate years after the end of the cold war, democratic transitions occurred disproportionately in Eastern Europe, since then they have been quite geographically diffuse.

Temporally, we find two clusters of democratic transitions. The first occurred around the end of the cold war. Interestingly, as shown in Figure 4.7, between 1987 and 1994 the type of authoritarian regime (closed, hegemonic, or competitive) does not seem to have made a significant difference in the likelihood of democratic transitions. In other words, the shock of the end of the cold war appears to have affected all authoritarian regimes similarly. In contrast, as shown on Figure 4.8, we find that between 1995 and 2006 competitive authoritarian regimes were more likely to experience democratic transitions than were other authoritarian regime types.

This finding is important in two respects. First, it suggests that longitudinal analyses, which cover both the cold war era and its aftermath without controlling for the great rupture caused by the end of the cold war, may overlook how the mechanisms and processes driving democratization over time have changed—from authoritarian collapse and bargaining to strategic inter-

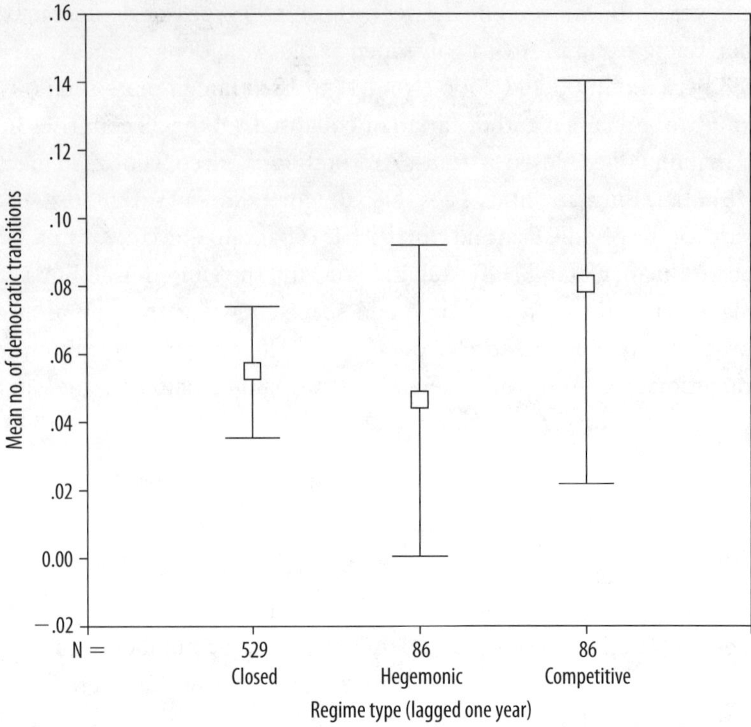

Figure 4.7. Democratic transitions across different types of authoritarian regimes, 1987–1994

actions in an electoral arena. Second, the finding justifies the disaggregation of the larger category of "electoral authoritarianism" based on the degree of prior contestation in their electoral processes (see also Brownlee, Chapter 5 in this volume). To maintain that these regimes are essentially the same—given that they are authoritarian and hold elections—runs the risk of conflating two subtypes that should remain conceptually, methodologically, and causally distinct.

The Relative Stability and Volatility of Regime Types

While the evidence from Figures 4.7 and 4.8 suggests that in the last decade competitive authoritarian regimes have been more susceptible to democratic transitions than other types of authoritarian regimes, in this section, we examine the relative stability or volatility of all regime types. Figure 4.9 depicts the stability of regimes based on *regime continuity* (whether a regime

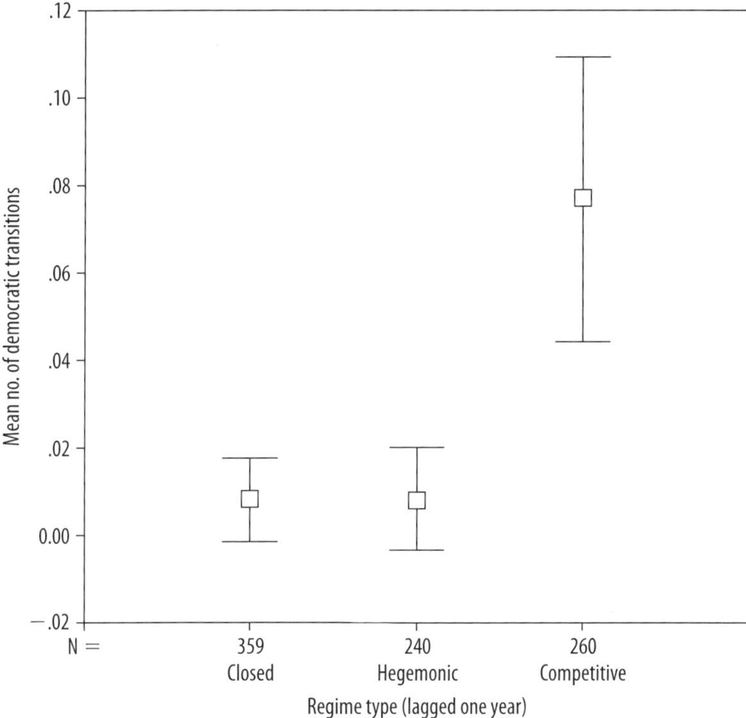

Figure 4.8. Democratic transitions across different types of authoritarian regimes, 1995–2006

is the same type from one year to the next). The figure reports data only from 1995 to 2006, in order to avoid the uncertainty surrounding the years immediately after the end of the cold war.

Figure 4.9 reveals the extraordinary stability of democratic regimes in the post–cold war period. Once a regime becomes a liberal democracy, it is almost guaranteed to remain one (with a 99% chance of staying the same the following year). Electoral democracies have proved similarly durable (with a 97% chance of staying the same). Between 1995 and 2006, there were only 14 incidences out of 630 country-years in which these regimes backslid into authoritarianism. But there have been even fewer incidences (7 out of 630) of electoral democracies becoming liberal democracies. In other words, once a country has reached the level of an electoral democracy, it rarely slides backwards—but it even more rarely improves to the level of liberal democracy. Although it may be too early to suggest that electoral democracies are

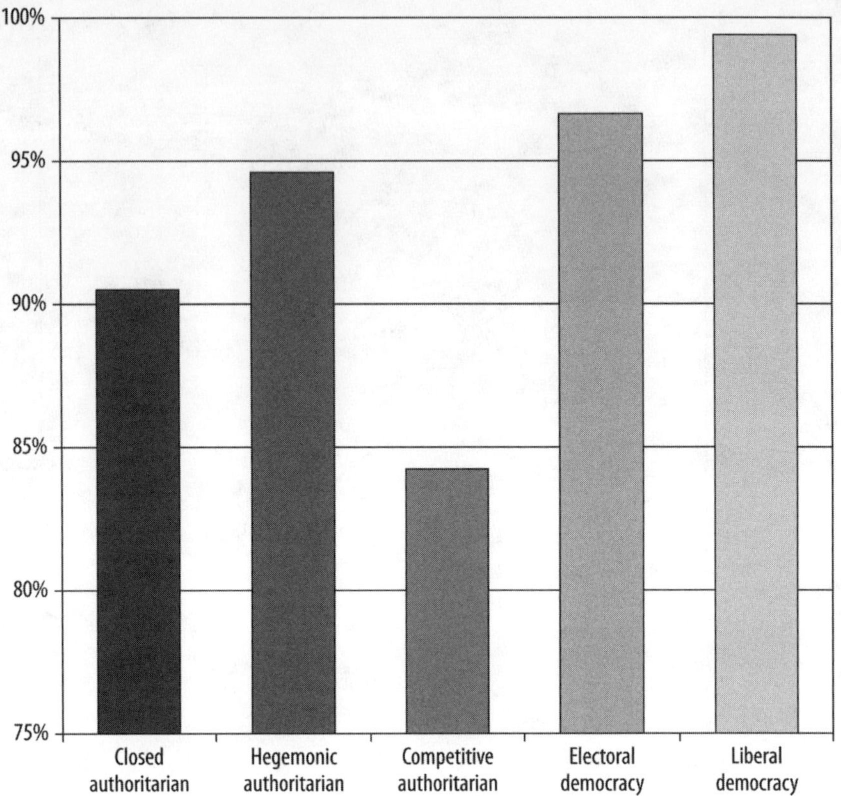

Figure 4.9. Regime continuity, 1995–2006

not consolidating into liberal democracies, the process is certainly not happening rapidly or regularly, if at all.

Figure 4.9 also shows that authoritarian regimes are more volatile from year to year. Hegemonic authoritarian regimes have the least instability (with a 94.5% likelihood of surviving the next year). While hegemonic regimes are susceptible to becoming competitive authoritarian regimes, they almost never become closed authoritarian regimes.[17] This suggests perhaps a surprising commitment to regular multicandidate elections in these regimes (though the average length of time in between elections in hegemonic authoritarian regimes is considerably longer than in other regimes with elections).[18] Closed authoritarian regimes have a somewhat lower level of stability (90.5%), and competitive authoritarian regimes are the most unstable (84%).[19]

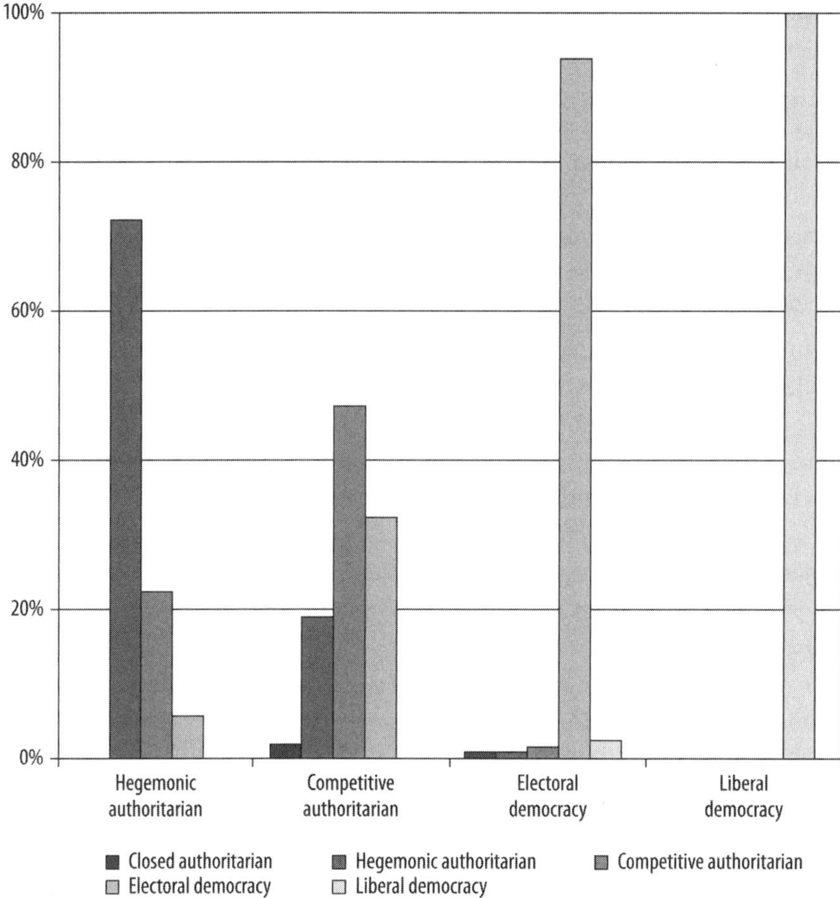

Figure 4.10. Change in regime type in the year after an election, 1995–2006

Figure 4.10 provides a more detailed perspective on the question of regime type continuity and change by showing not only the likelihood of change but also the actual direction and outcome of the changes that have taken place following elections between 1995 and 2006.[20] The figure confirms that competitive authoritarian regimes are particularly susceptible to political change from elections. One in two elections in competitive authoritarian regimes leads to a new regime type, with 10 elections (or 19%) leading to hegemonic authoritarianism, and 17 (32%) became electoral democracies. In contrast, 72% of the hegemonic authoritarian regimes stayed the same, whereas 22.2%

of them became competitive authoritarian, and 6% became electoral democracies. Finally, once again, liberal and electoral democracies rarely changed.

The Inherent Volatility of Competitive Authoritarianism

The analysis of the variation in the frequency and stability of regime types between 1987 and 2006 highlights several important trends, including the remarkable stability and distinctiveness of both liberal democracies and electoral democracies, as well as the decline in closed systems and the corresponding rise of hegemonic authoritarian regimes. Relative to the other regime types, however, competitive authoritarianism has shown to be particularly volatile. What accounts for this?

In some sense, it should perhaps not be surprising that competitive authoritarian regimes have proven to be the most volatile of the regime types, since these regimes are inherently contradictory: legitimate procedures (i.e., regular, competitive elections) clash with illegitimate practices (vote rigging, violent disenfranchisement, and media bias). Although the electoral process is certainly unfair, since the ruling party relies on fraud, coercion, and patronage to try to win the election, the opposition still has an opportunity to defeat the incumbent. Thus, elections generate a real struggle between the incumbent and the opposition that can sometimes lead to unpredictable or uncertain outcomes (Levitsky and Way 2002b; Bunce and Wolchik, this volume; Schedler, this volume).

Figure 4.10 illustrates the destabilizing effect elections can have on competitive authoritarian regimes relative to other regime types. Our previous research showed that elections in competitive authoritarian regimes are likely to lead to liberalizing outcomes under two conditions: when the opposition forms a coalition, thus increasing its probability of winning the election and raising the costs for the ruling party's use of force and fraud to rig the outcome, or if there is incumbent turnover, which can undermine extant patronage networks and lead businessmen and other elites to defect to the opposition (Howard and Roessler 2006). Of the 17 post–cold war elections in competitive authoritarian regimes that led to electoral democracies, almost two-thirds were due to opposition coalitions or incumbent turnover (based on data from Howard and Roessler 2006).

As Figure 4.10 also shows, elections in competitive authoritarian regimes can lead to backsliding into hegemonic authoritarianism. This can occur when the incumbent ruler or party decides that the competition is getting too close for comfort and increases its repressive measures to reduce the risk of defeat. For example, in Guinea prior to the 2003 presidential election the government, led by Lansana Conte, refused to allow the opposition to broadcast advertisements on state-run media, to participate on the electoral commission, or to campaign freely throughout the country. As a consequence, the opposition boycotted the presidential election, and Conte won more than 95% of the vote. In Gabon in 2005, Omar Bongo, the incumbent, made concessions to the opposition on the electoral commission (granting them a third of the seats) but instituted a new rule allowing members of the security services to vote two days before the rest of the country, which the opposition saw as an opportunity for vote rigging and double-voting.

One pattern evident in the data is that of the 10 competitive authoritarian regimes that regressed to hegemonic authoritarianism as a result of elections, 7 experienced this turnaround in the election immediately after the founding election (the 7 were Belarus, 2001; Cameroon, 1997; Mauritania, 1997; Tajikistan, 1999; Djibouti, 1999; Algeria, 2000; and Tanzania, 2000). After the cold war, incumbents in these countries were forced to bow to international pressure, open their political systems, and hold multiparty elections. But this opening would prove short-lived, for by the next election the incumbents had rigged the system, forced boycotts, and paved the way for complete electoral dominance.[21]

What these cases also suggest is that a state's income level and its access to economic resources may play a key role in determining whether the incumbent has the leverage to effectively control the electoral process and curtail contestation or remains vulnerable to an active opposition (see also Bunce and Wolchik, Chapter 10, for a discussion of the effect economic growth may have on regime vulnerability).[22] The mean levels of gross domestic product (GDP) per capita in the competitive authoritarian governments that became hegemonic authoritarian were nearly twice as high as in all other competitive authoritarian states ($2,553 versus $1,354).[23] Overall, competitive authoritarian states have a significantly lower mean level of GDP per capita than all other types of regimes.

Competitive authoritarianism can therefore be viewed as a residual category—neither liberal or electoral democracy nor closed or hegemonic authoritarianism—in which autocratic rulers of low-income countries find themselves in the post–cold war era. Desperate to stay in power in an era of multiparty elections, the rulers in these countries lack the material resources to effectively quash political contestation and find that each election represents a high-stakes game with their political survival on the line. These inherently unstable governments can "tip" in one direction or another depending upon the strategic interactions between the incumbent and the opposition. Where the opposition is able to coordinate a coalition or skillfully apply the "electoral model" described by Bunce and Wolchik in this volume, democratization is possible. But if the incumbent government is savvy and resourceful enough to divide its opponents, maintains the support of the military and security, and remains internally cohesive, the tenuous status quo will prevail until the next election. While it is not surprising that competitive authoritarian governments are susceptible to instability, and that the number of these regimes fluctuates extensively over time, there is little risk of the category becoming obsolete.

Conclusion

In this chapter, we have disaggregated the umbrella concept of political regimes into five specific types—closed authoritarianism, hegemonic authoritarianism, competitive authoritarianism, electoral democracy, and liberal democracy—each of which we have defined conceptually and operationalized empirically with clear and systematic criteria, which we submitted to various validity checks (see the appendix to this chapter). This alone is a contribution to a literature that for decades tended to be global and undifferentiated in scope, and in recent years has tended to focus more narrowly on specific types of systems. Moreover, by using GIS technology to present global maps of regime types at different points in time, the chapter provides an innovative means to identify and highlight trends across time and space.

The results introduce several intriguing findings that go beyond the well-documented observation that the third wave of democratization has seen the replacement of many formerly authoritarian countries with recent democracies. First, while the number of electoral democracies has more than doubled from 1987 to 2006, the increase in liberal democracies has been modest, suggesting the existence of a "glass ceiling" for countries that have passed the democratic threshold. Second, although the number of closed authoritarian systems has decreased tremendously over this time period, the growing and now modal authoritarian regime type is hegemonic authoritarianism, where the incumbent leader seeks to take advantage of the existence of elections without risking actually losing.

Third, by breaking down the longitudinal analysis into two time periods, we see that two distinct processes of democratization have occurred. From 1987 to 1994, democratic transitions occurred at relatively similar rates across all three types of authoritarian regimes. In other words, for the countries that quickly became electoral democracies in the early 1990s, it essentially did not matter whether their starting point was competitive, hegemonic, or closed authoritarian. The crucial factor was the end of the cold war and the sudden loss of external patronage and support, which led to authoritarian collapse. Since 1995, however, institutional arrangements have proven crucial. Democratization has occurred through the process of contested, but flawed, elections, and very few countries that were either closed or hegemonic authoritarian were able to make the leap to become electoral democracies. This finding reinforces the importance of disaggregating "electoral authoritarianism" based on the level of contestation, since this institutional variation has decisive consequences for democratization and other political phenomena.

Finally, on the issue of regime stability or volatility, the results show clear differences across the regime types. Electoral and liberal democracies are remarkably stable, with little backsliding. Hegemonic authoritarian regimes are also very stable, with almost no incidences of moving back to closed authoritarianism but also relatively few incidences of significant opening. Competitive authoritarianism is the most volatile regime type because it remains vulnerable to the destabilizing impact of elections that can either result in an opposition victory that will lead to an electoral democracy or cause the incumbent to fear defeat to the extent that he imposes even harsher measures that lead to a hegemonic authoritarian regime.

There are, of course, limitations to this study. Our coding is only as good as the data used in the sources we rely upon. And there will certainly be disagreements on the classification of some individual countries. Nonetheless, this analysis helps to provide a clear and systematic classification of the countries of the world from 1987 to 2006, to compare them across time and space, and to identify and account for important trends and developments in political regimes.

Appendix: Validity Checks of Measurement Scheme

The purpose of this appendix is to test the validity of our measurement criteria for distinguishing between regime types. As Adcock and Collier explain, "Measurement is valid when the scores . . . derived from a given indicator . . . can meaningfully be interpreted in terms of the systemized concept . . . that the indicator seeks to operationalize" (2001, 531). In our measurement scheme, therefore, we need to verify that the five categories of cases that our indicators define actually represent different types of political regimes.

The first check focuses on the cases our indicators define as subtypes of authoritarianism. We use the presence or absence of elections and the degree to which the elections allow for contestation to delimit closed, hegemonic, and competitive authoritarian regimes. If our indicators validly distinguish different categories of authoritarian regimes on these variables, we would expect this to be reflected in the average Freedom House political rights score and Polity scores across the types,[24] since a key component of each index is the degree to which the selection of the executive takes place by means of a competitive and open process. Table 4A.1 shows that our authoritarian subtypes reflect quite well different levels of authoritarianism according to these indices. It also suggests that our categories of competitive and hegemonic authoritarianism capture substantive and significant differences in types of authoritarian regimes.

A second validity check tests the assumption that our different regime types capture varying levels of contestation—that is, the degree to which the opposition has the possibility of winning. If our indicators validly distinguish contestation between different regimes, we should see varying rates of nonincumbent electoral victories across them. In hegemonic authoritarian regimes, the incumbent should win nearly all of the time; in competitive authoritarian regimes, the number of opposition victories should be signifi-

Table 4A.1 Mean level of authoritarianism across different authoritarian regime types

Regime type	Ave. Freedom House political rights score	Ave. Polity score
Closed	6.22	−6.79
Hegemonic	5.40	−2.74
Competitive	4.74	0.27

Table 4A.2 Nonincumbent electoral victory across different regime types

Regime type	Mean nonincumbent electoral victory
Hegemonic authoritarian	.06
Competitive authoritarian	.34
Electoral democracy	.56

cantly higher, though not as high in electoral democracies, where, given an even playing field, the opposition should win just as frequently as the incumbent. As Table 4A.2 illustrates, our different categories reflect contestation quite well. In hegemonic authoritarian regimes, nonincumbent electoral victory is extremely rare and is not distinguishable from zero.[25] In competitive authoritarianism, incumbent electoral victory is not guaranteed (in more than one-third of the elections the incumbent is not reelected), though the process is still rigged in the incumbent's favor. Finally, in electoral democracies opposition parties have a greater than 50% chance of winning.

In sum, these checks provide support for the internal and external validity of our measurement scheme. Using the selection of the executive to distinguish authoritarian regimes appears to capture clear differences in the level of authoritarianism as measured by Polity and Freedom House. Moreover, our assumption that the categories reflect different degrees of contestation is supported empirically, as there is a clear linear relationship between our measure of regime types and nonincumbent electoral victory.

CHAPTER FIVE

Harbinger of Democracy

Competitive Elections before the End of Authoritarianism

Jason Brownlee

On the question of the democratizing power of elections, this chapter takes a slightly different approach than the previous chapters. It builds upon recent literature on the origins and variations of authoritarianism (among others, Brownlee 2007a; Posusney and Angrist 2005; Schedler 2006a; Schlumberger 2007; Wedeen 1999). Recognizing stark contrasts in opposition performance among the world's nondemocracies, I investigate how variation in how "real" electoral contestation under authoritarianism bears upon the prospects that the next regime will be an electoral democracy rather than just another autocracy.

Premised on the synthesis of autocratic rule with democratic features (mainly elections), initial studies categorizing hybrid regimes distinguish between regimes facing viable opposition groups, in countries such as Iran and Malaysia, and those dealing with relatively marginalized challengers, as in Egypt and Turkmenistan. Whereas both kinds of regimes may be labeled "electoral authoritarian" due to the presence of multifactional polls (Schedler 2002a), Iran and Malaysia display the characteristics of "competitive authoritarianism," and Egypt and Turkmenistan's authoritarian systems are more "hegemonic," as discussed by Philip G. Roessler and Marc M. Howard in the first chapter of this book (see also Diamond 2002).

Much attention has been given to delineating these differences and labeling new forms of authoritarianism. But comparativists have invested less effort in testing whether and how such intra-authoritarian variations affect major political outcomes, particularly regime breakdown and democratization. Do more competitive elections under authoritarian conditions increase the likelihood that the regime, when it breaks down, will be replaced by a democratic system rather than another autocracy? While Roessler and Howard, in the preceding chapter, indicate that elections are the most powerful agents of democratic change in more competitive electoral authoritarian regimes, they do not test that proposition as such. Other authors in this book (e.g., Lindberg, and Bunce and Wolchik) also find suggestive empirical patterns without making a controlled large-*N* analysis.

Rather than looking at all countries and all years, as Jan Teorell and Axel Hadenius do in Chapter 3, the present chapter focuses on instances of regime breakdown. It provides quantitative tests of the impact of competitive elections on successor regime type in a dataset of 88 regimes that lost or withdrew from power during 1975–2004. Initial authoritarian regime codings were drawn from Barbara Geddes's dataset on authoritarian breakdown (1999a, 1999b, 2003). I then deployed a discrete measure to gauge whether the successor regime was democratic or nondemocratic, rather than using ordinal data from Polity or Freedom House. This method better matches extant concepts of Schumpeterian democracy and provides a more reliable assessment than its recent forerunners. A dichotomous dependent variable identified countries as having democratized if they experienced at least three consecutive years of electoral democracy (as reported in Freedom House's qualitative list of electoral democracies) beginning within two years of the prior regime's end. This operationalization yielded 48 regimes, out of 88 total regimes during 1975–2004, in which an authoritarian regime was succeeded by a minimally democratic one. The set of democratized regimes fit the field's concepts and includes the transitions treated by the leading studies of this period (Bratton and van de Walle 1997; Diamond, Linz, and Lipset 1988; Huntington 1991; Linz and Stepan 1996; O'Donnell and Schmitter 1986). The split in outcomes—with 45% of cases followed by more authoritarianism and 55% succeeded by electoral democracy—underlines the research question: Does attention to elections under authoritarianism help account for this wide divergence?

To answer this question, I developed a categorical independent variable for hybrid regime types, based on whether the regime held multiparty elections at all and whether or not the opposition performed strongly (winning at least 25% of the ballots) in those elections. This new variable then joined the existing battery of regime types and control variables from Geddes's tests. Tests of competitive authoritarianism and successor regime type show a statistically strong and positive relationship. Cases in which the opposition was performing strongly in elections before the regime change were substantially more likely to be followed by electoral democracy after the regime lost power. Predicted probabilities show the effect was substantial, raising the likelihood of democratic instauration from 48.2% to 88.8%. It follows that while competitive elections may be held for a long period without endangering an autocracy, they nonetheless bode well for the prospects of democracy taking hold in the country's subsequent regime.

The Debate over Elections, Authoritarianism, and Democratization

By the end of the 1990s the spread of democratization that comprised the "third wave" had begun to ebb, prompting many scholars of comparative politics to reexamine the persistence of authoritarian rule. Social scientists soon proposed new taxonomies to capture the resilient blend of electoralism and despotism that characterized regimes from Zimbabwe to Azerbaijan. In 2002 the *Journal of Democracy* crystallized many of the main labels in the new field of comparative autocracy, including the term *competitive authoritarianism*, which denoted a system where elections were meaningful enough that they reflected much of the electorate's preferences even if they were still plagued by problems of fraud and manipulation (Levitsky and Way 2002a, 2002b). These competitive authoritarian regimes faced strong opposition, in public and in government. As Larry Diamond put it: "One defining feature of competitive authoritarian regimes is significant parliamentary opposition. [By contrast,] in regimes where elections are largely an authoritarian façade, the ruling or dominant party wins almost all the seats" (2002, 29).

Although comparativists continue to debate the utility of fresh regime typologies (Armony and Schamis 2005; Snyder 2006), Diamond's categorization captures an important variance among a wide set of regimes, including autocracies in Africa, the Middle East, and Central Asia. For example, the notion of competitive authoritarianism speaks to the difference between Egypt and pretty much all of the Arab states on one hand, and Iran, on the other. Among authoritarian regimes in its region Iran is arguably the only government facing a viable democratic opposition that has demonstrated its ability to mobilize mass support. While the contrast between Iran's fractious Islamic Republic and Egypt's fortified police state is familiar to specialists of both countries, the implications of that variance have not been explored in the field of comparative democratization. Nor, for that matter, have scholars delved into the implications of analogous differences in competitiveness within regions such as sub-Saharan Africa and Central Asia.

Whereas electoral contestation has not received great attention, comparativists have long pondered whether elections in authoritarian circumstances can yield democratic gains. After regime-initiated elections in the Philippines, Chile, Poland, and Nicaragua produced opposition victories, Samuel Huntington remarked that "liberalized authoritarianism is not a stable equilibrium; the halfway house does not stand" (Huntington 1991, 174–75). Like Huntington, many other recent scholars have seen inclusion by means of limited elections as a path to change. In their definitive study of transitions away from authoritarianism, Guillermo O'Donnell and Philippe Schmitter contended that post–World War II autocrats "can justify themselves in political terms only as transitional powers" (1986, 15) and envisioned a slippery slope from liberalization to democratization: "Once some individual and collective rights have been granted, it becomes increasingly difficult to justify withholding others" (1986, 10). Along the same lines, Giuseppe DiPalma wrote that "dictatorships do not endure" (1990, 33), and Adam Przeworski reasoned that "liberalization is inherently unstable" (1991, 58).

However, even as rulers from Manila to Managua were ousted by the ballot box, their peers elsewhere remained in place. Autocratic incumbents learned to garb themselves in elections and thereby insulate themselves further, slowing the trend toward electoral democracy that Huntington had identified. If elections were not the "death of dictatorship" (Huntington 1991, 174), had they instead become the autocrat's livelihood? Some comparativists have made this argument, seeing liberalization as a reversible process that helps rulers manage their opponents (Chehabi and Linz 1998, 18; Gandhi and

Przeworski 2001, 15–16; Joseph 1997, 375; Remmer 1999, 349). In this view elections are not the lid of Pandora's box, unleashing a torrent of political change; they are a safety valve for regulating societal discontent and confining the opposition. The array of resilient dictators touting their electoral bona fides in Africa, the Middle East, and Central Asia suggests that in some circumstances elections are tightly bridled by those in power.

On balance, one can invoke cases in favor of either perspective: the notion of liberalization as regime control or the concept of liberalization as regime change catalyst. Certainly the setbacks dealt to opposition movements in the Middle East suggest an unpropitious setting for the "electoral revolutions" recently experienced in Eastern Europe (see Bunce and Wolchik 2006a, as well as their chapter in the present volume; Brownlee 2007b). At the same time, though, comparativists have delved less deeply into the long-term and post-regime effects of electoral competition—that is, the question of whether electoral contestation may lay the foundation for democracy even if it does not immediately topple the current autocratic government. In the remainder of this chapter I explore this possibility through a broad quantitative analysis. Popular assumptions about elections are largely driven by iconic cases, like the Philippines and Nicaragua. Rather than casting a spotlight on these familiar episodes, I widen the lens of analysis to see how well the competing arguments of elections under autocracy comport with general trends. With 30 years of data and 88 instances of autocratic regime breakdown, this approach offers one of the most systematic treatments of this topic to date and deliberately engages the contributions and limitations of prior work—which I consider next.

Recent Findings and Remaining Questions

Although case studies still constitute the bulk of work on elections and authoritarianism, cross-national statistical work on the subject has been progressing, fueled in part by the availability of relevant datasets.

Geddes's study of authoritarian breakdown, introduced as a conference paper and subsequently expanded into a monograph on research methods, distilled decades of scholarship on nondemocratic regimes and set a new baseline for cross-national studies of regime change (Geddes 1999a, 1999b, 2003). Intentionally developing a set of regime subtypes that matched the extant literature, Geddes eschewed a numerical range of authoritarianism in favor of a set of categories that reflected qualitative contrasts among different autocracies. Those differences primarily concerned the interests and power bases of incumbent rulers, whether they originated in the country's military (whence they could return after the regime ended), a party (upon which they depended for influence), or a personal clique. Geddes thus developed a tripartite typology of military, single-party, and personalist regimes, with various mixed types for regimes that spanned more than one category (Geddes 2003, 50–51). Consistent with Geddes's game theoretic elaboration of elites' interests in these different regimes, military regimes were the most likely to lose power (having an average duration of only 8.5 years), single-party leaders were least likely to relinquish power (22.7 years), and personalistic leaders lasted longer than military ones but not as long as single-party rulers (15.0 years) (Geddes 1999b, 37).[1] Her approach has since been employed in a series of regime change studies on which the present chapter builds (Kinne 2005; Peceny, Beer, and Sanchez-Terry 2002; B. Smith 2005).

One of the most ambitious successors to Geddes's project has been Axel Hadenius and Jan Teorell's cross-national study of regime change (see also Chapter 3 in this volume). In an earlier working paper and subsequent article Hadenius and Teorell (2005b, 2007) report on a new dataset that includes cases, variables, and outcomes not addressed by Geddes. Notably, their data encompass monarchies and classify democracies as well as autocracies. In all, they have five main types of regimes—monarchies, military, no-party, one-party, and multiparty—as well as hybrids that fall between categories (2006, 8). Combining these five subtypes with their coding of democracies, Hadenius and Teorell track both intra-authoritarian regime shifts—for example a change from no-party to multiparty autocracy—and extra-authoritarian transitions, from autocracy to democracy. The approach offers a substantial advance in our understanding of transitions not only *from* authoritarian regimes, but also within them. But its application in their accompanying statistical analysis elides the distinction between these kinds of change.

Hadenius and Teorell code intraregime periods of varying authoritarianism as distinct regimes and in some cases this has the effect of fragmenting one regime into several. For example, whereas Geddes is in accord with most area specialists in coding Mexico under the PRI as one regime from 1929 to 2000, Hadenius and Teorell identify two different cases: a dominant party regime (1960–87) and a multiparty regime (1988–98) (2006, 27–28). Likewise, most comparativists consider the dictatorial rule of Ferdinand Marcos in the Philippines one regime that lasted from Marcos's declaration of martial law in 1972 until his ouster following the "snap election" of 1986. For Hadenius and Teorell, the Marcos regime is counted three ways before its collapse: as a residual "other" (1972–77), as a dominant-party regime (1978–83), and as a multiparty regime (1984–86) (2006, 28, 30–31).

This coding decision departs from the conventional concepts of the comparative politics literature and undermines the reliability of the measures deployed. The PRI in Mexico and Marcos in the Philippines did not lose power multiple times; they each lost power once. Yet Hadenius and Teorell include these subperiods as separate regimes in their survival analysis and test of democratization (2006, 16, 21). By counting intra-authoritarian modulations as distinct instances of breakdown, Hadenius and Teorell risk biasing their results and overstating the potential for change. Mexico's democratization was not the conclusion of a 10-year-old multiparty autocracy, but the climax of a decades-old regime by a ruling party that had become more competitive in its final years. It is thus premature to conclude that "all other possible determinants of democratization being equal—limited multiparty systems are more likely to democratize" (Hadenius and Teorell 2007, 154). In order to recognize intra-authoritarian regime variations, comparative analysis must account for shifts within autocracies without obscuring the fundamental identification of regimes.[2] Two other recent works have approached the impact of regime competitiveness on regime change and democratization.

Using an original dataset on elections in sub-Saharan Africa, Staffan Lindberg argues that elections do not merely ratify preceding democratic development but actually facilitate democratization independently (2006a, 3). Over time, Lindberg contends, elections have a self-reinforcing effect that embeds and consolidates democratic practices in previously authoritarian settings: "My analysis of more than two hundred third-wave elections in Africa shows that an uninterrupted series of competitive elections imbues society with certain democratic qualities. Repeated elections—regardless of their relative freeness or fairness—appear to have a positive impact on human freedom and democratic values" (2007, 139). Lindberg reaches this conclusion by tracking "improvement in democratic qualities" as measured by changes in Freedom House civil liberties scores for the relevant countries (2006a, 18–19). Yet he leaves unexplored the relationship of these shifts in democratic quality to explore the arguably more monumental change from an electoral autocracy to an electoral democracy. The resulting implications are unclear; repeated elections may be accompanied by a flourishing of civil society, but we cannot be confident they spur regime change.

Finally, in a cross-national analysis of competitive authoritarianism, Marc M. Howard and Philip Roessler found that what they termed "liberalizing electoral outcomes" were most likely when the opposition coordinated around a single candidate and challenged a non-incumbent in the elections (2006, 375–76). These authors thus capture the importance of strategy for challenging competitive authoritarian regimes, illustrating their quantitative findings with the example of Kenya's transition from single-party rule in 2002 (378–79).

Howard and Roessler's study marks one of the first attempts to make careful use of the competitive authoritarian subtype to examine the dynamic question of how regimes become more politically open and pluralist, and their chapter in this volume makes a further contribution in this regard. Like Hadenius and Teorell, these authors combine Polity and Freedom House data to measure their dependent variable. An electoral outcome counts as having "liberalized" the regime if in that year "the Polity score increased by three or more points and the Freedom House political rights scored decreased by one point or more" (Howard and Roessler 2006, 370). This approach measures the significant shift from competitive authoritarianism toward electoral democracy while leaving open the issue of where such a regime change falls within the full spectrum of democratization: "An important question that will have to be left for future research is what explains transitions from more closed regimes to competitive authoritarian regimes, such that elections become competitive and the opposition has a greater opportunity to contribute to political liberalization through strategic electoral coalitions" (375, n. 26). In tandem with that question, one must also consider the prospect that some regimes may make the transition from closed autocracy to electoral democracy without lingering in the zone of competitive authoritarianism. In order to pursue such analysis, comparativists must set competitive autocracies alongside their noncompetitive and nonelectoral counterparts.

Coding Hybrid Regimes and Democratic Successors

The foregoing studies produced a set of valuable findings for our understanding of what variables undermine autocracy and generate democracy. I have attempted to integrate these gains in knowledge, compensate for some of the limitations in these prior works, and submit their implications to additional observation. Toward this end I have taken advantage of available measurements rather than constructing new ones (Snyder 2006, 227). Specifically, I have updated and expanded the regime data of Geddes; introduced categorical variables for electoral and competitive autocracy; and provided a measure for a dependent variable for gauging whether or not a successor regime is an electoral democracy. After dropping country-years for which the necessary economic data were unavailable, this dataset covers 88 authoritarian regimes that lost power during the period 1975–2004. Each unit in the sample is a country-year of regime breakdown (e.g., Haiti in 1986, Nicaragua in 1990). Here, I use "breakdown" in the simple sense of the end of a period of authoritarianism. It need not connote state collapse or other revolutionary outcomes but can simply convey that the basic political rules of the game have changed substantially, most often accompanied by an important shift in national leadership.

Geddes's Authoritarian Subtypes and Dependent Variable

The period covered in the dataset of Geddes (1999b) stopped with the year of publication. I updated the data through 2004 and introduced two cases of regime change under monarchies (Kuwait, 1990; Nepal, 1990). For each year, a regime is coded as one of Geddes's regime types (or as a monarchy), and the dummy variable of regime breakdown is coded as zero, except for a regime's final year. The seven regime types (military, military-personalist, personalist, single-party hybrid, single-party, military/personalist/single-party, monarchy) are mutually exclusive and collectively exhaustive. Personalist regimes are omitted from the regression analysis; coefficients for the other six regime type variables should be interpreted as the likelihood of the event (that the successor regime is an electoral democracy) relative to personalist regimes. Positive coefficients mean an increased likelihood of the event occurring, while negative coefficients indicate a reduced chance of democratization.

Electoral and Competitive Authoritarianism

Aside from Hadenius and Teorell's treatment, there has not yet been a comprehensive attempt at identifying which regimes, for which periods, are electoral and competitive autocracies. The works of Schedler, Levitsky, and Way specify the features of such regimes but do not as yet establish the full universe of such cases over the time period in question. In the spirit of not throwing the baby out with the bath water, I sought to introduce measures for these subtypes while retaining the data from Geddes's work. The most direct way of doing so was to create a separate set of dummy variable categories based on the characteristics of Schedler's electoral authoritarianism and Levitsky and Way's competitive authoritarianism. Electoral authoritarianism is defined as the foil of electoral democracy; it is a system in which elections are held but voting is systematically manipulated by incumbents (Schedler 2002a, 37–38). For a regime to be considered an electoral autocracy, some form of multiparty or multifactional polling must be allowed. The standard for competitive autocracy is higher: "Although incumbents in competitive authoritarian regimes may routinely manipulate formal democratic rules, they are unable to eliminate them or reduce them to a mere façade" (Levitsky and Way 2002b, 53). These regimes must exhibit a "meaningful" level of contestation, and Levitsky and Way explicitly excluded regimes like Egypt and Uzbekistan where rulers enjoyed hegemonic electoral dominance (54).

These categories may be seen as stacked tiers of autocracy above and beyond closed authoritarianism (in which rulers do not permit elections at all or allow only a single party to field candidates). In order to code all regimes in the dataset, one must apply some measure that sorts the regimes into one of three categories: closed autocracy, electoral (but noncompetitive) autocracy, and competitive autocracy. Although comparativists frequently use the numerical measures of Freedom House and Polity to reach such judgments, those datasets are intended to measure political contestation and thus match poorly with the particular institutional characteristics of Schedler, Levitsky, and Way's subtypes (see Munck and Verkuilen 2002). Further, Freedom House and Polity scores fail to capture the discrete changes that taxonomically partition the hybrid regimes.[3] Accordingly, I instead drew on the World Bank's Database of Political Indicators (DPI) and constructed dummy variables for the presence of limited multiparty elections and the competitiveness of those polls (Beck et al. 2001).

The latest version of DPI (released in 2005) covers the years 1975 to 2004 and includes seven-point indices of legislative and executive electoral competitiveness (Keefer 2002):

1 = no legislature
2 = unelected legislature/executive

3 = elected legislature/executive, one candidate/post
4 = one party, multiple candidates
5 = multiple parties are legal but only one party won seats
6 = multiple parties won seats but largest party received more than 75% of seats
7 = largest party won less than 75% of seats

DPI data on multipartyism cut across Geddes's regime types and are not endogenous to the outcomes of breakdown or continuity. They do not, per se, speak to the question of whether a regime is democratic or autocratic. They can thus be overlaid with Geddes's data to arrive at a system of authoritarian subtypes. Regime years that measured 1–4 in the DPI index were coded as closed autocracy; when at least two consecutive regime years received a score of 5–7 they were coded as electoral autocracy (as a combined category encompassing competitive and noncompetitive regimes). Electoral autocracies which were scored as a 7 on the indices of legislative and executive electoral competitiveness were further identified as competitive autocracies, producing three categories that offered a distinct and complementary typology to the existing regime divisions of Geddes.

Successor Regime Type: Electoral Democracy or Nondemocracy?

Although Geddes treated authoritarian breakdown with a dichotomous coding of regime maintenance and collapse, she refrained from creating a dependent variable for democratization. The prevailing method for doing so typically involves using Freedom House or Polity data and then identifying a numerical threshold or cut-off point at which a regime is said to have democratized. This is the tactic of Hadenius and Teorell, and their codings largely comport with general understandings in the field about which regimes have democratized.[4] Yet there is another source of data and another approach comparativists could adopt. Instead of trying to infer a dichotomous distinction from ordinal data, one could turn to the qualitative codings of electoral democracies that are now available.

Rather than assessing governments on a numerical spectrum, comparativists conventionally adopt a minimalist standard of democracy drawn from Joseph Schumpeter's emphasis on competition among elites by way of a popular vote. Seeking an alternative to concepts based on government effectiveness or economic equality, Schumpeter defined democracy in terms of the procedures for selecting leaders: "The democratic method is that institutional arrangement for arriving at political decisions in which individuals acquire the power to decide by means of a competitive struggle for the people's vote" (Schumpeter 1950, 269). Scholars subsequently added basic protection of civil liberties as another trait necessary for the exercise of democracy (Dahl 1971, 3; Diamond 2002, 21). The procedural definition of democracy—manifest through the rotation of top elites from competing groups—remains standard for judging whether or not a government is democratic (Schmitter and Karl 1991, 51). And the categorical distinction between democracies and nondemocracies is used annually in Freedom House's list of "electoral democracies." Applying Schumpeterian and Dahlian criteria, Freedom House identifies electoral democracies as those governments with

- a competitive multiparty political system;
- universal adult suffrage for all citizens;
- regularly contested elections under a secure and secret ballot and the absence of massive, outcome-changing fraud;
- significant public access of major political parties to the electorate through the media and open campaigning (Puddington 2007, 3).

Using these measures Freedom House has tracked global political trends since its coding of electoral democracies began in 1989. With these data I coded cases as being followed by electoral democracy if the regime in question experienced at least three consecutive years of electoral democracy beginning within two years of the prior regime's end. For example, Haiti 1986 is coded as 0 (no democratic successor) and Haiti 1994 is coded as 1 (democratic successor). The full list of regime changes and postregime change outcomes is provided in the Appendix.

Control Variables

In my model I included a number of economic and duration control variables, as well as a dummy variable for the Middle East.[5] For economic development and growth I utilized the Penn World Tables 5–2 (2006 dataset). One variable measures the natural log of GDP per capita in a given year; a second variable gauges GDP growth from the prior year. In tandem, the two address a country's development level and its government's economic performance (Boix and Stokes 2003; Haggard and Kaufman 1995; Lipset 1959; Przeworski et al. 2000). Similarly, in regard to longevity and the potential effects of age on regime change, I reproduced Geddes's variables—age, age squared, and age cubed—which enable the logistic regression to test for curvilinear effects of time, including whether the difficulty of remaining in power declines after a ruler's initial years (Bienen and Van de Walle 1991; de Mesquita et al. 2003).

Testing Whether Competitive Authoritarianism Portends Electoral Democracy

Table 5.1 presents results from four tests using the dependent variable of successor regime type. (As a reminder, the dependent variable, a 1 in a given year, means that the regime was followed by three consecutive years of electoral democracy.) Among the controls, per capita GDP and the Middle East dummy variable were significant, with GDP increasing the likelihood of democratic transition and location in the Middle East reducing it. These results accord with what scholars of democratization and Middle Eastern politics (Boix and Stokes 2003; Haggard and Kaufman 1995; Lipset 1959; Posusney 2004) have previously explored in great depth. The significance of the hybrid regime variables charts new terrain.

Turning first to the regime variables from Geddes's original project, only the military-personalist type evinces any significant positive effect on the likelihood of democratic transition. (Regimes that fall into this set include the Central African Republic and Pinochet's Chile.) Otherwise, there are no significant differences among the military, personalist, and single-party regimes in their tendency to be followed by nondemocracies or democracies. Whereas most of Geddes's categories showed no significant impact on subsequent regime type, the new hybrid regime categories emerged as salient predictors of electoral democracy after dictatorships had fallen. In model 3 the broad category of electoral autocracy (without regard to competitiveness) was weakly but significantly linked to democratic transitions. The underlying dynamics come into focus in model 4. Once the noncompetitive and competitive regimes of the combined electoral autocracy set are disaggregated, competitive autocracy emerges as a much stronger predictor of democratic transitions.

One further method for evaluating the effects of these variables is the measurement of predicted probabilities. Accordingly, I estimated the predicted probability that a typical authoritarian regime (with control variables set at the mean value or, for dummy variables, the mode) would be followed

Table 5.1 Tests of whether electoral and competitive autocracy lead to transitions to electoral democracy

Variable	Model 1 (Control variables)	Model 2 (Authoritarian subtypes)	Model 3 (Electoral autocracy, combined)	Model 4 (Electoral autocracy, disaggregated)
Regime type				
Electoral autocracy (combined)	—	—	1.107* (.596)	—
Electoral autocracy (non-competitive)	—	—	—	.448 (.703)
Competitive autocracy	—	—	—	2.112** (.919)
Military regime	—	.146 (.764)	.643 (.839)	.561 (.854)
Military-personalist	—	1.784* (.944)	2.039** (.979)	2.148** (.971)
Single-party hybrid	—	–.429 (.848)	–.257 (.872)	–.167 (.891)
Single-party	—	–.419 (.853)	–.278 (.894)	–.502 (.953)
Personal/military/single-party[a]	—	—	—	—
Monarchy	—	–.969 (1.707)	–.114 (1.722)	–.430 (1.768)
Per capita GDP_{ln}	.990** (.324)	1.054** (.370)	.907** (.371)	.931** (.388)
Lagged GDP growth	–.014 (.026)	–.021 (.027)	–.020 (.028)	–.018 (.029)
Middle East location	–3.479** (1.327)	–2.938* (1.587)	–3.007** (1.506)	–2.701* (1.566)
Age of regime	–.057 (.158)	–.068 (.166)	–.068 (.163)	–.105 (.164)
Age^2	.002 (.006)	.003 (.007)	.003 (.006)	.004 (.006)
Age^3	–.000009 (.00007)	–.00002 (.00008)	–.00002 (.00007)	–.00004 (.00007)
Constant	–6.749** (2.484)	–7.469** (2.697)	–6.972** (2.722)	–6.912** (2.811)
N	*88*	*86*	*86*	*86*

continued

Table 5.1 continued

Variable	Model 1 (Control variables)	Model 2 (Authoritarian subtypes)	Model 3 (Electoral autocracy, combined)	Model 4 (Electoral autocracy, disaggregated)
Pseudo R^2	.016	.199	.229	.254
Log likelihood	−51.014	−47.611	−45.809	−44.333

Note: The dependent variable is that the successor government is an electoral democracy. Results are from logistic regression. Entries are unstandardized coefficients. Standard errors are listed in parentheses. Two-tailed tests for all estimates.

[a] Two observations from the Personal/military/single-party category—Paraguay, 1992, and Indonesia, 1998—were dropped due to perfect prediction.

$*\ p \leq .10$ $**\ p \leq .05$ $***\ p \leq .001$

by electoral democracy. Even though these measures draw on data from prior regimes and thus do not address specific current cases, they provide an indication of what can be expected, given past experiences. The presence of significant electoral competition bolstered the prospects of democratization. Whereas the overall predicted probability of having a democratic successor regime was 48.16%, just shy of a coin toss, the probability was 88.75% in the context of substantial electoral competition.

These results speak to current literature in the field and many of the companion studies in this volume. To begin with Geddes's regime types, the sources of rulers' authority and the nature of their coalitions are poor predictors of what kind of government will follow their withdrawal from power. Military leaders may pass power to elected presidents, as has been the case in Argentina, Brazil, and Turkey. They may also be succeeded by elites no less autocratic than themselves, as occurred in the late 1970s in Chad and Ghana. It appears that very much the same diversity characterizes personalist and single-party regimes. Against that backdrop, the distinct post-transition legacy of competitive authoritarianism is striking. Among regimes that have lost power, competitive autocracies are significantly linked to the replacement of autocracy with electoral democracy. These results in turn illuminate Hadenius and Teorell's interpretation of relatively short-lived multiparty autocracies (such as Mexico under the PRI in the 1990s). Such regimes are likely to be followed by electoral democracy, yet that period of contested elections does not itself propel a transition.

This chapter also reinforces several points made by other contributors to this volume. As Lindberg notes in his introduction, there is a need for cross-regional attention to the general dynamics of elections in nondemocratic contexts, and my findings amplify his call. In a strong endorsement of Lise Rakner and Nicolas van de Walle's attention to opposition parties, the present study suggests that the vitality of challengers to authoritarianism matters a great deal for what kind of regime may follow a regime change and merits further scrutiny. Thus, the weakness of opposition movements in sub-Saharan Africa that Rakner and van de Walle identify bodes poorly not only for the obvious issue of removing incumbents from power but also for the future of electoral democracy in the event that current rulers are somehow ousted. Regarding regimes in power, this study echoes Howard and Roessler's message from their expansive survey of regime outcomes. Variations in the kinds of authoritarian rule bear upon the kinds of regimes that are most likely to follow. For this reason, hegemonic dictatorships, which pervade the Middle East and Central Asia, are some of the least likely candidates for democratization, given the vast power asymmetries between rulers and their opponents. There is also resonance between this study, which was not confined to one particular region, and Jennifer McCoy and Jonathan Hartlyn's careful examination of the record of "electoralism" in Latin America. Just as they find that repeated elections did not deliver democratization in the way Lindberg has observed in Africa, so too this chapter signals that the simple holding of elections is at best weakly correlated to the replacement of autocracy by democracy. What matters more is the level of contestation within those elections. In fact, in electoral authoritarian regimes where the opposition garnered less than 25% of the vote, elections had no statistically significant impact on democratization.

Conclusion

This chapter has delved into the effects of more and less contested forms of electoral autocracy. Quantitative analysis of 88 autocratic regimes indicates that competitive elections increase the likelihood that electoral democracy will succeed authoritarianism in the event of regime breakdown. It follows that ruling elites truly committed to democratic change would better serve that goal by opening the electoral arena, instead of repressing those trying to enter it.

The results suggest that a consideration of regime-sponsored elections—

including through the subtypes of electoral and competitive authoritarianism—provides both descriptive utility for politics within the gray zone and analytic value for understanding the long-term (post-transition) legacies of electoral contestation under authoritarian constraints. The analysis also calls for closer examination of the causal processes that propel these trends: *Why* is competitive authoritarianism propitious for the instauration of electoral democracy? A full answer to this question must await further study, but a provisional interpretation may be ventured.

The literature on hybrid regimes has often been treated apart from its forerunner in the "old" literature on authoritarianism, but this chapter suggests a resonance between Levitsky and Way's category and seminal works on democratic transitions and polyarchy. Years ago Dankwart Rustow posited that democracy began in nationally unified polities that experienced a "long and inconclusive struggle" and "a hot family feud" (1970, 352, 355). Writing in the same period, Robert Dahl argued that governments were more likely to become democratic as the opposition gained in strength and inclusion outweighed repression as a political tactic (1971, 16). The burgeoning opposition movements of today's competitive autocracies may display the kind of incipient pluralism that Rustow and Dahl deemed a boon to the establishment of democracy.[6] Seen in this light, systematic testing of competitive autocracy and regime change carries an implicit evaluation of earlier scholarship. Hence, the strongest contribution of scholars studying elections under authoritarianism may lie in cross-national research that recalls and systematically tests the propositions of an earlier generation. In this vein, this chapter provides substantial evidence to support the findings by Teorell and Hadenius and Roessler and Howard in this volume. This evidence also suggests that the many countries in Africa that Lindberg in his chapter finds have moved toward democracy through the "power of elections" were states that saw one or more competitive elections under authoritarianism. These are also the countries where autocrats face the "strategic dilemma" of manipulation that Andreas Schedler explores in the next part of this book. In short, approaching the same question of the power of elections from various angles and using different approaches, we see the emergence of a relatively consistent story: of elections as a mode of transition in competitive, but not hegemonic authoritarian regimes.

These points of analytic convergence in turn suggest a couple of fairly robust implications for practitioners concerned about elections and about promoting democracy during a period of possible "democratic recession" (Diamond 2008a). First, the so-called halfway house of elections and authoritarianism may not only not remain a stable equilibrium; it may not even portend democracy so long as elections are largely uncompetitive. Even if the ruling elite is pushed into relinquishing power, one hegemonic electoral autocracy is likely to be placed with another. The brightest prospects for democratization were in those cases in which the opposition performed respectably in the elections, garnering at least 25% of the vote. The lesson for those advocating democratic change is to be even more assiduous in demanding seriously contested elections rather than those dominated by one party, for therein lies the difference between the possibility for something more polyarchical and the prelude to more authoritarianism. This lesson suggests a second, and more counterintuitive point: Competitive elections are good not only for the opposition, but also for the ruling elite. By laying the foundation for an electoral democracy, participants in competitive authoritarianism provide a security policy for incumbents otherwise wary of relinquishing their posts. Such figures can be much more confident that they will have future opportunities at recontesting power and avoiding the kinds of arbitrary rule that might otherwise come back to haunt them after they leave office. In this sense competitive elections may constitute a first step toward the kinds of mutual guarantees that have traditionally been seen as a linchpin of democratization (Dahl 1973).

Appendix

Table 5A.1 Authoritarian regimes, 1975–2004, and successor governments

	Regime years (Geddes data)	Succeeded by electoral democracy?[a]	Democracy years (Freedom House)
Afghanistan	1979–1989	No	NA
	1996–2001	No	NA
Argentina	1976–1983	Yes	1989[b]–2007
Armenia	1991–1998	Yes	1999–2002
Burkina Faso	1966–1980	No	NA
	1983–1987	No	NA
Bangladesh	1971–1975	No	NA
	1975–1982	No	NA
	1982–1990	Yes	1991–2007
Benin	1972–1991	Yes	1991–2007
Bolivia	1971–1978	No	NA

continued

Table 5A.1 continued

	Regime years (Geddes data)	Succeeded by electoral democracy?[a]	Democracy years (Freedom House)
Brazil	1964–1985	Yes	1985[b]–2007
Burundi	1966–1987	No	NA
	1987–1993	No	NA
	1996–2003	Yes	2003–2007
Central African Republic	1966–1979	No	NA
	1981–1993	Yes	1993–2000
Chad	1960–1975	No	NA
	1975–1979	No	NA
	1982–1990	No	NA
Chile	1973–1989	Yes	1989–2007
Congo-Brazaville	1968–1992	Yes	1992–1997
Dominican Republic	1966–1978	Yes	1989[b]–1993
Ecuador	1972–1979	Yes	1989[b]–2007
El Salvador	1948–1984	Yes	1989[b]–2007
Ethiopia	1974–1991	No	NA
Guinea-Bissau	1974–1980	No	NA
	1980–1999	Yes	1994–2002
Georgia	1992–2003	Yes	2004–2007
Ghana	1972–1979	No	NA
	1981–2000	Yes	1996–2007
Guatemala	1970–1985	Yes	1989[b]–2007
Guinea	1958–1984	No	NA
Haiti	1957–1986	No	NA
	1991–1994	Yes	1994–1999
Honduras	1972–1981	Yes	1989[b]–2007
Hungary	1949–1990	Yes	1991–2007
Indonesia	1967–1998	Yes	1999–2007
Iran	1953–1979	No	NA
Iraq	1968–2003	No	NA
Ivory Coast	1960–1999	No	NA
Kenya	1963–2002	Yes	2003–2006
Korea, South	1961–1987	Yes	1989–2007
Kuwait	1950–1990	No	NA
Liberia	1944–1980	No	NA
	1980–1990	No	NA
	1997–2003	Yes	2005–2007
Madagascar	1972–1975	No	NA
	1975–1993	Yes	1993–2007
Malawi	1964–1994	Yes	1994–2007
Mali	1968–1991	Yes	1992–2007
Mauritania	1960–1978	No	NA

Table 5A.1 continued

	Regime years (Geddes data)	Succeeded by electoral democracy?[a]	Democracy years (Freedom House)
Mexico	1929–2000	Yes	2000–2007
Nepal	1950–1990	Yes	1991–2007
Nicaragua	1936–1979	No	NA
	1979–1990	Yes	1990–2007
Niger	1974–1993	Yes	1993–1995
	1996–1999	Yes	1999–2007
Nigeria	1966–1979	No	NA
	1983–1993	No	NA
	1993–1999	Yes	1999–2006
Pakistan	1971–1977	No	NA
	1977–1988	Yes	1989–1998
Panama	1968–1981	No	NA
	1981–1989	Yes	1990–2007
Paraguay	1954–1992	Yes	1993–2007
Peru	1968–1980	No	NA
	1992–2000	Yes	2001–2007
Philippines	1972–1986	Yes	1986[b]–2006
Poland	1947–1989	Yes	1990–2007
Qatar	1972–1995	No	NA
Romania	1945–1990	Yes	1992–2007
Rwanda	1973–1994	No	NA
South Africa	1948–1994	Yes	1994–2007
Sierra Leone	1968–1992	No	NA
	1992–1996	Yes	1998–2007
Senegal	1960–2000	Yes	2000–2007
Somalia	1969–1990	No	NA
Spain	1939–1979	Yes	1989[b]–2007
Sudan	1969–1985	No	NA
Taiwan	1949–2000	Yes	1996–2007
Thailand	1976–1988	Yes	1989[b]–1990
Tunisia	1957–1987	No	NA
Turkey	1980–1983	Yes	1989[b]–2007
Uganda	1971–1979	No	NA
Uruguay	1973–1984	Yes	1989[b]–2007
Zaire	1965–1997	No	NA
Zambia	1964–1991	Yes	1991–1995

[a] Answer based on whether end of authoritarian period (as defined by Geddes) was followed by three years of consecutive electoral democracy (as coded by Freedom House) within two years of the regime's end—i.e., without some separate regime holding power during the interim.

[b] In these cases of early democratization, the successor government was coded as electoral democracy on the basis of imputing a regime type for the period before 1989, the first year in which Freedom House published a list of electoral democracies.

CHAPTER SIX

All Elections Are Not the Same

Why Power-Sharing Elections Strengthen Democratization

Pippa Norris

Elections for the legislature and for the executive are a necessary but not a sufficient foundation for modern democratic states. Without elections, no state can be regarded as democratic. But at the same time, even with elections, not all states are democratic. Most contemporary autocracies have learned to use the façade of these contests in the attempt to legitimate the power of ruling elites at home and to forestall criticism from the international community. A series of fraudulent, rigged, or manipulated elections, even with some limited degree of multiparty competition, have been used in recent years by regimes which have been conceptualized, alternatively, as "electoral autocracies" (Diamond 2002), "illiberal democracies" (Zakaria 1997, 2007), or "competitive authoritarian regimes" (Howard and Roessler 2006; Levitsky 2003; Levitsky and Way 2002b; Schedler 2006a). In this volume, Roessler and Howard usefully distinguish between, and operationalize, closed, hegemonic, and competitive authoritarian regimes. Of these three regime types, the last two are characterized by the formal trappings of elections for legislative or executive office, but nevertheless the rules of the game for genuine multiparty competition, human rights, and civil liberties are sharply curtailed. These types of regimes have aroused considerable interest in recent years, although there is little agreement about the consequences of this such curtailed elections as either a preliminary step toward further democratization, or else as a cynical device used to deflect criticism and prevent genuine reform (Armony and Schamis 2006). The present volume is the first comprehensive attempt to answer the question if, and if so when and why, elections in nondemocratic regimes have democratizing effects. When can elections be a mode of transition?

In addressing one aspect of this volume's overall question, the first part of this chapter argues that all elections should not be treated as equivalent; instead, democratization by elections is most likely achieved by states holding nationwide elections that meet three power-sharing principles: multiparty competition, electoral integrity, and power-sharing rules (defined as those contests using proportional representation electoral systems and/or with positive action mechanisms for minorities). Logic suggests that regimes that meet these conditions should gradually become more democratic than equivalent states that have not employed these strategies, all other things being equal. To examine the evidence, the second part of the chapter operationalizes these conditions and classifies the major types of electoral systems. Evidence is derived from cross-national time-series analysis (with panel-corrected standard errors) covering 191 independent nation-states worldwide from 1972 to 2004. The third part of the chapter then analyzes the effects of this model on patterns of democratization, understood as a continuous process rather than a categorical end-point, measured by changes in the Freedom House and the Polity IV indicators (Marshall and Jaggers 2003) while controlling for many social and economic conditions which are commonly regarded as important for the process of democratization. The conclusion considers the implications for understanding democratic transitions, as well as for the practical interventions used by the international community when seeking to strengthen democratic governance.

The Analytical Framework

Electoral rules represent perhaps one of the most powerful instrument undergirding processes of regime change. Electoral rules have potentially far-reaching consequences for transitions from autocracy, patterns of party competition in the electorate and legislature, the inclusiveness of elected bodies, and the composition of cabinet governments, all of which can influence the transition to and the quality of democratic governance (Norris 2004, 2008; Sartori 1994). This book's core proposition, outlined in the introduction by Lindberg, suggests that elections provide a set of institutions which generate incentives conducive to strengthening democracy encapsulated in the expression of elections as a mode of transition. This chapter adds one dimension to the core thesis by arguing that elections that reflect conditions of multiparty competition, electoral integrity, and power-sharing principles, broadly defined, indeed serve these functions, while elections that do not meet these conditions will probably fail to strengthen the process of democratization. The type of rules matter—and not merely in trivial ways. Formal electoral rules are understood in this study, somewhat more broadly than is common in the literature, as the range of official policies, legal regulations, and administrative practices governing all steps in the process of nomination (determining the candidates and the parties listed on the ballot paper), campaigning (generating and mobilizing popular support), and election (translating votes cast into elected office). Studies comparing established democracies have usually focused most attention upon the final step in the process, including the basic type of proportional, combined/mixed, or majoritarian electoral system, the quota formula, the ballot structure, and the mean size of district magnitude, all of which determine how votes are cast and then converted into elected office. When elections are considered as part of a process of regime transition and democratic consolidation in a wide range of states, however, the conventional analytical framework needs to be widened to take account of the prior nomination and campaigning steps in the process of competing for elected office.

The core argument of this chapter is that the initial transition from autocracy, and the prospects for sustainable democratization, are strengthened most effectively by power-sharing principles where, after there is an initial agreement to hold elections for legislative and/or executive office, the following conditions are met:

1. The nomination, campaigning, and electoral rules facilitate multiparty competition for elected office, without restrictions on freedom of association and expression.
2. The contest is held under conditions that meet international standards of electoral integrity.

3. The electoral rules allocating votes to seats involve proportional presentation and/or minority representation, rather than either a combined/mixed electoral system, or else majoritarian/plurality rules.

The central argument is that each of these steps can be understood as involving progressively greater degrees of power-sharing. In particular, in deeply divided societies emerging from conflict, elections meeting all these conditions are most likely to stabilize fragile regimes and promote democratization. Power-sharing arrangements accommodate and thereby build trust and tolerance among diverse communities living within common national borders (e.g., Lijphart 1999, 2004). The argument implies that elections, rather being than a universal panacea, should be regarded as neutral mechanical tools which, like other institutions, can be used to good or ill. To clarify the underlying logic, the main steps in the process are outlined schematically in Figure 6.1. What is the reasoning behind these claims?

The Decision to Hold an Election

The first step in the sequence illustrated in Figure 6.1 relates to the decision by an autocratic government to hold an election for the legislature in parliamentary systems and/or for the executive office in presidential republics. This critical decision can arise for multiple reasons, which are regarded as exogenous and well beyond the scope of this study. In some cases, the election stage is purely nominal, once nominees are selected for the National

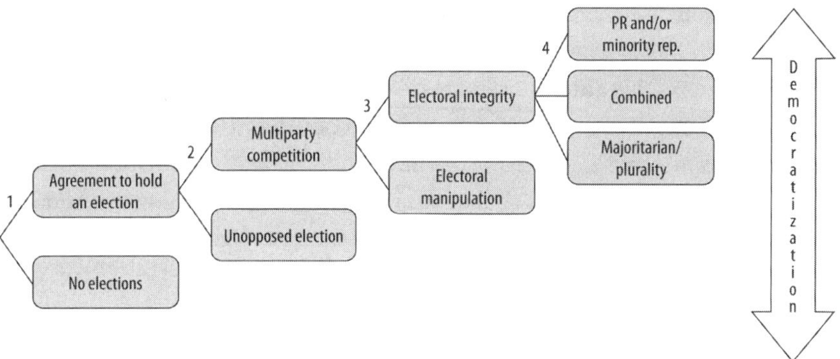

Figure 6.1. Four-step model of elections as a mode of regime transition

Assembly, as in Cuba. But there can still be limited competition among rival candidates and indeed among factions within the predominant party, as is the case with one-party elections in contests for the Ugandan parliament and for Chinese village elections. While one-party elections are often dismissed by independent observers and journalists as rigged plebiscites, they can still serve a function for the ruling elite by settling internal power struggles within the ruling party, by providing parties and candidates with incentives to mobilize popular grassroots support, and by providing the electorate with direct experience of voting participation. Local and provincial elections can also be part of a cautious incremental or evolutionary reform process which, if the experience is regarded as positive, ultimately leads to more liberal party competition and nationwide elections.

Multiparty Competition

Where there is an agreement to hold a nationwide election, party and candidate competition can be restricted through the formal rules and the election regulations governing all steps in the sequential process of winning elected office: the *nomination* stage (including party registration requirements and ballot access); the *campaign* stage (including the distribution of any public funds and subsidies, and access to the campaign media and any political broadcasts); and the *election* stage (including the major type of electoral system used, the effective vote threshold, the use of any positive action mechanisms such as reserved seats, and the processes of electoral management, such as polling and vote counting). Rules governing the process can be categorized into three broad ideal types:

1. *Autocratic regulations* are explicitly skewed toward the ruling party, restricting all opposition parties and dissident movements, to prop up repressive autocracies and one-party states. Communist China and Cuba are examples of states that continue to hold elections with unopposed candidates for the national legislature (the National Assembly). The most draconian restrictions on civil liberties and legal bans on opposition movements are exercised by one-party states and autocratic governments, such as Burma, Syria, Eritrea, Laos, and North Korea.
2. *Cartel regulations* limit party competition through a variety of restrictive practices designed to benefit established parties in

parliament or in government, including requirements for ballot access, regulations governing the allocation of public funding, limiting equal access to campaign broadcasts and to state subsidies for related services such as postage and staff, and excessively high minimal vote thresholds to achieve elected office. Cartels are designed to skew resources toward insiders, protecting against outside challengers.

3. *Egalitarian regulations* are designed to be more permeable and open, facilitating plural party competition among multiple contenders at all stages, with equal access to public resources and minimal legal restrictions on which parties and candidates appear on the ballot. Most liberal democracies attempt to strike a balance between totally egalitarian competition (which could, in principle, result in hundreds of parties and candidates on the ballot, extreme party fragmentation in parliament, and political instability in government) and unduly restricted cartels which limit basic political rights and civil liberties (Norris 2005).

Restrictions or outright bans on some or all parties at the nomination stage are the easiest cases to classify, since these practices place legal and constitutional limits on party registration and ballot access. In such cases, minor parties commonly experience problems in gaining ballot access; for example, some countries impose legal bans on extremist parties, such as laws restricting the expression of racial hatred by the radical right (Fennema 2000). Cases that are more difficult to categorize involve campaign restrictions on opposition parties and candidates which have at least nominal constitutional and legal rights to organize and to have access to the nomination process. States can restrict competition through partisan redistricting processes that limit ballot access to minor parties, or they can impose strict party and candidate registration requirements (Bowler, Carter, and Farrell 2003). Minor parties may also be disadvantaged by the official rules and statutory regulations governing direct public funding, indirect state subsidies, and access to campaign broadcasting (International IDEA 2003). Autocracies which hold flawed plebiscitary elections have employed a variety of tactics to restrict opposition party campaign activities and to limit challenges to their rule, including intimidation and imprisonment of party leaders and dissidents who challenge the government, illegal manipulation of campaign regulations, and severe limits on freedom of expression and association. Annual reports published by the Organization for Security and Co-operation in Europe (OSCE), Amnesty International, Freedom House, and Human Right Watch document multiple numerous cases of such malpractices and human rights abuses.

Electoral Integrity

Even where there are no outright bans or major restrictions on ballot access, a variety of techniques have often been used to undermine electoral integrity (Lehoucq 2003; Schedler 2002a, 2006a). Techniques include strong pro-government bias in election reporting; limits on independent journalism and control of the state media; the unequal and imbalanced distribution of campaign resources and state subsidies for parties; the widespread use of intimidation, coercion, or bribery by security forces at polling stations; and outright fraud or manipulation of the final vote tally and declaration of results. Other practices include stacking electoral commissions; bribing local officials and intimidating citizens at the polling place; kicking out independent electoral observers; rigging voting machines and holding fraudulent vote counts; gerrymandering district boundaries; and even, when an administration is finally defeated at the polls, rejecting the result and clinging to office. Even where contests meet international standards of electoral integrity, the outcome of majoritarian rules can still reinforce one-party predominance and limit minority representation.

There has been considerable progress in agreeing on the standards required for free and fair elections. For example, the OSCE *Election Observer Handbook* requires OSCE participating states to meet the following conditions:

- Hold free elections at reasonable intervals;
- Permit all seats in at least one chamber of the legislature to be elected by popular vote;
- Guarantee universal and equal suffrage;
- Respect the right of citizens to seek office;
- Respect the right to establish political parties, and ensure that the parties can compete on the basis of equal treatment before the law and by the authorities;
- Ensure that political campaigning can be conducted in a free and fair atmosphere without administrative action, violence, intimidation, or fear of retribution against candidates, parties, or voters;

- Ensure unimpeded access to the media on a non-discriminatory basis;
- Ensure that votes are cast by secret ballot and that they are counted and reported honestly, with the results made public in a timely manner; and
- Ensure that candidates who win the necessary votes to be elected are duly installed in office and are permitted to remain in office until their term expires. (OSCE 2007, 16)

Elections that fail to meet these standards are seriously flawed, and the outcome is unlikely to advance democratization.

Power-Sharing Electoral Systems

In addition, democratization processes are strengthened most effectively under power-sharing rules, understood here as electoral systems with proportional representation and/or positive action strategies for minorities. Proportional representation electoral systems are the simplest, least contentious, and most flexible way to facilitate the election of parties representing distinct minority communities, including those representing distinct ethnic minority groups that are scattered geographically. Unlike affirmative action policies, proportional representation electoral systems do not need to specify and thereby freeze the size of any such minority representation; instead, any groups and communities with a grievance may freely organize to mobilize voting support in proportion to their size (Lijphart 1997). Demographic shifts are also incorporated flexibly into the political process over successive elections (O'Leary and McGarry 2004, 2006).

Positive action strategies can also be used to achieve minority representation (Lijphart 1986, 1997). Such strategies include the creation of minority-majority districts (used in the United States to elect African Americans to the House of Representatives), the employment of communal rolls (such as those for Maoris in New Zealand), and the use of reserved seats (established in India for Scheduled Castes and Tribes) (Chandra 2001, 2004). Worldwide, such mechanisms have been employed in more than two dozen countries (Jarstad 2001; Reynolds 2005, 2006, 2007). Positive action mechanisms commonly recognize and institutionalize the claims of certain historical communities, such as the position of the Maoris as the original Polynesian settlers in New Zealand, the Hungarian community who first settled in Romania in the ninth century, and indigenous Indian populations in Venezuela.

At the same time, because of the contentious nature of affirmative action, these policies often fail to be equally inclusive for representatives and parties drawn from newer émigré communities, such as North African Muslims living in France, the Kurdish diasporas in Turkey, or Turkish "guest workers" resident in Germany.

The inclusion of community spokespersons in visible positions of power is expected to function as a safety valve for ethnic tensions, reducing intercommunal conflict, encouraging peaceful transitions, and thus strengthening the democratizing power of elections, especially in divided societies. It is theorized that under more inclusive electoral arrangements, the members of each distinct religious, linguistic, or nationalistic community will feel that their voice counts and that the rules of the game are fair and legitimate, as their leaders can articulate their concerns and protect their interests within the legislature and within government. In the long term, this process should serve to stabilize conflict-ridden societies and manage, or even reduce, broader ethnic tensions. The permanent exclusion of the leaders of any significant minority community from representative assemblies is thought to encourage alienation and violence. This situation is especially dangerous in divided societies and where politics is viewed by each community as a win-or-lose game.

The broad principles of power-sharing arrangements have been adopted in many negotiated peace-settlements. Nevertheless, it is by no means clear from the scholarly literature that proportional representation electoral rules will necessarily prove the most effective mechanism for promoting interethnic reconciliation and democratization. Two challenges have been widely debated: whether proportional representation is an incentive for community cooperation or for community rivalry, and that power-sharing arrangements require a trade-off among conflicting values.

One school of thought claims that it is dangerous to use proportional representation rules that empower leaders whose popular support is based exclusively within, rather than across, the boundaries of each community. Horowitz (1985, 1991) argues that this process provides an electoral incentive for populist leaders to appeal for popular support by reinforcing ethnic tensions and mistrust of other groups, and that it serves to institutionalize and thereby freeze existing ethnic identities and community boundaries. The political salience of communal identities may be unintentionally magnified by proportional representation electoral rules (which lower the nationwide voting threshold, facilitating the election of small parties) and by positive action strategies (which explicitly recognize specific linguistic, religious, or nationalistic communal groups as the basis for allocating seats) (Rothschild 2002). The dangers of such arrangements are exemplified, critics suggest, by elections in Bosnia-Herzegovina after the Dayton peace settlement, which reduced the incentive for cross-community cooperation and nonsectarian electoral appeals. Similarly, in Rwanda international efforts promoting ethnic power-sharing between Hutu and Tutsi may have unintentionally backfired by heightening ethnic tensions, reinforcing the incentive for extremist politicians to make sectarian appeals (Snyder 2000). The result was reinforcement of ethnic hatred within each community, generating disastrous bloodshed, and derailed democratization. Proportional representation systems facilitate the election of smaller parties, not just from ethnic minorities but also from the radical right; the newly empowered right exploit xenophobic fears about new immigrants, stoking racist tensions. These policies may therefore serve to rigidify the boundaries dividing ethnic communities, reinforcing and heightening political instability in deeply divided postwar societies (Collier and Sambanis 2005), thus undermining chances of a democratization-by-elections process.

By contrast, Reilly (2001, 2002) proposes that the incentives for community cooperation and reconciliation may be strengthened most effectively by the adoption of majoritarian electoral systems. Reilly advocates adoption of the alternative vote (AV, also known as "instant runoff"). The alternative vote system requires winning parties and candidates to gain an absolute majority of the vote (50% + 1), rather than a simple plurality. This hurdle is thought to have important consequences (Cox 1997, 1999). First, the need to gain support from a majority of the electorate encourages individual politicians to cooperate strategically with others within their party organizations. Even more importantly, higher thresholds also create strategic incentives for vote-pooling, as politicians and parties need to broad-based, moderate electoral appeals to win, emphasizing nonsectarian bridging issues and avoiding narrow polarizing and controversial policies Majoritarian electoral systems may thereby encourage politicians to adopt cross-identity appeals that target diverse sectors of the electorate.

Another common challenge to power-sharing principles emphasizes that the choice of electoral rules requires a trade-off among conflicting values, where the inclusiveness of all communities within the legislature is only one consideration (Dunleavy and Margetts 1995; Gallagher 2005). Majoritarian and plurality electoral systems systematically exaggerate the share of seats allocated to the winning party and reduce the share of seats allocated to smaller parties. The mechanical effect of these rules is to secure a decisive outcome for the first-ranked party, so that it can form a single-party cabinet government resting on a secure overall parliamentary majority, even in a closely balanced election. This arrangement may help to maximize the transparency and accountability of government policymaking, as well as serve to produce stable and durable governments empowered to serve their full-term in office. Effective government may be the overriding concern during democratization in societies emerging from deep-rooted internal conflict and in failed states, such as Liberia, Somalia, Iraq, and Eritrea. Societies emerging from a period of prolonged conflict which has destroyed intercommunity trust, and with many poorly institutionalized new parties and legislative factions elected to office, are likely to experience considerable problems in the postelection period, when bargaining and compromise are needed to create a workable governing coalition under proportional representation rules.

Comparing the Impact of Power-Sharing Rules

What evidence could help to support the argument about the positive effects of power-sharing developed in this chapter? Case studies of the apparent success of power-sharing elections in divided societies (South Africa?) and its apparent failure (Bosnia-Herzegovina?) can be cited by both sides. Yet case studies are limited, as these societies differ in many other fundamental ways, so it is difficult to isolate institutional effects arising from the electoral systems. Moreover, it is impossible to establish the long-term consequences of elections with any confidence in cases such as Iraq and Afghanistan, as well as the Democratic Republic of the Congo and Nepal, which have only recently held their first multiparty elections.

To examine the claims and counterclaims more systematically, we need broader comparisons. We can start by operationalizing the key variables; classifying power-sharing electoral arrangements; and identifying conditions of multiparty competition, electoral integrity, the type of electoral system, and the positive action strategies for minority representation, used in all nation-states worldwide. The analysis of the effects of these arrangements uses multivariate models with cross-national time-series data. Institutional effects are examined controlling for prior social and economic conditions, including levels of economic development and the degree of ethnic fractionalization within each society. The dependent variables include the indicators of democratization, measured as the annual change in the Freedom House and Polity IV indicators from 1972 to 2004, controlling for many standard factors commonly associated with patterns of democratization in the literature.

Trends in Elections and Multiparty Competition

The first step in the model involves the decision to hold elections. The growth in the number of countries holding legislative and executive elections was one of the most striking global phenomena during the late twentieth century. Trends can be compared utilizing the cross-national time-series classification of political institutions produced by Arthur S. Banks (2005). The Banks dataset classifies independent nation-states into three categories, defined by the mechanism used for recruiting members of the lower house of a national parliament in a bicameral system:

1. those with *no legislature;*
2. those with a *nonelective* legislature (for example, in which members are appointed by the executive or selected on the basis of heredity or ascription); and
3. those with *elective legislatures* (in which members are selected by means of either direct or indirect popular election).

Banks estimates that in 1972, out of 137 independent nation-states, 20% (28) lacked a national parliament, another 5% (7 nations) had an appointed parliament, and the remaining 75% had an elected national parliament. By 2003, out of 191 independent nation-states around the globe, 89% had an elected parliament (see Figure 6.2). Eight states (5%) lacked a national parliament, including those which were emerging from conflict, such as Afghanistan and Iraq, while a dozen states (6%) had an appointed legislative body. The latter category includes the states governed by the Persian Gulf royal families (Saudi Arabia, Qatar, and the United Arab Emirates), the monarchy-governed Brunei Darussalam and Bhutan, and some countries emerging from conflict, such as Burundi, Eritrea, Liberia, and DRC. The number of states without an elected national parliament is rapidly dwindling; Afghanistan, Iraq, Liberia, and DRC have all held successful elections in recent years. Bhutan, formerly a traditional absolute monarchy, held its first landmark

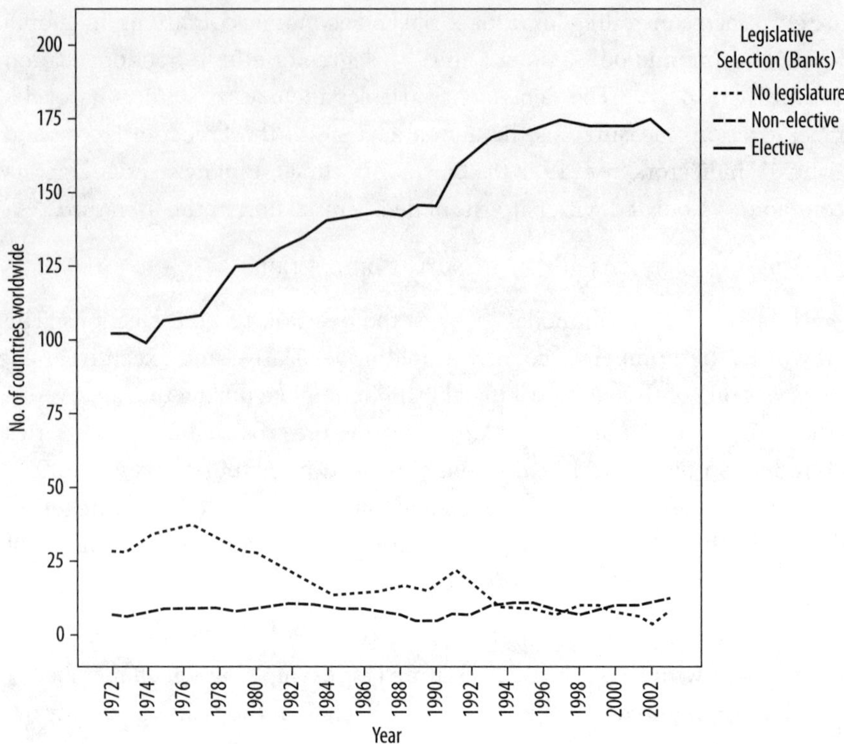

Figure 6.2. The rise in elective legislatures

Note: Classification of legislative selection from Arthur S. Banks's Cross-National Time-Series Dataset (CNTS)

legislative elections in March 2008 at the behest of the king. This contest established a two-party bicameral parliamentary democracy and a constitutional monarchy, peacefully ending a century of dynastic rule. Nevertheless, it is worth noting that under the single-member-plurality electoral system, the outcome was a lopsided win, with the Bhutan Peace and Prosperity Party (Druk Phuensum Tshogpa, or DPT) sweeping up a near monopoly in the National Assembly (43 of the 47 seats), leaving minimal representation by the opposition. In Qatar the 2005 constitution specifies direct elections for two-thirds of the members of the unicameral Advisory Council (Majlis al-Shura); it held its first direct elections for a national parliament in 2008. On the other hand, some elected assemblies have also been temporarily suspended or dissolved during recent years, for example, by the military coup in Thailand.

Figure 6.3 compares similar trends over time in the forms of executive

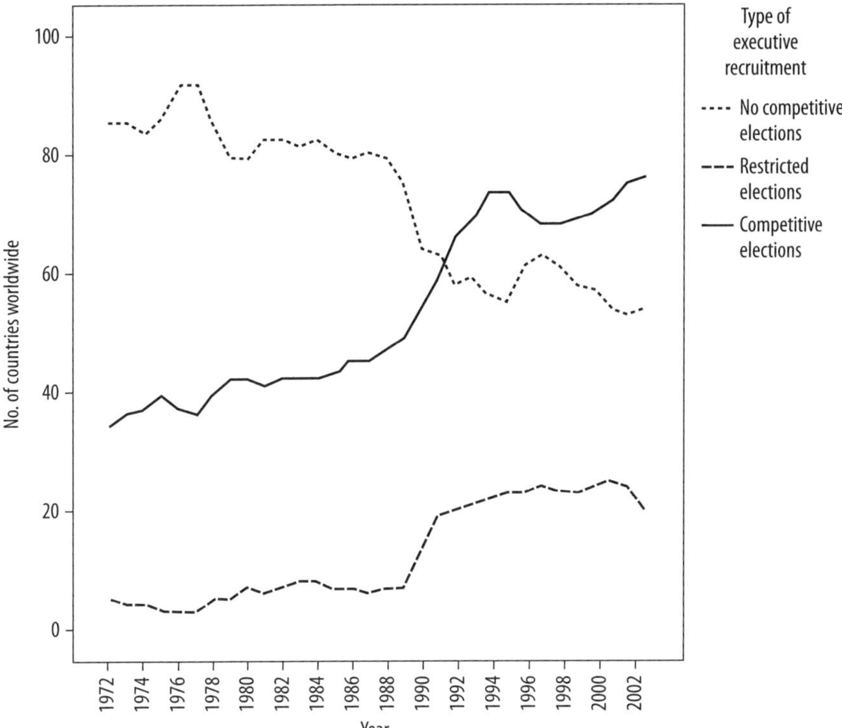

Figure 6.3. The rise in competitive elections for executive office

Note: Classification of executive recruitment derived from Polity IV. See Table 6A.1 for details.

selection. Elections that are held in one-party states, or with serious limits to party competition or electoral integrity, are unlikely to strengthen democratization. One indicator that can be used to monitor trends over time in patterns of multiparty competition is drawn from the Polity IV dataset, which classifies countries according to whether the selection of the executive is via a *closed selection* (for example, succession by dynastic birthright, seizure of power, or informal competition within the ruling elite), a *restricted election*, or a *competitive election*, (involving formal competition between at least two parties and at least two candidates). Moreover, only elections which are deemed to be free and fair by independent international and domestic observers, meeting the criteria of electoral integrity, are coded by Polity IV as competitive. Figure 6.3 shows the sharp rise in the number of executives chosen by competitive elections during the late twentieth century and the simultaneous erosion in the number of leaders rising to power through non-elected routes.

The Banks and Polity IV data suggest that not only are more elections being held today than 30 years ago, for both legislative and executive office, but the number of competitive multiparty contests for executive office has also risen significantly. Today, only a few repressive autocracies govern without even the fig leaf of any national elections; these are ruled either by military juntas, as in Burma; by one-party tyrants such as Kim Jong-Il in North Korea; or else by hereditary monarchies and emirs, such as the monopoly of power that has been held by the Al Saud family dynasty in Saudi Arabia since the eighteenth century.

Classifying Electoral Systems

The type of electoral system currently used for lower houses of parliament can be classified and then compared across all independent nation-states worldwide. The core typology used for this comparison is derived from the typology in the second edition of the *International IDEA Handbook of Electoral System Design* (Reynolds, Reilly, and Ellis 2005) covering electoral systems used in 2004. The handbook categorized electoral systems into three major families—proportional, majoritarian, and combined—each including a number of subcategories.

Proportional representation electoral systems are designed to translate the percentage of votes proportionally into the percentage of seats won, lowering the threshold facing smaller parties. Proportional representation systems defined in the present study to include the party list as well as the single transferable vote systems, the latter being less common (Bowler and Grofman 2000). The main institutional variations within proportional representation systems concern the use of open or closed lists of candidates, the quota formula for translating votes into seats, the level of the threshold for the legal vote, and the size of the average electoral district.

Majoritarian-plurality systems require a higher effective vote threshold, and they are essentially power-concentrating (by systematically squeezing the number of parliamentary parties). Majoritarian rules require the winning candidate or party to gain 50%+1 of the vote; systems using majoritarian rules include the alternative vote (instant-runoff) system and the second-ballot (runoff or two-round) system. Plurality rules require that the winning candidate or party gain more votes than any other but not necessarily a majority of ballots cast. Systems with plurality rules include the "first-past-the-post" (FPTP) design, also referred to as a single-member district (SMD) plurality system; the party block vote system; and the single nontransferable vote (SNTV) system (Norris 2004). Plurality rules generate a "manufactured" majority—that is, they have a systematic exaggerative bias that usually translates a plurality of votes for the party in first place into a majority of seats.

Finally, *combined* electoral systems (otherwise known as "mixed," "dual," "hybrid," or "side-by-side" systems) use two ballot structures within simultaneous contests for the same elected office (Shugart and Wattenberg 2001). This study follows Massicotte and Blais (1999) by classifying combined systems according to their mechanics, not by their outcome. Combined systems have become increasingly popular over the last decade and employ a variety of designs. This category can be further subdivided into combined-independent systems, where the distribution of seats is independent for each type of ballot, and combined-dependent systems such as those in Germany and New Zealand, where the distribution of seats is proportional to the share of the vote cast in the party list. Combined-independent systems are closer to the majoritarian end of the spectrum, while combined-dependent systems are closer to the proportional end (see also Colomer 2004).

Table 6.1 summarizes a series of indicators illustrating the characteristic impact of the major types of electoral systems on party systems and levels of proportionality. The results generally conform to expectations arising from the previous literature about the mechanical workings of electoral systems. Hence, as anticipated, the exaggerative bias common in majoritarian systems usually results in a decisive electoral outcome; on average, under these rules the largest party generally wins two-thirds of all parliamentary seats. This empowers single-party cabinet governments to implement their legislative program during their term of office assured of the support of a comfortable parliamentary majority, without the need for coalition partners. By contrast, proportional representation systems are more likely to generate coalition governments; the largest party usually wins less than a majority (44%) of seats. The indicators also confirm that proportional representation rules systematically lower the effective electoral threshold, thereby facilitating the election of many smaller parties. This pattern is consistent irrespective of the specific indicator of party competition; for example, the Rae party fractionalization index is twice as strong in proportional representation systems as in majoritarian elections.

Table 6.1 Characteristics of contemporary electoral systems, 2000

	Proportional representation	Combined	Majoritarian	*N*
(1) Largest governing party % of seats	44.4	53.7	68.1	158
(2) Rae party fractionalization index	65.2	54.6	34.6	189
(3) Mean number of all parliamentary parties	9.3	8.7	5.0	175
(4) Mean number of relevant parliamentary parties	4.7	4.4	3.2	175
(5) Herfindahl index for all parliamentary parties	.33	.39	.57	153
(6) Effective number of parliamentary parties	3.69	3.77	2.33	103
(7) Index of proportionality	90.4	83.2	83.1	110
(8) Effective electoral threshold	11.3	24.5	35.4	148

Notes and sources:

(1) Percentage of seats held by the largest governing party in the lower house of the national assembly. *Source:* Banks 2002.

(2) *Source:* Banks 2002.

(3) Mean number of parliamentary parties with at least one seat in the lower house of the national parliament. *Source:* calculated from elections around the world.

(4) Mean number of parliamentary parties with more than 3% of seats in the lower house of the national parliament. *Source:* calculated from elections around the world.

(5) Herfindahl Index for all parliamentary parties, ranging from 0 to 1, representing the probability that two randomly selected members of the lower house of parliament belong to different parties. *Source:* Keefer 2002.

(6) Effective number of parliamentary parties (ENPP), calculated to take into account not only the number of parties competing but also their size.

(7) Rose index of proportionality (a standardized version of the Loosemore-Hanby Index). *Source:* Rose 2001.

(8) Effective electoral threshold, using the formula $75/(m + 1)$, where m refers to the district magnitude or the number of members returned in the electoral district. Calculated from Rose 2001.

Based on this classification, the question that arises is whether there is systematic support for the core claims that democratization is strengthened in elections with multiparty competitions, electoral integrity, and proportional representation as the electoral system, and whether this pattern is particularly evident in divided societies. Is democratization by elections more likely under proportional representation than under combined or majoritarian electoral systems? To start to scrutinize the evidence, we can examine whether two indicators of democracy differ by the major types of contemporary electoral systems used worldwide, without introducing any prior controls.

Figure 6.4 compares the scores on Freedom House's indicator of liberal democracy and Polity IV's constitutional democracy. Regardless of the indicator used, the results confirm that countries using party list proportional

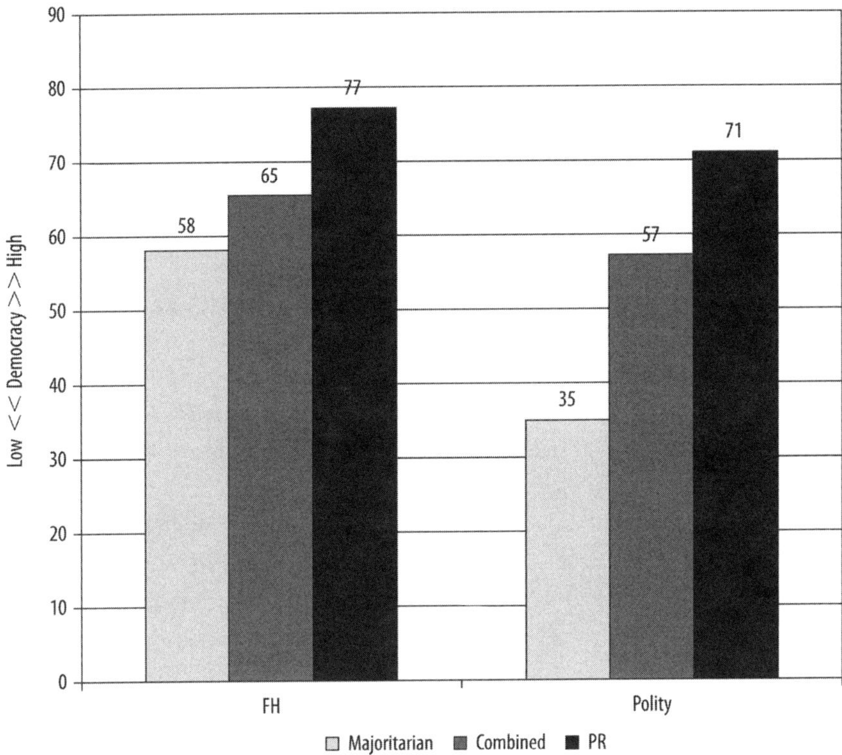

Figure 6.4. Democracy scores for contemporary electoral systems, 2000

Note: The standardized 100-point scales of democracy are described in the Table 6A.1. The two indicators are Freedom House's liberal democracy ratings (Freedom House 2000) and Polity IV's constitutional democracy (Polity IV 2000). When tested by ANOVA, the difference between mean scores are significant (at the $p = .001$ level). The three categories of electoral systems are *majoritarian/plurality* (including IDEA's single-member plurality, second ballot, block vote, alternative vote, and single nontransferable vote subsystems), *proportional representation* (with IDEA's party list and single nontransferable vote subsystems), and *combined* (in which more than one type of ballot is used in simultaneous elections for the same body). Contemporary electoral systems are classified in 191 nation states worldwide based on Appendix A in Reynolds, Reilly, and Ellis 2005.

representation electoral systems consistently rate as significantly the most democratic, as theorized. The combined types of electoral system are located in an intermediate position. By contrast, majoritarian electoral systems proved consistently less democratic; for example, according to the Polity scale, nation-states using proportional representation systems were on average twice as democratic as those using majoritarian rules. When tested by ANOVA, these differences by types of electoral system all proved moderately strongly associated and statistically significant (with the eta coefficient of association at .37 to .53, all at the $p = .001$ level).

But does this pattern also vary systematically by the type of ethnic cleavages within each society, with proportional representation proving most important in plural societies, the second and stronger claim? For a preliminary look at the patterns, Figure 6.5 compares societies which were classified as either heterogeneous or homogeneous, based on dichotomizing the ethnic fractionalization index developed by Alesina et al. (2003). This is a simple classification of plural societies, gauging whether populations are ethnically similar or different, but it cannot take account of whether such cleavages are politically salient. The comparison, without any prior controls, confirms that among homogeneous societies, nation-states using proportional representation electoral systems were consistently more democratic than countries with majoritarian elections, and that the difference in levels of democracy between proportional representation and majoritarian electoral systems was greatest in heterogeneous societies, as Lijphart (1999, 2004) theorizes. Consociational theory emphasizes that majoritarian systems can work well within homogeneous societies but that proportional representation elections are particularly important for consolidating democratization in divided societies; the comparison conducted so far provides preliminary support for this claim.

Positive Action Mechanisms for Ethnic Minorities

As an alternative proposition, Lijphart (1997) theorizes that democratic consolidation in divided societies will also be strengthened by electoral rules that incorporate positive action policies designed to ensure the election of representatives or parties drawn from minority communities. Two primary positive action mechanisms have been employed in different countries: district boundary delineation and reserved seats (Reynolds 2005, 2006, 2007).

District boundary delineation. In some countries, electoral boundaries are drawn to recognize certain communities of interest, creating specific single-member districts where minority electorates are concentrated. In the United States, for example, following the Voting Rights Act of 1965 and its amendment in 1982, racial redistricting processes have been based on identifying concentrations of black, Hispanic, Asian, and Native American minorities within the electorate. Boundaries are often drawn and revised periodically to maintain population equality between districts, but some countries have

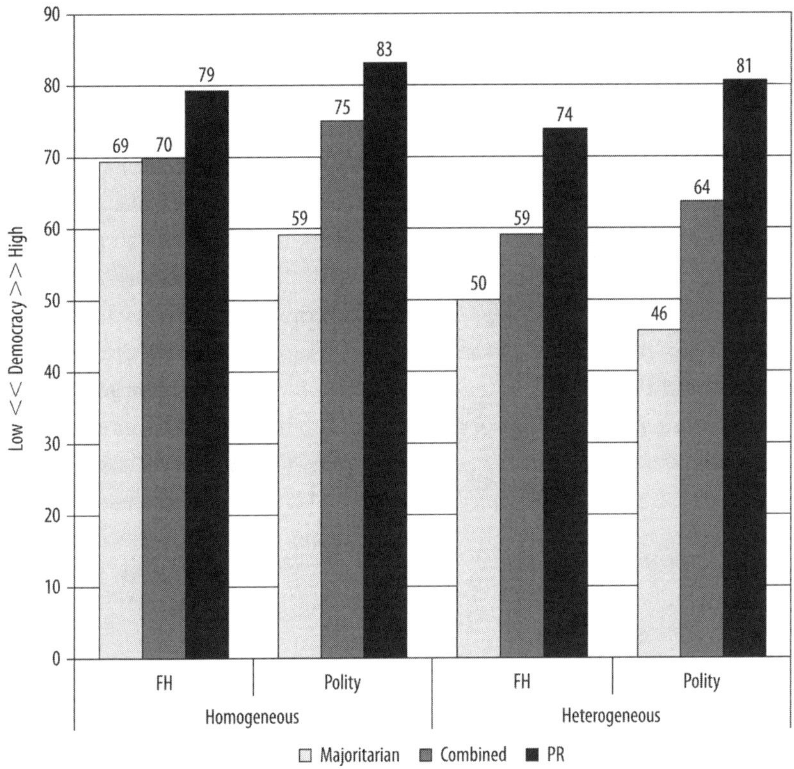

Figure 6.5. Democracy scores for contemporary electoral systems in heterogeneous and homogeneous societies, 2000

Note: Types of heterogeneous or homogeneous society classified according to the dichotomized index of ethnic fractionalization in Alesina et al. (2003). For the scales, indicators, and categories of electoral systems, see the note to Figure 6.4.

overrepresented specific territories by requiring smaller electoral quotas within certain regions.

Reserved seats. Another form of positive action is the use of reserved seats designed to give a voice to historically disadvantaged communities. This technique is used, for example, for indigenous minorities in New Zealand, Pakistan, and Fiji, where reserved seats are filled by appointees of the recognized group or elected by voters from a communal electoral roll. Reserved seats have been based on recognition of race or ethnicity, language, national identity, and religion, as well as for minorities on island territories detached from the nation-state land mass. A recent worldwide review found that at least 32 countries used reserved seats, communal rolls, race-conscious districting, or special electoral arrangements designed for communal or minority representation in parliament. Most countries using reserved seats have majoritarian electoral systems, including within FPTP systems such as those in Pakistan, India, Samoa, Iran, and Kiribati. But countries with proportional representation and combined electoral systems also use this mechanism, particularly in cases of postconflict power-sharing agreements, as in Rwanda, Kosovo, Cyprus, Bosnia and Herzegovina, and Lebanon.

What is the effect of these mechanisms for minority representation on democratic consolidation? We can start by comparing levels of democracy, using the two indicators already employed in this study, in the countries which do and do not use at least one of these positive action mechanisms. Figure 6.6 illustrates the patterns, confirming that the 29 countries employing positive action policies for minority representation are consistently more democratic across each of these indicators. ANOVA shows that the pattern is statistically significant, with the most substantial contrast found using the Polity index.

Multivariate Analysis

The preliminary comparisons so far appear to support the argument favoring more proportional electoral systems and/or positive action strategies for minorities. But are the contrasts we have observed the product of the institutional arrangements, or can they be attributed to other features in the nation-states being compared? Multivariate analysis is needed to determine whether these patterns persist even after the use of a battery of prior controls which are closely related to patterns of democratization (Norris 2008). One of these concerns the past colonial legacies which continue to shape the contemporary distribution of electoral systems. Thus, three-quarters of the former British colonies still use a majoritarian electoral system for national elections to the lower house of the legislature, as do two-thirds of the former French colonies. By contrast, proportional electoral systems are employed by three-quarters of the former Portuguese colonies, two-thirds of the former Spanish colonies, and all the former Dutch colonies. The post-Communist states freed from rule by the Soviet Union divide almost evenly among the three major electoral families, although slightly more countries (37%) have adopted proportional systems. While Eastern Europe leans toward majoritarian arrangements, Central Europe adopted more proportional systems. To examine the impact of electoral systems on democracy, we need to control

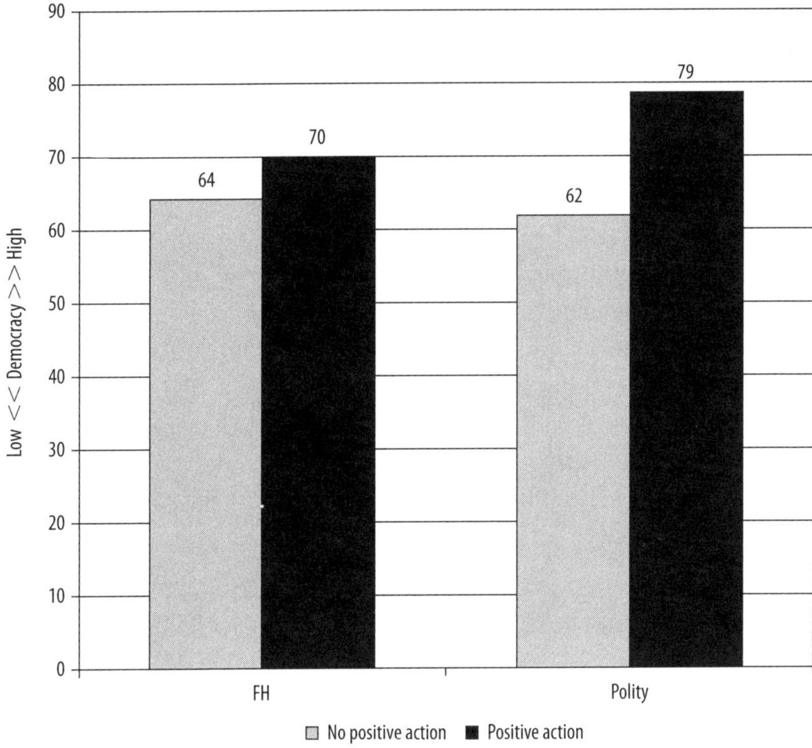

Figure 6.6. Effect of strategies for better ethnic minority representation on democracy

Note: The use of positive action strategies in 29 out of 191 nation states, including through reserved seats and district boundary delineation, is described in the text. For the scales, indicators, and categories of electoral systems, see the note to Figure 6.4.

for past colonial histories, as well as for degrees of ethnic fractionalization, levels of economic development, regional diffusion, location in the Middle East region, and the physical and population size of the country. In these models, combined (mixed) electoral systems are the default (comparison) category.

Table 6.2 presents the results of the OLS regression models, based on analysis of the pooled time-series cross-sectional data with panel-corrected standard errors. The coefficients confirm that, compared across all societies worldwide, countries using proportional representation electoral systems are positively associated with democracy, even after controlling for the range of economic and cultural factors associated with democracy. By contrast, majoritarian electoral systems have a worse democratic performance on each of the indicators (although this was not statistically significant for the Polity IV indicator). Moreover, the use of positive action strategies was also positively related to levels of democracy across all the indicators, as were multiparty competitive contests. Overall, the multivariate analysis confirms the comparisons observed earlier, supporting the argument that countries using competitive elections, proportional representation electoral systems, and positive action strategies are the most successful democratically.

Power-sharing theory predicts that these institutional forms are valuable in general, but nowhere more so than in divided societies. Accordingly, Table 6.3 repeats the analysis but limits the comparison to plural societies, defined by dichotomizing the Alesina et al. (2003) measure of ethnic fractionalization. The results confirm that the positive impact of proportional representation electoral systems on democracy is far stronger in plural nation-states: for example, the use of proportional representation produces a 5–10 percentage

Table 6.2 Effects of electoral systems on level of democracy: all societies worldwide

	Liberal democracy (Freedom House)		Constitutional democracy (Polity IV)	
	b	(pcse)	b	(pcse)
Majoritarian	–2.74***	(.377)	–.042	(.503)
Proportional representation	1.60*	(.801)	3.19***	(.290)
Positive action strategies	2.24***	(.296)	4.85***	(.391)
Multiparty competitive contests	19.78***	(.786)	54.86***	(1.477)
Log GDP/capita	10.56***	(.792)	1.50***	(.602)
Ex-British colony	9.06***	(.646)	1.11*	(.596)
Middle East location	–12.80***	(1.24)	–8.61***	(1.05)
Regional diffusion	.513***	(.027)	.293***	(.028)
Ethnic fractionalization	–9.57***	(.917)	–3.57**	(1.52)
Population size	–.001***	(.001)	–.000***	(.001)
Area size	.001***	(.001)	.001***	(.001)
Constant	–10.76		10.71	
Adjusted R^2	.559		.813	
N of observations	5125		4221	
N of countries	187		156	

Note: Entries for liberal democracy and constitutional democracy 100-point scales are unstandardized Prais-Winsten regression coefficients (with their panel corrected standard errors) and the significance (p) of the coefficients for the pooled time-series cross-national analysis obtained using Stata's xtpcse command. The default (comparison) is mixed electoral systems. For details of all the variables see Table 6A.1.

$^*p < .10$ $^{**}p < .05$ $^{***}p < .01$

Table 6.3 Effects of electoral systems on level of democracy: plural societies only

	Liberal democracy (Freedom House)		Constitutional democracy (Polity IV)	
	b	(pcse)	b	(pcse)
Majoritarian	−2.45***	(.814)	−3.15***	(.611)
Proportional representation	6.41***	(1.391)	7.28***	(1.58)
Positive action strategies	−.053	(.833)	8.28***	(1.38)
Multiparty competitive contests	20.46***	(.654)	47.59***	(1.55)
Log GDP/capita	9.27***	(.577)	1.13**	(.845)
Ex-British colony	3.92***	(.714)	1.54	(.851)
Middle East location	−12.24***	(.888)	−11.72***	(1.53)
Regional diffusion	.585***	(.024)	.436***	(.039)
Ethnic fractionalization	5.73	(4.18)	11.05***	(3.08)
Population size	−.001***	(.000)	−.001***	(.001)
Area size	.001***	(.001)	.001*	(.001)
Constant	−19.9		−1.94	
Adjusted R^2	.626		.743	
N of observations	2380		2069	
N of countries	86		75	

Note: Entries for liberal democracy and constitutional democracy 100-point scales are unstandardized Prais-Winsten regression coefficients (with their panel-corrected standard errors) and the significance (p) of the coefficients for the pooled time-series cross-national analysis obtained using Stata's xtpcse command. Only plural societies are selected (based on dichotomizing Alesina's ethnic fractionalization index). The default (comparison) is mixed electoral systems. For details of all the variables see Table 6A.1.

$*p < .10$ $**p < .05$ $***p < .01$

point increase in democracy on the 100-point scales. Multiparty competitive contests were strongly related to indicators of democracy, not surprisingly, and majoritarian electoral systems were negatively related.

Conclusions

All elections should not be treated as equivalent; instead, the underlying conditions facilitating the process of democratization by elections is most likely to be maximized with rules reflecting power-sharing principles. The results of the analysis confirm that elections which meet the conditions of multiparty competition, electoral integrity, proportional representation electoral systems, or with positive action mechanisms for minority representation are indeed the most effective in strengthening democratization. This pattern is replicated irrespective of the democratic indicator used, and the effect is particularly marked in divided societies.

With regard to elections as a mode of transition, therefore, the international community should recognize more clearly that not all contests are equally effective; instead, the types of electoral rules have important consequences for this process. International agencies are often relatively neutral about the type of electoral system adopted in post-conflict constitutional negotiations and peace settlements, believing that the principle of national ownership should be respected for any viable long-term solution. Imposing any agreement on a country carries the danger of triggering a backlash, and this also means that the major actors may not be fully committed to implementing the settlement. Nevertheless, while active external intervention is inappropriate, if the international community is concerned with peace-building and democratic governance, it should not be neutral when providing technical advice and assistance about the choice of electoral systems and processes; instead, it should seek to encourage stakeholders to consider and adopt power-sharing agreements in transitional and subsequent elections.

Appendix

Table 6A.1 Technical appendix: variables, coding, and sources

Name	Description and source	Obs
Ethno-linguistic fractionalization	The share of languages spoken as "mother tongues" in each country, generally derived from national census data, as reported in the *Encyclopedia Britannica 2001.* The fractionalization index is computed as 1 minus the Herfindahl index of ethnolinguistic group share, reflecting the probability that two randomly selected individuals from a population belonged to different groups. *Source:* Alesina et al. 2003	181
Religious fractionalization	The share of the population adhering to different religions in each country, as reported in the *Encyclopedia Britannica 2001* and related sources. The fractionalization index is computed as 1 minus the Herfindahl index of ethnoreligious group share, reflecting the probability that two randomly selected individuals from a population belonged to different groups. *Source:* Alesina et al. 2003	190
Ethnic fractionalization	The composite measure calculated on the basis of the two measures above, ethno-linguistic and religious fractionalization. *Source:* Alesina et al. 2003	

Table 6A.1 continued

Name	Description and source	Obs
Freedom House liberal democracy index	The Gastil index, the 7-point scale used by Freedom House, measuring political rights and civil liberties annually since 1972. The scale was standardized to 100 points. *Source:* Freedom in the World, www.freedomhouse.com	191
Polity IV constitutional democracy index	The Polity IV project classifies democracy and autocracy in each nation-year as a composite score of different characteristics relating to authority structures. The dataset constructs a 10-point democracy scale by coding the competitiveness of political participation (1–3), the competitiveness of executive recruitment (1–2), the openness of executive recruitment (1), and the constraints on the chief executive (1–4). Autocracy is measured by negative versions of the same indices. The two scales are combined into a single democracy-autocracy score varying from –10 to +10. The democracy-autocracy index for 2000 was recoded to a 20-point positive scale from low (autocracy) to high (democracy). The scale was standardized to 100 points. *Sources:* Marshall and Jaggers 2003; "Polity IV Project: Political Regime Characteristics and Transitions, 1800–2003," www.cidcm.umd.edu/inscr/polity	
Human Development Index (HDI)	Based on longevity, as measured by life expectancy at birth, educational achievement, and standard of living, as measured by per capita GDP (PPP $US). *Source:* UNDP *Human Development Report*	170
Population size	Estimates of total population per state (in thousands) *Source:* World Bank 2007	187
BritCol	The past colonial history of countries classified as those with a British colonial background (1) and all others (0) *Source:* CIA, *The World Factbook*, www.cia.gov	191
Middle East	The regional location of nations classified as those Arab states in the Middle East and North Africa (1) and all others (0)	191
Electoral systems parliament	The type of electoral system used for the lower house of the national parliament: *Majoritarian formulas* include the subcategories first-past-the-post, second ballot, block vote, single nontransferable vote, and alternative vote. *Proportional formulas* are defined to include party list as well as single transferable vote systems. *Combined* (or mixed) *formulas* use both majoritarian and proportional ballots for election to the same body. *Source:* International IDEA, *Handbook of Electoral System Design*, 2nd ed., 2005	191

continued

Table 6A.1 continued

Name	Description and source	Obs
Legislative selection	Arthur S. Banks, Cross-National Time-Series Data, S22F5, coded as follows: (0) None: no legislature exists (1) Nonelective: examples are the selection of legislators by the effective executive or by means of heredity or ascription (2) Elective: legislators (or members of the lower house in a bicameral system) are selected by means of either direct or indirect popular election	
Executive selection	Polity IV's variable "Executive recruitment" is here recoded into three categories: no competitive elections (including 1, ascription; 2, dual executives; 3, designation; 4, self-selection; 5, gradual transition from self-selection), restricted election (6), and competitive elections (7).	
Competitive elections	Polity IV Component Coding Scheme: XRREG (3) Regulated XRCOMP (3) Election XROPEN (4) Open *Description:* Chief executive (de facto head of government) is chosen through competitive elections matching two or more candidates from at least two major parties. Elections may be popular or by an elected assembly. The electoral process is transparent and its outcomes are institutionally uncertain. *Checklist of attributes with coding decisions:* 1. Elections are deemed to be "free and fair" by independent international and domestic observers. a. Not coded: If no international observers are allowed to monitor the elections b. Coded: If domestic opposition groups claim fraud but these claims are not independently substantiated by international and domestic observers c. Not coded: If there appears to be no consensus among international and domestic observers regarding the transparency of the electoral process d. Coded: If an independent electoral commission verifies electoral results 2. The outcomes of elections are not "significantly" influenced by the incumbent, nonelected officials (e.g., the military, the monarch, etc.), or foreign powers	

Table 6A.1 continued

Name	Description and source	Obs
	a. Not coded: If the incumbent uses his/her official powers to alter the constitution or unduly influence the electoral process to benefit himself or his party; included in this category are attempts by the incumbent to extend his term in office by "dubious" constitutional means, efforts to manipulate competition through new residency laws or changing the timing of elections, and the imposition of a "state of emergency" in opposition strongholds b. Not coded: If nonelected and foreign actors rig the electoral processes so as to predetermine the election of their favored candidates; these actors may, however, influence the electoral process c. Not coded: If elections are held under conditions of direct military occupation by a foreign state d. Not coded: If the military threatens a coup if specific candidates or parties are elected 3. Major opposition parties participate vigorously in the electoral process a. Not coded: If the major opposition party boycotts the election, for either strategic reasons or as a political protest b. Not coded: If there are significant restrictions on major opposition parties to nominate candidates, mobilize followers or access the media	

PART II / Determinants of the Power of Elections

Autocrats and Opposition Strategies

Part I of this volume explored the questions of the democratizing power of elections, focusing to a large extent on descriptive and causal large-*N* analysis covering the entire globe and much of the modern era. While the overall picture emerging from those studies portrays elections as in fact having an important causal role in democratization, ambiguities and divergences persist. This leaves open the well-known questions of causal mechanisms and necessary and sufficient conditions. *How* do elections and electoral processes become modes of transition furthering democratization? *Which* are the causal mechanisms and under *what conditions* do elections become tools of autocratic regime reproduction? This second part of the book seeks to provide answers to these questions. We do not claim to have all the answers or to be able in the limited space available to address all the relevant factors involved. Yet, we think the following chapters capture the most important issues in terms of strategic interactions between incumbents and opposition.

CHAPTER SEVEN

Sources of Competition under Electoral Authoritarianism

Andreas Schedler

Electoral authoritarian regimes are regimes in which opposition parties lose elections—often by a landslide, sometimes by a hair's breadth. Given their structural disadvantage, opposition actors face the challenge of changing the correlation of strength in the electoral arena by simultaneously countering manipulation and persuading voters. While democratization is a matter of institutional change, not substantive outcomes, electoral transitions cannot get moving as long as ruling parties remain unassailable behind the protective walls of electoral dominance. If we wish to assess the state as well as the prospects of democratization in an electoral autocracy, we need to gauge the given level of authoritarian manipulation as well as the given degree of interparty competition. [1]

The present chapter explores the impact of government and opposition strategies on the balance of power in the electoral arena. Initially, it was motivated by the question of whether electoral manipulation is an effective strategy to keep opposition parties weak and thus to keep levels of electoral competitiveness low. In this sense, the original research question was *x*-centered. The focus was on the effects of a determinate explanatory variable *x* (electoral manipulation) rather than on the causes of a determinate dependent variable *y* (electoral competitiveness). Yet, like any serious *x*-centered analysis, this investigation had to take into account alternative explanations of *y*, the supposed consequences of *x*. In the present explanation of electoral competitiveness, governmental manipulation will compete against its closest theoretical (as well as political) competitor, opposition protest.[2]

In its theoretical part, this chapter discusses the potential dilemmas both governments and opposition parties confront in authoritarian elections: the government's dilemma of manipulation and the opposition's dilemma of protest. In its empirical part, it explores the sources of electoral competitiveness in electoral authoritarian regimes on the basis of an original dataset that covers (almost) the universe of authoritarian elections in the world from 1980 through 2002, including 123 legislative and 74 presidential elections. Of these 197 authoritarian elections, almost two-fifths were held in sub-Saharan Africa and close to one-fifth in Latin America. The rest were distributed rather evenly among the remaining world regions (see Tables 7.1 and 7.2).

Strategic Dilemmas

Acting before the large audience of the citizenry, the two main antagonists in the game of authoritarian elections—the government and the opposition—are engaged in a two-level competition for votes. At the *game level of electoral competition* they campaign to win popular support. At the *metagame level of institutional struggle* they fight over the rules and practices that govern the electoral process. At this meta-level, the government manipulates elections to ensure outcomes favorable to itself, while the opposition mobilizes protest to counteract manipulation and extract liberalizing concessions (either by withdrawing from the electoral arena or by convoking contentious mass action). Political conflict unfolds simultaneously and interactively at both levels of this complex "nested game" (Tsebelis 1990).[3]

In this complex two-level interaction, neither party can be certain of success. Both may fail for analogous reasons: (a) their strategies of electoral competition at the game level may fail to persuade voters (unpopularity); (b) their metagame strategies may fail to shape the electoral arena in an effective manner (ineffectiveness); and (c) their metagame strategies may bear counterproductive effects at the game level of voter evaluations (strategic dilemmas). Declaring itself largely agnostic on the popularity of electoral contend-

Table 7.1 Authoritarian elections around the world, 1980–2002

Albania
1991 L
1992 L
1996 L
1997 L
Algeria
1995 P
1997 L
1999 P
2002 L
Armenia
1995 L
1996 P
1998 P
1999 L
Azerbaijan
1993 P
1995 L
1998 P
2000 L
Belarus
1994 P
1995 L
2000 L
2001 P
Burkina Faso
1992 L
1997 L
1998 P
2002 L
Cambodia
1993 L
1998 L
Cameroon
1992 C
1997 C
2002 L
Chad
1996 P
1997 L
2001 P
2002 L
Colombia
2002 C
Cote d'Ivoire
1990 C
1995 C
2000 C
Croatia
1992 C
1995 L
1997 P
Egypt
1984 L
1987 L
1990 L
1995 L
2000 L
El Salvador
1984 P
1985 L
Ethiopia
1995 L
2000 L
Gabon
1990 L
1993 P
1996 L
1998 P
2001 L
Gambia
2001 P
2002 L
Georgia
1992 L
1995 C
1999 L
2000 P
Ghana
1992 C
Guatemala
1985 C
1994 L
1995 C
Guinea
1993 P
1995 L
1998 P
2002 L
Haiti
1990 C
1995 C
1997 L
2000 C
Indonesia
1982 L
1987 L
1992 L
1997 L
1999 L
Kazakhstan
1995 L
1999 C
Kenya
1992 C
1997 C
2002 C
Kyrgyzstan
1995 C
2000 C
Macedonia
1994 L
Malaysia
1982 L
1986 L
1990 L
1995 L
1999 L
Mauritania
1996 L
1997 P
2001 L
Mexico
1985 L
1988 C
1991 L
1994 C
Moldova
1994 L
Nicaragua
1984 C
Niger
1996 C
1999 C
Pakistan
1990 L
1993 L
1997 L
Panama
1984 C
1989 P
Paraguay
1983 C
1988 C
1989 C
1998 C
Peru
1995 C
2000 C
Philippines
1981 P
1984 L
1986 P
Romania
1990 C
1992 C
Russia
1999 L
2000 P
Senegal
1983 C
1988 C
1993 C
1998 L
Singapore
1980 L
1984 L
1988 L
1991 L
1997 L
2001 L
Sri Lank
1994 C
Tajikistan
1999 P
2000 L
Tanzania
1995 C
2000 C

continued

Table 7.1 continued

Togo		Tunisia		Yemen		Zimbabwe	
1993	P	1999	C	1997	L	1985	L
1994	L	Turkey		1999	P	1990	C
1998	P	1983	L	Zambia		1995	L
1998	L	1995	L	1996	C	1996	P
2002	L	1999	L	2001	C	2000	L
						2002	P

Source: Author's database on authoritarian elections in the world.

P = Presidential elections, L = Legislative elections, C = Concurrent elections (within one calendar year)

Table 7.2 Distribution of authoritarian elections by world region, 1980–2002

World region	Legislative elections	Presidential elections	Total	% of total
Latin America and Caribbean	21	18	39	19.8
Eastern Europe	13	7	20	10.1
Central Asia and Caucasus	12	10	22	11.2
Northern Africa and Middle East	12	4	16	8.1
Sub-Saharan Africa	42	32	74	37.6
South and East Asia	23	3	26	13.2
All regions	123	74	197	100.0

Source: Author's database on authoritarian elections in the world.

ers (their success at the game level of electoral campaigning), the present chapter strives to estimate the causal effects their metagame strategies (government manipulation and opposition protest) have on electoral results.

Ineffective Strategies

Whatever type and level of manipulation authoritarian governments choose in order to contain the uncertainty of multiparty elections, their manipulative intentions may be frustrated by unwilling or incapable executioners down the line of command. For the successful implementation of their blueprints, the masterminds of electoral manipulation depend on battalions of political, administrative, and judicial allies who may be less than fully reliable. Just like all mortals in the world of strategic interaction and stochastic uncertainty, authoritarian incumbents can choose strategies but not outcomes.[4] They decide upon a bundle of authoritarian strategies to be deployed and the intensity of electoral manipulation to be implemented. They do not, however, fully control the effectiveness of their strategic moves. For political, administrative, or financial reasons, they may suffer severe agency losses along the extended chain of command that runs from the centralized design of manipulative strategies to their local execution.[5] Electoral authoritarian governments that lack the personnel, infrastructure, and resources to put their nondemocratic strategies into effective practice may eventually enlarge the spaces of interparty competition "by default" (Way 2006), as the benign outcome of their political and administrative failure.

The effectiveness of authoritarian maneuvers does not depend on reliable state agents alone. Through acts of protest and vigilance, opposition actors, too, may subvert or even revert the electoral impact of manipulation. They may engage in civic education, they may monitor the preparation of voter rolls, they may denounce acts of intimidation and other violations of the electoral law, they may organize comprehensive election monitoring, they may take bribes and still vote their conscience, and so forth. For all their efforts, opposition campaigns may still fail to mitigate the redistributive effectiveness of repression and manipulation. In the race of technological innovation, in which authoritarian governments deploy ever more sophisticated techniques of manipulation and opposition actors ever more sophisticated techniques of monitoring (see Beaulieu and Hyde forthcoming; Hartlyn and McCoy 2006), the latter may well fail to counteract either the subtleties or the brutalities of the former.[6]

The Dilemma of Manipulation

In the production of authoritarian election outcomes, popular support and government manipulation are substitutes. If regimes have more of one, they need less of the other. Yet there are limits to substitution. While other types of dictatorships (in particular, military regimes and totalitarian regimes) may know few constraints on the intensity of repression they unleash on their subjects, electoral authoritarian regimes do not rely on naked repression. They engage in a game of illusions and contradictions. Officially, they give citizens a voice; informally, they retain the capacity of distorting "the will of the people" as it emanates from the ballot box. Their rule is built on fraudulent foundations. Playing the game of democracy (on the front stage), they juggle (behind the scenes) with the tools of authoritarianism. While the authoritarian control of elections is designed to ensure easy governmental victories at the polls, it suffers the perennial possibility of overextension. Authoritarian excesses may destroy the regime's foundational illusion of democratic foundations. At some ill-defined point, electoral manipulation may turn counterproductive.[7]

To the extent that citizens value democratic political goods and perceive the existing political regime to violate democratic precepts, they create a dilemma for electoral authoritarian regimes.[8] By manipulating the electoral arena, electoral authoritarian incumbents may compensate for their deficits of popular support. At the same time, they aggravate these deficits to the extent that manipulation makes democratic voters turn their backs on the government. Manipulative substitutes for popular legitimacy may thus end up deepening the very problem they are supposed to solve. The dual goals of control and legitimacy may turn into "conflicting imperatives" (Gould 1999). To survive, electoral authoritarian governments need both, but their efforts to obtain one hurt their chances of attaining the other.

Figure 7.1 illustrates the space of possible outcomes. The vertical axis depicts the gains of manipulative maneuvers, the horizontal axis their costs. Both dimensions are conceived in concrete electoral terms. The *y*-axis, "regime effectiveness," depicts the vote shares rulers gain through manipulation; the *x*-axis, "legitimacy costs," the vote shares they lose through manipulation. The net effects of manipulation are nil along the dotted line that divides this two-dimensional space at 45 degrees. Along this neutrality line, the costs and benefits of manipulation hold a balance, whether they are small or large. Below the neutrality line, delegitimizing effects prevail; above, manipulative benefits predominate.

If citizens are indifferent toward liberal-democratic goods, or unwilling to recognize the existing regime as authoritarian, manipulative maneuvers are costless and incumbents are free to deploy authoritarian strategies at their convenience, moving up and down the vertical axis unhampered by cost considerations. By contrast, if citizens are firm in their democratic convictions, convinced of the nondemocratic nature of the existing regime as well as somehow (miraculously) able to counteract the deleterious effects of manipulation, authoritarian maneuvers become pointless; by picking from the repertoire of manipulation, rulers do no more than choose a location at the horizontal axis of legitimacy costs. The upper-left and lower-right corners of the graphic show the extremes of these polar possibilities: effective and cheap manipulation versus ineffective and costly manipulation. In these opposite corners, governments face clear structures of incentives. In the area of

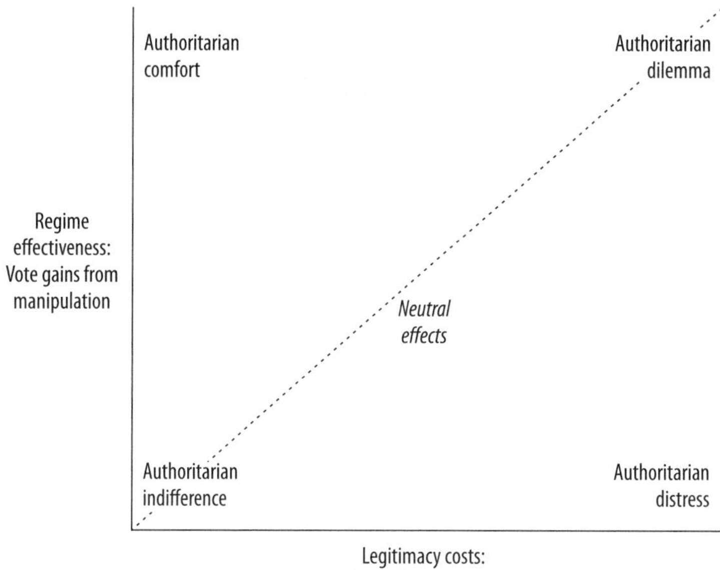

Figure 7.1. Electoral costs and benefits of regime manipulation

"authoritarian comfort," the reasonable thing to do is to manipulate. In the area of "authoritarian distress," the reasonable course of action is to democratize.

As long as the net effects of manipulation stay close to either the vertical or the horizontal axis, authoritarian rulers will know what to do. The structure of choice turns more uncertain as net effects approximate zero. The closer they lie to the line of neutrality, the more difficult it is for the government to decide upon its choice of instruments. Again, Figure 7.1 shows two polar possibilities. Rulers may expand or intensify their measures of authoritarian control in a manner that yields few redistributive benefits, while at the same time the legitimacy costs of their metagame strategies may be limited, too, as citizens may be distracted or forgiving. The lower-left area of "authoritarian indifference" points to such a situation of small contradictory effects. By contrast, ruling parties may be able to manipulate the electoral arena in a highly effective manner, either by securing large vote swings, or earning decisive margins, or freezing a favorable status quo. At the same time, voters may be alert as well as allergic to authoritarian manipulation. They may respond with massive defection, active mobilization, and vote swings toward the challengers. In such situations of large contradictory effects, as illustrated by the upper-right area of our figure, rulers act under the promise of decisive gains and the simultaneous threat of decisive losses. With the final and precise balance of both being uncertain, the situation turns indeterminate. It places rulers before a genuine "dilemma of manipulation" in which whatever they do to further their goals of survival may end up undermining these very goals.

The Dilemma of Protest

Just as with governments, opposition actors may pursue metagame strategies (boycott, protest, or acquiescence) that may generate counterproductive effects at the game level of electoral competition. If voters believe the current regime is essentially democratic, they will give little credit to contentious opposition parties that cry fraud, boycott elections, and mobilize active protest. By contrast, if they believe the existing regime is deeply authoritarian, they will question the credentials of tame opposition parties that quietly play by the rules of the nondemocratic game. If the legitimacy effects of governmental metagame strategies depend primarily on the attitudes of voters (their levels of normative commitment to democracy), the credibility costs of opposition strategies depend fundamentally on the perceptions of voters (their cognitive judgments about the nature of the existing regime).

In analogy with the previous graphic, Figure 7.2 shows the space of possible outcomes. The horizontal axis depicts the electoral costs that opposition protest may carry by affecting voter support, the vertical axis the electoral benefits it may generate by triggering democratizing reform. The upper-left corner describes an area of opposition success where opposition strategies create a virtuous circle of increasing institutional fairness and increasing voter support. The lower-right corner indicates an area of opposition failure where opposition protests leave existing conditions of repression and manipulation unchanged while provoking rejection among the electorate. Again, the diagonal line of mutually neutralizing effects points to situations of contradiction. Below, the credibility costs of protest prevail; above, its gains predominate.

The closer opposition parties lie to the diagonal and the farther away from zero, the more dramatic is the dilemma they face. In the lower-left corner, "opposition powerlessness," there is little they can do about the nondemocratic conditions they confront, and there is little they have to fear from voters in terms of credibility costs. In the upper-right corner, by contrast, oppo-

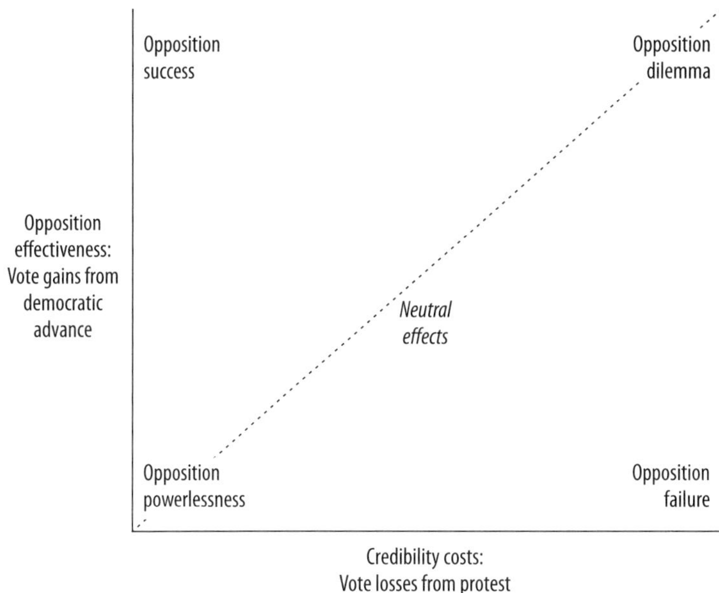

Figure 7.2. Electoral costs and benefits of opposition protest

sition parties face a true dilemma of protest. Here, the democratizing gains they achieve through protests are counteracted by the adverse reactions these strategies provoke among voters. The dilemma of protest is particularly acute when opposition parties consider boycotting an election. Authoritarians wish to be conferred electoral legitimacy without making democratizing concessions. Democrats struggle to achieve the opposite. They wish to extract democratic concessions without legitimizing the authoritarian manipulation of elections. But often they can not have one without the other. They "find themselves caught between the need to run and garner votes and the feeling that they are taking part in a charade" (Monga 1997, 158). If they enter the game they legitimate it. If they stay outside, they miss an opportunity for accumulating strength and opening up spaces of liberty and plurality. Contesting manipulated elections may perpetuate their authoritarian nature. But it may well be the only way of subverting authoritarianism.

The dual obstacles to authoritarian success created by state agents and citizens motivate the *x*-centered research question the present chapter pursues: What are, on average (across a medium number of cases), the empirical consequences of the metagame strategies carried out by electoral authoritarian governments (manipulation) and opposition parties (boycott and protest) in terms of electoral outcomes (levels of interparty competitiveness)?

Oblique Observations

In established democracies, in election after election, students of voting behavior work hard to unearth the long-term and short-term factors, the social, political, and institutional forces, that drive voter decisions. In electoral authoritarian contexts, by contrast, scholars tend to assume that the preferences and decisions of voters matter too little to deserve extensive study. Most empirical analyses of authoritarian elections are concerned with issues of electoral manipulation. Issues of popular legitimacy and the complex logic of voter decisions have received much less attention, and the same is true for the dynamics of electoral campaigning.[9]

Endemic—indeed overwhelming—information problems may explain at least in part the relative neglect of voter behavior in the study of authoritarian elections. Under nondemocratic conditions, the study of electoral behavior is irredeemably hampered by the scarcity of reliable data on both its dependent variables (the choices of voters) and its independent variables (the beliefs and desires of voters). Neither can election results be taken at face value, as aggregate expressions of the decisions of free citizens. Nor can public opinion polls, where they exist, be taken as faithful reflections of voter attitudes. In the absence of shared knowledge claims that would be acceptable across antagonistic political communities, political actors (including international election observers) tend to engage in intense public contention both about prevailing levels of manipulation and prevailing levels of regime support.

Authoritarian elections generate irritating mixtures of noise and silence, rhetoric and rumor, absolute certainty and absolute distrust. No cross-national quantitative dataset can ever do justice to the level of detail and sophistication, or to the amount of confusion and controversy, that tends to reign over local actors' efforts to draw "descriptive inferences" both on levels of manipulation and on levels of legitimacy from such informational disorder. The present enterprise, of disentangling the causal effect of manipulation on electoral outcomes across a medium number of cases, does not pretend to introduce unshakable factual knowledge into a field marked by deep epistemic uncertainties. Its statistical explorations rest modestly upon (a) thin data on a small set of strategies of manipulation, (b) partial and indirect measures of popular legitimacy, and (c) a single measure of interparty competitiveness (my dependent variable).

Governmental Manipulation

Given my original "*x*-centered" interest in assessing the (potentially contradictory and thus dilemmatic) consequences that authoritarian manipulation may bring to bear on electoral outcomes, governmental strategies of manipulation constitute my primary explanatory variables. The repertoire of electoral manipulation that authoritarian rulers have at their disposal is wide, multifaceted, and open (see Schedler 2002b). In this chapter, I wish to explore the individual impact of four specific strategies: physical repression, media restrictions, the exclusion of parties and candidates, and electoral fraud. To reduce problems of endogeneity, I measure repression and media restrictions in pre-election years. In addition to absolute levels of electoral manipulation, I also capture changes in levels from previous to current elections.[10] Table 7.3 contains summary descriptions of my measures, while Table 7.4 provides some descriptive statistics. (For more extensive explications of coding rules, coding processes, and data sources, see Schedler 2006b, 2006c.)

Opposition Protest

Several thin indicators of public protests by opposition actors prior to elections allow me to trace manifestations of "behavioral illegitimacy" (Diamond 1999). From the "conflict event" data of the Cross-National Time-Series (CNTS) Data Archive (www.databanksinternational.com), I use event counts of three types of contentious mass action: riots, strikes, and antigovernment demonstrations (calculating averages for the five years preceding each election). In addition, I employ news-based data on election protests that capture, in a coarse, dichotomous way, the intensity of pre-electoral protest by the opposition. I also include information on the most dramatic nonviolent strategy of election protest that opposition actors have recourse to: the boycott of an election.

Generally speaking, opposition actors more often choose to acquiesce to authoritarian elections than to protest against them. For a remarkable number of cases, CNTS data do not register any instance of contentious mass action in the five preceding years: no riots (51.0%), no general strikes (71.4%), and no antigovernment demonstrations (35.4%). Similarly, according to my

Table 7.3 Authoritarian manipulation and opposition protest: description of variables

Variables	LM[a]	Categories	Sources
Physical repression: Violation of physical integrity (extrajudicial killings, disappearance, torture, and political imprisonment)	Ordinal	Range 0–8 0 = full respect for basic human rights 8 = gross violation of human rights	Cingranelli-Richards (CIRI) Human Rights Data Project: Physical Integrity Rights Index (inverted) http://ciri.binghampton.edu
Media restrictions: Restrictions on freedom of speech and mass media	Ordinal	Range 0–2 Original categories (recoded): CIRI: 0 = no 1 = some 2 = frequent violations Freedom House: 0 = free press 1 = partly free 2 = not free	Arithmetic mean of CIRI Freedom of Speech and Press (inverted) and Freedom House press freedom (author calculation) http://ciri.binghampton.edu www.freedomhouse.org
Electoral fraud: Administrative redistribution of votes	Ordinal	0 = No fraud 1 = Irregularities 2 = Fraud	Author's database on authoritarian elections in the world (1980–2002)
Exclusion: Exclusion of parties and candidates from elections	Nominal	0 = Openness 1 = Exclusion	Ibid.
Opposition boycott: Participation or withdrawal from the electoral process by main opposition parties	Ordinal	0 = Participation 1 = Boycott threats 2 = Partial boycott 3 = Full boycott	Ibid.
Pre-electoral protest: Mobilization of followers by opposition (e.g., through public demonstrations, street blockades, strikes) in protest against upcoming elections	Nominal	0 = Acquiescence 1 = Active protest	Ibid.

[a]LM = Level of measurement

Table 7.4 Dependent and independent variables: descriptive statistics

Dimensions and variables	*N*	Min.	Max.	Mean	St. dev.
Regime manipulation (absolute levels)[a]					
Violations of physical integrity (pre-election year)	149	0	8	4.20	2.08
Violations of media freedom (pre-election year)	148	.5	2.0	1.36	.41
Legislative exclusion	121	0	1	.46	.50
Presidential exclusion	75	0	1	.36	.48
Legislative fraud	121	0	2	.93	.72
Presidential fraud	75	0	2	1.13	.74
Regime manipulation (changes since past election)[a]					
Violations of physical integrity	93	−5.00	3.00	−.26	1.62
Violations of media freedom	94	−1.00	1.00	−.03	.37
Legislative exclusion	62	−1	1	−.05	.38
Presidential exclusion	28	−1	1	−.14	.52
Legislative fraud	62	−1	2	−.02	.66
Presidential fraud	28	−2	2	.07	.90
Opposition protest[a]					
Legislative election boycott	121	0	3	.87	1.08
Presidential election boycott	74	0	3	1.07	1.27
Legislative pre-electoral protest	121	0	1	.31	.46
Presidential pre-electoral protest	74	0	1	.45	.50
Opposition protest (previous 5 years)[b]					
Riots	147	.00	5.40	.39	.76
General strikes	147	.00	1.80	.12	.27
Protest demonstrations	147	.00	7.80	.70	1.17
Economic cycle[c]					
GDP per capita, annual change (pre-election year)	152	−27.50	12.17	−.02	6.97
Interparty competition (dependent variable)[a]					
Legislative margin of victory	121	.00	100.00	48.90	28.84
Presidential margin of victory	74	.18	97.96	45.87	28.68
Lagged legislative margin (previous election)	64	.00	100.00	54.54	29.20
Lagged presidential margin (previous election)	28	.18	97.96	47.49	27.96

[a] Author's database on authoritarian elections in the world.
[b] CNTS Cross-National Time-Series Data Archive.
[c] World Bank, World Development Indicators.

data, opposition parties in electoral authoritarian regimes actively protest only 30.6% of legislative and 44.6% of presidential contests. They organize either partial or full boycotts in 31.4% of legislative and 37.8% of presidential elections.

Although I cannot measure base levels of popular legitimacy to control for the "genuine" popularity of government and opposition, I include one indicator of short-term economic performance that may have an impact on the "material legitimacy" political regimes enjoy. From the IBRD World Development Indicators, I take annual percentage changes in GDP per capita in the year preceding each election (for descriptive statistics, see Table 7.4).

Electoral Competitiveness

For mapping variations in interparty competitiveness, comparative election studies work with a broad variety of quantitative indicators. For the present purpose, I choose one simple measure of my dependent variable: margins of victory. For legislative elections, I take the difference in seat shares between the largest and the second-largest party. For presidential elections, I use the difference in valid vote shares separating the winning candidate from the runner-up (in the first round of presidential elections, in ballotage, also known as two-round systems). Margins of victory are simple and intuitive, and they seem relevant to political actors themselves (who may or may not spend their time computing the arcane indicators of the comparative scholar, such as fractionalization indices or effective numbers of parties and candidates).

Margins of victory also offer a straightforward linear measure of competitiveness: the larger they are, the less competitive is the party system. While electoral authoritarian parties may reduce interparty competitiveness either by concentrating power (the creation of hegemonic party systems) or by fragmenting power (the creation of nonparty systems), most conventional counts of parties suggest that more is better. Yet, higher numbers of parties may not always indicate higher levels of competitiveness. Where ruling parties block the formation and consolidation of opposition parties by promoting the boundless proliferation of nominally independent candidates, as in the Central Asian successor nations of the former Soviet Union, very high numbers of competitors are symptomatic of very low levels of competition. As the descriptive statistics in Table 7.4 show, mean margins of victory are rather high, both for legislative elections (48.9%) and presidential contests

(54.54%). Nevertheless, as the high standard deviations indicate, electoral authoritarian regimes differ substantively in the lead the governing party enjoys over its nearest competitor. Margins of victory, however, do not seem to vary systematically from one election to another.[11]

Cautious Inferences

In the present statistical explorations, I employ simple OLS regression to examine the linear relations between my dependent variables (legislative and presidential margins of victory) and my explanatory variables (levels and variations of authoritarian strategies, opposition protest, and macroeconomic fluctuations). Given the high number of variables I am working with (about a dozen), relative to the low numbers of cases in which none of them is missing (as few as 64 in the legislative and 28 in the presidential arena), I employ stepwise regression through backward elimination to identify the most significant and robust explanatory variables.[12]

In principle, my underlying causal expectations seem straightforward: A positive association between manipulation and vote margins would suggest that electoral manipulation is not an idle activity but an effective tool of power. A negative association between protest and vote margins would suggest that opposition protest is not a hopeless waste of time but an effective tool of contention. A significant association between economic growth and interparty competitiveness would indicate that electoral authoritarian regimes are vulnerable to short-term macroeconomic fluctuations. However, before plunging into the presentation and interpretation of results, I wish to highlight the disquieting possibility of inverse causality.

Authoritarian elections are haunted by endogeneity (a problem for the statistician and a resource for the politician). As outlined before, they constitute complex two-level games in which the struggle for citizen support (at the game level of electoral competition) is embedded in a struggle over rules (at the metagame level of electoral reform). The conflictive interaction between government and opposition evolves in a simultaneous as well as interactive fashion at both levels. What happens at one level affects the other (see Schedler 2002a). For the purpose of estimating the causal effects of manipulation on competitiveness, the close interaction between the two game levels implies that electoral manipulation may indeed affect electoral competitiveness—and the other way around: competition may very well affect manipulation, too. Correlations of strength between government and opposition may be a direct result of authoritarian manipulation, while authoritarian manipulation may be a direct response to present or anticipated correlations of strength.

Naturally, as soon as we conceive of variables as interacting, blurring their neat separation into dependent and independent factors, their patterns of association turn ambiguous. Thus, a positive association between manipulation and margins of victory may be indicative of manipulative effectiveness—or of preventive manipulation, where tight authoritarian controls are intended to keep the threat of opposition low. Similarly, a negative association between the two variables may speak of manipulative ineffectiveness—or of defensive manipulation, where increasing authoritarian controls respond to rising competitive threats. Analogous ambiguities hold for opposition protest. A positive relationship between protest and margins of victory may be reflective of counterproductive opposition strategies—or of courageous, calculating opposition actors who take to the streets when grievances are deepest, and take electoral competition seriously when the odds are best. Similarly, a negative relationship between protest and margins of victory may be evidence of effective contention—or of prudent opposition actors who recognize the futility of protest as long as regimes look too strong.

Because I have been careful to select explanatory variables that are prior in time to the election results I want to explain, I may be minimizing problems of endogeneity. Temporal priority provides limited insurance against endogeneity, though. Human intelligence is forward-looking, and political actors' dense "local knowledge" (Geertz 1983) may enable them to anticipate structural trends that take years to crystallize in the ethereal matter of election figures. With these methodological caveats in mind, we can begin our exploratory walk through the results of multivariate regression.

Legislative Competitiveness: The Magic of Protest

Let us start by examining legislative elections. Table 7.5 presents the results of regressing legislative margins of victory on my battery of explanatory variables through backward elimination. As outlined above, the rather extensive list of independent variables in the equation includes measures of levels and level changes of four authoritarian strategies (physical repression, media restrictions, exclusion, and electoral fraud), five indicators of opposition protest (boycott, pre-electoral mobilization, riots, general strikes, and antigovernment demonstrations), and one indicator of the macroeconomic context (growth in GDP per capita in the year before the election). The lagged value of legislative margins of victory (in the preceding election) is meant to control for party-system "inertia," for the effects of previous elections on later levels of competition.

The results are quite stunning, as can be seen in Table 7.5. Accounting for more than two-fifths of the variance in legislative competitiveness (adjusted $R^2 = .44$), only four variables survive the process of stepwise elimination. None of my eight measures of manipulation is among them. Apparently, levels of electoral manipulation and levels of legislative competitiveness are unrelated. The same is true for the three counts of contentious mass action recorded by CNTS for the five years previous to the election. My two election-related protest measures are highly significant, though, and carry substantively large effects. The measure of pre-electoral protest mobilization is dichotomous. If opposition parties shift from passive resignation (coded 0) to active protest mobilization (coded 1), they can expect to reduce the seat gap that separates the incumbent party from its nearest contender by almost 21%. A bit less coarse, the boycott variable contains four ordinal values: full opposition participation, the issuance of boycott threats, a partial boycott by some of the major opposition parties, and a full boycott by all relevant opposition parties. Each step in the four-point scale from full participation to full

Table 7.5 Explaining legislative margins of victory in electoral authoritarian regimes (stepwise linear regression)

Significant explanatory variables	β	*p*
Opposition boycott	8.764	.002
Pre-electoral protest	−20.979	.001
Annual change in GDP per capita (pre-election year)	.846	.063
Margin of victory (previous election)	.433	.000
Constant	31.250	.000
Standard error	20.890	
Adj. R^2	.436	
N	60	

Note: Estimation of linear effects. OLS stepwise regression by backward elimination (retention of variables at p (≤ 0.1). *Excluded variables:* Manipulation variables (absolute levels): legislative fraud, legislative exclusion, violations of physical integrity (pre-election year), and violations of media freedom (pre-election year). Lagged manipulation variables (changes since previous legislative election): violations of physical integrity, violations of media freedom, legislative exclusion, and legislative fraud. CNTS protest variables (previous five years): riots, general strikes, and anti-government demonstrations.

boycott increases the ruling party's legislative margin of victory by 8.8%. At this point, I am agnostic about the long-term consequences of election boycotts. They may retard the prospects of democratization, as Staffan Lindberg finds (2006a). Or they may trigger democratizing reform, as Emily Beaulieu suggests (2006). The immediate negative impact of opposition boycotts on legislative interparty competitiveness, though, is dramatic.

Lagged values of interparty competition also remained in the small basket of statistically significant variables. While considerable, the effect of inertia is not overpowering, however. One additional percentage point in margins of victory in the past yields less than half a point in the present. Pre-electoral variations in GDP per capita survived the contest of variables, too, even if the magnitude of their effect must be considered modest. Each additional percentage point of per capita growth translates into less than one additional percentage point in legislative margins of victory. In times of economic bonanza, ruling parties may appreciate the extra bonus. In times of economic crisis, they may find comfort in the fact that even harsh economic downturns may have only modest electoral consequences. For instance, if they happen to engineer a serious economic debacle with GDP per capita decreasing by 5%, they can expect to lose only a little more than 4% of legislative seats to the largest opposition party.

Presidential Competitiveness: The Mechanics of Censorship and Exclusion

In the presidential arena, as in the legislative arena, levels as well as level changes of authoritarian controls show loose associations only with levels of electoral competitiveness (see Table 7.6). The two big exceptions are restrictions on media freedom (in the year previous to the election) and changes in the inclusiveness of elections (when compared to the previous presidential election). Both show statistically and substantively significant effects on presidential margins of victory. In regimes that impose wholesale restrictions on media freedom (a score of 2), incumbents may expect to retain the presidency with vote margins that are about 15% higher than in regimes implementing partial restrictions only (a score of 1). Similarly, incumbents who abandon inclusionary stances and move toward the arbitrary exclusion of opposition candidates from presidential contests may expect to widen their vote margins of victory by an additional 20%.

While media controls and exclusion seem to work as effective tools of gov-

Table 7.6 Explaining presidential margins of victory in electoral authoritarian regimes (stepwise linear regression)

Significant explanatory variables	β	*p*
Violations of media freedom (pre-election year)	15.204	.098
Opposition exclusion (change)	22.895	.003
Opposition boycott	15.073	.000
Pre-electoral protest	–15.175	.058
Constant	18.565	.156
Standard error	18.194	
Adj. R^2	·589	
N	27	

Note: Estimation of linear effects. OLS stepwise regression by backward elimination (retention of variables at p (≤ 0.1). *Excluded variables:* Manipulation variables (absolute levels): presidential fraud, presidential exclusion, violations of physical integrity (pre-election year), and violations of media freedom (pre-election year). Lagged manipulation variables (changes since previous legislative election): violations of physical integrity, violations of media freedom, and presidential fraud. CNTS protest variables (previous five years): Riots, general strikes, and anti-government demonstrations. Control variables: GDP per capita change (pre-election year), and lagged presidential margin of victory (previous election).

ernment power, opposition actors need not watch the electoral game helplessly. Again, boycotts dramatically widen the vote gap between the official candidate and the strongest opposition candidate. Each step toward full boycott on our four-point scale is likely to increase the winner's vote margin by 15%. The self-exclusion of opposition parties seems to be a quicker road to governmental landslides than the exclusion of opposition candidates by the rulers. Somewhat surprisingly, presidential vote margins seem to be impervious to medium-term popular mobilization (the CNTS counts of riots, general strikes, and protest demonstrations). By contrast, short-term pre-electoral mobilization by the opposition (a dummy variable) is likely to reduce the government's margin of victory by about 15%.

Finally, neither changes in GDP per capita nor lagged margins of victory survived the competition of variables by backward elimination. Presidential elections in authoritarian regimes seem to be immune to short-term macroeconomic oscillations, and they appear to be less determined by the past than legislative elections. Past levels of competitiveness do not foreshadow present levels of competitiveness. Taken together, our four significant variables—one pair of authoritarian strategies and one of protest variables—account for a considerable portion of variations in presidential margins of victory (adjusted R^2 = .59).

Conclusion

This statistical inquiry into the sources of competitiveness in authoritarian elections has yielded some remarkable findings, some positive, others negative.

Disconnected manipulation. With few exceptions, the levels of electoral manipulation show no systematic, statistically significant relation to the ruling party's margins of victory, our measure of electoral competitiveness. This striking lack of statistical significance may be highly significant both theoretically as well as practically. It seems to confirm the idea that the effectiveness of electoral manipulation may be structurally problematic. Because of agency losses, manipulative maneuvers may generate limited vote gains for the incumbent; and thanks to their potentially negative impact on citizen support, they may even turn counterproductive. The remarkable empirical disconnect between levels of manipulation and levels of competitiveness reaffirms the potential importance of these mediating factors. It strongly suggests that strategies of manipulation may be much less important in explaining the official distribution of votes under electoral authoritarian conditions than we have been inclined to believe. Of course, we may raise a fair number of cautionary objections. Most prominently, the friendly elephant of endogeneity is still walking on our argumentative premises. However, for all the well-advised inferential caution we may practice (and for all the comforting congruence of our finding with hypothetical expectations), it remains a striking discovery that levels of electoral manipulation have little to do with levels of electoral competition. If nothing else, these findings suggest that the "dilemma of manipulation" may be more than a hypothetical possibility for electoral authoritarian governments. It seems to be real and pressing.

Presidential safeguards. The two significant exceptions to the rule of authoritarian ineffectiveness are exclusion and censorship. Both strategies give substantial boosts to the winning margins of authoritarian incumbents in presidential elections. Blocking the access of opposition parties to the office of chief executive is a universal concern of electoral authoritarian governments. Controlling the public space and controlling the field of competition seem to constitute effective tools for keeping opposition candidates at a safe distance from the presidential office. The relative personalization of presidential elections, in comparison to more party-based legislative contests, could help explain the relative effectiveness of both strategies of authoritarian containment. Controlling the media may be a more effective authoritarian tool in presidential elections, where challengers tend to depend more on media exposure than do opposition parties participating in legislative elections. The same may be true for the exclusion of uncomfortable contenders in presidential elections, where voters tend to depend more on individual candidates than in legislative contests.

Asymmetric arenas. I did not enter the present analysis with explicit expectations about systematic differences in the determinants of competitiveness between legislative and presidential elections. Yet, in addition to the causal asymmetry of manipulation in legislative and presidential elections, two further differences did emerge serendipitously. First, pre-electoral changes in GDP per capita, while moderately important in the legislative arena, are of no consequence in the presidential arena. This seems to be excellent news for authoritarian macroeconomic populists. Secondly, legislative elections are more tightly tied to the past than presidential elections. For both sides, the relative indeterminacy of presidential contests contains an optimistic message: miraculous shifts in presidential vote shares may occur regardless of the outcome of the previous election.

Defeat by boycott. Whatever the normative grounds and potential long-term benefits of opposition boycotts, at least their immediate effects are as bad as one would expect. Boycotts give a massive vote boost to the authoritarian incumbent, forcing opposition actors to face a simple choice: Unless they are willing to trade the certainty of defeat in the present for the uncertain prospect of future gains, they should stay within the electoral arena. They should keep struggling within the game, while taking their protest against the game to the streets.

Magical protest. In contrast to the consistently weak and ambiguous effects of manipulation, our measure of pre-electoral opposition protest shows strong, significant, and robust associations with levels of competitiveness. The active mobilization of opposition parties on the eve of national elections goes hand in hand with large downward swings in ruling parties' seat and vote margins. If there is a causal story behind these findings, it is one that is immensely encouraging for opposition parties: Those parties strong and bold enough to take their followers to the streets have impressive chances of reducing official margins of victory. When deciding to boycott, opposition parties seem to face a genuine dilemma. When deciding to protest, their structure of choice seems to be straightforward. If the two-level game of democratization by elections is supposed to be propelled by governmental manipulation on the one side and opposition protest on the other, my findings strongly suggest that the real motor that drives authoritarian electoral outcomes may not be government decisions, but opposition strategies. If we wish to understand the dynamics of electoral authoritarian regimes, perhaps we should turn more decisively to the study of opposition politics, instead of maintaining our relative fixation on government policies.[13]

Asymmetric dilemmas. While authoritarian elections can pose tantalizing decision dilemmas for governments as well as opposition parties, empirically only the former seem to confront a genuinely dilemmatic structure of choice. The empirical disconnection I found between manipulation and regime strength is persuasively consistent with the idea that electoral authoritarian governments face a dilemma of manipulation. By contrast, the empirical association I found between protest and opposition strength strongly contradicts the notion that opposition parties face a serious dilemma of protest. This asymmetry may have a single source: the presence of democratic citizens who are neither infinitely tolerant of nor infinitely ignorant of authoritarianism. Popular rejection of authoritarian governance (which is a matter of evaluations), in conjunction with popular awareness of authoritarian governance (which is a matter of perceptions), create high legitimacy costs of governmental manipulation, while keeping low the credibility costs of opposition protest. In addition, to the extent that popular norms and beliefs put into question the solidity of regime support, they force ruling parties, and encourage opposition parties, to struggle for the minds and hearts of citizens. By inhibiting governmental manipulation, inviting opposition protest, and encouraging voter persuasion, citizens' pro-democratic norms and perceptions are likely to push political actors onto the track of democratization by elections. To the extent that these norms and perceptions are universal, the democratizing power of authoritarian multiparty elections should be expected to be universal, too.

Strategic implications. Finally, my empirical conclusions invite a couple of practical recommendations for opposition parties (and for incumbents, too, if someone wished to formulate these recommendations in a Machiavellian spirit). First, don't boycott. Protest instead. Build up mobilizational capacities and take your followers to the streets. Withdrawing from the electoral arena hurts you in the short run (which hurts a lot) and probably also over the long haul (where everything is more uncertain). Counteracting authoritarian manipulation through active protest, by contrast, pays tangible benefits within one electoral cycle. Second, in preparing for presidential elections, fight for media freedom and an open field of competitors. Censorship and exclusion, more than anything else, are likely to debilitate you in the personalist competition for the presidential office. Third, take legislative elections seriously. While media restrictions and exclusionary policies debilitate you in the presidential arena, your relative immunity to manipulation in the legislative arena provides golden opportunities for conquering congressional positions of power and publicity. All in all, even if weather conditions look less than inviting, keep protesting in the rain.

CHAPTER EIGHT

Opposition Parties and Incumbent Presidents

The New Dynamics of Electoral Competition in Africa

Lise Rakner and Nicolas van de Walle

Like the other chapters in this book, this one examines the impact of elections on democratization, in our case, of the fledgling multiparty systems in sub-Saharan Africa. More specifically, we examine the ability of opposition parties in the region to compete in elections. We show that the strength and strategies of opposition parties are intrinsically linked to the dynamics of contemporary democratization in Africa. Although our focus is not designed to be prescriptive, it seems clear that strengthening opposition political parties and their position in the national legislature is a central component of any strategy of "democratization by elections."

Several authors in this volume (Schedler, Roessler and Howard, and Brownlee) argue in some way that elections represent an important instrument for democratization in regimes which already allow a good deal of competition, but not necessarily in the most autocratic of the electoral autocracies. This power of elections in Africa seems irrefutable, as shown also by Lindberg in this volume. Certainly, in historical terms, the emergence of multiparty elections in the early 1990s has proved both contagious and resilient. Only Botswana and Mauritius could claim regular elections before November

1989, the date of Namibia's independence and the generally accepted beginning of sub-Saharan Africa's democratization wave. Yet, between 1989 and 2007, the region witnessed some 120 presidential elections in 39 countries, and 137 legislative elections in 41 countries.[1] More than half of the countries in the region have institutionalized elections enough to have convened at least four presidential and legislative elections over this period. As Lindberg (2006a), Posner and Young (2007), and others have argued, the quality of these elections appears to be improving over time, and a number of countries can claim to have become more democratic since they first started to convene multiparty elections.

At the same time, a number of signs point to a difficult and incomplete process of democratization. Very few African incumbents have actually lost an election in which they competed. Probably more than half of the region's multiparty systems are not democratic, even by the most generous definition, and few of these appear to have made any discernable progress toward liberal democracy during this period. Freedom House's 2007 report identifies 13 sub-Saharan African countries as not free, more than a quarter of the region's 48 countries. In some, like Somalia or the Democratic Republic of the Congo (DRC), conflict and state collapse can be argued to have prevented democratization. In several other "not free" states like Eritrea or Angola, a more traditional autocratic regime has simply refused to countenance regular multiparty elections. But in countries like Chad, Equatorial Guinea, or Zimbabwe, it is hard to argue with confidence that the regularization of elections over the course of the last 20 years has advanced democratization, though admittedly it is conceivable that a capital of democratic experience and values is being developed even in these countries, to be redeemed at some later time.

This second part of the present volume investigates causal mechanisms for when elections indeed lead to further democratization, and when they do not. Addressing this, we do not find compelling, clear-cut evidence that the regularization of elections has strengthened legislative oppositions since 1989. Instead, this chapter argues that the continuing weakness of the opposition is both a consequence of democratic deficits in African countries and a cause of their continuation. Weak opposition parties are highly correlated to imperfect democratization, but the causality is not always clear. Broadly, it appears that autocratic rule over the last several decades has prevented the emergence of a viable opposition, and in turn strengthened the ruling elite.

Thus, identifying the weakness of the opposition and the cross-national correlates of its relative strength is a critical task for scholarship, a task to which this chapter is dedicated.

There are remarkably few studies of opposition parties in contemporary Africa (Lindberg, 2006b). Studies of political parties have typically focused on the parties in power (e.g., van de Walle 2003), on party systems (e.g., Kuenzi and Lambright 2001, 2005; Manning 2005; Mozaffar, Scarritt, and Galaich 2003; Randall and Svåsand 2002), or on the general dynamics of electoral competition (e.g., Basedau, Erdmann, and Mehler 2007; Salih 2003). Studies of the opposition in Africa since the recent wave of democratization have also tended to focus on the broader category of civil society (Olukoshi 1998) and have mostly ignored electoral competition and legislative politics.

This neglect of opposition parties seems unfortunate. For one thing, the evolving ability of opposition parties to compete politically should be quite instructive about the level and quality of democratic practice. Legislative dominance by one party over time is often associated with misuse of state resources and authoritarian tendencies. Electoral turnover and declining legislative dominance should therefore be considered positive for democratic competition and the institutionalization of democracy more generally. Second, the incentives and resources available to opposition parties are quite different from those available to the party in power. Though this will clearly vary across the region, opposition parties are likely to have much more circumscribed access to state resources and thus, it can be hypothesized, a lower ability to resort to patronage strategies. The implications for both party organization and programs, and for the institutionalization of the party system more generally, are issues that have received surprisingly little attention in the scholarship on African parties.

According to democratic theory, the presence of a stable and numerically viable opposition in the legislature is a key requisite for horizontal accountability, through legislative checks on executive power. We could therefore assume that the ability of the opposition to win elections is in large part a function of the degree of democracy existing in the political system. Working on this assumption, we initially hypothesized a positive correlation between the strength of democracy and the progress made in democratization, on the one hand, and the strength of opposition parties in the region. In fact, the data we describe below suggest a weak or even nonexistent relationship.

The weakness of opposition parties in Africa today is a striking characteristic of the multiparty systems in the region largely irrespective of their level of democratic performance.

Another preliminary issue needs to be mentioned. One of the difficulties that confronts the scholar of opposition parties in the less than completely democratic multiparty systems of Africa, and presumably in electoral autocracies in all regions of the world (in this volume see Lust-Okar on similar systems in the Middle East, or Bunce and Wolchik on post-Communist countries), is that legislative elections are largely a sideshow in what are strong presidential systems. The key political competition inevitably concerns the presidency, in which resides a disproportionate amount of institutional power and resources. As Prempeh (2008) has recently argued, the African state continues to be characterized by "untamed" presidential power, and mechanisms to limit presidential power or indeed to move toward parliamentary rule have barely been discussed in the region since the wave of democratization first emerged nearly two decades ago. The presidency influences the parties of the opposition in a wide variety of ways, and thus the latter cannot be studied without reference to the former. For example, turnover of the executive has a powerful influence on the degree of competition and turnover at the legislative level. As a result, our analysis tries to integrate the study of legislative elections into the analysis of presidential politics in the region.

We start by presenting our findings on opposition parties in sub-Saharan Africa. Linking presidential and legislative election statistics to Freedom House scores, we find few significant differences in the strength of the incumbent and the number of opposition parties represented in the legislature between polities with high and low political freedoms and civil rights. We then explain these finding by describing a set of formal and informal institutional impediments to the development of opposition parties in the region. In each case, we examine the interplay of formal and informal institutions which are shaping the likely evolution of party politics in the region. As key causal mechanisms for undermining elections as a mode of transition in these countries, we suggest that the limited resources of opposition parties, combined with the pervasive ability of presidential parties to draw on state resources for clientelism, largely explain the weakness of opposition parties in sub-Saharan Africa. These African political systems thus remind us of what Lust-Okar finds in the Middle East (Chapter 9 in this volume). However, shifting forms of clientelism, and the institutional rules of term limits for the presidency and the two rounds of presidential elections, offer some potential for the emergence of stable and viable opposition in the region.

Opposition Parties in Africa Today

Some summary statistics of electoral results motivate our discussion. Table 8.1 shows the number of parties winning seats, as well as the share of total votes and total seats won by the winning party and by the second biggest party, in each country's first four elections, and, in three cases, the fifth election.[2] It also tabulates the combined Freedom House political freedom and civil liberties scores for each country in the year that the election was held. The last column in the table shows that the average combined Freedom House scores have improved steadily in the countries convening regular elections, since countries convening their fifth election had average Freedom House scores of 5, compared with 8.5 for the countries convening their first elections back in the early 1990s. Finally, the table offers calculations of average "effective number of parties" scores for each election. As the table indicates, some 21 countries had convened fourth elections between the end of 1989 and mid-2007, providing eloquent testimony to the routine nature of elections in Africa today. Indeed, these data offer evidence for a democratization by elections thesis.

The winning party, more often than not an incumbent party, has continued to win handsome majorities of both votes and seats. Some observers might note optimistically that the winning party's margin has not increased over time. Nor does it appear that the degree of disproportionality between votes and seats is growing over time, if we compare the first and second columns. It should be noted, however, that the percentage of votes going to the winning party includes a number of missing values; these missing values tend to come from less democratic systems, so the data almost certainly understate the level of actual disproportionality. On the other hand, given the region's significant economic problems, the persistence of poverty, and the poor performance of governments, it is remarkable that incumbents have continued to do so well; their success points to the advantages of office, as the literature has tended to argue.

The most useful and least deceptive variable for assessing the strength of the opposition is probably the proportion of seats going to the opposition. The "effective number of parties" statistic is often used instead, but the very

Table 8.1 African legislative election results, first through fifth elections, 1989–2006

Election	*N*	Winning party % seats	Winning party % votes	No. of parties in legislature	Mean effective no. of parties	2nd party % seats	FH score[a]
1	41	62.4	55.4	6.7	3	18.9	8.5
2	38	68	60.4	6.8	2.6	16.2	8.4
3	34	64.6	53.4	6.4	2.4	21.4	7.9
4	21	61.6	56.5	6.8	6.8	27.5	7.2
5	3	41.9	37	9.0	9.0	27.5	5.0

Source: van de Walle database of legislative elections.

Note: Fifth elections have been held in Benin, Niger, and São Tomé. These totals do not include elections in Botswana and Mauritius, the two countries in the region that regularly held competitive elections for at least a decade before 1989. In bicameral systems, the data concerns only the lower house.

[a] Mean combined ratings of Freedom House political rights and civil liberties.

large number of independent candidates in some countries, which leads to anomalous scores for fourth and fifth elections (discussed below), has lessened its usefulness over time. In brief, it is hard to distinguish between small parties and independents, both of which appear to be expanding. To cite just two examples: In the 2006 DRC elections, 63 independents are reported to have won seats, as well as 56 parties with five or fewer seats (in a legislature of 500 deputies!). In Mauritania, the winning party claimed only 16% of the seats following the 2006 elections, but there are 41 independents.

What, then, can be argued about these second parties? They appear to have gained in strength over time, if just barely, from under a fifth of total seats allocated in the first two elections, to just over a quarter in fourth elections. Still, second parties remain relatively small, gaining a third of the legislative seats in only 22 of the 137 elections (in comparison, the majority party had 66% of the seats in 68 elections).

Table 8.2 categorizes the same legislative elections data by the Freedom House scores of the country in the year of the legislative election being held. The first category, of 34 elections, are the most democratic countries, categorized as "free" by Freedom House. The second set, with 55 elections, are countries characterized as hybrid regimes, mostly what Freedom House calls "partly free." The third category, with 44 elections, are the least democratic countries, which Freedom House scores categorize as "not free." As indicated above, our initial expectation was that the opposition parties would do much

Table 8.2 African legislative elections results by level of democracy, 1989–2006

Mean FH score[a]	*N*	Winning party % seats	Winning party % votes	No. of parties in legislature	Mean effective no. of parties	2nd party % seats
Free (<6)	34	58.5	53.1	5.9	2.7	25.6
Partly free (6–9)	55	60.0	53.0	7.1	3.6	20.1
Not free (≥10)	44	73.0	62.2	6.1	2.0	15.2

Source: van de Walle database of legislative elections.

Note: Elections after 2006 are not included because of unavailability of Freedom House scores for 2007. Civil rights and political freedom scores have been summed.

[a] Mean combined ratings of Freedom House political rights and civil liberties.

better in the first category of countries, given that political freedoms and civil rights are the highest. In fact, we do find a weak correlation between the quality of the democracy and the strength of the opposition. Still, we expected to find much sharper contrasts between the three categories; the weakness of opposition parties in even the most democratic systems does appear striking.

The election statistics presented here correspond to findings by Lindberg (2007), among others. He found that of 21 electoral democracies in sub-Saharan Africa, 11 may be characterized as stable/institutionalizing; of these 11 democracies, 8 are one-party dominant. Thus, stable party systems in Africa seem to mean stable one-party dominance (Lindberg 2007, 237). From the perspective of democratic accountability, this is problematic. As reported in much of the literature, dominance is very often associated with misuse of state resources and authoritarian tendencies (Manning 2005; Randall and Svåsand 2002; van de Walle 2003). In other words, if the only political systems capable of providing mass patronage through their party system as "electoral machines" are one-party systems, the question is whether multiparty democracy is really emerging in the region. In countries like Tanzania, Botswana, South Africa, and Mozambique—all characterized as either stable or institutionalizing (Lindberg 2007)—the dominant party has not been subjected to serious electoral contestation. The increasing degree of horizontal and vertical accountability observed in these regimes exists in the context of one dominant party that has not been subject to serious electoral challenge.

How does this compare with opposition scores in presidential competitions over the same time period? Table 8.3 calculates similar data for presi-

Table 8.3 African presidential election results, first through fourth elections, 1989–2007

	Mean no. of candidates	% of votes		
		1st candidate	2nd candidate	3rd candidate
All presidential elections				
First elections (*N* = 39)	3.3	59.4	24.2	10.4
Second elections (*N* = 35)	3.5	63.9	21.4	9.1
Third elections (*N* = 32)	3.5	56.9	26.2	9.7
Fourth elections (*N* = 14)	3.8	50.6	30.8	8.6
Second-round runoffs only				
First elections (*N* = 10)	2	60	40.1	
Second elections (*N* = 7)	2	60.9	39.1	
Third elections (*N* = 10)	1.9	63.7	40.3	
Fourth elections (*N* = 4)	2.3	62.8	33.8	
Mean	3.1	59.5	27.7	9.6

dential elections between 1989 and 2007, as they have evolved from the first election convened in some 39 countries after the transition to—in some 14 cases—the fourth election. Because a number of countries conduct a second-round runoff when no candidate has won a clear majority in the first round, this table also tallies results for second-round elections. Presidential elections are discussed in greater length below, but several features in the table are worth highlighting here. First, over time, the results for presidential elections do suggest increasing competition, as the totals for the winner and the runner-ups appear to be converging slightly. In contrast to the case for legislative elections, winning margins appear to be getting smaller, though again, as for legislative elections, they remain quite healthy, at about 20%. Second, the quality of democracy appears to have a clearer effect in presidential elections than in legislative elections. Presidential elections appear to follow two somewhat different modal paths: some 25 countries use a two-round majority system (TRM), while 13 countries have simple majority (SM) rules in their presidential elections. Presidential elections are clearly more competitive in the TRM systems. The winner in these elections on average received 54.4% of the vote in the first round and 61.7% in the second round, compared with 67.5% of the vote in the SM system elections. The equivalent scores for the runners-up were 25.8%, 39.1%, and 22.6%. Similarly, of the 45 elections in which the runner-up won at least 35% of the presidential vote, only 5 were in SM systems.

Understanding Opposition Weakness

Our statistical findings highlight averages and hide major exceptions and developments over time, within a given country and the region. Nevertheless, looking at individual electoral results and countries, one first tentative finding is that there is a slight but not overwhelming relationship between the strength of the opposition and the quality of the electoral competition. A second finding is the pervasive weakness of electoral opposition in Africa. Below we investigate three signs of opposition party weakness.

The Small Size of Opposition Parties

First, as suggested in Tables 8.1 and 8.2, the leading opposition party is often relatively small compared to the ruling party. Even in the region's most democratic countries, the opposition often has fewer than half the number of seats of the winning party: in Benin in 2003, for instance, the opposition had 15 seats compared with the government's 31, and in Cape Verde in 2006, the numbers were 29 versus 41. Since the majority party can often count on the legislative support of smaller parties and independents, these data understate the strength of the majority party relative to the opposition. Moreover, most of these countries have constitutions with wide discretionary powers for the executive and no requirement that the parliamentary majority be the party of the president (Prempeh 2008). Yet, a difference in party between the executive and the legislature has actually been the case in only a very small number of cases, most notably Niger and São Tomé, where successive presidents have not consistently been able to count on a stable parliamentary majority.

The Limited Durability of the Opposition

As argued by Randall and Svåsand (2002), functioning democracies require an institutionalized party system such that voters are able to choose between alternative parties and to vote on the basis of the parties' performance in previous elections. Underlining the weakness of African opposition parties are the striking number of changes in parties and in the number of parties from one election to the next. Lindberg (2006a, 13) has compiled the number of parties registered in legislative elections in 44 sub-Saharan African countries. While the number ranges from a low of 7 (Botswana) to the 100 registered parties in Congo (DRC), more than half of the multiparty democracies in the region are reported to have more than 15 registered parties in legislative elections. In only a handful African countries have the same parties—apart from that of the incumbent—contested all three (or four) elections since multiparty elections were reinstituted. In Zambia, for instance, the Movement for Multiparty Democracy (MMD), the party that won the first multiparty elections in 1991, is the only party to have run in all four legislative elections since 1991. In the Gambia, no parties have participated in legislative elections in more than three elections. Even the relatively institutionalized multiparty system in Senegal has not produced a stable party system to the extent that the majority of the electorally significant parties are represented in consecutive elections.

In addition, though we could find no systematic study of the phenomenon, a number of observers (Joel Barkan, personal communication) have remarked upon the fact that incumbent parliamentarians are fairly often defeated in legislative elections, including parliamentarians in the president's own party, so there is added volatility within the elected officials of the different parties, including those parties that survive the election cycle.

On the other hand, the absence of presidential turnover means that the president's own political organization exhibits considerable political stability. Incumbents have been defeated only eight times in presidential elections since 1989, including three times in Madagascar. Moreover, five of the eight defeats occurred in "transition" elections in the early 1990s, when the sitting incumbent was swept away in the wave of democratization spreading through the region. The remaining three defeats of a sitting president occurred in 1996 in Benin and Madagascar and in 2001 in Madagascar. In the first two cases, the winner was the pre-democratization strong man; in the latter, international intervention and a lengthy conflict were needed to convince the incumbent to step aside. In sum, while the literature has emphasized the volatility in African party systems (Kuenzi and Lambright 2001, 2005), in fact this volatility largely excludes the president's party.

The Independent Candidate Phenomenon

Throughout the region, political parties appear to dominate the political scene. Nevertheless, in countries as varied as the Ivory Coast, Gabon, Malawi, Madagascar, Mauritania, and Uganda, independent candidates have constituted more than 10% of members of parliament. In the 1998 elections in Madagascar, independent candidates garnered a higher percentage of the vote (26.8%) than did the largest party.[3] In Uganda's 2006 multiparty elections, independent candidates gained the same number of seats as the largest opposition party, Forum for Democratic Change (FDC). With 20% of the vote in the 2004 elections, independent candidates constituted the third largest group in the parliament of Malawi (Rakner, Svåsand, and Khembo 2007). These totals are, of course, hard to interpret comparatively. The voting behavior of independent legislators and their relationship to the majority vary both within and across legislatures. The numbers also do not tell us much about the role of these independents in the legislature between elections. Candidates may be elected as independents but eventually join the presidential majority.

The functional difference between independents and parties represented by a single parliamentarian is not entirely clear. Clearly, at least some parties with only one effective candidate for the legislature are equivalent in political effect to an independent candidacy. The large and apparently growing number of independents in legislative elections throughout the region serves to weaken all parties, since it lessens their discretion over candidate selection; at the same time, the effect seems clearly more negative for opposition parties and their ability to contest presidential power. Several distinct individual motivations appear to be at the root of the phenomenon.

First, a substantial number of candidates do not think that running as part of a party increases their chances of winning a seat. They choose to run on their own and count on their own prominence within the community and their own resources to win. This suggests that parties often do not provide candidates with additional resources, one reason candidates might prefer to run as a member of a party. Second, a number of independents initially sought to run as members of a party, but lost a primary or were not chosen by the party to be a candidate. Dissatisfied with the results of the primaries or disagreeing with the party's decision, they choose to run as independents instead. The party that rejected them cannot assert party discipline and convince them not to run.

Finally, and concurrently with both of these logics, the decision to run as an independent can be part of a strategy to negotiate one's entrance into the winning party after the election, perhaps to buttress the presidential majority. At least some independent candidates believe that winning on one's own enhances the leverage to negotiate a good deal for oneself after the election (Rakner, Svåsand, and Khembo 2007). For instance, in the case of Malawi provisions in section 65 of the constitution intended to strengthen the role of parties by preventing MPs elected on a party ticket from changing party affiliation during the electoral term without having to recontest their seat may have led to an increase in the number of independent candidates. MPs may leave their party group and declare themselves as "independent"; MPs elected as independents may join an existing party group.[4] Thus, standing as an independent provides individual MPs with incentives in terms of striking bargains with the main party.

Explaining the Weakness of Opposition Parties

The scholarship on African political parties has increased markedly in the past decade, and in particular, we now have a number of valuable case analyses of party systems in Africa's emerging multiparty systems. Nevertheless, there are still few systematic studies of party-legislative relations, and we know little of how opposition parties (and independents) vote in parliament and the level of horizontal accountability. The numeric weakness of the opposition—demonstrated by the rarity with which the opposition gains more than 20% of parliamentary seats even in Africa's most institutionalized multiparty systems—the limited durability of opposition parties, and the unclear role of independents in parliament suggest that many legislatures in the region are relatively weak checks on executive power. The weakness of opposition parties remains perhaps the key factor in making elections "powerless" rather than leading to further democratization. What may explain the continued weakness of opposition parties throughout the region, not only in the electoral autocracies but also in relatively democratic multiparty states?

An analysis of a number of excellent case studies of party system development and electoral policies in sub-Saharan Africa over the past two decades reveals three sets of factors that generally appear to weaken opposition parties throughout the region: incumbency advantages related to the dominance of the executive, limited access to resources, and the low legitimacy attached to the notion of opposition politics in the region. Each is the result of both informal and formal mechanisms that serve to weaken opposition parties. In each case, there is clearly dual causality as well, insofar as the weakness of parties itself has allowed the continuation of old patterns in African politics. In the sections below, we trace each of these challenges facing opposition parties.

The "Untamed" Presidency

The third wave of democratization in the African region has often resulted in only limited increase in actual political competition. Ishiyama and Quinn (2006) show that political parties that were dominant in the period before democratization, typically in competitive single-party systems, were systematically more likely to emerge in power following democratization, though this trend was tempered by the number of political parties in the system and the degree of ethnic fractionalization. Across sub-Saharan Africa, even when there has been real alternation, the weak institutionalization of legislative parties is linked to the political framework in which the presidency is overwhelmingly important. Parliamentary office and control of committee leadership remain poor bases for parties to promote their own policies. Legislatures, in which opposition parties might gain a power foothold and enhance their popularity, are institutionally weak across Africa, with only a few exceptions, as suggested by Fish and Kroenig's Parliamentary Powers Index scores (Fish and Kroenig 2008). Barkan (2008) may be right to suggest that there are signs of increasing power and political influence in some African legislatures, but the modal legislature remains weak, and even in those that Barkan surveys, the balance of power remains strongly tilted toward the executive.

Furthermore, in many of the countries in the region, the absence of regionally elected assemblies and weak local government structures imply that there are few alternative arenas where parties can groom prospective candidates or affect the formulation or execution of public policies. Thus, the weakness of the parties, and in particular of the opposition, is embedded in excessive power concentration in the political system.

The use of the executive office to maintain control over the legislature is illustrated by recent developments in Malawi. Shortly after the 2004 election President Bingu Wa Mutharika resigned from the UDF and formed a new party, the Democratic Progressive Party (DPP). The president then faced a parliament in which "his" party did not have a single representative and with the largest party seeing him as an enemy. In order to secure control over parliament, President Mutharika has sought to limit the role of parliament by drastically reducing the number of times it convenes and has used cabinet positions as a survival instrument. As a result the number of cabinet positions increased from 24 (in 2004) to 42 (by June 2007) (Gloppen, Rakner, and Svåsand 2007). The cumulative effect has been increased costs and the paralyzing of parliament.

Another source of presidential power is the ability to control the electoral calendar. The data suggest that presidents in sub-Saharan Africa have been able to defer having to face the voters, so that on average, across the region, there have been 1.5 fewer presidential elections a year than legislative elections. A number of the less democratic states—such as Cameroon, Gabon, or Rwanda—combine a 7-year presidential term with a 5-year legislative term. In other cases, the constitution enables the president to convene legislative elections earlier than the end of the 4- or 5-year term.

In sum, a strong presidency and an authoritarian legacy serve to weaken political parties as well as the opposition. In an earlier essay, van de Walle noted that the democratization of politics in Africa is changing the nature of political clientelism in the region (van de Walle 2007); this change is likely to strengthen the position of political parties over time. The introduction of greater rule of law, regular competitive elections, and greater vertical accountability do not necessarily eliminate clientelism, since we can see that various practices of patronage, selective benefits to key constituencies, and influence peddling are all common features of the most respectable democracies of the OECD countries. Instead, we hypothesize that, first, democratization shifts the locus of clientelism from the central state apparatus to the political parties. Whereas the presidency typically controls clientelism in an authoritarian regime, the exigencies of competitive elections may force incumbents to shift clientelist practices to the parties to help them compete for votes. Secondly, we hypothesize that the movement to democratic politics increases the amount of redistribution that takes place, thanks to clientelism. The need to win elections may therefore result in an expansion of clientelism away from just a small minority of elites, where this practice was more likely to be controlled in authoritarian regimes.

There are important caveats to this prediction. In Africa's poor and stagnant economies, politically motivated spending and patronage possibilities are actually quite limited. Despite conceptions to the contrary, African state structures are comparatively small and cheap (Goldsmith 2000). Thus, even while the shift to electoral politics may create a need for expanding social services and patronage, the need does not in itself lessen the sharp fiscal constraints of governments that have never been very good at taxing their citizens and are relatively dependent on the donors. Nonetheless, and in comparison to the sleepy days of noncompetitive single-party elections and foreordained presidential referenda, the move to electoral politics certainly reinforces the importance of the party in power. To win elections, the president needs to strengthen his party, both in order to maintain party discipline and to campaign effectively. This process is not without its problems, and there is plenty of evidence that incumbent parties have a hard time maintaining party discipline and are not necessarily able to campaign effectively all over the territory, especially in rural areas far from the capital. Nonetheless, access to state resources, and to the infrastructure of the state throughout the territory, offer a huge advantage to the party in power, in contrast to opposition parties, which have neither.

In sum, the single biggest impediment to more competitive democracies in the region is the dominance of the presidency. Only Ethiopia, Lesotho, and South Africa opted for parliamentary systems in the 1990s, even though many other African countries had emerged from colonialism with parliamentary systems. It is even more striking how little the formal mechanisms of presidential power were questioned and undermined through constitutional tinkering in the early democratization period.

Limited Access to Resources

As anyone who has ever visited a party office in an African country will attest, most parties are poor, characterized by few resources, poor organizational capacity, and little mobilizational capability. While parties in Eastern Europe and Latin America have developed party structures tied to functional interests in society (e.g., the ties of working class parties to trade unions, the links of Christian parties to the Catholic churches, and the ties between agricultural parties and farming interests), few such linkages between party structure and interest groups can be found in Africa. The strength of incumbent parties is very often explained by their access to public funds and their use of state instruments to their own advantage (Randall and Svåsand 2002; van de Walle 2003). The extent to which opposition parties can sustain themselves without access to central state resources is key to their ability to compete. In countries where opposition parties have been weak, there is much evidence that party finance and the party's ability to project itself throughout the territory have been key issues (on the latter, in Togo, see Toulabor 2005).

Generally, personal ambitions and ethnic differences, rather than social and economic issues, drive political parties (Burnell 2001). The prevailing levels of economic development in the region, coupled with weak private sectors, have long led ambitious young men and women to view politics as the most realistic channel for upward mobility. Political positions are often the route to business opportunities (e.g., licenses, contracts with the state and donors). The predominance of personal ambition over policy platforms may be a driving force in the fragmentation of the party system. The 2006 presidential and parliamentary elections in Uganda offer some insights into the constraints on opposition parties in the face of incumbency control of state resources (Kiiza, Makara, and Rakner 2008). There, the incumbent greatly affected the outcome of the election, from deciding to call an election, to changing the electoral laws, to the actual conduct of the election itself. The so-called Movement system remained in operation until the February 23, 2006, elections, so that the incumbent party was funded as a government entity through the 2006 elections. The failure to ensure a distinction between the National Resistance Movement Organisation (NRM-O) and the state was shown in the use of public resources, public servants' campaigning for the NRM-O, the lack of balance in media coverage, and the harassment of the main opposition candidate and his supporters. Because of these advantages of the NRM-O, none of the opposition parties were able to challenge its hegemony in even a fraction of the 945,351 seats contested at various levels of government in Uganda.

The Low Legitimacy of Legislative Opposition

A third major challenge for opposition parties concerns their legitimacy. In one manner or another, the legitimacy of the back bench is questioned in many African political systems, as the role of a legislative opposition is not yet widely accepted in the region. To be sure, surveys like the Afrobarometer suggest that large majorities of Africans now reject one-party rule and support multiparty rule (e.g., Bratton 2007). Nonetheless, and somewhat paradoxically, these same surveys point to the relatively low esteem in which political parties are held, and interestingly, the particularly low esteem of opposition parties (Afrobarometer 2004). Piet Konings (2004, 305–6) argues convincingly, for instance, that the Social Democratic Front (SDF) in Cameroon lost popular legitimacy when it agreed to enter into parliamentary opposition because many people, including some of its own rank and file, believed that a party out of power would participate in parliamentary processes only in order to benefit from various perks and prebends. Public financing for parties inevitably leads to accusations regarding the use of that money by party leaders, and participation in legislative politics engenders accusations of compromise and lack of vision. Notably, while international donors finance as much as 50% of the budget in many African countries, financial support to political parties has remained a marginal and controversial area of aid (Carothers 2006).

We know relatively little about elite behavior and why politicians either run for office on the opposition side or choose to join the government, but it is evident that the nature of representation in sub-Saharan Africa to a large degree favors the dominant party. A number of studies have emphasized that African politicians are expected to act as spokespersons and financial providers in their communities. Being in opposition is of limited political value because politicians are expected to represent and benefit their constituencies, notably with materials goods and services. Opposition politicians therefore have limited incentives to coalesce because individual politicians are more likely to gain access to state resources if they associate with the president's party (van de Walle 2007). Burnell (2001) notes that in Zambian politics party formation is driven by political careerism, competition over spoils, and personal traits rather than serious disagreements over ideology or program. Bierschenk (2006) makes much the same point about elections in Benin, and Rakner, Svåsand, and Khembo (2007) about Malawi. Opportunistic backbencher behavior in systems in which political finances are largely patronage-based is often viewed in a negative light by the citizenry and leads to the bad reputation of parties, even as such behavior is consistently individually rewarding.

Institutional Variables

Several institutional variables appear related to the strength of the executive branch and thus indirectly impinge on the ability of the opposition to compete.

Electoral Rules

The electoral rules in effect appear to have a role in shaping the power of the presidency. As suggested earlier in this chapter, the TRM system used in a number of African countries is a formal mechanism that facilitates presidential alternation and thus provides more favorable possibilities for opposition parties. Certain kinds of electoral rules probably facilitate incumbency turnover (van de Walle 2006). In particular, the defeats of incumbents in Benin and Senegal suggest that the TRM system of presidential elections increases the chances of an opposition coalition forming to defeat an incumbent. In both those countries, the vulnerability demonstrated by the incumbent in the first round created the sense that an opposition coalition could win the election, which encouraged a movement of defection from the presidential camp to the opposition. In addition, the vote results from the first round act as a coordinating device for the opposition. These results settle who the most popular opposition party candidate is and thus who has the greatest claim to be the coalition candidate for president. The first round also provides leverage and a formula for the other parties to claim position in the cabinet and government if they have established some ability to deliver votes in the first round.[5] The brief period between the two rounds of voting facilitates deal-making to encourage this process. In Benin and Senegal, an SM system would probably have resulted in the plurality victory of the incumbent president over opposition candidates who won instead.

The case of Zambia illustrates well, on the other hand, how a first-past-the-post (FPTP) electoral system tends to discourage the opposition from entering into coalitions and thus makes defeating the president harder. Before the 2001 elections, opposition efforts to form a coalition that would compete in both the presidential and legislative elections failed, in spite of repeated calls in the press for such a coalition. As Burnell noted, "In Zambia many politicians like to conceive of themselves as the president of a political party and envisage being the next republican president, and treat parties as a personal vehicle to that end" (2001, 245).

In general, TRM systems are associated with francophone states, since it is believed that the inspiration for this electoral mode was the French Fifth Republic, though a small number of anglophone systems, notably Zimbabwe, have also used TRM systems. Interestingly, some of the less democratic francophone states have moved to the SM system, including Gabon, Cameroon, and Congo-B. In the last, incumbent president Dennis Sassou-Nguesso lost power to opposition figure Pascal Lissouba as the result of the fairly democratic, two-round election of August 1992. Sassou-Nguesso came in third, with just under 17% of the vote. When he returned to power in 1997, thanks to an armed takeover, Sassou-Nguesso changed the electoral system to an SM system. The constitutional change was probably a case of overkill, since Sassou-Nguesso gave himself a comfortable victory with 89% of the vote, in an election marked by intimidation and fraud.

Term Limits

As part of the democratic transitions of the early 1990s, most African countries introduced presidential term limits as a response to the president-for-life situation that had been associated with the one-party state. Term limits provide the best chance to limit the accumulation of power in the hands of the executive. Term limits may also prevent an electoral authoritarian regime's descent into dictatorship (Maltz 2007; Posner and Young 2007). Perhaps more important in terms of the prospects for opposition parties, term limits promote the alternation of power both for individuals and political parties. This is because term limits entail the periodic exit of incumbent presidents; the opposition parties and candidates then tend to fare better against successor candidates than against the incumbent. Presidential term limits thus reduce incumbency advantages and improve the chances of political alternation in power.

Ghana's president Jerry Rawlings set a precedent in 2000 when he retired after two terms in office, and his successor lost the elections (Nugent 2001). Similarly, in Mali, the constitutional limit of two presidential terms decreased the dominance of the ADEMA party that came to power in the 1992 elections as a result of internal rivalry. The legislative elections that followed produced a parliament divided among a number of parties and without a clear presidential majority (Villalón and Idrissa 2005, 51). The 2002 elections in Kenya broke the dominance of the Kenya African National Union (KANU), which had been in power since independence in 1963. President Daniel Moi had ruled since 1978. As part of a package of democratic reforms, the president agreed to term limits to the presidency in the early 1990s and under domestic and international pressure bowed to these limits in the 2002 elections. His successor candidate, Uhuru Kenyatta, won only 31% of the vote, and the opposition, facing Kenyatta rather than Moi, was able to stand behind one candidate, thereby breaking the one-party dominance that had prevailed since independence.

Most Latin American republics instituted term limits in the nineteenth and early twentieth centuries, apparently in an effort to limit presidential powers, in what were highly presidential and personalistic systems (see Bienen and van de Walle 1991; Carey 2000). This appears to have been one pragmatic solution to dealing with the patron-client tradition of the region. It was very hard to limit presidential prerogatives while the president was in power, but it became part of the formal rules to set a clear limit on how long the president might stay in power. It is conceivable that the same clear-eyed pragmatism is developing in Africa's imperfectly democratic systems today.

Opposition Strategies

We now turn to strategies used by opposition parties to overcome their electoral weaknesses. Clearly, opposition movements are involved in long-term attempts to level the playing field of formal institutions, as discussed by Schedler in Chapter 7. They demand independent and well-funded electoral commissions; they lobby for constitutional reforms. At the same time, opposition groups often accept the nature of the formal rules as a given; they appear remarkably pragmatic and focus instead on informal mechanisms that will allow them to compete in elections.

Mobilizing Resources

How can opposition parties address their systematic funding disadvantage? They are adopting at least two pragmatic approaches to the funding quandary. One is the financing of parties by private business. In Madagascar, for instance, Marc Ravalomanana used his own personal fortune as owner of the island's biggest dairy company to finance his party and his own successful campaign for the presidency in 2002. In Benin, the winner of the presidential elections of March 2006, Yayi Boni, had been president of the West African Development Bank (or BOAD, in its French acronym), a financial development institution of the West African Monetary Union, for a decade before he ran for the presidency. BOAD's projects in Benin were broadly publicized in the months before the election to enhance Boni's technocratic image and his ability to deliver the goods to the population. He also appears to have relied on the financial support of businessmen with whom he had had business relations while at BOAD (see Mayrargue 2006, 167–68). Morrison (2004) describes similar tactics by political candidates in Ghana, where businessmen invest in candidates.

A second pattern is for opposition parties to seek to get candidates elected to office at the subnational level as a platform from which to compete at the national level. In Uganda, John Kizito Ssebaana, the head of the Democratic Party, has been mayor of Kampala. Nicephore Soglo, leader of the opposition in Benin, following his own presidential term in office from 1991 to 1996, became mayor of Cotounou, the capital city, a base from which he has promoted his own son, now that his age excludes him from the presidency. For an opposition party, control of a mayoral office provides significant resources for the party faithful as well as a core base of supporters, both of which are sure to prove very useful when the time comes to compete for national office. Financial resources are only a part of the motivation. Ravalomanana's entry into Malagasy politics was as mayor of the capital, Antananarivo. In his case, the political resources afforded by such a position were probably more important than the financial resources. Moreover, Krutz (2006) has shown that opposition parties have systematically polled best relative to incumbents in major urban areas, suggesting that these cities offer a natural power base from which to compete for national office. But even if they were not fertile areas for generating political support, cities would also be attractive for the budgetary and patronage resources they offer to opposition parties.

Political Rhetoric

The other strategy parties can use to increase their legitimacy is to abandon traditional clientelistic approaches in favor of a mobilizational political rhetoric, which compensates for their relative inability to compete with the government party on material resources and improves their reputations. The absence of programmatic politics in sub-Saharan Africa has been much remarked upon. Its absence is not inevitable, however, and some parties are beginning to experiment with a public discourse that would set them apart from the incumbent party and make them attractive to voters. Two approaches appear to be emerging. One is the distinctive African populism being followed by Michael Sata and his Patriotic Front (PF) party in Zambia, which emphasizes class differences and economic nationalism to mobilize voters. The evidence from Zambia suggests that such political rhetoric can be quite effective, particularly in urban areas (Krutz 2006). Though it has a strong ethnic component as well, the discourse of Laurent Gbabgo's Ivorian Popular Front (IPF) also appears to fit in this category, notably in its strident nationalism. Indeed, there is no reason to believe that manipulating ethnic identities will not combine quite effectively with economic populism as an electoral device. Nor is there much reason to believe that politicians like Sata and Gbabgo are particularly sincere about their rhetoric, or that they will resort less to traditional forms of clientelism if and when they get to power. The point is that opposition parties can compensate for their weaknesses with rhetoric, and we should expect more and more parties to do this.

Another, more problematic approach is posed by the emergence of doctrinaire Islamic parties, which has been widely predicted for West Africa (Miles 2007) and Northeastern Africa. A number of groups have sought to mobilize Muslim voters with an Islamic-tinged social critique of traditional politics and have also sought to deliver social services to prove their attention to voters' everyday concerns. Electoral breakthroughs have not yet been much in evidence, but precedents in the Middle East suggest this may well be a viable political strategy.

In the West, the adoption of programmatic politics was accompanied by major investments in party organization (Shefter 1994), dramatically enhancing the mobilizational capacity of these parties. Superior organization, Shefter has shown, was a key instrument for countering the incumbency advantages of parties in power, particularly when it was combined with a new and popular political rhetoric. This was notably the case for the very successful labor-based organization that rose to prominence toward the end of the nineteenth century. This paradigm is unlikely to be replicated in Africa, however, because African parties cannot rely on the dues of very large memberships to fund organizational growth. In most countries, economic structure militates against the emergence of large working-class movements, at least in the short to medium term.

Concluding Comments

An aspect of our topic that requires more research is the relationship between formal and informal institutions in the democratization of sub-Saharan Africa. The impact of electoral rules and other formal institutions have been a favorite object of study in the current phase of research on political parties (Bogaards 2000; Mozaffar, Scarritt, and Galaich 2003; Reynolds 1999). Arguably, this turn to institutionalism has been a breath of fresh air for a literature too often marked by the parochialism of African exceptionalism. But this exclusive emphasis on formal institutions remains problematic. With the contemporary Western experience as the theoretical referent, the literature has not tended to take into account the actual level of democracy in the political system. Yet, in less than fully democratic electoral regimes, characterized by substantial incumbency advantages and abuses of power, formal political institutions are clearly at least in part the endogenous product of the balance of political power in the system. As a result, in many African states, it is problematic to study the effects of formal institutions on political outcomes (Erdmann and Basedau 2007).

Moreover, formal rules interact in a variety of ways with informal institutions in all political systems to mediate how the rules shape political behaviors and outcomes (Helmke and Levitsky 2006). In some cases, informal political institutions like political clientelism undermine the formally specified political rules. In others, the working of formal political institutions is facilitated or accommodated by a set of informal rules and conventions. Competing informal institutions typically predominate in the new democracies, while complementing informal institutions normally prevail in the more established democracies. But as Latin American case studies show, in emerging democracies informal institutions can have a positive effect on governance, especially in presidential systems with multiparty or fragmented party systems, and can increase the likelihood of governability (Helmke and Levitsky 2006, 11). Thus, it is important to describe these informal political institutions and analyze their potential impact on the emergent African democracies. Studies of African democratic developments have tended to associate nondemocracy with informality and democracy with formal rules (e.g., Bratton 2007). As an electoral democracy matures, more weight will be given to rule-based behaviors, in which formal political institutions will take pride of place. Nonetheless, it is important to emphasise that democracy will thrive in Africa only if political actors develop a set of informal norms, rules, and standards that uphold, legitimize, and strengthen the formal rules. The real test of democratic consolidation on the continent then is whether such complementary informal norms are emerging in party competition or whether competing informality largely undermines democratic developments. Clearly, more research is needed to identify these informal institutions.

Our data suggest at best a weak and uneven relationship between the extent of democratization and the size of opposition parties across the region. Arguably, cross-national data are sensitive to the limited time series, and sometimes to the sheer weakness of the data. Nevertheless, comparative and case analyses of sub-Saharan African elections confirm the weakness of opposition parties in Africa as a striking characteristic of the multiparty systems in the region. Indeed, our reading of chapters in this book on other regions of the world suggests that many of the features discussed above are not unique to Africa, but appear to be present in both the Middle East (Lust-Okar) and the post-Communist countries (Bunce and Wolchik).

Our analysis of factors that may explain the weaknesses of opposition parties has emphasized the links between formal institutions and political strategies. While it is clear that reversals to authoritarian forms of rule are not proving particularly attractive to Africans, our analysis of the role of opposition parties in the region suggests that we should perhaps question the assumption that Africa's multiparty systems are progressing in any direction (Herbst 2001), or at least that the pace of democratic progress is exceedingly slow. It seems that African incumbents are quite efficient in handling the strategic dilemma outlined by Schedler in this volume. Regardless of the nature and quality of electoral institutions, opposition parties have remained numerically weak and fragmented. As a result, the essential element of democratic accountability has not yet emerged in many cases.

It is interesting, and perhaps not surprising, that some of the most stable political regimes in the region, and also some of the regimes now rated as "most promising" from a developing aid perspective, have one-party-dominant systems that have not experienced alternations in power. There are a number of reasons for questioning this tendency to favor stability over power alternation. For one thing, the prospects of future power alternation change the incentives for key actors. If the ruling party faces a real prospect of losing power, it may be induced to create institutions that protect it when out of power, such as a strong, independent judiciary. Studies of former Communist countries also suggest that businesses tend to invest less in buying influence in countries with party alternation. Thus, there are strong empirical reasons to believe that power alternation will increase the quality of governance through strengthening both horizontal and vertical accountability mechanisms. The role of opposition parties and the formal and informal institutional mechanisms that enhance their prospects for electoral success should therefore be emphasized in future research.

CHAPTER NINE

Legislative Elections in Hegemonic Authoritarian Regimes

Competitive Clientelism and Resistance to Democratization

Ellen Lust-Okar

Authoritarian regimes often hold elections for decades without these elections providing a mechanism for transition to democracy. Even in hegemonic authoritarian regimes, in such countries as Syria, North Korea, and Zimbabwe, citizens have consistently gone to the polls, casting ballots for representatives at the local and national levels. Indeed, as Jason Brownlee argues in Chapter 5, elections appear to have an impact on the possibility and stability of transition only in competitive authoritarian regimes. It is in these regimes, as Philip Roessler and Marc M. Howard note (Chapter 4), that there is the greatest possibility of change—either toward democracy or toward hegemonic authoritarianism. By contrast, in hegemonic regimes, elections do not appear to foster democratization. There is fairly consistent evidence that authoritarian regimes which hold elections remain in power longer than those that fail to hold them (Gandhi and Przeworski 2001; Geddes 1999a; Hadenius and Toerell 2005b).[1]

Why is this the case? Why do elections in hegemonic authoritarian regimes reproduce rather than undermine the regime, and under what conditions do they do so? To examine these questions, this chapter focuses on national legislative elections in the Middle East and North Africa (MENA) because these are held frequently, are sometimes perceived to offer the hope for transition and, consequently, are a focus of democratization programs.

The analysis proceeds as follows. The first section provides an overview of elections in MENA. The second section sets forth a framework for understanding the role that elections play in these regimes, arguing that elections are best thought of as an arena for competition over access to state resources, or "competitive clientelism." The third section shows how competitive clientelism drives the behavior of voters and candidates in systematic ways and, more importantly, how this behavior promotes inherently pro-regime parliaments. The fourth section examines how incumbent elites therefore can manage elections, largely using institutional mechanisms rather than extralegal manipulation to maintain power. Finally, the conclusion reconsiders the relationship between elections in hegemonic authoritarian regimes and the possibility for democratization through elections, paying particular attention to the conditions under which elections may fail to reinforce hegemonic authoritarian regimes.

Overview of Elections in MENA

Elections in MENA are not a new phenomenon. As shown in Table 9.1, citizens have long engaged in elections, and they did so in some countries even while those countries were still under foreign rule. Both dominant-party regimes and monarchies hold elections, and while some regimes have reinstituted elections and parliaments in the post–cold war period, many held elections in earlier periods as well. For decades, voters have gone to the polls and cast their ballots for a variety of institutional bodies—trade unions, student bodies, municipal councils, national legislatures, and the head of state—as well as to voice their opinions on referendums.

In this region, however, citizens engage in elections within an environment that maintains tight control over the political sphere. MENA countries are consistently rated as "not free" or only "partly free," according to Freedom House analysts. Rights are restricted, and government responsiveness is among the lowest in the world, according to World Bank indicators.

How citizens behave in elections, the ways in which incumbent elites attempt to manage citizens' participation, and the extent to which these elections can promote democratization depends to a degree on the type of

Table 9.1 Elections in authoritarian regimes of MENA, 1975–2005

Country	Regime type	Voice and accountability rank (1996)	Presidential election, years held	Legislative elections			Freedom House indicators[a]	
				Year	Seats held by largest government party	Seats held by largest opposition party	PR	CL
Algeria	Dominant-party state	24.5	1976, 1984, 1995, 1999, 2004	1977	261	0	6	6
				1982	281	0	6	6
				1987	291	0	6	6
				1992	NA[b]	NA	7	6
				1997	156	0	6	6
				2002	199	43	6	5
Bahrain	Monarchy	27.4		2002	40	5	5	
Egypt	Dominant party	17.8	1981, 1987, 1993, 1999, 2005[c]	1976	280	125	4	
				1978	310	12	5	5
				1979	302	29	5	5
				1984	302	58	4	4
				1987	346	37	5	4
				1990	348	6	5	4
				1995	316	6	6	6
				2000	353	7	6	5
				2005	311	6	6	5
Iran	Dominant party	10.1	1993, 1997, 2001, 2005	1975	268	0	5	5
				1980	270	0	5	5
				1984	270	0	5	6
				1992	270	0	6	6
				1996	270	0	6	7
				2000	290	0	6	6
				2004	156	39	6	5

Iraq	Dominant party	7.7		1979	250	0	7	7
				1984	250	0	7	7
				1989	250	0	7	6
				1996	250	0	7	7
				2005	128	11	6	5
Jordan	Monarchy	28.8		1989	31	20	5	5
				1993	47	16	4	4
				1997	60	8	4	4
				2003	87	17	5	5
Kuwait	Monarchy	35.6		1976	NA	NA	6	5
				1981	NA	NA	4	4
				1992	7	10	5	5
				1996	7	10	5	5
				1999	7	10	4	5
				2003	21	3	4	5
Libya		1.9						
Morocco	Monarchy	28.4		1977	49	16	3	4
				1984	83	41	4	5
				1993	63	58	5	5
				1997	50	57	5	5
				2002	50	42	5	5
Oman	Monarchy	26.4						
Qatar	Monarchy	31.7						
Saudi Arabia	Monarchy	9.1						
Syria	Dominant party	5.3	1978, 1987, 1991, 2000	1977	159	1	5	6
				1981	195	0	6	7
				1986	151	9	6	7
				1990	166	1	7	7

continued

Table 9.1 continued

Country	Regime type	Voice and accountability rank (1996)	Presidential election, years held	Legislative elections			Freedom House indicators[a]	
				Year	Seats held by largest government party	Seats held by largest opposition party	PR	CL
				1994	166	1	7	7
				1998	166	83	7	7
				2003	167	83	7	7
Tunisia	Dominant party	13.9	1989, 1994, 1999	1981	136	0	5	5
				1986	110	1	6	5
				1989	141	0	5	3
				1994	141	0	6	5
				1999	144	10	6	5
				2004	152	14	6	5
UAE	Monarchy	25.5						
Yemen	Dominant party	18.8	1999, 2006	1993	123	56	4	5
				1997	187	84	5	6
				2003	228	48	5	5
YAR	Dominant party			1982	1000	0	6	5
PDR	Dominant party			1978	111	0	6	7
				1986	111	0	6	7

Sources: Keefer 2007; Freedom House 2006b, June 15, 2008.

[a] PR = political rights rating; CL = civil liberties rating.

[b] Parliament interrupted.

[c] First competitive presidential election.

election. Elections for student councils, trade unions, municipal councils, national legislatures, and the head of state all have very different dynamics. A full discussion of the differences in these elections is beyond the scope of this chapter, but a brief example is warranted. Presidential and legislative elections in dominant-party, hegemonic authoritarian regimes differ significantly. Presidential elections appear largely intended to signal support for the incumbent leader, dissuading potential opponents from challenging the ruling government.[2] To be effective, the message must be not only that voters will cast their ballots for the incumbent, but also that the incumbent can *mobilize* the people. Both the preponderance of votes cast for the incumbent and high turnout are critical. Consequently, we find in Syria, for instance, official reports that 95.7% of eligible voters came to the polls in 2007, with 97.6% approving the referendum granting President Bashar al-Asad a second term (SANA 2007). By contrast, as we shall discuss shortly, legislative elections play a very different role in reproduction of the regime, and they rarely see such high turnout levels or such sweeping victories for individual candidates.[3]

Legislative Elections in Hegemonic Authoritarian Regimes: Competitive Clientelism

Understanding the extent to which legislative elections foster or hinder prospects for democratic transition requires that we understand what is at stake in the elections. In general, elections are competitions over policy (including ability to determine who controls the policymaking arena and the rules of the game), and over gaining benefits for elected officials and their constituents. This is true in democracies as well as in competitive and hegemonic authoritarian regimes; pork-barrel politics and constituency service are part and parcel of electoral politics in both democracies and authoritarian regimes. In hegemonic authoritarian regimes, however, elected officials' control over policymaking is nearly absent, and particularly over the policy arenas that matter most. Rather, elections are best thought of as competitions over access to state resources, or "competitive clientalism."

Before examining competitive clientelism in more detail, let us begin by clarifying what elections are *not*. Elections in hegemonic authoritarian regimes are not intended to choose the key decision makers or fill top cabinet posts. Even in monarchies, such as Jordan and Morocco, where the legislature is not dominated by a single party, the parliament does not have any significant input into government formation. The king chooses the prime minister, who then appoints the government. The parliament may bring down the government through a no-confidence vote, but the fact that the king can dissolve the parliament at any time, and has at times chosen to do so, means that this power remains more theoretical than substantive. Moreover, the appointed prime minister does not systematically consult with the parliament in forming the government. There is a significant disjuncture between the appointment of figures to key political posts and electoral results.

Elections are also not intended to serve as battlegrounds for policymaking over key policy arenas. In Jordan, for instance, members in the lower house do not legislate; rather, the government formulates laws and presents them to the lower house for consideration. The elected members of the lower house vote on the legislation and then pass it on to the fully appointed Senate, which effectively holds veto power. In other cases, there is little daylight between the executive and legislative branches. In Syria, members of the ruling party officially dominate the parliament, and the party elite carefully vet the candidates. Parliament's role is so limited that one Syrian parliamentarian reportedly exclaimed, in response to questioning on legislation: "We're Members of Parliament. We don't make laws!" (Lust-Okar 2005). In Egypt, the party has lost much of its ability to control party candidates but continues to dominate the legislature. Moreover, through the use of emergency laws and other repressive measures, ruling elites can threaten to disband parliament or use various other means to hold individual representatives in check. Thus, particularly on the most important issues—sensitive domestic policies, economic policies, and foreign affairs—the parliament is limited.

Citizens recognize that parliaments are not lawmaking bodies. In Jordan, a survey conducted by the Center for Strategic Studies (CSS) in 2004 found that only 7.34% of respondents believed that parliament played a major role in policymaking, and 28.29% believed that it played no role whatsoever. Less than one-quarter of Jordanian respondents believed the parliament was capable of solving the major problems of unemployment, poverty, corruption, and inflation (CSS 2004).[4] In Algeria, less than one-third of respondents surveyed believed that the parliament played a significant policymaking role (Benstead and Lust-Okar 2006). In a similar vein, only 19% of Moroccans surveyed in 2002 said that they would choose their candidate based on his or her party platform. Anecdotal evidence suggests that these views are held in Egypt and Syria as well (Lust-Okar 2006a; Shehata 2008).

In addition, elections in hegemonic authoritarian regimes are not usually the arenas in which opposition and incumbent elites struggle over the rules of the game. Only infrequently, and only for some people, are elections in these regimes two-level games—a first competition over the offices and the resources associated with them, and a second competition over the rules of the game (Schedler 2002b). More often, the question of democratization is not even on the table in hegemonic authoritarian regimes. Indeed, it is important to realize that in many cases, elections were instituted entirely independently from a discussion of "democratization." In Syria, Tunisia, and Egypt, ruling elites used elections as a mechanism for cooptation and increased political participation, but not with the promise of democratization.

Moreover, even where elections are announced in the context of promised, or expected, democratization, citizens lose hope for this over time. Consequently, as we shall see, candidates and voters do not focus on democratization. Indeed, in the 1997 Jordanian elections, when opposition to the 1993 electoral law was at its height and the retrenchment of democratization was being hotly debated, less than a third of the candidates discussed strengthening democratic life in Jordan, and fewer than 10% discussed reforming electoral law, strengthening political parties, or further democratizing Jordan (Sari 2002, 72, 74, 80).

Rather, both voters and candidates recognize that what is "at stake" in these elections is access to a pool of state resources. Parliamentarians may not be able to make laws, but they can use their position and influence to pressure ministers and bureaucrats into giving jobs, licenses, and other state resources to their constituents. They do so, in part, by using the floor of the legislature, and their access to media, "threatening state institutions of scandalizing them in parliament if they did not react positively to their requests" (Kilani and Sakijha 2002, 58). Consequently, many call parliamentarians *na'ib khidma* ("service deputy"), referring to their role of providing services rather than legislation or executive oversight.

This role is extremely important. Given the weak rule of law and the nontransparent nature of these autocracies, finding a mediator (or *wasta*) between the citizen and the state is often the key to entering university or obtaining government licenses, public housing, employment, and a broad range of other state resources. Finding someone who can clear the path between the citizen and services he needs simply to make it through the day is a critical concern.[5]

Citizens recognize this. In Algeria, for instance, when asked how they would resolve a dispute with the government, only 59% percent of survey respondents said that they would first take the issue to the government agency, and only 24% believed that this approach would be most effective. Even more strikingly, only 39% said that they would first approach the government employment agency if they wanted to seek employment in the public sector, and less than 20% believed that this was the most effective approach (Benstead and Lust-Okar 2006a). Similar results are found in Jordan, where surveys conducted in 2000 and 2005 both found that the majority of respondents believe that they need a *wasta* in order to succeed in conducting business with government agencies or obtain public-sector employment.[6] More anecdotal evidence from Egypt, Iraq, Lebanon, Morocco, the Palestinian Authority, and Syria suggests that this phenomenon is widespread.[7]

Elected officials are not the only possible source of *wasta*. Citizens also call on friends and family members, religious leaders, and other intermediaries to navigate through bureaucracies and maintain their survival. Yet, they do see the parliamentarians' major role as providing services, not making policy or holding the government accountable. As Sa'eda Kilani and Basam Sakijha (2002, 58) conclude: "Parliament, whose main task is to monitor government's performance and legislate laws, is gradually becoming the haven for *Wasta* practices. Voluntarily or out of social pressure, parliamentarians' role in mediating, or, in other words, using *Wasta* between the citizen and the state is . . . becoming their main task." Legislators also have some resources directly available to them that they can distribute to their supporters. Some of these are in the form of parliamentary advantages, such as the hiring of staff and access to personal discretionary budgets.

Indeed, at stake is not only access to a set of resources that the parliamentarian can help to mediate on behalf of their constituents, but also access to a set of resources that directly benefit the elected official. Parliamentarians routinely enjoy the prestige of being parliamentarians and, for some, a sense that they can make a marginal contribution to the public welfare; they also receive cars, drivers, offices, and a set of attractive benefits. Even more importantly for many, parliamentarians can often use their direct access to government ministries that dole out public contracts to their own benefit. Thus, for example, a factory owner may use his connections with the ministries to bypass import duties or to obtain large public contracts. Finally, in most cases parliamentarians are granted immunity, which can be quite lucrative. Ruling elites sometimes withdraw parliamentarians' immunity, as they did in Syria during fall 2001, if parliamentarians choose to challenge the government. Those who do not challenge the leadership, however, benefit greatly. Samer Shehata's description of this mechanism is worth quoting at length:

> Many in Egypt, however, believe that the reason people are willing to spend millions of pounds running for parliament is because membership in the chamber provides legal immunity (hasana) which can be extremely rewarding financially.[8] The immunity that parliamentarians receive, in fact, can only be lifted by the People's Assembly itself. And it sometimes is.[9] Immunity from prosecution, it is said, allows some parliamentarians to engage in all sorts of extra and sometimes illegal practices and business ventures, making significant sums of money in the process. In addition, membership in the Assembly, it is believed, opens up all sorts of other opportunities for pecuniary gain (e.g., selling favors, including jobs, licenses, access to government land at below market price). (Shehata 2008, 100–101)

Engaging in Elections

Understanding elections as competitive clientelism, in which access to a pool of state resources is what is fundamentally at stake, can help to explain electoral behavior. Most importantly for our purposes, it helps to explain why candidates are rarely those who most oppose the incumbent rulers, and how voters help to reinforce the pro-regime bias of parliaments. In short, it explains why, in the absence of political or economic shocks, elections inherently help to maintain the status quo.

Voters

Citizens recognize that elections are primarily about obtaining access to state resources, and this affects both their choice of candidates and their willingness to vote. Most fundamentally, citizens vote for candidates whom they believe can deliver services. They also want to be sure that the services are directed to them. When they feel that candidates do not meet these conditions, they choose to stay home.

Voters see candidates who are connected with, or are "willing to work with," the state as being able to deliver. Thus, for instance, a 2006 Algerian survey found that 64.2% of respondents cast their ballots for the "helpful candidate" (Benstead and Lust-Okar 2006). Similarly, a 2003 survey by the Center for Strategic Studies (CSS 2003) found that more than two-thirds of Jordanian respondents voted for candidates who "work effectively with government."

In contrast, voters choose not to vote for candidates who have shown themselves unwilling to cooperate with the incumbent elites. Thus, for instance, a Jordanian voter argued: "I came to seek a job from the deputy of our district. He told us that the government does not listen to them these days . . . I wonder why the deputies oppose the government. They should comply with and obey the government's policies so that we can take our rights, because it is up to the government to pass anything. Frankly speaking, I will not elect anyone unless the government approves of him because we want to survive" (Khaled, quoted in Kilani and Sakijha 2002, 59). Voters also want to ensure, however, that the parliamentarians will deliver the services to them, not others. In many cases, given the importance of kinship ties, voters prefer candidates who are from their own family or tribe. The Jordanian CSS survey in 2003 thus found that more than a third of voters cast their ballots for a candidate who was a member of their tribe or family, and almost half (49%) voted for a candidate with whom they had close personal ties. In other cases, emphases are placed on whether or not the candidate is a committed *ibn al-balad* ("son of the community").[10] The goal is the same, however: voters want to elect parliamentarians who can and will deliver services to them.

Voting for services is not unique to authoritarian regimes, but the extent to which it overshadows concerns with ideology, policymaking, and elite turnover may be. Recognizing the limited role that parliaments play in policymaking, and even more so in replacing the existing elites, voters pay little attention to political parties and party platforms. When asked if they considered party membership in choosing their candidate in the 2003 Jordanian elections, only 13.38% of respondents stated that they supported their candidate, in part, because he or she was in the Islamic Action Front (the major Islamist party in Jordan), and only 6.27% supported their candidate because he or she was a member of another political party (CSS 2004). For the vast majority of Jordanians, party membership was not an issue.

Perhaps even more surprising is the extent to which party membership and platforms are insignificant factors determining voting in dominant-party states. Only 5.8% of Algerian respondents stated that they cast their ballots for candidates with "a good program." Similarly, in a detailed study of Fatah infighting during the 2005 municipal elections, Dag Tuastad (2008) demonstrates how Fatah leaders recognized that it was credible commitment to service provision, not party platforms, that would determine their success or failure in the elections, and Samer Shehata (2008) shows similar dynamics in Egypt.

Understanding authoritarian elections as competitive clientalism yields insight not only in whom voters elect but also in which citizens choose to go to the polls. Voting in the parliamentary elections of authoritarian regimes is not compulsory. Indeed, as Table 9.2 shows, turnout in the latest parliamentary elections ranged from a low of 23% in Egypt to nearly 90% in Tunisia. Moreover, there is great variation across districts, with some registering turnout rates as low as 7% (LCPS 2003, 15).

Individuals will abstain from voting when they believe there is nothing to gain from participating in elections. Given the authoritarian nature of the governments and the limited role of legislatures, some believe that voting simply is not relevant. Asked why they do not vote, they say that "elections are not useful in this political system," or "elections are a fraud."[11] Not surprisingly, election turnout in the early elections following announcements of liberalization or the reintroduction of multipartism tends to be higher than subsequent elections. Across the region, voter turnout tends to decline over time.

Table 9.2 Turnout in recent MENA parliamentary elections

Country	Year of election	Election round	Turnout (% of registered voters)
Algeria	2002		46.2
Bahrain	2002		52
Egypt	2005		23
Jordan	2003		58.8
Kuwait	2006		80
Lebanon	2005	1	28
		2	43
		3	55
Morocco	2002		51.6
Palestinian Authority	2006		77.7
Syria	2003		63.5
Tunisia	2004		86.4

Sources: LCPS 2003, 15; International IDEA 2009.

Citizens are also less likely to vote if they believe their candidates cannot deliver services. In Jordan, therefore, where individuals of Palestinian origin have historically had tense relations with the incumbent rulers, turnout in elections is lower than in areas where voters—and their representatives—have traditionally not had close relations with the government (Lust-Okar 2006a). In Iran too, candidates from outside the government have lower voter turnout (Tezcur 2008). Voters, believing that their candidates can deliver neither *wasta* nor policies, prefer to stay home.

Citizens are also less likely to vote if they believe their representative, while able to provide *wasta*, will not do so for them. Consequently, turnout in rural areas tends to be higher than that in urban areas. This pattern is evident in the Iranian, Egyptian, and Jordanian parliamentary elections (Lust-Okar 2006a; Lust-Okar and Masoud, in progress; Tezcur 2008). These findings stand in contrast to some of the common wisdom, which suggests that voters will use elections to push for greater democratization. In actuality, more conservative voters are likely to go to the polls, reproducing, rather than undermining, the authoritarian regime.

Candidates

Individuals who either have developed, or can anticipate developing, close relations with the state are the most likely to enter electoral races, while those who are most opposed to the regime will abstain. Moreover, in their campaigns candidates emphasize their personal relations to the ruling government, and their ability to provide services, not party platforms and hotly debated policy issues.

Importantly, the majority of candidates in the Middle East finance their own campaigns, often at astounding expense. This is partly because of the potential financial gains that successful candidates can reap from their position. Again, Shehata (2008, 100–101) nicely argues: "The money that candidates spend getting elected are recovered through the benefits of holding office; the money spent on political campaigns, at least in part, becomes a business expense." Indeed, in Egypt, candidates will spend millions of pounds to run in campaigns, despite a legal campaign limit of 70,000 LE (approximately US$12,300) in a country where the average GNP per capita is less than 9,000 LE per year (approximately US$1,500) (Shehata 2008). This is true elsewhere as well. In Jordan and Syria, for instance, I found that candidates generally finance their own campaigns, often drawing extensively on their own personal funds, at sums that both candidates and observers agree are many times the average annual income.

Understanding elections as a business investment in a competition to serve as an intermediary helps explain what types of elites choose to run in elections. Those who are most opposed to the authoritarian nature of the regime are also the most unlikely to enter the race. This is partly because they see running in elections as legitimizing and supporting a nondemocratic regime. For reasons I will describe shortly, they also recognize that they are likely to lose if they choose to run. Voters do not elect candidates whom they perceive as unable to work with the government (Lust-Okar 2006a). Thus, running in elections is both ideologically distasteful and a poor investment for ardent opponents of the ruling government.

Rather, elites enter the race when they believe they can win, or at least when they can raise their social prestige through campaigning. Consequently, a Jordanian survey of candidates found that candidates entered the race at the encouragement of family, friends, and the tribe. Encouragement by political party elites and government officials to enter the race were much less important (Lust-Okar 2008.) Moreover, candidates who are members of parties other than the ruling party often choose to run as independents, deemphasizing their party affiliations. Recent elections in Palestine and Egypt, where a large number of Fatah and the National Democratic Party (NDP) members ran as independents, demonstrate the extent to which service provision and individual connections dominate party affiliation and platforms in elections.

Candidates also emphasize their ability to deliver services and their willingness to do so. In Jordan, candidates are more likely to discuss their tribal ties and family relations than their political platforms. Similarly, in Egypt, even candidates who are committed to discussing the legislative and oversight roles of the parliament recognize that services, not legislative records, interest voters (Shehata 2008).

Elections can be expensive enterprises, but they also have relatively low barriers to entry. Political parties remain weak and unable to play an important role in coordinating among potential candidates. Rather, elites need to expect that the votes of their personal supporters are enough to achieve victory; in elections with large numbers of candidates, individuals with a relatively small number of supporters can win the race. In Jordan, on average, seven to eight candidates have contested each seat in the four elections since 1989 (Hourani et al. 2004, 198). This number of candidates per seat remained high (and the parties continued to be weak) despite changes toward a more majoritarian electoral law. In Iran more than 5,000 candidates campaigned for 290 seats in the 2000 parliamentary elections (Esfandiari 2003, 124), and in Egypt 5,133 candidates ran for the 444 parliamentary seats (Shehata 2008).

Managing Elections

Ruling elites can manage elections with relative ease. Elections are fundamentally about access to state resources—not about changing the rules of the game through a process of democratization—and the logic driving both candidates' and voters' choices tends to reproduce the regime. Moreover, because of this, ruling elites can shape elections through institutional mechanisms, rather than by relying primarily on repression.

Incumbents can fashion district maps that funnel resources (and parliamentary seats) to the districts which contain traditional supporters of the ruling elite. Thus, in Jordan, we find that districts are drawn such that they disproportionately favor areas of predominantly East Bank Jordanians (Lust-Okar 2006a, 2008). Similarly, the 2000 electoral law governing Lebanese elections under Syrian influence was "mainly to ensure that Syria's supporters would reach Parliament, irrespective of their religion" (Haidar 2005). Anecdotal evidence suggests that Saddam Hussein's autocracy in Iraq engaged in similar manipulation. Through districting, the government pushed seats and the opportunity to gain access to state resources toward supporters of the authoritarian regime.

Electoral rules also shape outcomes in the ruling elites' favor. In Jordan, the palace weakened the Islamic Action Front (IAF) by decreeing a one-person, one-vote clause in the electoral law in 1993. The law reduced the number of votes per person from the number of seats in the district to a single vote, favoring conservative forces over the opposition. Even in Egypt, where the Supreme Court has a degree of latitude and has ruled in favor of opposition parties challenging electoral laws, ruling elites have managed to draft new legislation that essentially maintains the dominance of the ruling NDP. The precise rules, and the resulting distribution of power among parliamentary forces, may vary across authoritarian regimes. Indeed, monarchies are more likely to prefer rules that lead to the fragmentation of power, while dominant-party states seek to maintain the ruling party's dominance (Lust-

Okar and Jamal 2002). In both cases, however, competitive clientalism gives voters and candidates rational incentives that enable ruling elites to use election laws to manage outcomes.

Despite these important differences, the fundamental lesson remains: in the absence of fiscal or political crises, state elites are able to rely primarily on electoral institutions to shape electoral outcomes. When this tactic appears to fail—as happened in the 2005 Egyptian elections—ruling elites can turn to repression. Amr Hamzawy and Nathan Brown (2005) explain how Egypt had to "resort to clumsy tools" to guarantee continued NDP dominance:

> Independents who had defeated NDP candidates were rushed into the party. In districts where opposition candidates were strong, police were used to surround polling stations to prevent voters from reaching the polls. Journalists covering voting were physically attacked. Supervising judges who publicly criticized official behavior were threatened with prosecution, while the perpetrators of violence were allowed to act unimpeded. The result was something of a schizophrenic election: The campaign itself saw freer discussion and media coverage, limited but real willingness to accept some domestic monitoring, discrete arrangements for international observers, and the creation of at least the form of an independent election omission. But as the extent of the Brotherhood's strength became clear, the gloves came off. By that time, only the crudest of tools were left to produce the regime's desired outcome. Far more thuggery and manipulation were necessary than was healthy to protect the regime's reputation.

Yet, such occasions are striking because they are rare. The experiences of Iran, Jordan, and Syria are much more common: fraud, repression, and government intervention in elections exist, but on a limited scale (Esfandiari 2003; Lust-Okar 2006a). Ruling elites manage electoral outcomes predominantly through institutions and the logic of competitive clientelism, which is inherently biased toward returning conservative, pro-regime parliaments.

Prospects for Democratization by Elections in Hegemonic Regimes

Not only do elections in hegemonic authoritarian regimes fail to push the transition process forward, but they also tend to reproduce the incumbent regime. They create political dynamics that undermine public support for institutions and individuals associated with democracy. They also provide a more efficient mechanism for distribution of patronage, allowing incumbents to remain in power at a lower cost. Only in the presence of economic or political crisis are these elections likely to serve as mechanisms by which transitions take place, with at least the possibility of democratization.

Undermining Pro-Democratic Forces

The limited space for policymaking in hegemonic authoritarian regimes means that elections are more frequently contests over access to state resources than debates over policy. Voters recognize this, casting their ballots for those who can best deliver services. Parliamentarians know this as well, seeking to maintain good relations with the government, meeting constituents' needs, and sometimes enriching themselves in the process. Consequently, elections based on the logic of competitive clientelism foster public disillusionment with democratic institutions.

Citizens develop a cynical view of parliament, seeing parliamentarians at worst as a body of privileged pawns, willingly supporting incumbents' policies in return for personal enrichment, and at best as ineffective. Opposition elites who do run in elections, and particularly the few who win seats, are often seen as accepting (and benefiting from) the system. Moreover, parliamentarians, unable to make policy, become part of the patronage network, providing selective benefits.

Parliaments are also weakened by low incumbency rates. Turnover rates of parliamentarians are typically more than 75%. For example, in Iran, only 83 of 275 parliamentarians returned in 1992, and fewer than 60 of 290 parliamentarians returned in 2000 (Kayhan, cited in Tezcur 2008). In Jordan, only 19 of the 110 members elected in 2003 were returnees from the 1997 parliament, and only 20 of the deputies who won in 1997 elections were returning from the 1993 parliament (Hourani 1998, 204).

The high turnover is the outcome of weak parties, high candidate entry rates, and patronage-based voting. It is much easier for candidates to promise (or voters to expect) that they will receive selective benefits from their parliamentarian than it is for the parliamentarian to distribute selective benefits to all of his constituents. The resulting disappointment with incumbent parliamentarians coupled with the large numbers of candidates translates to high numbers of wasted votes. In fact, according to the Jordan Parliament Elections Web site, more than 60% of the ballots in Jordan's 2003 parliamentary elections were cast for candidates who failed to win seats (www.electionsjo.com).

Similarly, elections in hegemonic authoritarian regimes tend to weaken political parties and undermine opposition leaders. Parties come to be seen as personalistic cliques, focused on their own interests. Fewer than one-fifth of Algerians surveyed in 2006 believed that the parties served the people's interests, compared with 79% who believed that they served the leader's interests (Benstead and Lust-Okar 2006). Similarly, only 12.8% of Jordanian respondents in a CSS survey (2004) believed that parties served the people's interests, while 49.1% believed they served the party leaders and 35.3% did not know.

Citizens also view parties as unable to field candidates effectively or influence government. For instance, fewer than one-fifth of Jordanians believed their parties had been somewhat or very successful from 1992 (when Jordanian parties were legalized) until 2004. Moreover, 84% of respondents believed that no parties were capable of forming a government in Jordan, while fewer than 5% of respondents named a party they believed capable of forming the government (CSS 2004).[12] Similar attitudes were expressed in Morocco, where the palace, recognizing the crises of weak parties in the 1990s, sought to shore up the opposition parties (Lust-Okar 2005a). Even in dominant-party states, the public does not view parties as successful. In Algeria, only 5.5% of respondents in a 2006 survey believed political parties were "very successful," 49.6% saw them as somewhat successful, and 36.9% saw them as not very successful (Benstead and Lust-Okar 2006). In Egypt, when asked about the importance (not the success) of political parties, 54.5% of respondents in an al-Ahram survey saw them as important and 24.5% somewhat important. Even here, however, 21% of respondents believed that parties in a state dominated by the ruling NDP party believed that political parties were not important (al-Ahram 2000a).

Not surprisingly, then, citizens are not interested in joining political parties. In Jordan, the 2004 CSS survey found that only 1.3% of respondents were or planned to become a member of a political party.[13] Similarly, in Egypt, two surveys conducted by al-Ahram in 2000 found that only 4.7% and 5.4% of respondents claimed to be members of a political party, surprisingly low given the role of the NDP (al-Ahram 2000a, 2000b).

As a result of weak party support, political parties tend to splinter into even weaker offshoots. Political party activists understand that most voters cast their ballots on the basis of a candidate's profile, not the candidate's party affiliation. Thus, when party elites find themselves in conflict, members find it easy to leave and form a new party. The costs of defection are low, since the party label is of little value and most parties have minimal funding. Islamist parties appear to be an important exception to this rule, probably because they control significant resources and they focus on social issues, which parliament is given more power to influence. More frequently, however, weak parties become even weaker and less effective through a series of splits and splinters (Lust-Okar 2001).

Lowering Costs of Rule

Elections not only help to undermine pro-democratic forces, but they also provide an efficient mechanism for the distribution of patronage that lowers the cost of rule. Elections allow elites an opportunity to vie with each other over access to state resources; in addition, the frequency of turnover in the legislatures gives those who remain outside the legislature the hope that they can win in the future, even if they have lost today. As a result, elections co-opt potential counter-elites even without distributing benefits to them today and therefore gain support for the authoritarian regime.

Elections also provide an important mechanism that links the countryside to the capital. For rural populations, which may otherwise find it difficult to have links to the center of power, elections provide a way to gain access to patronage networks. Not surprisingly, then, rural dwellers are much more likely to vote than their urban counterparts. For the ruling elite, elections provide an efficient mechanism for patronage distribution. They can find and reward local elites, even in the absence of detailed information about social networks in the countryside.

Finally, autocrats may receive a "democracy dividend" for holding elections. The international support for holding elections increased after the end of the cold war, although it is certainly not available to all countries. Syria, for instance, has had a difficult time gaining kudos from the international community for holding elections. Egypt and Jordan, in contrast, received international support for holding elections, even though these elections arguably did not move Egypt and Jordan any closer to a full democratic transition than did elections in Syria.

The Potential for Authoritarian Breakdown

Generally, the very support that the international community gives to incumbent elites following the initiation or expansion of elections will also keep them in power. This does not mean that elections can never be mechanisms of transition in hegemonic authoritarian regimes. However, elections are likely to promote regime transitions only when they are held in the context of declining political and economic resources.

The reason for this is simple. The stability of elections in hegemonic regimes depends on the ability of ruling elites to deliver resources. Voters cast their ballots for pro-regime candidates and potential candidates choose whether or not to run as pro-government candidates, based on whether or not they believe the ruling elites will continue to monopolize resources and are secure in power. If the incumbents become unable to deliver or if the government appears vulnerable for political reasons (e.g., defeat in war, economic crises), voters and candidates may defect, and the elections become much more contested. This possibility is entirely consistent with the findings of Valerie Bunce and Sharon Wolchik (Chapter 10) that elections (if exploited by opposition coordination) can push toward democratization.

In the absence of such shocks, however, we can expect that elections will help shore up hegemonic authoritarian regimes. Parliament serves as an arena of patronage distribution, not as a locus for producing legislation or engaging in struggles over democratization. Elites who are only moderately opposed to or supportive of the existing regime choose to run in elections, while more radical opponents abstain. Moreover, parliamentarians often become invested in maintaining the status quo, including the need for *wasta*. For many parliamentarians, a move away from patronage functions and toward policy-making roles would only serve to weaken their influence. Elections may, in the face of a precipitous decline in state resources or extraordinary political crises, provide a focal point around which opposition forces may rally. Yet, in the absence of such crises, elections in hegemonic authoritarian regimes are unlikely to serve as a potential mechanism for democratization.

CHAPTER TEN

Oppositions versus Dictators

Explaining Divergent Electoral Outcomes in Post-Communist Europe and Eurasia

Valerie J. Bunce and Sharon L. Wolchik

In this volume, Staffan Lindberg, Axel Hadenius and Jan Teorell, Philip Roessler and Marc Howard, and Andreas Schedler explore the relationship between elections and democratic performance. While there are some differences of opinion about whether the very repetition of elections invests in improved democratic performance, there is agreement on one issue: democratic performance seems to be quite sensitive to the electoral calendar (also see Bunce 1994, 2007; Fish 1998). As a result, the key question before us is specifying both when and how elections contribute to democratic change.

This chapter seeks to identify some of the mechanisms involved by comparing two sets of electoral episodes in post-Communist Europe and Eurasia.[1] The first group is composed of eight elections that led to the defeat of authoritarian leaders and the victory of more democratic political forces. The cases in this group are Romania (1996), Bulgaria (1997), Slovakia (1998), Croatia (2000), Serbia (2000), Georgia (2003), Ukraine (2004), and Kyrgyzstan (2005). The second set is composed of six elections in which the opposition mounted a strong challenge to dictatorial rule but failed nonetheless to win power. The electoral episodes falling into this category are the 2003 and

2008 elections in Armenia; the 2003 and 2005 elections in Azerbaijan; and the 2001 and 2006 elections in Belarus.[2]

Several aspects of this comparison make it particularly illuminating with respect to teasing out the relationship between elections and democratic development. First, as we will argue in greater detail below, these elections did not just have contrasting outcomes. They also featured contrasting patterns of democratic change after the elections. Second, all the cases analyzed in this chapter are drawn from the same region—a region that, among other things, shares a Communist past and began to confront at roughly the same time the possibility of both a radical and a simultaneous transition to completely new political and economic regimes. There are also a number of less obvious similarities across our two sets of cases that help us eliminate some plausible explanations for success and failure. For example, with the exceptions of Bulgaria and Romania, all of the states being analyzed are new, having arisen from the dissolution of the Soviet, Czechoslovak, and Yugoslav states from 1991 to 1992. All else being equal, new states are less likely than more established states to support democratic development, given differences, for example, in state capacity to extract resources, monopolize coercion, and define and defend boundaries. In addition, as we will discuss in greater detail below, there are a variety of structural and institutional factors, such as level of economic development, economic performance, regime type, and degree of corruption, that are well-represented on both sides of the electoral divide and that are, as a result, limited in their explanatory power. Perhaps the most surprising example is the range of regime types that served as sites for the defeat of dictators. Put simply: while dictators may be easier to dislodge in more democratic settings (though even in these contexts reelection of authoritarian leaders has been the norm), they can also be defeated in relatively authoritarian contexts. Thus, there seem to be relatively elastic regime parameters on the electoral defeat of dictators in the post-Communist region—a conclusion that contrasts to some extent with the conclusions of Jason Brownlee and Andreas Schedler in this volume (and also see Brownlee 2007a).

Our comparison also includes two more "controls" that are helpful for locating the sources of electoral stability and change. One is the fact that in 10 of our 14 electoral confrontations between authoritarians and the opposition, public protests played a critical role. Such protests have been linked to democratic change in several recent studies (Ackerman and Karatnycky

2005; Bunce 2003; Hadenius and Teorell 2007; as well as Andreas Schedler's contribution to this volume). The complication is that such protests took place in *all* of the failed cases but in only half of the successful ones. Protests arose primarily because of widespread perceptions that authoritarian incumbents or their anointed successors tried to steal the election—though in the Bulgarian case from 1996 to 1997, large-scale demonstrations played a different role by bringing down the Communist-led government and forcing new elections that brought the liberal opposition to power (Ganev 2007; Petrova 2007).

Second, every electoral episode analyzed in this chapter featured a united opposition (though this is less true of the 2008 Armenian presidential election). Indeed, this was a primary consideration when selecting our "negative" cases, because the presence of a united opposition in an election differentiates "serious challenges" to authoritarian rule from elections where the opposition collaborates with the ruling government, runs lackluster campaigns, or stands on the sidelines. Unity of the opposition is rare in these settings, as it is in most regimes that fall in between the extremes of democracy and dictatorship, and a unified opposition has been identified as a key factor—if not the key factor—accounting for the defeat of dictators in regimes that tolerate, but also discourage, if not sabotage, political competition.[3] Moreover, there are competing interpretations of why a united opposition is so important for electoral turnover. Does a united opposition "cause" electoral turnover, or does unity itself reflect expanded optimism about the prospects for winning power?[4]

Our analysis is divided into five parts. In the first section, we highlight similarities and differences between our two sets of cases, focusing on indicators of democratic change after elections. We then examine several plausible explanations for contrasting electoral outcomes that do not vary consistently between our two groups of cases. In the next two sections, we discuss factors that seem to differentiate well between successful and failed attempts to defeat dictators: regime vulnerability and implementation of what we term the "electoral model." While the first factor refers to regime weakening as a result of some combination of poor economic performance, withdrawal of support for the regime by powerful international allies, and leadership violation of political norms, the second factor refers to a new approach to winning elections that solved many of the collective action problems that had long prevented citizens from supporting the opposition and the opposition from winning both a significant number of votes and political office. In conclusion, we discuss several implications of our findings by returning to the key question motivating this volume: What are the conditions under which elections contribute to democratic development?

Electoral Change and Democratic Development

We begin by noting that the contrast between our two sets of electoral outcomes also translated into contrasts in democratic performance after the elections. Table 10.1 provides a summary of democratic performance in the 14 post-Communist states in our study before and after the elections of interest in, first, the failed cases of electoral change and, second, the successful cases. Several aspects of this table need to be highlighted. One is that the political impact of electoral turnover varies among our successful cases. This outcome is hardly surprising, given differences in political context between, for example, the relatively democratic nature of Romanian, Slovak, and especially Bulgarian politics on the eve of pivotal elections in these countries, where the key issue was either consolidating a democratic project already relatively elaborated by defeating former communist presidents or, as in Slovakia, ending a dangerous de-democratizing episode and, on the other hand, the far more authoritarian politics of Ukraine, Georgia, and especially Croatia, Serbia, and Kyrgyzstan. Yet, even taking these differences into account, it is still striking that the two relatively authoritarian polities in the group that were also emerging from years of warfare—Croatia and Serbia at the end of the 1990s—show dramatic democratic improvements after their breakthrough elections in 2000.

Another important pattern in this table is not just the absence of democratic improvements in the failed cases but indeed some democratic deterioration following the electoral episodes (and see Brownlee 2002). As our interviews with participants suggested, the failure of democratizing elections had a number of consequences that strengthened authoritarianism. In particular, these elections alerted authoritarians to the costs of "tolerating" electoral competition (given, for example, public protests). They also provided ample opportunities for authoritarian incumbents and their allies to identify and harass the opposition and their supporters and gave authoritarians the information they needed to recalibrate their patronage networks (Lust-Okar 2004, 2006a, and her chapter in this volume; Bunce and Wolchik

Table 10.1 Elections and democratic performance in 14 post-Communist European and Eurasian states

		NIT		CS		IM		EP		Corruption	
		Before	After	Before	After	Before	After	Before	After	Before	After
Failed cases											
Armenia	2003	4.83	5.09	3.50	3.50	4.75	5.38	5.50	5.75	5.75	5.75
	2008	5.68	NA	3.50	NA	5.68	NA	5.75	NA	5.75	5.75
Azerbaijan	2003	5.59	5.75	4.50	4.63	5.68	5.88	5.75	6.18	6.25	6.25
	2005	5.55	5.97	4.48	5.13	5.68	6.18	5.88	6.50	6.25	6.25
Belarus	2001	6.25	6.38	6.00	6.68	6.75	6.75	6.75	6.75	5.25	5.38
	2006[a]	6.59	6.68	6.75	6.50	6.75	6.75	6.88	7.00	5.89	6.25
Successful cases											
Bulgaria	1997[b]	3.90	3.57	4.00	3.75	3.75	3.50	3.25	2.50	NA	NA
Croatia	2000	4.36	3.54	3.50	2.75	4.88	3.50	4.25	3.25	5.25[c]	4.50
Georgia	2003	4.46	4.90	4.00	3.50	3.68	4.18	4.75	5.00	5.38	5.88
Kyrgyzstan	2005	5.67	5.68	4.50	4.50	6.00	5.75	6.00	5.75	6.00	6.00
Romania	1996	NA	3.90	NA	3.75	NA	4.18	NA	3.25	NA	NA
Serbia	2000[d]	5.67	4.52	5.18	3.50	5.13	4.00	5.25	4.25	6.25	5.75
Slovakia	1998[e]	3.80	2.71	3.25	2.25	4.25	2.25	3.75	2.00	NA	3.75
Ukraine	2004	4.82	4.34	3.68	2.88	5.50	4.25	4.25	3.38	5.88	5.75

Sources: Freedom House, *Nations in Transit* (New York: Freedom House, 1997–98, 2000–2007).

Note: The assessments in this table are two-year averages, for two years before the electoral breakthrough and two years after the breakthrough. For example, for Armenia in 2003, the scores for 2001 and 2002 were averaged for the "before" entry, and the scores from 2004 and 2005 were averaged for the "after."

Nations in Transit's democracy, civil society, independent media, electoral process, and corruption scores are an average of political rights and civil liberties scores, with 7 indicating most repressive and 1 indicating most free.

NIT = Nations in Transit democracy score; CS = civil society; IM = independent media; EP = electoral process

[a] Scores for "after" include results from 2007 only; the scores for 2008 were not yet available. [b] Score for 1997; scores for 1995 and 1996 not available. [c] Scores for 2000/1999; scores for 1998 not available. [d] Scores for 1999/2000; score for 1998 not available. [e] Score for 1997; score for 1996 not available.

2007c). Once the votes were counted, moreover, the very fickle international community that promoted democracy was free to shift its focus to elections taking place in other countries. Just as international democracy promoters often consider elections to be key indicators of democratic development, so their support for free and fair elections has the advantage of being far less controversial than intervening in the domestic politics of foreign countries to promote democratic change (Bunce and Wolchik 2008a, chaps. 3–4). The interpretation of regime "hardening" after failed efforts to use elections to promote democratic change is made even more convincing by the cases of Slovakia and especially Kyrgyzstan, Serbia, and Ukraine, where in the years leading up to the pivotal elections, incumbent authoritarian regimes had become more, not less authoritarian.

It seems fair to conclude, therefore, that successful challenges to authoritarian rule contributed to democratic improvements. While we would not argue that elections "produce" democracy, especially given variations in the electoral effects noted on Table 10.1, we would suggest that a necessary condition for democratization is the removal of dictators from office. In this sense, elections can be defined as a mode of democratic transition for the simple reason that they are well-defined political episodes that hold the promise of improving subsequent prospects for democratic change (Lindberg 2006a and Chapter 1 in this volume). While elections do not guarantee democratic improvements, neither do the other two commonly cited modes of transition—pacting and mass mobilization (Jones-Luong 2002; Karl 1990). Moreover, in the post-Communist region as a whole, the best predictor of democratic improvements is the election of the democratic opposition—an argument that is less tautological than it sounds, given the emphasis in the earlier transitions literature on the importance for future democratic development of electing former allies of authoritarian leaders, such as Suarez in Spain, to bridge dictatorship and democracy and to reassure authoritarians that democratic change would neither destabilize the country nor eliminate them from the political game (Bunce 2003; also Bunce 1994, 1999; Fish 1998).

Structural and Institutional Factors

We now turn to the puzzle of explaining different electoral outcomes. In Table 10.2, we have provided a summary of a number of factors that would logically provide insights into the puzzle of why some countries became

Table 10.2 Structural and institutional comparisons in 14 post-Communist European and Eurasian states

	GDP per capita (US$)							
	1995	Year prior	Economic growth (%)	Border conflicts	FH scores	Voice and accountability	Presidential power	Corruption
Failed cases								
Armenia	522.2	740.3	11.4	Yes	4/4	−0.52	16	5.75
Azerbaijan	312.9	760.5	11.2 / 26.4	Yes	6/5	−0.82	18	6.25
Belarus	1035.4	1042.8	4.7 / 9.9	No	6/6	−1.35	21	5.25
Successful cases								
Bulgaria	1563.1	1257.2	−3.25	No	2/3	+0.09	1	NA
Croatia	4029	4371.1	0.8	No	4/4	−0.29	9	5.25
Georgia	534.6	741	5.1	Yes	4/4	−0.58	13	5.50
Kyrgyzstan	330.6	434.5	7.0	No	6/5	−0.96	16.4	6.00
Romania	1564.1	1564.1	5.5	No	4/3	NA	6	NA
Serbia	1730.4	2319.2	0.05	Yes	5/5	−1.11	NA	6.25
Slovakia	3615.7	3935	5.35	No	2/4	+0.28	4	NA
Ukraine	721.5	1053.3	7.2	No	4/4	−0.66	13	5.75

Sources: European Bank for Reconstruction and Development, "Economic Statistics and Growth," www.ebrd.com/country/sector/econo/stats/index.htm; Freedom House, "Comparative Scores for All Countries from 1973 to 2006," www.freedomhouse.org/uploads/fiw/FIWAllScores.xls; Freedom House, *Freedom in the World 2008*, www.freedomhouse.org/uploads/fiw08launch/FIW08Tables.pdf; Daniel Kaufmann, Aart Kraay, and Massimo Mastruzzi, "World Governance Indicators, 1996–2006" World Bank, http://info.worldbank.org/governance/wgi2007/home.htm; Freedom House, *Nations in Transit* (New York: Freedom House, 1997–98, 2000–2007).

Notes: GDP per capita scores include 1995 and the year prior to the election, or for countries with multiple elections, the year prior to the first election.

Economic growth scores are an average of the two years prior to the pivotal election. Where there were multiple elections, scores are reported for both.

Freedom House scores comprise political rights and civil liberties scores based on a scale of 1–7, with 1 indicating most free and 7 indicating most unfree. Scores are taken from the year prior to the pivotal election. In cases where there were multiple pivotal elections, the scores from the first elections are used.

Voice and accountability scores are measured on a scale of +2.5 to −2.5. Higher scores correspond to better governance. Where there were multiple pivotal elections, the scores from the first elections are used.

For presidential power, higher scores represent higher levels of power. Where there were multiple pivotal elections, the scores from the first elections are used.

Nation in Transit's corruption scores are an average of political rights and civil liberties, with 7 indicating most repressive and 1 indicating most free. In cases of multiple pivotal elections, the scores from the first elections are used.

more democratic and others did not. The figures in this table suggest, first, that there is no consistent pattern with respect to level of economic development, type of government (as indicated by presidential powers), level of corruption, or the location of the regime on a continuum defined by democracy on one end and dictatorship on the other—though all of the elections that failed to unseat dictators took place, we must recognize, in relatively authoritarian contexts. Moreover, wars generated by secessionist struggles and the instability, economic dislocations, and demobilization of the liberal opposition such wars tend to produce (Gagnon 2004) do not differentiate well between our two sets of cases, as both the "failed" elections in Armenia and Azerbaijan and the "successful" elections in Georgia and Serbia testify. In all four countries, there were prolonged conflicts between the center and secessionist regions or between the country and its neighbors, or in some cases both.

There is some support in this table for the argument that strong economic performance protects dictators from defeat; Armenia, Azerbaijan, and Belarus all experienced relatively strong economic growth in the years leading up to the elections examined. However, there are reasons to be skeptical about the explanatory power of this variable (Shephard 2007). One is that economic growth in both Slovakia and Croatia was relatively strong before the elections of interest. Another is that economic performance in Georgia and especially Ukraine—also "successful" cases—had improved substantially in comparison with the disastrous decade of the 1990s prior to the elections that brought the victory of the opposition. Thus, the "Putin principle"—the argument that citizens will embrace authoritarians if they bring order and growth after a prolonged period of disorder, economic decline, and more robust but chaotic democracy—does not seem to apply in a consistent way in our cases. In addition, as we saw in both Azerbaijan and Armenia in the 1990s in particular, poor growth can lead not simply to turnover in leaders but also to the rise to power of more, not less authoritarian politicians.

A final amendment to the economic interpretation is that, in the post-Communist context as in other regions where regimes have been in transition, the norm, even when the economy is failing, is for leaders in competitive authoritarian regimes to win one election after another. For example, if the economy were critical, three long-serving dictators in the region—Askar Akaev in Kyrgyzstan, Slobodan Milosevic in Serbia, and Eduard Shevardnadze in Georgia—would have lost power far earlier than they did. Especially in the last two cases, these leaders managed to stay in power when their economies, by many estimates, declined by approximately 30%.

As Table 10.2 suggests, structural and institutional factors fail to give us much causal purchase on why some elections defeated dictators, whereas others did not. However, there are two variables that seem to be more helpful. The first is regime vulnerability, and the second is implementation of what we term the *electoral model* of democratization. Put more concretely: we see electoral change as a two-stage process. In the first stage, successful challenges to authoritarian rule present themselves as political possibilities when there is widespread recognition among opposition leaders and the citizenry that incumbents (or their anointed successors, as in Ukraine in 2004) have become too dangerous, unaccountable, corrupt, or incompetent to remain in office.

What we see, in short, are defections from the ruling circle—by former allies and by ordinary citizens. However, the long tenure of incumbents, the resources at their disposal to manipulate elections, the difficulties for citizens of ascertaining whether their negative sentiments are widely shared and whether substantial numbers of other citizens will act upon them, and, perhaps most importantly, widespread skepticism about whether the opposition is worthy of support and capable of winning an election—all lead to the same problem. Citizens need to be *convinced* that authoritarians can be defeated, that the opposition is worthy of their support, and that voting for the opposition and using protests to defend the vote are actions that can and should be taken and that have a reasonable probability of success. Thus, it is one thing to argue that authoritarians are losing support and another thing to establish the necessary conditions for oppositions to win elections and take power.

It is precisely at the intersection between these two considerations—that is, the key distinction between regimes weakening and regimes falling—that the electoral model comes into play. As we discuss in greater detail below, the electoral model is a constellation of difficult, often tedious, and sometimes dangerous tasks that, if implemented by oppositions and citizens, increase the likelihood that authoritarians will be defeated at the polls and leave office. While varying in details from country to country, given differences in both local preparations and the constraints and opportunities presented by each political context, these tasks nonetheless have a common core: they pressure incumbent governments to reform election procedures and oppositions to collaborate in support of common candidates for office; build ties with organizations in civil society in order to pursue the common goal of holding free and fair elections; carry out large-scale voter registration and turnout drives; run ambitious nationwide campaigns that take opposition candidates throughout the country and that energize voters; expand the use of the media, public opinion polls, campaign rallies, marches, and various types of street theatre (where allowed); organize parallel vote tabulation (again, where allowed); and prepare for political protest in the event that authoritarians refuse to leave office (Bunce and Wolchik 2008a, chap. 4; Garber and Cowan 1993). Put more simply, the electoral model is distinctive in furnishing opposition parties, civil society groups, and citizens with three factors noticeably absent from previous elections: an electoral strategy for success, extensive citizen engagement in campaigns and voting, and optimism about the ability of oppositions and citizens to challenge authoritarian rule.[5]

Vulnerable Regimes

In one sense, all of the regimes examined in this chapter were at least potentially vulnerable, for the simple reason that they felt compelled to hold regular and at least semicompetitive elections. The leaders of each of these regimes, therefore, opened themselves up to the possibility of losing power (Brownlee, Chapter 5, this volume; Schedler 2006, and Chapter 7, this volume). Whether dictators did lose power in elections, however, seems to have depended in part, but only in part, on regime strength. Regimes, we must remember, can be vulnerable for a wide range of reasons, both objective and subjective.

Perhaps the most obvious threat to regime survival is economic hardship, which, as we argue above, was somewhat variable in the "success" cases but was certainly far less apparent in the failed cases, given, for example, very high rates of growth in both Armenia and Azerbaijan. Yet, the data in Table 10.2 fail to highlight some other aspects of the economic story. The first is that economic decline had generated enormous inequalities in the once quite egalitarian countries of Bulgaria, Georgia, Serbia, Kyrgyzstan, and Ukraine. There is also evidence that long-term economic decline was making it harder and harder for "patronal presidents," such as the leaders of Georgia, Serbia, Ukraine, and Kyrgyzstan, to maintain their networks of political support (Hale 2004, 2005, 2006). Indeed, this is one reason that it is precisely in these cases where we see the combination of unusually authoritarian leaders, popular mobilization against fraudulent elections, and electoral turnover; it is also the reason that Heydar and Ilham Aliyev of Azerbaijan, Alexander Lukashenka of Belarus, and Robert Kocharian and his designated successor, Serzh Sarkisian in Armenia, were able to withstand popular protests challenging their elections to office. What this argument does not explain, however, is why these elections and not earlier ones were so successful in unveiling the bankruptcy of patronage networks. Moreover, there is ample evidence from public opinion surveys that citizens were extremely concerned about economic issues not just, for example, in Georgia, but also in Azerbaijan—which, like most petro-states, failed to distribute widely the gains from rising oil prices and its strategic position with respect to the location of both pipelines and fossil fuel shipping.

Although economics no doubt played some role in weakening or protecting regimes, there were other factors, far harder to express in numbers, that differentiated between our successful and failed electoral contexts. One has already been suggested: the defection of key allies of the rulers. It was very important for the electoral breakthroughs in Georgia and Ukraine, for example, that former and quite popular cabinet ministers—Mikheil Saakashvili and Viktor Yushchenko—left the Shevardnadze and Kuchma governments, respectively, and became leaders of the democratic opposition. Moreover, several years before the 2003 election in Georgia, the ruling party attached to President Eduard Shevardnadze, the Citizen's Union of Georgia (CUG), disintegrated. This also happened in the case of the Croatian Democratic Union in the months following Tudjman's death and preceding the presidential and parliamentary elections in 2000. Serbia also saw the defection of key supporters, including the Serbian Orthodox Church, which had played a central role since the late 1980s in supporting Slobodan Milosevic as the defender of the Serbian nation. Milosevic's abuse of power and his failed drive to build a greater Serbia were good reasons for the church to defect. However, the youth movement, Otpor (Resistance), also played a facilitating role in moving the church toward the opposition. In Kyrgyzstan, future president Kurmanbek Bakiyev was fired as prime minister by Akaev in May 2002 after the 2002 protests, and later Prime Minister Felix Kulov, who was released from jail during the March 2005 protests, became an opposition leader after having served as the former head of the secret police and later as vice-president under Akaev. In all of these cases, former supporters of the ruling elite moved to the opposition camp after either being fired or leaving positions they had held under the incumbent.

By contrast, Azerbaijan, Armenia, and Belarus on the eve of their elections do not exhibit a similar pattern. The question then becomes, what caused defection of government allies? Here, the answer is more complex than economic considerations. One reason is the failure to institutionalize power (Levitsky and Way 2007; Silitsky 2005; Way 2005a, 2005b). The leaders of Azerbaijan, Armenia, and Belarus are distinctive in having devoted considerable energy to building political machines that penetrate the polity and the economy and that defend their powers. The same could not be said of either Milosevic or Shevardnadze in particular—which is remarkable, given their long tenure in office and their rise to power through the Communist party-state apparatus in the "old days."

Regimes are also weakened by changes in the international environment that involve either a withdrawal of external support for the ruling elite or growing pressures on the government for reform, including introducing or improving electoral practices. In Slovakia, Serbia, Georgia, and Ukraine, a wide range of actors—including the United States government and a variety of organizations supported by the government (such as the National Endowment for Democracy, the National Democratic Institute, and the International Republican Institute), the European Union, OSCE and ODIHR, and European and American foundations and nongovernmental organizations—provided substantial electoral assistance, while making it clear before, during, and after the election that free and fair elections were an extremely high priority. In Slovakia, where Vladimir Meciar's policies from 1994 to 1998 had resulted in the country's exclusion from the first round of NATO expansion, it was quite clear that future membership in the EU and NATO depended on his defeat (Fisher 2006; also Vachudova 2005). In Ukraine, the United States responded very quickly to the attempt by Viktor Yanukovych, Leonid Kuchma, and their Russian allies to steal the election. By the same token, during the summer of 2003, President George W. Bush sent James Baker to Georgia to press Shevardnadze to reform Georgian elections.

The Serbian case provides perhaps the most dramatic example of the importance of changing international support for both regime strength and electoral turnover. In the mid-1990s, with the war in Bosnia moving into its fifth year, the United States was seeking some way to forge peace. To do so,

Milosevic, like Franjo Tudjman of Croatia, was needed as an ally. Thus, the three-month-long Serbian protests of 1996–97, in reaction to Milosevic's failure to abide by local election results, did not receive much U.S. attention—or, for that matter, assistance. However, by the end of the 1990s, following the bombing of Serbia during the crisis in Kosovo, and with Dayton Peace Accords no longer a serious constraint, the United States redefined Milosevic as the problem, not the solution, with respect to Balkan stability. As a result, U.S. assistance to Serbia skyrocketed, more than tripling from 1999 to 2000 (Finkel et al. 2006) once Milosevic made the mistake of calling early elections and, even more surprisingly, making himself a candidate.

The United States and the European Union, as well as promoters of democracy from various countries in the post-Communist region, collaborated closely to defeat Lukashenka in Belarus, but failed to make much headway in 2006. Western support for free and fair elections and electoral change in Azerbaijan, however, was quite limited in 2003 and 2005—though overall democracy and governance assistance to Armenia, the third country where elections failed to unseat autocrats, was the highest on a per capita basis over the course of the transition of any country in the post-Communist region, save Bosnia, where high levels of assistance were connected to the Dayton Peace Accords (Bunce and Wolchik 2006a). U.S. support was joined, however, with uneven pressures on both Armenia and Azerbaijan to clean up their electoral processes. For instance, U.S. democracy promoters believed that further democratic change was unlikely in these two countries and that such change could be destabilizing (an argument that became easier to make with the victory of Hamas). They also believed that further progress on the democratic front in this part of the world was not so critical to U.S. interests, given, in the case of Azerbaijan, in particular, the combination of a border with Iran, oil and very recently discovered gas deposits, and the country's status as a transit area for pipelines connecting Central Asia to Turkey and the Black Sea.[6]

A final indicator of regime weakness is one that received considerable attention in our interviews but is very hard to nail down. What Milosevic, Shevardnadze, Kuchma, Akaev, and Meciar in particular shared—and what certainly distinguished them from leaders in countries where elections failed to bring about change—was a behavioral pattern leading up to the breakthrough elections that involved violating widely accepted norms for political behavior. The authoritarian leaders who lost power all went too far in the abuse of their powers—not just harassing the opposition and journalists, but also murdering them; relying on increasingly blatant interventions to prevent people from voting and to steal elections; introducing a series of constitutional changes that were widely viewed as self-serving and contrary to accepted political and constitutional practices; and beating up and jailing large numbers of young people (actions that were in stark contrast to the peaceful and often humorous protests mounted by such youth organizations as Otpor, Kmara, and Pora).

These actions produced, to use the language of the youth groups, a sense that "enough" is "enough" (*Kmara*); that "it's time" (*Vremena* in Serbian and *Pora* in Ukrainian); and that "he is finished" (*Gotov je*). Rising despotism, moreover, was linked in the public mind with desperation. It is often assumed that an increase in despotism, by making both opposition groups and citizens more fearful, dampens anti-government mobilization. However, as the Serbian, Ukrainian, Georgian, and Kyrgyz cases in particular remind us, despotic acts can encourage popular resistance—because of a widespread understanding that using extreme measures to safeguard power is a clear sign that the leader is losing both legitimacy and power (Francisco 2004; Lichbach 1998; Wintrobe 1998).

At the same time, while not true for Kuchma and the candidate he chose to succeed him, Viktor Yanukovych, for Akaev, Shevardnadze, and even Milosevic, the abuses of power running up to the election did not translate into an ambitious political campaign. This was particularly true of Shevardnadze, who was largely disengaged from the 2003 parliamentary elections in Georgia, despite clear indications that the opposition was unusually committed and capable. Moreover, in Croatia, Serbia, Georgia, and Ukraine, earlier protests and local elections had provided concrete evidence of popular dissatisfaction. Why did so many of these authoritarian leaders run lackluster campaigns? One reason was that there was no precedent in these countries for ambitious campaigns. Incumbents, in short, were merely behaving "as usual" in these elections, whereas the opposition was moving in new directions. Another reason is that all the incumbents seemed to assume, precisely because of their ability to weather so many challenges to their power in the past and the long history of fragmented and ineffective oppositions, that the most recent round of elections would play out in the same ways as earlier elections. A third consideration was also important, especially for Milosevic, Akaev, and Shevardnadze: long tenure in office can lead leaders to take their powers for granted, in part because they become captives of the very support networks they have constructed.

We see a very different story in the cases of Aliyev, Kocharian, and Lukashenka. While all three have clear records of abuse of power, these three leaders never took their power or opposition weakness for granted. They were active stewards of authoritarian rule, orchestrating electoral details ranging from control over voting processes and media to control over public spaces in anticipation of public protests. While we elaborate on this issue below, the key point is that each of these leaders assumed that power had to be won. In fact, in all three cases we see a history of electoral turnover during the transition—though this was also true, we must remember, for some of our success cases, including the turbulent politics of Georgia in the 1990s, along with Slovakia, Bulgaria, and Ukraine. In Ukraine, Kuchma and his hand-picked successor, Yanukovych, went to extreme lengths, including the murder of a journalist and the poisoning of Yushchenko, to silence critics and later win the 2004 election.

Regimes therefore weaken in a number of ways, and vulnerable regimes are those that combine at least several of the factors we discuss above—that is, economic stress, lack of institutionalization of their powers, defection of key allies, changing international pressures with respect to free and fair elections, despotic excesses, and an unwillingness to campaign for power. When these characteristics are combined, and especially when they occur in exceedingly corrupt ruling elites (as all of the countries in this study had; see Table 10.2), these factors have several important consequences for the regime's future. First, they lead to growing public dissatisfaction with the ruling government. By all accounts, the popularity of the leaders in cases where elections led to the defeat of the old regime had either declined significantly (in Bulgaria, Romania, Serbia, Croatia, Georgia, Kyrgyzstan, and Ukraine) or remained stable (in Slovakia), whereas in Azerbaijan, Belarus, and Armenia, Aliyev, Lukashenka, and perhaps Kocharian seemed to have been in a position to win elections even without manipulating them.[7] Second, vulnerable regimes generate not just growing resentment but also expanding optimism—on the part of the public, opposition groups, and civil society organizations.

While there is an increased possibility in vulnerable regimes that dictators will be defeated, such vulnerability does not lead necessarily or directly to breakthrough elections. Most obviously, the Bulgarian, Georgian, Serbian,

Kyrgyz, and Ukrainian regimes had been in serious trouble for many years, yet their leaders remained in power. Moreover, as already noted, all of these countries in the "success" category with the exceptions of Romania and especially Bulgaria had significant democratic deficits. Competitive authoritarian regimes in general and in the post-Communist region, along with the more democratic polities in place in Bulgaria and Romania on the eve of their elections, benefit from having considerable incentives and resources to protect themselves from electoral challenges. Even quite poorly performing autocracies tend to have a solid group of supporters who depend upon the incumbent government for protection and money and who, more generally, may also prefer the devil they know to the devil they do not know; they may also fear the prospects of both political instability and legal actions against them, should the dictator lose power. These considerations explain in part why all of the breakthrough elections except those in Georgia were relatively close.

At the same time, opposition groups in all of these countries have had a long history of being urban-centric, divided, incompetent, and disorganized; their leaders have often been tainted by past association with the rulers; the parties have in some cases been in power, only to demonstrate their inability to govern effectively (as in Bulgaria and Slovakia); and they have been quite distanced from—and often disinterested in—either the electorate or nongovernmental organizations supporting democratic change. This is a major reason that the fall of most authoritarian regimes has been followed not by democracies but, rather, by authoritarian polities (Hadenius and Teorell 2007). At the same time, given the poor track record of both the ruling government and the opposition, citizens have had few reasons to vote or, if they have voted, to necessarily prefer the democratic opposition over the incumbents or other parties independent of either group.

All of this leads to a simple conclusion. Vulnerable authoritarian leaders in competitive authoritarian regimes or even in largely democratic polities are unlikely to lose power through elections until the nature of the elections themselves changes.

Implementing the Electoral Model

This is precisely what happened in the pivotal elections of 1996 to 2005 in Bulgaria, Romania, Slovakia, Croatia, Serbia, Georgia, Ukraine, and Kyrgyzstan. More precisely, in these eight countries we find full implementation of what we termed earlier the electoral model—specific tasks and approaches that the opposition and citizens can undertake to increase the likelihood that authoritarians will be defeated at the polls. The model was less fully implemented in elections at the beginning of the wave, such as those in Bulgaria and Romania, where aspects of the electoral model were first introduced, and in the country that served as the final site for the wave of electoral change, Kyrgyzstan, where, as is typical of diffusion dynamics, demonstration effects, or the power of examples elsewhere, outpaced local actions (Beissinger 2002; Bunce and Wolchik 2007c, 2008a). However, in the elections that have taken place in Armenia, Azerbaijan, and Belarus since 2000, core elements of the electoral model have been missing, including, for example, rigorous election monitoring, ambitious political campaigns and get-out-the-vote and voter registration drives, preparations for protests that included consultations with security forces prior to protests, and the generation of a second set of election results to compare with the official results offered by the incumbent government. What we saw, in short, was a radical break with "elections as usual" in the first group of countries and far more continuity with the electoral past in the second group.

The electoral model requires, first, the creation of a unified opposition. Thus, opposition leaders must put aside their own individual ambitions and desires for power to work together and, in most successful cases, agree on a common candidate to support. Such agreement is generally extremely difficult to achieve—not just because of the ingrained habits of going it alone, but also because expanded opportunities for electoral success can have the effect of feeding individual ambitions while starving collaborative ventures, a dynamic opposite the one offered by van de Walle (2006). In the case of Serbia, for example, Zoran Djindjic agreed to support Vojislav Kostunica after public opinion polls in the summer of 2000 showed that citizens trusted Kostunica, who had never been involved in any way with the Milosevic government and who, in contrast to Djindjic, had spent the entire Milosevic years in Serbia. In Kyrgyzstan, collaboration took another form. Leaders of the opposition agreed to cooperate to divide up the spoils—in this case, top offices.

In most of our successful cases, moreover, but not in any of our unsuccessful cases, the opposition had experimented earlier with various forms of collaboration that had produced some partial successes. For instance, we see cooperation among members of the opposition in local elections in Serbia, Croatia, Ukraine, and Georgia leading up to the "big" election, as well as joint protests in Ukraine, Georgia, and Serbia that forced the governments to back off on unpopular policy initiatives. These developments demonstrated the benefits of cooperation while reassuring citizens that the opposition parties could both work together and achieve some results. At the same time, ample evidence had accumulated before the pivotal elections to convince opposition leaders that the absence of cooperation was costly—as in the "Ukraine without Kuchma" and "Arise, Ukraine!" campaigns in 2002 and 2003, and in the defeat of the parties that had formed a broad coalition government in mid-1994 in Slovakia but failed to run together in the September and October elections. These earlier episodes of contestation also gave the activists who would later emerge as leaders experience with mobilization and in many cases solved another problem. In all of these cases, until these experiments with challenging the regime there had been little contact between the political opposition and the nongovernmental sector; the opposition was embroiled in its own world, and the third sector had long defined itself as a force operating outside of the political sphere, in part because that definition was an understood condition for external funding.

The electoral model also provided a powerful answer to the question of how to overcome the apathy and alienation of citizens (IRI 2006; Tucker 2007). By mounting energetic election campaigns and using innovative techniques such as door-to-door campaigning and citizens' fora, political leaders sought to energize the population; increase turnout, especially of those voters public opinion polls indicated would support democratic change; and create a sense of both possibility and optimism. The effort to create the belief that change was not only desirable but possible was supported by campaigns organized by nongovernmental organizations. In all of our successful cases except for Krygyzstan, nongovernmental organizations, often including youth organizations or actions directed at mobilizing youth, played an extremely important role in empowering ordinary citizens to take part in politics (Bunce and Wolchik 2007b, 2007c; Kuzio 2006). The model provides a rationale that allowed NGO activists, many of whom were adamantly opposed to being involved in partisan politics, to see political activity aimed at ensuring free and fair elections and ousting autocratic leaders not as a betrayal of their mission but integral to it.

The electoral model also included efforts to force the ruling elite to agree to improvements in the quality and transparency of electoral procedures to reduce fraud in candidate selection, construction of voter rolls, and vote tabulation. Typically preparations were made to use exit polls, parallel vote tabulation, and both internal and external election monitoring, when the incumbent government allowed this. The model also involved exploitation of media openings and institutional loopholes favorable to the opposition where these existed. In Serbia, for instance, the opposition made good use of a law that required election results to be posted outside each precinct, and in Ukraine the relatively independent Supreme Court called for new elections.

In the more authoritarian states, where incumbents were expected to "steal" the elections, the electoral model also included preparations for mass demonstrations to protest the fraudulent results and call upon the incumbents to resign.[8] These preparations included discussions with leaders of the army and security forces in Serbia, Ukraine, and, to a lesser extent, Georgia (and even in Croatia, where such actions proved to be irrelevant) to make sure they would not fire on peaceful protestors. Civil society groups were also often involved in preparation for and in the actual protests (and see Trejo 2004, on temporal ties between the electoral calendar and protest cycles). In Ukraine, for example, the advance planning for street protests after the first round of elections involved not only the Yushchenko campaign staff but also the leaders of Pora and other civic society groups as well as the financial backing of some of Ukraine's oligarchs. In Georgia, activists from the Liberty Institute, the Georgian Young Lawyers Association, Kmara, and other NGOs participated in the march on parliament that led to Shevardnadze's resignation as president.

As this discussion illustrates, the electoral model is very demanding. It requires a good deal of those who wish to employ it in terms of hard, often tedious work, coordination, and willingness to take risks. In those cases where the opposition failed to oust autocrats, some aspects of the model were at least partially applied—most obviously, the unification of the opposition. But important aspects were missing. Much of the opposition in Belarus in 2006, for example, united to support Milenkevich just as several opposition groups had supported a common candidate in 2001. Youth groups, including Yeni Fakir, attempted to stage rock-the-vote campaigns and other actions to appeal to young voters in Azerbaijan in 2005. But other critical elements of the model were not implemented. Thus, the opposition made little headway in Belarus, Armenia, or Azerbaijan in changing electoral procedures to prevent fraud or in gaining acceptance for election monitoring. Nor was there, in these three countries, parallel vote tabulation, which would have provided independent data on election results for the opposition that these groups could then use to confront the rulers, demonstrate fraud to the electorate, and mobilize significant public outrage. This was a critical difference between our "failure" and "success" cases because citizens, especially in new democracies, tend to associate democracy with free and fair elections and to resent, as a result, clear evidence that elections were stolen (Dalton, Shin, and Jou 2007). Moreover, in our failed cases, there were no get-out-the-vote campaigns or massive electoral campaigns that moved out of the capital or the main cities to reach voters in rural areas and smaller towns. When 20,000 citizens showed up in Minsk to protest voting fraud in the 2006 elections in Belarus, for instance, opposition leaders were both surprised and unprepared to sustain the momentum of the initial protest. Similarly, when part of the opposition continued its protest of electoral fraud in Armenia in 2005 beyond the time allowed by the government, there was no coordinated plan by the opposition to use this protest to mobilize large numbers of citizens to support the demonstrators, who were subsequently beaten by the police and, in many cases, arrested.

The importance of the electoral model is that it undermines the ability of anti-democratic leaders, whether operating in relatively democratic or relatively authoritarian settings, to win elections and, if losing, to stay in power. On the one hand, it reduces the control that authoritarian leaders have over the media, political campaigns, voter registration and turnout, tabulation of the vote, and sometimes even the security forces. On the other hand, the electoral model invests in a more effective opposition, one that is able to convince voters to take the necessary steps of registering to vote, voting, supporting the opposition, and, if necessary, defending their votes in the streets. Thus, the electoral model has the potential of solving two collective action problems: the difficulties oppositions have in coordinating their campaigns and in focusing their attention on actions that have direct electoral payoffs and the difficulties citizens have in believing their votes will count, in supporting the opposition, in demanding free and fair elections, and, more generally, assuming that others will act in similar ways. Thus, the electoral model plays a key role in linking regime vulnerability to electoral change—a linkage that was by no means easy to establish, as so many of the elections that failed to unseat dictators, whether in earlier electoral rounds in our successful cases or in our failed cases, amply demonstrate.

Conclusions: Elections and Democratization

In our comparison of 14 electoral episodes in post-Communist Europe and Eurasia from 1996 to 2008, two factors emerged as critical in explaining why dictators were defeated in some of these elections but not in others. The first is whether the regime was vulnerable—for example, as a result of economic difficulties and growing evidence that leaders were becoming more isolated at home and abroad, as well as more despotic and desperate. The second is whether the opposition and civil society organizations, in clear contrast to previous practices, carried out what we have termed the electoral model of democratic change. Both sets of factors seem to be critical. While the first opens up the possibility that rigged but competitive elections could lead to the defeat of dictators, the second removes important and long-standing obstacles to such an outcome by creating a more united and more competitive opposition and by increasing the likelihood that voters will vote, vote for the opposition, and where necessary, defend their preferences in the streets.

We can draw several implications from our comparison about the mechanisms underlying the relationship between elections and democratic change. First, because the unity of the opposition was evident in both the successful and the failed cases and because both failed and successful breakthrough elections were followed by massive political protests, we would counsel caution when attributing too much explanatory power insofar as democratic development is concerned to either a united opposition or elections that generate sizeable protests (but see Schedler and Roessler and Howard in this volume, along with Howard and Roessler 2006; van de Walle 2006, 2007). In particular, we would suggest that other factors in addition to the unity of the opposition must be included in any argument that explains the success of electoral challenges to authoritarian rule. Moreover, there is limited evidence to support the claim that it is a chance for victory that leads oppositions to coalesce. It is not just that the opposite is equally likely to occur; it is also that pressures on the opposition from civil society organizations and from the donor community play an extremely important role in determining whether opposition groups will decide to cooperate and whether they will continue collaboration for the duration of the electoral campaign.

Our findings also contribute to discussions about competitive authoritarianism. Here, our study supports through a comparative case study the statistically based arguments made by Philip Roessler and Marc Howard in this volume that such regimes are, in comparison with other types of polities, unusually unstable in the particular sense that they tend to move back and forth over time along the continuum anchored by democracy on one end and dictatorship on the other, and that these fluctuations seem to be particularly common in the post-Communist region. Moreover, it is clear from their study and from our comparative exercise that elections have played a critical role in this dynamic. Here, however, we need to be clear. As we have shown, elections in competitive authoritarian regimes contribute to *both* democratic and authoritarian development. What seems to differentiate the two is whether authoritarians, or their anointed successors, lose power or win. Elections, in short, can serve as both an investment in and a pretext for consolidation of authoritarianism (and see Ellen Lust-Okar and Jason Brownlee in this volume) as well as facilitating democratization.

At the same time, however, we found less support for what seems to be a relatively obvious claim and one that has empirical foundations—that is, that more authoritarian settings are less hospitable to democratizing elections. Here, we would argue that while fully authoritarian regimes such as that in Uzbekistan, for example, have the ability to block democratizing elections, if only because competition is limited to parties supporting the Karimov regime, even in relatively authoritarian settings elections can produce democratic breakthroughs—as the cases of Serbia and Croatia demonstrate unusually well (and see Ackerman and Duvall 2004). This is not just because vulnerable regimes can be ended through implementation of the electoral model, but also, more generally, because agency—in this case, the availability of a successful model; the hard, creative, and often tedious work of opposition parties and the third sector; and the willingness of citizens to demand democracy while taking a chance on the opposition—can transform a political setting well-situated to defend authoritarianism into one more supportive of electoral change.

In this sense, the interest in making more and more fine-grained distinctions among competitive authoritarian regimes may miss the larger point that was implied in earlier arguments about the instability of competitive authoritarian regimes (Epstein et al. 2006; Levitsky and Way 2007; Roessler and Howard in this volume). These regimes are not very "regime-ish" in that they often feature, especially when power is more personalized than institutionalized, remarkably elastic parameters on the kinds of political shifts that can occur over time. They can become more competitive not simply because they are designed to be more competitive but also because of how the electoral process plays out. While the accumulated weaknesses and strengths of the regime matter, so do the shorter-term consequences of more effective challenges to its political monopoly. Such challenges, however, are the exception, not the rule—as indicated by the high rates of reelection of dictators in regimes that tolerate some, if only limited, political competition for office. Moreover, as in the cases of Azerbaijan, Armenia, and Belarus, vigilant leaders can keep themselves fully abreast of the threats posed by the successes of the electoral model in their neighborhood. This is a primary reason, for example, why the wave of electoral change may have ended in the post-Communist region, at least for the time being.

CHAPTER ELEVEN

Judicial Complexity Empowering Opposition?

Critical Elections in Armenia and Georgia

Bryon Moraski

Scholars and policymakers alike tend to agree on democracy's electoral components: elected officials, free and fair elections, inclusive suffrage, the right to compete for elected office, freedom of expression, freedom of association, and access to alternative sources of information (see Dahl 1989, 222). Yet, as many of the previous chapters in this volume suggest, the relationship between elections and democratization is more complicated. While casual observers may equate elections with democracy, the first part of this book emphasizes that the two are distinct. For example, Roessler and Howard depict the boundary between liberal democracy and electoral democracy as a "glass ceiling" for many states transitioning from authoritarian rule, even though both are characterized by regular, as well as free and fair elections. Lindberg, meanwhile, finds evidence to indicate that elections in Africa are themselves "a powerful force of political change," yielding direct improvements in the quality of political freedoms and civil rights. The generalizability of these conclusions remain in doubt, however. Not only do McCoy and Hartlyn find little evidence of such a "democratization by elections" dynamic in Latin America, but Teorell and Hadenius find that elections have relatively small effects on democratization when the number of cases is expanded temporally as well as spatially. Rakner and van de Walle, in the second part of this volume, depict the viability of opposition parties as an essential element of democratic accountability. Yet, the absence of durable and competitive opposition parties in Africa reflects, among other things, political frameworks on the continent that concentrate significant power in the presidency while providing little opportunity for the opposition to groom politicians or gain policymaking experience.

Naturally, the contention that elections can spur democracy must confront a myriad of intervening variables. For neo-institutionalists (March and Olsen 1989), choosing among the plethora of institutional combinations could prove instrumental to democracy's prospects. Not surprisingly, though, a lack of consensus also exists as to how ancillary institutions assist "democratization by elections."[1] For example, O'Donnell (2004, 37) notes that in addition to electoral accountability, democracies must have societal accountability, in which groups, and possibly even individuals, can mobilize the legal system to place demands on the state or government.

Among the ancillary institutions that frame the backdrop of elections, courts stand out both for being prominently mentioned in the literature and for receiving relatively little attention. Political scientists have directed a substantial amount of energy toward understanding how electoral systems, executive-legislative arrangements, and federalism shape democratic politics (Amoretti and Bermeo 2004; Bunce 1999; Coppedge 1994; Cox 1997; Duverger 1954; Filippov, Ordeshook, and Shvetsova 2004; Fish 2006; Lijphart 1994; Linz 1990; Mainwaring 1993; Rae 1967; Taagepera and Shugart 1989). Comparativists have increasingly analyzed how the composition, organization, and operation of the judicial branch shape the rule of law in transitioning states (Eisenstadt 2004; Epstein, Knight, and Shvetsova 2001; Ginsburg 2003; Helmke 2002, 2005; Herron and Randazzo 2003; Staton 2006), but Shapiro and Stone Sweet (2002, 137) submit that social science scholarship on the judicial branch remains far behind the "global expansion of judicial power" identified by Tate and Vallinder (1995a).

Given the willingness of incumbents in the "gray zone" between democracy and dictatorship (see Carothers 2002b; Diamond 2002) to tilt the field of electoral politics in their favor while facing the strategic dilemma between the benefits and the costs of manipulation (see Schedler in this volume), it seems reasonable to assume that the judiciary may be critical both as an actor and as a institutional structure in the struggle over whether elections should be allowed to have democratizing power. Accordingly, an investigation into how democracy's proponents utilize courts and judges in seeking to dislodge the incumbents of an entrenched illiberal regime represents a fruitful endeavor. This topic is conspicuously absent in the budding literature on electoral revolutions in the post-Communist countries (Anabele 2006; Beissinger 2007; Bunce and Wolchik 2006a; D'Anieri 2006; Kuzio 2005b; McFaul 2005; Mitchell 2004; Tucker 2007; Way 2005b). To address this topic, the chapter capitalizes on recent developments in the post-Soviet region to conduct a most-similar-systems analysis of the role that judicial design can play during electoral revolutions.[2] This chapter also supplements Bunce and Wolchik's contribution in this volume by highlighting a crucial factor in two of their cases: one found among their class of successes (Georgia) and one among their failures (Armenia).

I begin with a review of some of the key literature linking judicial activism and judicial independence. I then examine whether variations in judicial design and reform in Armenia and Georgia help account for the different outcomes in the two cases. There are two main findings. First, electoral revolutions take on a legal character in states with a surprisingly low level of judicial independence. Second, whether a judiciary is used effectively depends on aspects of institutional design rarely considered in the literature, such as the number of judicial access points available to those claiming fraud. I am not arguing that court action is the sole, or even the primary, explanation for regime change in places like Georgia, Kyrgyzstan, or Ukraine.[3] Rather, the goal is to determine whether certain judicial configurations provide better opportunities than others for those pursuing democratization by elections.

Mobilizing Courts

Even in the advanced industrialized countries of the West, the willingness of courts to act as defenders of individual rights is a relatively new phenomenon. For much of its history the U.S. Supreme Court focused on business disputes, often supporting property-rights claims of businesses and wealthy individuals. While the court emerged as a guardian of individual rights in the late 1960s, as late as the mid-1930s, "less than 10 percent of the Court's decisions involved individual rights other than property rights" (Epp 1998, 2). To a large extent, existing literature links the ability of courts to protect individual rights to judicial autonomy and review. After 1949, as dozens of authoritarian and totalitarian states transitioned to democracy, the use of judicial review increased notably, and today, "the rights and review tandem is an essential, even obligatory component of any move toward constitutional democracy" (Shapiro and Stone Sweet 2002, 136).

Still, the spread of constitutional review is somewhat controversial and paradoxical. It is controversial because, as democratic theorists observe, the presence of a judiciary empowered and willing to strike down national policies adopted by popularly elected bodies—even in the name of preserving fundamental rights—smacks of quasi-guardianship (Dahl 1989, 188). It is paradoxical because, as Shapiro and Stone Sweet (2002, 142) point out, the decision to grant courts the power of judicial review comes from those whom it will constrain, raising questions such as why politicians would freely give the judiciary the authority to control their activities. Shapiro and Stone Sweet offer what they call a "naively straightforward" answer. When a constitution is designed, designers cannot negotiate rules that govern all possible contingencies. Since the interests of parties (and even the parties themselves) will evolve and change over time, review mechanisms ensure that constitutional bargains and commitments made during a constitution's founding stick. Thus, an independent judiciary with the power of judicial review resembles "a fierce dog kept confined during business hours and set loose to roam the junkyard all night attacking all and any interlopers" (164). But not all courts bite their "masters" should they venture into forbidden territory. So the relevant question for studies of countries in transition is what factors differentiate an obedient judiciary from one that is willing and able to take action against any and all violators?

Most accounts consider independent courts as those most likely to protect the constitution and the people from a ruling elite bent on overstepping its legal bounds. Although judicial independence is a slippery concept,[4] at its core judicial independence entails the resolution of conflicts by a neutral third party. By utilizing judges with no interest in the case and no bias toward the parties, all citizens—regardless of their wealth or position in society—stand on equal footing before the law and possess the opportunity to protect their rights and security. Similarly, when the government is a party to a dispute, courts can be entrusted to arrive at a principled position only if they are not biased in favor of the government. Therefore, judges should be shielded from threats, interference, or manipulation that could lead them to rule unjustly in the state's favor. Larkins (1996) calls the former aspect of judicial independence, impartiality, and the latter, insularity. When elections become strategic processes of contested political reform, judicial autonomy can reasonably be assumed to be a critical factor determining when elections have democratizing effects, and when they do not.

Constitutional provisions promoting impartiality and insularity are common in transitioning states. Their quality and effectiveness, however, vary substantially. Russell (2001a, 13–23) divides encroachment upon judicial independence into four categories: structural, personnel, administrative, and direct. Structural encroachment occurs when governmental bodies outside the judiciary create, modify, or threaten to modify judicial institutions as a way to shape adjudicative outcomes. Examples include court packing, stripping courts of their jurisdiction, and altering judicial jurisdictions. Personnel encroachment happens when governmental bodies use appointment, remuneration and removal, as well as promotions, transfers, training, professional evaluations, and disciplinary action short of removal, to influence judicial decisions. Administrative encroachment entails manipulating the assignment of judges to cases and courtrooms, the sittings of courts, and court lists so as to attain favorable legal rulings. Finally, direct encroachment on judicial independence involves blatant attempts to influence judges. They range from death threats to bribery to personal meetings behind closed doors with the intent of swaying members of the judiciary.

Of course, judges may not behave independently even when the formal relationships that exist between the judiciary and other political institutions permit such behavior (Russell 2001b, 6–7). Likewise, judges may defy the odds and act independently even where the formal structures enabling such autonomy are absent (see especially Helmke 2002, 2005). Yet Russell (2001b, 8) submits that emerging democracies are better off making constitutional provisions for judicial independence than not: Since one has little influence over the minds and behavior of individual judges, scholars and policymakers should focus their efforts on institutional mechanisms that impede relational violations of judicial independence. Similarly, Dodson and Jackson (2001, 255) argue that where behavioral manifestations of judicial independence are rare, the reforms that are most likely to make a difference are structural ones.[5] Dodson and Jackson promote methods of selection that, as much as possible, limit partisan intrusion into judicial appointments; provide relatively long tenures with adequate remuneration and legal safeguards against retaliation for unpopular decisions; set conditions for removal from office for misconduct that are well grounded in the procedures of due process; provide adequate court resources in the form of professional staff support, facilities, and finances; and establish a legal and political culture supportive of the rule of law, particularly the notion that all individuals and groups are under the law and will abide by judicial decisions (256–57).

As Dodson and Jackson's list suggests, the ability of institutional designers to empower or constrain the judiciary is multidimensional. Indeed, the final point—the existence of a legal and political culture supportive of the rule of law—highlights the degree to which manifestations of judicial independence depend upon state-societal relations. Epp (1998) makes this point more explicit. He argues that an overlooked component of the rights revolution in the United States was the support structure for legal mobilization. While constitutional guarantees of individual rights and judicial independence—as well as the existence of activist judges and increased rights consciousness—facilitated the rights revolution, "sustained judicial attention and approval for individual rights grew primarily out of pressure from below" (2). Pressure from rights-advocacy organizations, rights-advocacy lawyers, and new sources of litigation financing were instrumental in democratizing access to the U.S. Supreme Court and leveling the legal playing field. Likewise, McCann (1994) demonstrates how legal discourses and tactics act as crucial tools for social movements seeking to alter the practices of those in power.

While most existing studies on judicial power depict it either as being provided from above or as being expanded from below, Woods (2008) notes that these approaches, in isolation, fall short. She argues that levels of judicial power reflect both the *supply* of judicial tools and powers (like judicial review) from elected politicians as well as the *demand* for greater judicialization of politics, often thanks to the legal mobilization of social movements. Understanding judicial power and independence as a reflection of supply and demand meshes quite nicely with O'Donnell's (2004) view that higher-quality democracy requires both horizontal and societal accountability. The role of the courts in election disputes not only depends on whether constitutional provisions supply courts the power to oversee elections, but also on mobilized and assertive groups or individuals in society willing to take claims of election fraud to the courts.

O'Donnell and Schmitter (1986, 65–70) make this point clear when they compare political transitions to a multilayered chess game. While the analogy is far from perfect, its limitations prove illustrative and instructive. Unlike chess, the rules structuring political transitions are in flux and are malleable. The players and teams not only seek to establish rules that work to their advantage, but at least in the short run, these actors may attempt to change the rules of the game as play continues, producing a "nested game" (Schedler 2002b). Also, while chess is a single game in which two players compete for complete domination, political transitions more closely resemble a tournament of matches and multiple boards played among multiple teams composed of multiple players who may cooperate, enjoy mutual victories, and even switch sides. While O'Donnell and Schmitter depict much of the game of transition politics as being played among elites, they acknowledge that resurrecting civil society can change the game's trajectory: A strong popular upsurge may introduce new, possibly impulsive players, thus complicating the carefully laid plans of the incumbents.[6] Meanwhile, Schedler (Chapter 7 in this volume) emphasizes that where transitions have given way to electoral authoritarian regimes, the incumbents face a strategic dilemma between benefits and costs of manipulation. Such strategic calculations should be significantly influenced by the existence of an autonomous and impartial judiciary.

To the extent that players in political transitions are willing to cheat whenever they can (O'Donnell and Schmitter 1986, 66) and that some willingness to cheat continues on at least until democracy is consolidated, one should not be surprised to see players asserting any leverage they possess over those empowered to enforce the rules of the electoral game. In other words, the prospects for democratic consolidation depends not only on consensus that elections should be used to distribute political power (i.e., electoral accountability) but also on the presence of electoral referees with enough power and independence to preserve the elections' integrity (horizontal accountability). And in the game of democratic politics these referees are often courts and judges. At the same time, society's willingness to utilize these referees (i.e., societal accountability) during election disputes may prove to be watershed moments in democracy's evolution. It is at these points in history that more authoritarian players may decide to (a) abide by the rules of the game, thus conveying legitimacy upon the democratic process; (b) exert undue pressure on the electoral referees, thus undermining the prospects for, or at least popular faith in, free and fair elections for the foreseeable future; or (c) kick over the chessboard(s) and reestablish a more authoritarian system of government. Recent electoral disputes in the post-Soviet region provide the opportunity to explore these dynamics more closely.

Courts in Post-Soviet Countries

While both McCann (1994) and Epp (1998) focus on the relationship between courts and rights in the common law states, the collapse of Communism in Europe led to a proliferation of civil law states. The difference between common law and civil law states is an important one. The emphasis of the former on precedent creates a political and legal culture that is more likely to spawn the judicialization of politics. On the other hand, those states that give pride of place to monolithic codes and stress norms of deference to legislative interpretation impede judicial intervention and creativity.[7] Yet, legal action, even in the most favorable of institutional settings, often depends on the existence of structures in civil society that support private-party litigation. Soviet annihilation of independent civil society (see among others, Bernard 1993; Di Palma 1991; Javeline 2003; Kubicek 1999; Skilling 1983) should be a major impediment to the judicialization of post-Soviet politics. Thus, an investigation of the judiciary's role in post-Soviet electoral disputes provides a novel opportunity to consider the relationship between judicial design and judicial activism. Any factors that can facilitate the judicialization of electoral politics in this rugged terrain should be of notable import to other countries around the globe.

Among the post-Soviet states, Georgia, Ukraine, and Kyrgyzstan are obvious candidates for analysis, as each of these three countries experienced so-called "colored revolutions." In addition, the judiciaries emerged as noteworthy players in the Rose, Orange, and Tulip Revolutions, respectively. The Supreme Court of Georgia nullified the results of the country's 2003 parliamentary elections; the Supreme Court of Ukraine ordered a repeat election for its country's 2004 presidential runoff; and the Kyrgyz Supreme Court declared its country's February to March 2005 parliamentary elections invalid. In each instance, nationwide protests accompanied claims of electoral fraud, with popular protests turning violent in Kyrgyzstan.

Among these three cases, I focus on Georgia's Rose Revolution because it was the first to reveal that an electoral revolution could produce regime change in the post-Soviet space. And while these electoral revolutions surely learned lessons from revolutions elsewhere—with the Rose Revolution benefiting from graduates of the 2000 Serbian election (Bunce and Wolchik 2006a, 12)—diffusion dynamics were arguably lower in Georgia than in Ukraine and Kyrgyzstan. Focusing on Georgia is also useful because it permits comparisons with a strikingly similar case with a different outcome, Armenia.

Armenia and Georgia are both former Soviet republics located in the Caucasus. They both are largely Christian and are of roughly similar size.[8] In addition, civil society and democracy had been developing at roughly the same pace in the two states. Both Armenia and Georgia scored the same—receiving aggregate scores of 4.2—on the 2002 NGO Sustainability Index for Central and Eastern Europe and Eurasia.[9] Meanwhile, Freedom House labeled both as "partly free" in 2002, giving each scores of 4 on both its civil liberties and political rights dimensions. Equally important, Armenia experienced a controversial election in the same year as Georgia. Widespread allegations of vote rigging followed the 2003 reelection of Armenian president Robert Kocharian. Calls for Kocharian's resignation led thousands of demonstrators to take to the streets. But, unlike in Georgia, the Armenian judiciary neither nullified the 2003 election nor did it call for a revote. And, in the end, claims of electoral fraud and mass protest did not produce a change of regime.

To what degree can the different outcomes in Armenia and Georgia be attributed to the design of the judicial branch? Based on preexisting research on post-Communist courts, one might conclude "not much." In fact, according to Smithey and Ishiyama's judicial power index (2000), Armenia possesses a much more powerful and independent judiciary than Georgia.[10] Armenia scores 0.83, while Georgia receives a 0.56 on a scale of 0 to 1.0, with 1.0 indicating a judiciary with all of the constitutional provisions identified by the authors needed to ensure power and independence. A detailed audit of the judiciaries in both states confirms this assessment.

The American Bar Association's Central European and Eurasian Law Initiative (ABA/CEELI) rates the institutional factors shaping judicial independence and judicial activism in Armenia and Georgia separately. In particular, the ABA/CEELI devised a judicial reform index (JRI) and has used the JRI to evaluate the judicial systems in the post-Communist region. The index is intended to assess aspects of judicial reform that should facilitate the development of an accountable, effective, and independent judiciary (ABA/CEELI 2002, ii). To evaluate these judicial systems, the ABA/CEELI presented 30 standardized statements to judges, lawyers, journalists, and outside observers with detailed knowledge of the system. After evaluating the responses, the organization gave each statement a score of positive, neutral, or negative. According to the ABA/CEELI: "Where the statement strongly corresponds to the [perceived] reality in a given country, the country is . . . given a score of 'positive' for that statement. However, if the statement is not at all representative of the conditions in that country, it is given a 'negative.' If the conditions . . . correspond in some ways but not in others, it [is] given a 'neutral'" (ABA/CEELI 2005, ii–iii).[11] Table 11.1 provides a summary of how the two states' judiciaries compare on 10 dimensions of judicial independence using 16 JRI statements that reflect the conditions commonly identified in the literature.[12]

As one can see from the table, judicial independence in both Armenia and Georgia is, at best, a mixed bag. Armenia's courts are neither sufficiently impartial, nor are they significantly insulated from external pressure. While the situation is better for Armenia's Constitutional Court, which is the key judicial actor in electoral disputes, even its independence suffers from areas of vulnerability. Neither the appointment process for Constitutional Court justices nor the existing judicial codes of conduct in Armenia ensures that the court will decide cases in an impartial manner. Thanks to the political situa-

Table 11.1 Comparison of institutional safeguards advancing judicial independence in Armenia and Georgia

Judicial characteristics	Armenia	Georgia
Impartiality of constitutional court selection	Questionable, but appointed by previous administration	Questionable, and appointed by incumbent administration
Criteria for constitutional court membership	Average qualifications	Minimal qualifications
Protection from external pressure	Medium to low	Medium to low
Code of ethics	Limited	Limited
Process for complaints against the judiciary	None	Exists but used improperly
Judicial transparency	Medium	Medium
Financial support	Underfunded	Underfunded
Judicial salaries for constitutional court justices	High relative to other public officials	Low relative to other public officials
Job security	Medium to high	Medium to high
Personal security	Low	Medium to low

Sources: ABA/CEELI 2002, 2005.

tion at the time, however, there are at least reasons to believe that the court was not biased in favor of the Kocharian camp during the 2003 electoral dispute. Specifically, Kocharian's predecessor, Lev Ter-Petrosian, not Kocharian, appointed the court. However, the financial position of the Constitutional Court in Armenia raises questions about whether its members were adequately insulated from political pressure emanating from the incumbent president. By comparison, Georgian judges actually experienced greater financial and professional insecurity in 2003 than did Armenian judges at the time. At the same time, the incumbent appointed the justices on Georgia's high courts, which should have yielded courts more likely to favor the incumbent government.

With this information in hand, then, the surprise does not appear to be why Armenia's judicial branch failed to contribute to regime change during Armenia's 2003 presidential elections but, rather, how Georgia's opposition was able to obtain a favorable ruling from the judiciary during its 2003 parliamentary election. Answering this question requires a detailed comparison of the legal maneuvers employed during these two disputed elections.

Contesting Elections in Court: Lessons from Armenia and Georgia

Schwartz (2000) finds that election issues are among the most common subjects on the docket of post-Communist constitutional courts. At the same time, he notes that in almost all of the countries of Eastern Europe, the constitutional courts are not given the discretion to refuse to issue a ruling on a case brought before them. The courts may devise ways to avoid a case, but in general they follow the Continental practice of deciding every question properly brought before them. And, in Eastern Europe, a large number of political actors possess the right to bring cases to their constitutional courts. In fact, actors with standing before Eastern Europe's constitutional courts are commonly "those with the greatest interest and best opportunity: members of the opposition, and other officials unhappy with the actions of other public officials, governments, or legislative majorities" (Schwartz 2000, 29).[13]

Armenia's 2003 Presidential Election

As in other post-Communist countries, in Armenia judicial review of the constitutionality of laws and government decrees operates separately. Armenia's nine-member Constitutional Court alone possesses judicial review powers. Of these nine members, the president appoints four members and the parliament (or National Assembly) appoints the remaining five (Constitution of the Republic of Armenia 1995, art. 99). The Court's jurisdiction includes "matters related to the constitutionality of law, National Assembly, government resolutions, orders and decrees of the president, and international treaties" (ABA/CEELI 2002, 1). According to Article 100 of the Armenian constitution, the Constitutional Court also has the authority to "rule on disputes concerning referenda and the results of presidential and parliamentary elections."

Leading up to the 2003 presidential election, standing before Armenia's Constitutional Court was severely limited. Only the president or one-third of the deputies sitting in the National Assembly had free reign to initiate cases before the Constitutional Court that challenged the constitutionality of laws (Constitution of the Republic of Armenia 1995, art. 101).[14] Due to these restrictions on standing, the Constitutional Court was relatively inactive from its creation in 1996 to 2002, rendering only 350 decisions (ABA/CEELI 2002, 2).[15] However, both presidential and parliamentary candidates have the constitutional right to bring disputes over election results to the court (Constitution of the Republic of Armenia 1995, art. 101), which means not only that Armenia's Constitutional Court is responsible for resolving election disputes but also that the natural litigants in such a suit have access to the court.

On March 5, 2003, the runoff to Armenia's presidential ballot occurred. Official results listed incumbent president Robert Kocharian as winning 67.5% of the vote and his challenger Stepan Demirchian, 32.5%. Not only did Kocharian's vote total prove to be the highest that any presidential candidate in Armenia had recorded since independence, but Western observers from the Council of Europe and the Organization for Security and Cooperation in Europe stated that balloting "fell short of international standards" (Danielyan 2003). In particular, controversy marked the two-week period between the two rounds of the presidential election. Roughly 200 Demirchian campaign aides were arrested, and the OSCE's Office for Democratic Institutions and Human Rights noted that state-controlled mass media outlets heavily favored Kocharian. Following the runoff, the Demirchian camp claimed that roughly 400,000 votes were "falsified in favor of the incumbent president" (Eurasia Insight 2003). Meanwhile, a report published in the newspaper *Aykakan Sha-*

manak claimed that as many as 600,000 ballots had disappeared the day before the runoff election. The Central Election Commission denied receiving any reports of stolen ballots, however (Eurasia Insight 2003). In an attempt to oust President Kocharian, the Demirchian-led opposition challenged the results before the Constitutional Court. The challenge coincided with ongoing street protests, including a march of an estimated 12,000 to 15,000 people marking International Women's Day (Hakobyan 2003).

The first round of the 2003 presidential election also was not without controversy. On March 14, the court ruled on complaints from first-round presidential contender Artashes Geghamian (ARKA News Agency 2003a). On March 19, the court asked the Central Election Commission to inspect a number of polling stations over the course of three days (ARKA News Agency 2003b). By March 25, the Constitutional Court's chairman, Gagik Harutiunian, issued the verdict that the plaintiff's side did not have sufficient grounds for the court to declare the first-round results invalid. He also announced that the court would begin hearing Stepan Demirchian's suit regarding the second round the following day (ARKA News Agency 2003c).

The results of Demirchian's case differed notably from that of Geghamian's suit. On April 16, even while upholding the results of the 2003 presidential election, the court also questioned the election's legitimacy. Specifically, the court noted that violations "that are incompatible with the further development of democracy" had occurred at different polling stations, both during the vote as well as during its tabulation (Khachatrian 2003). Moreover, it suggested that the controversy could be seen as a potential violation of Armenia's obligations under international treaties, such as the Universal Declaration of Human Rights. However, the court also ruled that the number of proven violations was not sufficient to warrant voiding the election, since Demirchian and his supporters could only document irregularities in fewer than 300 of the 1,864 precincts. So, while anecdotal evidence and popular reports indicated violations throughout the country and echoed concerns expressed by monitors from the Council of Europe and the OSCE, the court ultimately upheld the Central Elections Commission's decision to declare Kocharian victorious. Still, in an attempt to address the opposition's grievances, the court issued a nonbinding recommendation that a popular referendum be held on the election results. Not surprisingly, this tactic annoyed the opposition as well as the Kocharian camp (Khachatrian 2003).[16]

The decision by Armenia's Constitutional Court to recommend that a referendum be held on the validity of the 2003 presidential runoff led some opposition groups to conclude that the court had conceded, even if indirectly, that Kocharian's reelection was illegitimate. Demirchian himself submits that, by proposing a referendum as part of its decision, the Constitutional Court demonstrated that "even under pressure from the authorities, [it] could not reject the complaint" (interview with the author, June 2, 2008). Others at the time, though, like the anti-Kocharian newspaper *Aravot,* reacted to the decision with hostility. Following the decision, in a headline *Avarot* denounced the Constitutional Court as a "puppet of Kocharain" (Khachatrian 2003). In other words, Armenia's 2003 election dispute provides a striking illustration of how the question of judicial impartiality can take center stage in an election dispute, as well as of the potential for political suspicions to overshadow debates about the legal appropriateness.[17]

Georgia's 2003 Parliamentary Elections

Georgia, like Armenia, declared its independence from the Soviet Union in 1991 and adopted a constitution in 1995. In another similarity to Armenia, Georgia has a nine-member Constitutional Court that alone possesses judicial review powers.[18] Of these nine members, the president appoints three, the parliament chooses three (by a three-fifths majority), and the Supreme Court appoints three (Constitution of the Republic of Georgia 1995, art. 88). To be a Constitutional Court judge in Georgia, one only need be 30 years of age and have a university degree in law. Neither the Law on the Constitutional Court nor the Constitution stipulates that appointees have any legal experience.

The Supreme Court's role in the selection of Georgia's Constitutional Court justices differs markedly from the Armenian case, where only the president and parliament appoint justices. Presumably, the Supreme Court will ensure that some well-qualified justices find their way onto the court. Members of Georgia's Supreme Court, on the other hand, are nominated by the president and confirmed by a majority vote of parliament. They must be at least 28 years of age, be able to speak the state language, and have a university degree in law with at least five years of experience (ABA/CEELI 2005, 9–12).

Georgia's Constitutional Court has the authority to determine the constitutionality of laws, international treaties, and governmental actions as well as the power to "consider disputes connected with the Constitutionality of referenda and elections" (Constitution of the Republic of Georgia 1995, art.

89). Specifically, issues related to the constitutionality of the elections include the right to vote (art. 28), the right to compete for office (art. 49), and the scheduling and time of the elections (art. 50). Constitutional issues can make their way to the Constitutional Court through various routes in Georgia. The president or no fewer than one-fifth of the members of parliament may bring a case before the court. However, common courts also may seek a ruling from the Constitutional Court if a court finds, during the course of a hearing, that there is ample reason to believe a law or normative act contravenes the Constitution. In addition, the Plenum of the Supreme Court may ask the Constitutional Court to rule on the constitutionality of a normative act. Finally, the Public Defender of Georgia, or anyone whose rights and freedoms are violated, may file a claim with the Constitutional Court (ABA/CEELI 2005, 18–20). Thus, a very important distinction is that there were many access roads to the Constitutional Court in Georgia whereas there was only one in Armenia in 2003. This aspect of judicial design later proved crucial to the divergent outcomes in these two disputes.

McFaul (2005, 6) points out that one remarkable aspect of post-Communist electoral revolutions is "how few analysts predicted them." As Georgia's 2003 parliamentary election approached, corruption was rampant, growth in the private sector as well as foreign investment had slowed, and many public officials enjoyed privilege and wealth thanks to years in office under President Shevardnadze. So, while the president enjoyed substantial prestige on the international stage—often by defying Russia—and many foreign policy makers and diplomats seemed to accept the flawed electoral process in Georgia, Shevarnadze's domestic support eroded significantly after his 2000 re-election. In fact, members of Shevardnadze's camp broke with the president, forming the core of the opposition during the 2003 election. These members included the former and acting speakers of parliament, Zurab Zhvania and Nino Burjanadze, respectively, and former justice minister Mikhail Saakashvili (Mitchell 2004, 343). Even under ripe conditions, however, revolutions require agency. And, the deciding factor in Georgia's Rose Revolution was how the agents of the opposition acted (see also Bunce and Wolchik in this volume).

During Georgia's November 2, 2003, parliamentary elections there was ballot stuffing, multiple voting, polls being held open late, ballots not being delivered to certain polling stations, and voter lists that included the dead and excluded the living. Since pro-government forces controlled the Central

Election Commission (CEC) as well as the local and district-level election commissions, the opposition used parallel vote and turnout counts (under the auspices of the International Society for Fair Elections and Democracy, a Georgian election monitoring organization) to combat election fraud. Data from the group suggested that the CEC inflated support for pro-government parties in the aggregation of precinct-level results. The opposition also contended that among opposition parties, Saakashvili's National Movement was the decisive winner even though Burjanadze's and Zhvania's party, the Burjanadze Democrats, did not perform as well as expected (Mitchell 2004, 343).

On November 4, 2003, the opposition took to the streets, holding vigil in front Georgia's parliament and calling for the president's resignation. In response, pro-government blocs warned that the protests were destabilizing the country. President Shevardnadze, meanwhile, belittled the protests, saying he would not resign because of "a few hundred kids" (Mitchell 2004, 344) On November 14, however, the demonstration that began with anywhere from 500 to 5,000 protestors had swelled to over 20,000 people.[19]

Armed with the evidence collected by voting monitors and exit polls, the opposition used the court system to challenge the results of the elections. Opposition groups began by contesting the results of the Bolnisi election district—a stronghold of the pro-government's political machine—as well as the count of absentee ballots for Georgian voters living abroad. The Tbilisi District Court overturned both sets of results (Zullo 2003). Meanwhile, a district court annulled elections in Kutaisi, Georgia's second-largest city (Radio Free Europe 2003a). By November 17, courts had ordered repeat elections in nine districts (*Turkish Daily News* 2003). These decisions were critical because the opposition used them to challenge the CEC's November 20 confirmation of the parliamentary election results. Specifically, the opposition argued that the CEC confirmed the election outcome based on district results that had already been legally overturned, which made the confirmation itself illegal (Zullo 2003). Georgia's Supreme Court affirmed the opposition's stance on November 25, annulling the proportional representation portion of the election, which was responsible for allocating 150 of the 235 seats in the new parliament (Radio Free Europe 2003b).

Many members of the opposition hailed the Supreme Court's ruling as a victory not just for democracy but also for the judiciary. Saakashvili, in particular, was quoted as saying the decision "proves that judicial reform was a success. Of course there are still some problems, but it proves that we did the right thing in reforming the courts" (quoted in Zullo 2003). The fact that Saakashvili was intimately aware of how Georgia's judiciary operated prior to the Rose Revolution merits mentioning. Not only did he serve as a former justice minister under Shevardnadze, but he also helped initiate judicial reform in 1998 as a member of parliament (ABA/CEELI 2005, 38). Thus, the opposition's knowledge of the legal system helps explain its use at critical junctures in Georgia's Rose Revolution.[20]

Mitchell (2004, 344) describes Shevardnadze's attempt to seat the new parliament on November 22 as a vital turning point leading to his downfall. He points out that if Shevardnadze had succeeded, "the moment of opportunity would have passed because the new legislature would have immediately elected a new pro-government speaker," important because it is the speaker of parliament who becomes interim president in Georgia if the incumbent is incapacitated or resigns. Replacing the acting speaker of parliament, Nino Burjanadze, with a Shevardnadze supporter, then, would have made demands for the president's resignation following the flawed parliamentary election more or less meaningless. To preempt this, members of the opposition entered the parliamentary chamber and disrupted the first session. The opposition justified its entry, which otherwise might have been considered illegal, by citing their legal right to accompany the 65 opposition MPs who had just been elected. Similarly, the opposition's disruption of parliament prevented the ratification of a presidential decree issuing a state of emergency, which needed to be ratified within 48 hours to be considered valid.[21]

In sum, then, an easily overlooked aspect of Georgia's Rose Revolution is the opposition's reliance on court cases and legal maneuvers. The design of Georgia's judicial system and the opposition's knowledge of that system provided it with the opportunity to use legal tactics alongside populist ones. Still, given the sequence of events, it is difficult to argue that the Georgian Supreme Court itself played a decisive role in Rose Revolution: The Supreme Court's decision was issued only after the opposition's disruption of the first session of parliament and only after President Shevardnadze's November 23 resignation. When the events in Georgia are compared with those in the Armenian case, it appears that a genuine change in the political winds may be necessary before the judiciary—or at least, the members of its highest courts —feel at liberty to strike down election results. And, in these cases, it becomes difficult to distinguish judicial independence from political opportunism.

Conclusion

To what extent do judicial design, actors, and legal maneuvers matter in making elections a mode of transition? This chapter seeks to provide some preliminary answers by focusing on the role of the law and courts in two election disputes in the former Soviet Union. While the number of cases considered is small, their relevance to an understanding of the development and operation of contemporary democracy is significant. In the past few years alone, one can list several notable instances in which the judiciary emerged as a prominent player making critical rulings that shaped perceptions about, if not the outcome of, elections. These range from the unanimous ruling of Mexico's Federal Election Tribunal (TEPJF) denying Andres Manuel Lopez Obrador, the 2006 presidential candidate of the Party of the Democratic Revolution (PRD), a full recount of votes, to the May 2007 decision by Turkey's Constitutional Court to halt balloting for its country's president. In post-Soviet Ukraine, the Supreme Court continues to be a forum for resolving disputes among parties that had defined the Orange Revolution, while Armenia's Constitutional Court was again charged with evaluating election fraud during that country's 2007 parliamentary and 2008 presidential elections.

Reconsidering Armenia's 2003 presidential election and Georgia's 2003 parliamentary elections from the perspective of judicial design and judicial activism reveals that law and courts can matter even in places where they lack a history or tradition of influence. In both cases, the post-Soviet constitutions designed judiciaries with the power and opportunity to oversee elections. Thus, not only did the judiciary play the role of electoral referee in both cases, but also the referees' decisions proved to be critical junctures in the election disputes, even though the final outcomes differed. In Armenia, the Constitutional Court upheld the election but expressed its doubts about its legitimacy and the impact that such elections could have on Armenian democracy. This decision illustrates how political pressure may limit the degree to which judges in hybrid regimes are willing to play decisive roles in election disputes: even when courts acknowledge that fraud has occurred, they are rarely in a position vis-à-vis an incumbent government to annul elections. In Georgia, meanwhile, lower court rulings helped justify the opposition's cause while key legal maneuvers were critical in keeping the cause alive. Finally, the Supreme Court's decision overturning the election results granted the Rose Revolution legal legitimacy.

Still, some argue that, by overturning the 2003 parliamentary election results, Georgia's Supreme Court exceeded its authority. For example, despite being a member of the opposition at the time, Natelashvili of Georgia's Labor Party argued that the Georgian Supreme Court overstepped its jurisdiction in 2003, since Georgia's Constitution grants the Constitutional Court, not the Supreme Court, explicit powers to determine the constitutionality of elections and referenda (Chikhladze 2003). Yet, it is likely that critical institutional differences between Armenia's Constitutional Court and Georgia's Constitutional Court shaped the tactics that Georgia's opposition employed and determined the legality of the Supreme Court's actions. First, as discussed above, the selection process for Georgia's Supreme Court, and even for its lower courts, is more likely to produce a professional and qualified bench than the selection process for the country's Constitutional Court. As a result, Georgia's opposition had reason to believe that relying on common courts rather than the Constitutional Court would increase its chances of a fair hearing. Second, the electoral jurisdiction of Georgia's Constitutional Court is linked explicitly to the "constitutionality" of elections and most of the associated text in the Constitution focuses on the timing of elections. In fact, according to the Law on the Constitutional Court of Georgia (1995, art. 17), the court is responsible for breaches in individual rights and freedoms only "if the decision of the dispute is not within the competence of any other court." In other words, those issues with which one could challenge the legality of election results are *not* the sole jurisdiction of Georgia's Constitutional Court. With the right legal argument, cases regarding election fraud could be brought before common courts, for which the Supreme Court is the highest court of appeals.

While Armenia's common courts also rule on cases related to civil rights and civil liberties, the constitutional provision outlining the electoral jurisdiction of its Constitutional Court is more encompassing and specific: the Court "shall rule on disputes concerning referenda and the results of presidential and parliamentary elections" (Constitution of the Republic of Armenia 1995, 100). At the same time, the main parties in any election dispute—the candidates in the presidential and parliamentary elections—are expected to file suits directly with the Constitutional Court (art. 101). Moreover, Armenia's opposition was well aware of this limitation.[22]

Ultimately, then, Armenia's constitution is written so that Armenia possesses just one electoral referee, the Constitutional Court. That is, Armenia's formal institutions create a single-shot game for the opposition, and its prospects for emerging victorious depended on the decision that these justices reached. Georgia's constitution is more ambiguous, and in 2003 the Georgian opposition capitalized on the multiplicity of options available—that is, the opposition turned the election dispute into a multi-shot game. In terms of strategic games, then, the judicial structure made for multiple series of parallel games in which victory in a few games at the lower level, where the incumbent's control of the rules is less evident, could undermine the games at higher levels and assist the opposition's victory. In such a situation of multiple games with uncertain significance and uncertain outcomes, it becomes hard for the incumbent to have enough information and leverage to control all games simultaneously.

Drawing policy implications from this analysis, which relies on a comparative study of these two similar systems, is a risky proposition. Most-similar-systems approaches allow one to isolate theoretical relationships while controlling for other, possibly intervening factors at the expense of generalizability. Thus, it is never clear how findings from two cases with similar degrees of democratic development or comparable levels of civil society, for example, might be altered when such *ceteris paribus* assumptions are relaxed. At a minimum, however, my analysis suggests that the electoral model of democratization (see Bunce and Wolchik in this volume) may benefit greatly from engaging the courts. Judicial design matters, however. Where electoral jurisdiction is narrowly circumscribed, the legal options available to the opposition will be circumscribed as well. However, where many courts are empowered to resolve election disputes, locating and utilizing sympathetic venues to challenge election results could be a critical step toward legitimizing opposition demands and forcing the hand of the incumbent rulers. Of course, it remains to be seen whether the 2003 judicial rulings in favor of Georgia's opposition actually advance the cause of democratic consolidation there. Certainly, such instances reveal a commitment to institutionalized mechanisms of conflict resolution, which is a boon for democracy. Yet scholars and policymakers alike must remember that regime change is not the same thing as democratization, and much depends on the inclinations of the opposition.

PART III / Reflections and Conclusions

CHAPTER TWELVE

The Contingent Power of Authoritarian Elections

Andreas Schedler

Over the past years, responding to the expanded use of multiparty elections in authoritarian regimes, we have seen growing scholarly interest in deciphering "the power of elections" (Di Palma 1993, 85) under authoritarian governance. In conceptual, theoretical, and empirical terms we have been learning a lot from this new and blossoming literature on the causal role of authoritarian elections. However, defying the scientific goal of accumulation of knowledge, we have seen a disquieting bifurcation of debate. On the one hand, the literature on the political economy of dictatorship has been emphasizing the *regime-sustaining* value of authoritarian elections. On the other hand, comparative studies of democratization by elections have been stressing their *regime-subverting* potential. These two strands of theoretical inquiry and empirical analysis have been developing in a state of peaceful coexistence and mutual ignorance. Happily divorced from each other, almost *incomunicados*, they have been generating seemingly incompatible empirical findings.

This chapter offers brief reviews of both debates, arguing that despite appearances their theoretical arguments and empirical findings are fundamentally consistent with each other. The seemingly contradictory claims of these two strands of literature—the *probabilistic* claim that authoritarian multiparty elections strengthen the survival capacity of the incumbent and the *possibilistic* claim that they create opportunities for opposition forces to weaken, or even topple, the incumbent—are in fact essentially compatible with one another. The focus of this book lies on the democratizing power of authoritarian elections. Whether authoritarian elections can assume democratizing roles is, I argue, subject to double contingency. It is contingent on the type of authoritarian elections the ruling elite orchestrates (only multiparty contests can be expected to get the transition game moving); and it is contingent on the balance of power and the conflictive interaction between government and opposition (only political actors can turn structural opportunities into realities).[1]

I develop my argument in four steps. Assuming that our capacity to estimate the causal effects of authoritarian elections depends on our capacity of analytic differentiation, I first lay out the relevant spectrum of authoritarian elections: single-party, hegemonic multiparty, and competitive multiparty. In a second step, I synthesize some basic theoretical arguments and empirical findings put forward by the political economy literature on authoritarian institutions. Drawing on a recent study by Gary Cox (2007), I conclude that multiparty elections are rational institutional devices for self-serving autocrats, despite their ostentatious inferiority to single-party elections. While single-party elections are not a viable option for contemporary autocrats, multiparty elections grant them higher job security than democratic elections while protecting them from violent job losses through military intervention. Still, they render them vulnerable to processes of democratization by elections. There is no such thing as a free electoral lunch.

In the third section, I describe two major outcomes that democratization by elections may produce: alternation of power in the wake of gradual reform ("democratic revelations") and alternation of power in the wake of mass protest ("democratic revolutions"). I also outline broad causal mechanisms that explain the vulnerability of competitive authoritarian regimes to electoral transitions: agency losses, defections by members of the ruling elite, and structural opportunities for contentious action. The fourth and final section tries to make sense of the diverse empirical patterns comparative studies on the democratizing power of elections have demonstrated. Some authors have dismissed elections as irrelevant to democratization, while others have identified them as powerful motors of democratic transitions. I suggest three major reasons to explain the divergence of results: divergent specifications of the dependent variable, divergent definitions of scope conditions, and divergent assumptions of causality.

The Spectrum of Electoral Regimes

When debating the empirical power of elections, we need first of all to be clear about the type of elections we are discussing. Much of the debate on the democratizing power of elections has been limited to nondemocratic elections. Yet, even within the realm of authoritarian regimes, not all elections are equal. Some are more meaningful than others. Some are more democratic, more competitive. Others are less so. Some allocate power; others do not. Some are regular, others sporadic. Some subject the chief executive to electoral confirmation; others do not. Not all of them serve authoritarian purposes equally well. Not all of them represent plausible starting points for electoral transitions. Not all of them should be expected to carry democratizing consequences.

Figure 12.1 represents the spectrum of electoral regimes within which current debates are situated. At the left-hand extreme, we find regimes that do not hold elections to fill positions of national power. For the sake of simplicity, I label them nonelectoral. Some of them literally do not hold any kind of elections. Others organize occasional referenda, and still others conduct elections only at subnational levels of power. At the right-hand extreme, we find elections that take place in either liberal or electoral democracies. As a matter of course, democratic elections vary enormously in their societal context, their institutional setup, their party-systemic configuration, their competitive dynamic, and many other dimensions.[2] For the present purpose, though, it is sufficient to place them into a single conceptual box, stored outside the warehouse of authoritarian elections.

In the broad middle of the spectrum, the extensive family of authoritarian elections stretches across three distinct categories: single-party elections, hegemonic elections, and competitive multiparty elections. Single-party regimes sometimes allow for intraparty or nonparty competition. They do not, however, open up national elections to formal contestation by independent opposition parties. By contrast, both hegemonic and competitive authoritarian regimes allow for multiparty competition at the national level, in legisla-

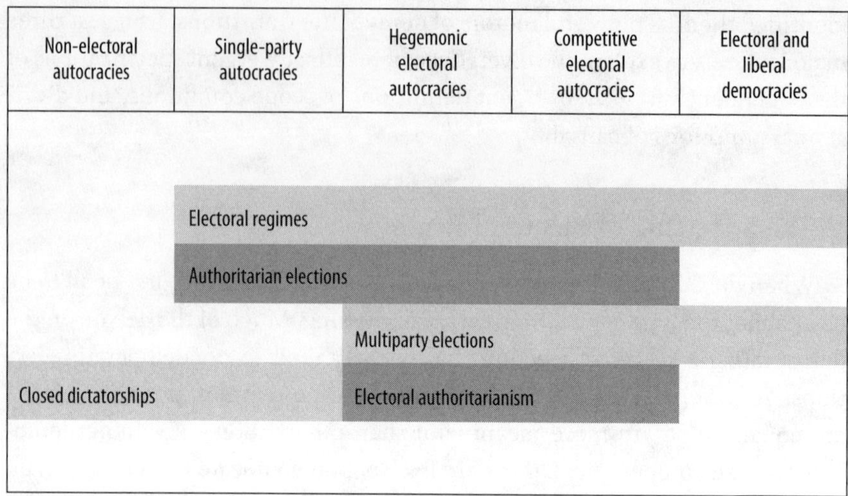

Figure 12.1. The spectrum of electoral regimes

tive as well as presidential contests (in presidential systems of government). The big difference between the two lies in their level of institutionalization. Hegemonic regimes are in equilibrium; competitive regimes are not.

Grounded in an uncertain mixture of genuine popularity and resolute manipulation, hegemonic parties always win and win big—and are expected to keep winning and winning big in the foreseeable future. Their twin presumption of popular support and authoritarian resoluteness creates an equilibrium of dissuasion in which defection by either citizens or politicians seems not just cost-intensive, but simply futile. Of course, social expectations are a soft "tissue that can easily tear" (Kurzman 2004, 171). Edifices of interlocking expectations are fragile social constructions that may collapse like a house of cards when fissures appear in their self-sustaining foundations. Political regimes may look inevitable one day and on the brink of collapse a couple of days after. In this sense, hegemony is like love: eternal while it lasts.[3]

Competitive regimes do not enjoy similar levels of consolidation. Often, they look more like "authoritarian situations" (Linz 1973) than authoritarian regimes: they are fluid, insecure, inconsistent, and improvisational in response to recurrent challenges from within and without. The security and tranquility that hegemonic systems are able to enjoy is denied to competitive authoritarian systems, caught up in a constant tug-of-war with opposition forces. Accordingly, when analyzing the dynamics of "competitive authoritarianism" (Levitsky and Way 2002b), authors often choose earlier insights of the transition literature on the inherent instability of authoritarian liberalization (Przeworski 1991, 57–60) as their theoretical starting point.[4] In the transitions from military rule in southern Europe and South America, the contradictory mix of authoritarian governance and liberalization systematically failed to produce a sustainable equilibrium. The same may be true for the contradictory mix of authoritarian governance and multiparty elections that characterizes contemporary cases of competitive authoritarianism.

As the shaded areas in Figure 12.1 indicate, our four broad categories of elections may be grouped in various ways. Whether the three types of authoritarian elections belong to the same or to different classes of institutions depends on our criteria of classification. At the highest level of abstraction, we may locate all authoritarian elections side by side with democratic elections in the catchall category of "electoral regimes." The less comprehensive notion of multiparty elections similarly puts authoritarian and democratic elections into one abstract conceptual box, although it excludes single-party elections. Finally, the concept of "electoral authoritarianism" covers nondemocratic multiparty elections only, marking off the territory of democratic elections, while banning single-party regimes into the residual category of "closed regimes," where it shares company with military and personalist dictatorships. Depending on their theoretical frames and analytical concerns, students of elections and regime change choose different levels of conceptual differentiation. As I argue below, the conceptual lenses they wear have direct implications on the empirical patterns they observe.

Authoritarianism by Elections

Over three decades ago, in their edited volume *Elections without Choice* (1978), Guy Hermet, Richard Rose, and Alain Rouquié called upon scholars to pay more attention to the empirical relevance of authoritarian elections. As one of the editors wrote, back then "state-controlled elections" were often "denied any significance." Observers tended to dismiss such elections as hollow, fraudulent, predetermined rituals; to view them with "objective contempt"; and to ignore the "numerous functions" they perform (Hermet 1978, 1). Among the manifold roles that Hermet and his colleagues attributed to "elections without choice" were regime legitimation, voter education, communication between rulers and subjects, and resolution of conflict within the ruling class (13–17).

For quite some time, *Elections without Choice* represented the state of the art in the comparative study of authoritarian elections. It was well-received and often-cited—yet inconsequential in its impact on the research agenda of comparative political studies. Hermet and his coauthors had identified and surveyed a research lacuna the discipline was not capable of filling at the time. It is only in recent years that we have seen a new generation of largely quantitative empirical research that studies the use of elections (along with other formal institutions) as instruments of authoritarian rule. Subsequent to the creation of longitudinal cross-national datasets on political regimes and political institutions, the new research on the formal institutional underpinnings of authoritarian governance is broad in its temporal and geographic scope, subjecting to statistical analysis large numbers of cases, spread across the globe and through contemporary history. Following the strategic turn in comparative politics, with its passionate embrace of rational choice as the explanatory paradigm of political action, current students of authoritarian politics have no trouble accepting the notion that authoritarian rulers are not fools who would set up formal institutions that are irrelevant or even harmful, or that promise aesthetic gains only ("window dressing"). Whatever institutions dictators establish can be assumed to serve their material strategic goals.

According to most of the literature, political elections under a dictatorship serve one overwhelming purpose: the political survival of the dictator. The basic assumption is simple: authoritarian rulers want to survive in office, and political institutions like parties, legislatures, and elections help them accomplish this.[5] They do so by containing structural threats to their hold on power. In principle, these threats to political survival may be either *vertical* or *horizontal*. The former originate from below, from the citizenry, the latter from within the ruling coalition. Popular rebellions are the classic instance of vertical threats, military coups the typical manifestation of horizontal threats. Given the reality that "most of the time the most serious challenge to dictators' survival in office comes from high level allies, not from regime opponents" (Geddes 2005, 6), much of the literature on the political economy of dictatorship focuses on horizontal rather than vertical threats.[6]

Within this elite-centered perspective, authoritarian elections are not conceived of as deceptive devices to create popular legitimacy, but as tools of elite persuasion, designed to nudge potential challengers from within the ruling circles into continuing acquiescence. Often, the underlying "mechanisms through which [elections] promote regime survival remain opaque" (Pepinsky 2007, 1), and authors have in fact been proposing different ways through which elections are supposed to stave off lateral threats by authoritarian allies. According to the account offered by Barbara Geddes, authoritarian elections work as instruments of deterrence. To the extent that they provide demonstrations of popular support that are credible to members of the elite (who know all about the dirty tricks of the government), they "serve to deter rivals" from challenging the incumbent (Geddes 2005, 10). According to the almost opposite account more recently introduced by Beatriz Magaloni, authoritarian elections serve as mechanisms of self-restraint. To the extent that incumbents credibly commit themselves to keep playing the electoral game, authoritarian elections offer "a credible exit option" for internal challengers who may leave the ruling party in case the dictator fails to pay and protect them properly (Magaloni 2008, 728).

A variety of statistical studies have confirmed the theoretical expectation that links authoritarian elections with authoritarian longevity (see Gandhi and Przeworski 2007; Geddes 2005; Magaloni 2008). And, it seems, authoritarian elections work. They do what they are expected to: extend the life span of nondemocratic regimes.[7] Quite remarkably, any election does the job, whether regular or irregular, single-party or multiparty. Furthermore, elections serve the noble purpose of prolonging authoritarian governance in any kind of dictatorship, whether military, personalist, or single-party (see Geddes 2005). And yet, not all authoritarian elections are equal. Single-party elections stand out among all others. They are the champions of longevity among twentieth-century authoritarian regimes (even if few of them survived the end of the cold war).

The "exceptional durability" (Gandhi and Przeworski 2007, 1292) of regimes that hold single-party elections creates a challenge for strategic explanations of authoritarian elections that the literature has not quite resolved yet. If the primordial goal of authoritarian rulers lies in prolonging their grip on power, why do they ever choose anything other than the institutional formula that works best for their purpose, single-party elections? In particular, why should they ever choose to establish multiparty elections, if these are less effective in diffusing threats to their political survival than single-party rituals?

In a recent paper, Gary Cox (2007) introduced an important distinction into the debate on authoritarian elections that allows us to resolve the puzzle of ostensibly irrational dictators who choose suboptimal institutional arrangements. Distinguishing between *violent* and *nonviolent* exits from power, he stipulates that rulers care about their political welfare and survival—but even more so about their physical welfare and survival. The average dictator hates losing power but hates even more going to jail or losing his life. His first preference will be to remain in power. Yet when confronting the alternative of being evicted from office through peaceful or violent means, he will opt for the former as the lesser evil. Political survival matters, that is, but forms of death do, too.

As Cox hypothesizes, it is the potential trade-off between preferring to survive (politically) and not wishing to die (physically) that motivates the organization of elections under authoritarian rule. Elections come with a cost. They "always involve some risk" (Geddes 2005, 4) and may end up shortening the life span of the regime. Rational rulers may trade this marginal risk against the benefit of lowering the probability of suffering a violent overthrow. To test his theory of exit preferences, Cox collected annual data for 1975 through 2000 on the global incidence of all three outcomes: the survival of national leaders in office, their peaceful exit, and their violent exit from office. Table 12.1 shows the frequency distribution he finds across four types of political regimes: nonelectoral regimes, single-party regimes, multiparty electoral autocracies, and democratic regimes.[8] The data suggest some compelling regularities. Democratic leaders are most likely to exit office peacefully and least likely to do so violently. Dictatorships without parties or elections have few peaceful exits and are most vulnerable to violent ones. Single-party dictatorships are the best of all authoritarian worlds: they suffer the fewest exits from power, be they peaceful or violent. On all accounts, multiparty autocracies fare worse than single-party regimes. Why, then, should autocrats ever conduct multiparty contests instead of single-party elections?

The answer, I believe, is simple: With few exceptions, single-party rule is no longer a part of the set of choices available to contemporary autocrats. At the end of the Cold War, most sub-Saharan countries and all post-Soviet countries had already lived through long nights of single-party rule in the second half of the twentieth century. Finding themselves under multiple domestic and international pressures after the disintegration of the Soviet Union, they simply could not choose to perpetuate the old political monopoly that had steered their countries into political oppression and economic ruin. Since the fall of the Berlin Wall, authoritarian regimes adopt multiparty elections not because they are preferable to single-party elections but because they are preferable to the remaining feasible alternatives: military rule without elections or a full transition to genuine democracy. Gary Cox's data show why. Although multiparty autocracies do assume some degree of electoral risk, their annual vulnerability to electoral turnovers is only about one-third that of democratic governments. And although they face marginally higher risks of violent exit than democracies, their exposure to irregular removals from office is only one-fourth that of nonelectoral regimes (see bold figures in Table 12.1).

In sum, if single-party rule is not a feasible option, authoritarian rulers chose multiparty arrangements over democracy because they want to survive in office; and they chose multiparty arrangements over nonparty regimes because they do not want to die in office. The Cox dataset does not distinguish between hegemonic and competitive electoral autocracies, nor does it separate horizontal from vertical threats to authoritarian survival. Introducing these finer conceptual distinctions, Table 12.2 offers rough estimates of the intensity of political threats under various conditions.[9] These threat estimates are speculative, yet broadly consistent with the empirical litera-

Table 12.1 Continuity in office and peaceful and violent exits from office, by regime type, 1975–2000

		Nonelectoral autocracies	Single-party autocracies	Electoral autocracies	Electoral and liberal democracies
Continuity	*N*	793	785	722	1,633
	%	84.5	93.9	90.3	78.3
Peaceful exit	*N*	51	44	58	432
	%	5.4	5.3	**7.3**	**20.7**
Violent exit	*N*	94	7	20	20
	%	**10.0**	0.8	**2.5**	1.0
Total	*N*	938	836	800	2,085
	%	100.0	100.0	100.0	100.0

Source: Cox 2007, fig. 1.

Note: Data are annual event counts of the fate of national leaders (chief executives), worldwide, 1975–2000. Bold figures highlight the core differences between electoral autocracies and their viable alternatives: nonelectoral regimes and democratic regimes. Differences between regime types are statistically significant (Somers' $d = -.059$, $N = 4.659$, $p = .000$).

Table 12.2 Intensity of threats to political survival by regime type

	Horizontal threats		Vertical threats	
Regime type	Violent: Military coup	Peaceful: Ruling coalition split	Violent: Armed rebellion	Peaceful: Electoral rebellion
Nonelectoral autocracies	**High**	Low	Medium	—
Single-party autocracies	Low	Low	Low	—
Hegemonic electoral autocracies	Low	Low	Low	Low
Competitive electoral autocracies	**Low**	High	Low	**Medium**
Electoral and liberal democracies	Low	High	Low	**High**

ture. According to this quasi-synthesis of the literature in tabular form, nonelectoral regimes leave few spaces for peaceful challenges, while suffering a high level of violent threats; single-party regimes face low levels of threat throughout and zero levels in the electoral arena; hegemonic regimes look similarly tranquil, running only some slight risks in the electoral arena; and democratic governments expose themselves to high risks of losing power in civil, institutional ways. Competitive autocracies, finally, display systematic competitive advantages over their viable competitors. They are less vulnerable to electoral turnovers than democratic regimes, and less vulnerable to military coups than dictatorships without elections. By comparison, though, hegemonic regimes look more advantageous; in these regimes both the likelihood of elite splits and the likelihood of electoral surprises are reduced to a minimum. Political hegemony, however, cannot be chosen, only constructed. The strategic advantage of hegemonic rule explains why governing parties in competitive autocracies frequently strive over time to transform their (more or less) precarious electoral dominance into electoral hegemony.

According to available cross-national evidence, then, multiparty elections serve to prolong the longevity of authoritarian regimes. Regimes with multiparty elections suffer fewer military coups than nonelectoral regimes and fewer electoral changes of government than democratic regimes. As a matter of course, though, all these effects are probabilistic, not deterministic. Multiparty elections prolong the expected life span of nondemocratic regimes. They do not buy them immortality. They depress the risk of military coups but do not eliminate it (see Clark 2006). They depress the risk of electoral defeat yet do not eliminate it either. It is here that the literature on democratization by elections sets in. Electoral transitions are not the predictable, lawlike outcome of authoritarian multiparty elections. They are the marginal risk authoritarian rulers assume when convoking multiparty elections for the purpose of political (as well as physical) survival. Recognizing the general capacity of multiparty elections to raise the average life expectancy of authoritarian regimes therefore does not imply denying their potential of shortening the lifespan of concrete regimes by triggering "democratic revolutions" (Thompson 2004).

Democratization by Elections

Rulers at times describe their political adversaries in medical terms as diseases that menace the health of the body politic. Extending the medical metaphor, we may conceive of multiparty elections as vaccines against certain categories of threats to the life and welfare of authoritarian regimes. In public health, effective vaccination protects a fair number of recipients from a particular disease and lowers its average incidence in the population. In an analogous manner, multiparty elections protect the average autocracy from military intervention and popular rebellion and augment the mean life expectancy of the electoral authoritarian regime population. Yet, all vaccination includes risks. Some people who may never have acquired the disease otherwise fall ill due to the vaccination. Similarly, electoral authoritarian regimes may perish as a consequence of having accepted the vaccine of multiparty elections.

The metaphor of the electoral vaccine helps us to understand the essential compatibility of approaches that emphasize the regime-sustaining effects of authoritarian multiparty elections with those that focus on their regime-subverting consequences. The former highlight *probable* effects of authoritarian elections that are *general* (context-invariant), the latter *possible* consequences that are *contingent* (context-dependent). The discussion on the democratizing power of authoritarian elections goes beyond electoral alternations, though. It covers a broader range of possible democratizing effects. These include a gradual erosion of the authoritarian quality of elections through democratizing reforms that may eventually lead to electoral alternations in power (see Schedler 2002a). They also include possible spillover effects into nonelectoral arenas, in particular, the expansion of civil liberties (see Howard and Roessler 2006; Lindberg 2006a, chaps. 5–6; Pop-Eleches and Robertson 2008). Given the close conceptual association between electoral alternation and democracy we find in the literature, I wish to clarify the idea of democratizing (transitional) alternation, as distinct from both democratic (post-transitional) and authoritarian (nontransitional) alternation, before I offer a synthetic discussion of the causal mechanisms that may push actors either toward prolonged journeys or into sudden leaps of "democratization by elections."

Types of Alternation

Under democratic conditions, the occurrence of electoral alternation in government testifies both to the vigor of interparty competition and to the vitality of the democratic system. The achievement of power by opposition parties is the crowning act of interparty competition, the acceptance of defeat by governing parties the crowning act of democratic consolidation.[10] In addition, according to mainstream liberal democratic theory, the possibility that elections will turn power over to the opposition constitutes the very foundation of democratic accountability and responsiveness (Powell 2000; Sartori 1987). Given the central role both actual and possible government turnovers play in democratic practice as well as in democratic theory, some scholars have been including alternation in power in their operational definitions of democracy.

Most prominently, the well-known "alternation rule" codified by Adam Przeworski and his collaborators stipulates a close association between the occurrence of alternation and the presence of democracy.[11] Based on the attractive conception of democracy as "a system in which parties lose elections" (Przeworski 1991, 10), this rule rests upon the twin assumptions that (a) democracy requires alternation and (b) alternation requires democracy. Thus, under this rule, if we see a regime that holds elections it never loses, we should not classify it as democratic. Inversely, if we observe a regime holding elections and actually losing them, we should infer that the regime had been democratic all along (since its last fundamental change of rules). Since the possibility of electoral alternation is conceived as being contingent on the reality of electoral democracy, electoral turnovers count as the ultimate proof of the democratic pudding. While the causal association of alternation with democracy must be regarded a solid empirical generalization, it does allow for exceptions. In authoritarian contexts, alternations in power may happen, and their significance is less clear and predetermined than under democratic conditions. Depending on the integrity of the election and the identity of the winner, turnovers under authoritarian (or post-authoritarian) rule may belong to one of three categories: democratic revelations, democratic revolutions, or authoritarian reshuffles.

Democratic revelations: post-transitional alternation. In cases in which electoral authoritarian governments oversee a process of democratizing reform, their final defeat in national elections serves to confirm the seriousness of the democratic advances they allowed to happen before. In such instances of post-transitional alternation, the defeat of the ruling parties at the polls fulfills an epistemic function: it reveals the presently democratic nature of a previously authoritarian system. The 2000 presidential victories of opposition candidates Vicente Fox in Mexico, Abdoulaye Wade in Senegal, and Chen Shui-bian in Taiwan were neat examples of such "democratic revelations" (Schedler 2000). Under the alternation rule, we would classify these regimes (correctly) in a retroactive fashion "as democratic for the entire period [the outgoing] party was in power under the same rules" (Przeworski et al. 2000, 24).

Democratic revolutions: transitional alternation. Even if electoral autocracies are systems in which opposition parties are supposed to lose elections, and actually do lose elections most of the time, alternation in power may occur even under authoritarian conditions. Electoral autocrats expose themselves to some degree of electoral uncertainty, however small. Through institutional design, authoritarian manipulation, and electoral persuasion they may be able to contain electoral uncertainty but are rarely able to eliminate it altogether. However remote and wafer-thin, the possibility of suffering defeat in "stunning elections" (Huntington 1991, 175; Thompson and Kuntz 2006) remains alive. More often than not, opposition parties must take to the streets and stage "electoral revolutions" to make their surprise victories stick, as in the Philippines in 1986, Ivory Coast and Serbia in 2000, Georgia in 2003, and Ukraine in 2004. More occasionally, as in Olusegun Obasanjo's victory in the 1999 presidential elections in Nigeria, opposition candidates may emerge victorious from fraudulent elections and be able to take office without large-scale conflict.

In all these cases, alternation does not reveal the democratic nature of the regime—but only its *unpopularity* (its lack of popular support) as well as its *weakness* (its lack of resources and resolve to ensure its own survival). Instances of democratizing or "transitional" alternation do not serve as *indicators*, but *causal forces*, of democratic advance.[12] When opposition parties manage to win the uphill race of an authoritarian election against all odds, we should not infer from the failure of authoritarian manipulation that the process was free and fair from the very beginning. Of course, the temptation is high to reassess the procedural quality of elections in retrospect, in the light of their substantive outcomes. Even with everybody complaining about the ruling party before election day, nobody cares seriously about its foul play anymore if the opposition ends up winning the election. There is no better washing powder than alternation to launder a dirty election of its bad image.[13]

Authoritarian reshuffles: alternation without transition. In exceptional cases, nondemocratic elections may lead to changes in government without changing the nature of the authoritarian regime. Such rare instances of authoritarian alternation in government tend to happen under three partially overlapping circumstances: (a) in cases where ongoing civil wars undermine the democratic foundations of electoral competition, as in Sri Lanka in 1994, Algeria in 1999, or Colombia in 2002; (b) in cases where military tutelage drains the authority of elected officials, as in Guatemala in 1985, Pakistan in 1990, 1993, and 1997, or Niger in 1999; and (c) in cases of inaugural, yet still authoritarian, elections in the wake of civil war or military rule, as in Turkey in 1983, Georgia in 1992, or Cambodia in 1993. Needless to say, in such governmental reshuffles under continuing authoritarian conditions, elections do not assume the democratizing role that they play in the so-called electoral revolutions.

Causal Mechanisms

If multiparty elections on average tend to work as they are intended to, prolonging the lifespan of authoritarian regimes, why should we expect them to produce counter-intentional consequences: either democratic alternation in the wake of democratizing reform or democratizing alternation in the wake of electoral rebellion? Are either gradual or sudden electoral transitions no more than stochastic accidents, or can we identify causal mechanisms and rational motives that produce them with predictable regularity? I would like to propose three "causal mechanisms" (structures of constraint and opportunity) that explain why elections tend to empower opposition actors (relative to their strength in the absence of elections), enabling them potentially either to push the electoral game step by step along a path of democratizing reform or to break the authoritarian grip on power by electoral rebellion. The decision-theoretic explanation Staffan Lindberg offers in Chapter 13 in this volume focuses on *rational motives* for electoral transitions. His approach centers on the cost-benefit calculus of repression versus toleration that may lead electoral autocrats to either widen or narrow the space of electoral contestation. In contrast, my brief revision of causal mechanisms is meant to highlight *structural sources* of electoral transitions.[14]

Problems of agency control. Popular elections are huge bureaucratic undertakings. They entail "the largest peacetime mobilization of the national population in a short time span and require the coordination of millions of individuals engaged in hundreds of different activities" (Mozaffar and Schedler 2002: 5). Especially in poor, large, and diverse countries, elections pose enormous administrative and logistical challenges to governments, be they democratic or nondemocratic. For authoritarian governments striving to contain the uncertainty of electoral outcomes, multiparty elections with universal suffrage involve additional problems of agency control at a massive scale. Their strategies of electoral manipulation depend on the active cooperation of state agents capable of and willing to carry them out in an effective fashion. They require "usable states" (Linz and Stepan 1996), but they also need pliable citizens who let themselves be persuaded, intimidated, or corrupted in order to make the electoral authoritarian machinery run smoothly. Their authoritarian schemes may fail because of the incapacity of state actors (Way 2006), the political unreliability of state actors (see Moraski in this volume), or the resourceful resistance by citizens (McFaul 2005; Bunce and Wolchik in this volume). It is purely and simply a problem of large numbers. Just imagine. If electoral autocrats had to control a small face-to-face electorate only, such as an assembly of notables, the central committee of the ruling party, or a town hall meeting, they would have (almost) none of the troubles they face when trying to domesticate competitive mass elections—that savage modern invention, egalitarian, bureaucratic, and decentralized.

Elite desertion. Hegemonic parties are practically immune to internal splits so long as they can convince (temporarily) discontented members of the ruling alliance that they can maintain "a fair chance they will win posts and privilege in the future" only within the hegemonic party but that if they leave the party, "a high probability exists that that they will win nothing in the cold outside" (Langston 2006, 60). Competitive autocracies, by contrast, face the perennial threat of ambitious insiders defecting to the ranks of the opposition. Existing opposition parties and candidates are often too disorganized and unpopular to unseat the incumbent at the polls. If anyone is capable of defeating the incumbent, it is someone from the inner ranks of the ruling elite. The Ukrainian electoral rebellion of the year 2004 nicely illustrates these dynamics, as virtually "the entire leadership of the Orange Revolution had . . . been closely allied with the president" until just a few years before the collapse of the regime (Way 2008, 63).

Opportunity structures for collective contention. Few areas of political research possess anything resembling a unifying paradigmatic core. The study of social movements is an exception. Students of social movements have a basic knowledge of what is needed to get protesters onto the streets. They know what to look for if they want to explain the emergence of contentious collective action: grievances (appropriately framed to resonate with relevant audiences), repertoires of collective action (such as public demonstrations, strikes, and street barricades), mobilizing structures (such as social networks or formal organizations), and political opportunities (positive expected utilities of collective action under given circumstances, a favorable balance between expected success and expected repression). Authoritarian elections provide all this. They create profound democratic grievances as well as a powerful master frame of protest: the defense of democracy. They provide the opposition with a simple, low-cost medium of communication (the vote) and a simple common message (a protest vote against the government and/or the regime). They circumscribe the time and place for collective action. They energize political parties, the organized pillars of competitive elections; mobilize civic associations; and activate social networks in alliance either with parties or with civil society organizations. They offer a range of roles citizens may assume, as voters, grassroots activists, party leaders, or candidates, as well as a range of collective activities they may carry out, such as campaigning, voter education, electoral observation, and protest demonstrations.

Authoritarian elections, in a word, place many constraints on opposition actors and yet, crucially, provide *structural opportunities for collective challenges*. In the absence of such electoral focal points of elite as well as mass coordination, regime dissidents would have a much harder time getting together and making themselves heard. As a matter of course, political opportunities are not self-realizing, though. They must be seized by political actors. The weaker the authoritarian regime, the larger the opportunities to further weaken it at the polls. The stronger the opposition, the more resourceful, imaginative, and energetic, the larger its chances to grasp these opportunities. Thus the centrality of politics, and the centrality of opposition politics, in electoral transitions.[15]

The Diversity of Findings

Over the past years, several large-*N* studies have put the hypothesis of the democratizing power of elections to statistical testing. The results have been mixed, with some studies confirming and others rejecting the notion that political elections further democratization. To some degree, the divergence of findings may be due to differences in data, model specification, statistical procedures, and spatial and temporal coverage. More importantly, though, these divergences seem to originate in differences in research questions (the definition of dependent variables) and theoretical reach (the definition of scope conditions). On the one hand, empirical studies have been analyzing a broad *range of democratizing effects* authoritarian elections may have: the transformation of regimes through gradual reform, the collapse of regimes through electoral rebellions, and the expansion of civil liberties. Contradictions among studies that work with different dependent variables may be optical illusions only. Causal inferences that are valid for one of these broad effects may not be valid for others. On the other hand, empirical studies sometimes overstep the *scope conditions* (the range of plausible causes) that delimit our theoretical expectations regarding the democratizing consequences of authoritarian elections. They run the risk of "theoretical stretching" when they include either categories of authoritarian elections or types of democratic elections that bear little relationship to the original hypothesis of "democratization by elections." In the following, I briefly illustrate such problems of "theoretical stretching," while keeping in mind, yet leaving undeveloped, the previous caveat regarding different specifications of the dependent variable.[16]

Scope Conditions

As argued above, the democratizing effect of elections is not supposed to be universal, but contingent on the type of election convoked by the incumbent government. Not any kind of election should be expected to have democratizing effects; only multiparty contests in electoral authoritarian regimes should. Statistical tests that either overaggregate different categories of elections or overgeneralize the theoretical expectations regarding the power of elections are likely to confirm the original premise: elections do not *in general* bear democratizing consequences.

In the introductory statistical chapter to his insightful comparative study on the conditions of authoritarian longevity, Jason Brownlee (2007a) illustrates the potential substantive implications of conceptual overaggregation. To examine the impact of elections on the breakdown of nondemocratic regimes, he constructs a dummy variable that registers the presence of formal multiparty elections whatever the degree of the competitiveness they permit de facto single-party elections where opposition parties are legally admitted but win no legislative seats, hegemonic party elections where opposition parties win less than a quarter, and competitive authoritarian elections where these parties win more than 25% of seats—all are counted as equal. Since the first two categories of elections are associated with stable, nondemocratic rule sustained by strong parties, the statistical analysis produces a predictable finding: in the explanation of regime change, elections, thus conceived, are of "secondary" importance at best; they do not appear to represent an "independent causal factor" (Brownlee 2007a, 32; see, however, Brownlee's contribution in this volume).

The comprehensive, careful study Jan Teorell and Axel Hadenius offer in this volume indicates the potential consequences of stretching the scope of empirical inquiry beyond authoritarian elections. Even if authors appropriately exclude single-party elections by conducting separate tests for multiparty contests, their multivariate regressions are almost bound to produce disappointing results, since they still include several categories of elections we should *not* expect to exert a democratizing pull: inaugural elections, democratic elections, limited elections, and postconflict elections.

Inaugural elections. When single-party regimes or military regimes undergo transitions to democracy, the "founding elections" (O'Donnell and

Schmitter 1986, 57) they convoke are symptoms of democratization, not its motor. Rather than preceding democratic breakthroughs, they follow them.

Democratic elections. Liberal democratic theory holds that electoral accountability constitutes the core mechanism ensuring the continual responsiveness of political elites to citizen demands (see Sartori 1987). High normative expectations rest on the shoulders of democratic elections. Yet the extent to which elections actually work as "instruments of democracy," making real on the democratic promises of accountability, representation, and responsiveness is contingent on institutional arrangements, party-systemic configurations, and political dynamics (see Powell 2000, 2004). Although meaningful elections are vital to the quality of democracy, they cannot sustain the open-ended project of "democratizing democracy" on their own. If unsupported by "horizontal accountability" (O'Donnell 1994) as well variegated forms of "societal accountability" (Smulovitz and Peruzzotti 2000), elections may be powerless to protect even basic rights and liberties, not to speak of the deepening or extension of democracy (see McCoy and Hartlyn in this volume). In electoral democracies, elections in and of themselves have been patently insufficient to move regimes toward democratic completion. As Philip Roessler and Marc Howard find in this volume, most electoral democracies are stuck where they are, neither progressing toward liberal democracy nor reverting to authoritarian governance. In liberal democracies that have already reached the ceiling of cross-national democracy scores, truncated scales like Freedom House or Polity would be unable to register further democratization, even if elections were actually able to advance the deepening of democracy.

Limited elections. Authoritarian regimes may restrict multiparty elections to the legislative arena, thus sparing the chief executive position from formal popular approval. Under such limitations of scope, elections are unlikely to develop into serious contests for power. They will tend to serve as arenas of competition for access to state patronage (see Lust-Okar in this volume; Weber 1988, 536–45).

Postconflict elections. In postconflict, post-independence, or post-totalitarian elections, where state institutions are weak, political parties fluid, and mass media free of professional restraints, electoral campaigns may serve aggressive leaders as convenient vehicles to create and exacerbate ethnic conflict and sectarian violence (Snyder 2000). Rather than promoting democracy, ill-designed and ill-timed transitional elections may reignite civil violence and sweep exclusionary ethnic autocrats to power.[17]

Tracing the causal effects of political elections across these diverging contexts, Teorell and Hadenius quite expectedly find rather weak evidence only for the context-independent expectation that "elections have a democratizing potential" (Teorell and Hadenius, Chapter 3 in this volume). In general, statistical studies on the power of elections may have come to diverging conclusions because they have focused on different objects of study: different kinds of elections conducted in different political contexts. Too, they may have come to negative conclusions because they have looked at the wrong objects of study—that is, various kinds of elections that we would not expect to have democratizing consequences.

By contrast, large-*N* studies that cover (roughly) the kinds of electoral authoritarian regimes in which electoral transitions are supposed to take place are more likely to confirm the democratizing power of elections. In his research on electoral cycles in sub-Saharan Africa since 1989, Staffan I. Lindberg (2006c) concluded that the regular conduct of multiparty elections tends to cause steady improvements in their integrity, legitimacy, and competitiveness. In addition to increasing the "democratic qualities" of elections, he found, uninterrupted sequences of electoral contests tend to have effects in nonelectoral spheres as well. In particular, they appear to have "a significant and positive causal effect" on the improvement of civil liberties (144). In short, "the more successive elections, the more democratic the regime" (2006c; see also Lindberg, Chapter 1 in this volume). Relying on a different notion of political liberalization centered on the expansion of political rights, Grigore Pop-Eleches and Graeme Robertson examined the capacity of authoritarian elections to generate "liberalizing moments" in the post–cold war era. They found that most elections do not have liberalizing effects (and "sham elections" do not have any at all), yet most instances of liberalization are "closely associated with elections" (2008, 5). Their statistical findings are elegantly consistent with the idea of authoritarian elections I am proposing here: Authoritarian elections constitute arenas of unequal struggle between government and the opposition that grant governments the tools to win most of the time (the probable outcome), and opposition actors the opportunity to advance or even to win sometimes (the possible outcome).

In their recent study of discrete regime transitions (rather than incremental changes in democracy scores) from 1972 to 2003, Hadenius and Teorell

(2007) discovered that electoral authoritarian regimes are less durable than either single-party regimes or military dictatorships. Furthermore, a majority of transitions from hegemonic regimes lead to competitive authoritarianism—and from there a majority of transitions lead to democracy. Overall, competitive electoral regimes appear to form "a typical stepping-stone to democratization" for all other types of nondemocratic regimes (150–53).[18] Similarly, Jason Brownlee, in his contribution to this volume, concludes that transitions from competitive authoritarianism are more likely to lead to democracy than transitions from any other kind of authoritarian regime (except personalist military dictatorships). The analysis of post–cold war political regimes presented by Philip Roessler and Marc Howard in this volume points in the same direction. While they find both hegemonic party regimes and democratic regimes to be "remarkably stable," they find competitive authoritarianism to be "the most volatile regime type because it remains vulnerable to the destabilizing impact of elections."

The twin properties of competitive authoritarian regimes that these studies identify—their relative instability and their democratizing proclivities—lend credence to the notion that authoritarian elections regularly work as engines of democratization. Despite appearances, these findings do not undermine the notion that elections serve to prolong the lifespan of authoritarian regimes. Governments that preside over competitive autocracies cannot realistically aspire to achieve the longevity of either single-party or hegemonic regimes (unless they succeed in developing a hegemonic party). They can only aspire to last longer than they would in a hypothetical democratic scenario (and to enjoy their retirement more fully than they might had they established a coup-prone military dictatorship). All in all, by respecting the scope conditions of the democratizing power of elections (circumscribed to authoritarian multiparty elections) and by introducing higher levels of analytic differentiation (by distinguishing between hegemonic and competitive regimes), these studies have been adding analytic precision to earlier findings regarding the inherent instability of "inconsistent regimes" located between the poles of democracy and closed dictatorships (see Gates et al. 2006).

Contingent Generalization

While statistical studies have been searching for context-invariant effects of authoritarian elections, a growing number of small-*N* comparisons have been striving to uncover their context-dependent effects. Rather than testing the democratizing impact of elections across contexts, they have tried to identify the contingent political conditions that turn authoritarian elections into effective levers of democratic change. To cite just a few examples: Conceiving of manipulation as an art form, in a faint echo of William Riker (1986), William Case (2006) explained the fate of electoral authoritarian regimes by the degree of skill with which governments execute their manipulative maneuvers. Nicolas van de Walle (2006) and Joy Langston (2006) studied the interdependent coordination problems of government and opposition. The more divided the government, and the more united the opposition (with one depending on the other), the more likely it is that authoritarian elections change the correlation of force between the two antagonists. Similarly, in their embedded case study of Kenya, Howard and Roessler (2006) emphasized the role of opposition coalescence in producing "liberalizing electoral outcomes." In his explanation of democratic breakthroughs in post-Communist countries, Michael McFaul (2005) analyzed the broader correlation of force between civil society and the state. In essence, he inferred from examining commonalities among successful electoral transitions, if civil society is strong and able to mobilize and the incumbent government is weak and paralyzed, electoral rebellions are likely to happen and likely to be successful. Valerie Bunce and Sharon Wolchik tell a similar story in this volume: If authoritarian rulers become vulnerable and complacent, while their opponents take seriously the twin challenge of attracting voters and counteracting manipulation, electoral revolutions have fair chances to succeed.

Taking stock: Those studies, be they quantitative or qualitative, that focus narrowly on the democratizing power of multiparty elections under competitive authoritarianism seem to be consistent with the "empirical teleology" Staffan Lindberg cautiously embraces (Lindberg 2006a, 98 and 144). Empirically, we can observe that elections tend to push competitive authoritarian regimes, however gently and slowly, toward the *telos* of electoral democracy. Unless locked into an equilibrium of hegemonic party rule, authoritarian multiparty elections do seem to work as triggers of democratizing change. Their power to propel the processes of democratization by elections is not mechanical, though. There is nothing automatic or inevitable about it. The transformative power of elections is essentially political.

Conclusion

As M. S. Gill, former president of India's federal election authority, once wisely stated, an "essential condition for making democracy secure is never to take it for granted" (1998, 167). Something similar applies to electoral autocracies. An essential condition for making them secure (as well as for rendering them insecure!) is never to take their security for granted. Autocrats know that and maneuver incessantly to stave off latent and emerging threats to their continuity in power. Those who preside over single-party regimes have nothing to fear from the arena of electoral acclamation. They can aspire to live a long and comfortable political life—as did the figures of the past, who enjoyed their power and privilege before the collapse of the Soviet Union and the end of the cold war extinguished with a stroke almost the entire species of single-party dictatorships. Those who command hegemonic party regimes are destined to lead a tranquil life of authoritarian comfort, too. Nevertheless they have to be on their guard against internal turbulence or external shocks that threaten to upset their institutional equilibrium, artfully sustained by their double reputation of popularity and manipulative skill. Finally, those rulers who sit atop a competitive electoral autocracy are those who struggle most to keep the contingent democratizing power of elections under control. For democratic actors and observers, the bad news is that these autocrats succeed more often than they fail. The good news is that they do fail, and can be made to fail.

CHAPTER THIRTEEN

A Theory of Elections as a Mode of Transition

Staffan I. Lindberg

It is astounding to think that what eventually became known as the third wave of democratization started almost 35 years ago after the death of Franco, the demise of his regime in Spain, and the overturn of the military regime in Portugal in 1974–75. The number of individuals who analyze the phenomenon has increased exponentially from the days in the late 1970s when Juan Linz and a few others, beguiled by the events in Southern Europe, began to revisit the transition from authoritarian rule—after having just finished the study of the breakdown of *democratic* regimes (Linz and Stepan 1978). The (mostly military) authoritarian regimes in Latin America soon started to give in to pressures for change, beginning with the Dominican Republic in 1978,[1] and Guillermo O'Donnell and Philippe Schmitter took the lead in the *Transitions* project analyzing Latin America's return to democratic rule. Focusing more generally on the so-called Third World, Larry Diamond, Seymour Lipset, and Juan Linz followed with another massive effort (the *Democracy in Developing Countries* project) in the mid- to late 1980s and early 1990s, increasing both our knowledge and the number of students in the field. This was just in time; the Berlin Wall was coming apart, ushering 27 new post-Communist states into the world, and Africa's almost 50 states, as well as Asia's 15, started swaying and in many cases moved toward more democratic dispensations. As a result, and for the first time in world history, about 65% of the countries in the world today are electoral democracies, compared to around 30% in the mid-1970s. This change is even more impressive taking into account the increasing number of states in the world, from 148 nations in 1973 to 193 recognized states at present. A monumental shift has occurred over these past 35 years.

No wonder the literature on democratization has expanded accordingly, with literally dozens of books and hundreds of articles published every year now. Twenty years ago we were lucky if there were a couple of good books and a few articles published in any one year. Yet, there seems to be little substantial debate any longer about the normative preference for representative, liberal democracy and that its most fundamental value is self-government. This is not to deny that there are other democratic values as well but only to say that the freedom of citizens to rule over themselves through a concerted collective process is logically prior; without it other democratic values cannot be fulfilled other than in minute entities. Democracy, after all, means rule by the people.

While the Schumpeterian tradition emphasizes competitive selection of political leaders as the main criterion of democracy, and this book is a concerted effort to investigate the role of elections in furthering democracy beyond electoral procedures, the basic rights and procedures of electoral democracy are not "mere procedures." The right to self-government, as Dahl reminds us, is neither a trivial nor merely a procedural right (Dahl 1989, chap. 12). It constitutes in itself substantive societal power sharing and an increase in individual autonomy ultimately for the realization of freedom of both the individual citizen and the collective people. The redistribution of even some aspects of decision-making from the few to the many constitutes an increase in choice and freedom.[2]

Most of the contemporary comparative work on democratization is conducted in reference to Dahl's understanding of polyarchy as the minimal but also empirically possible expression of democratic ideals. Given the foundational nature of Dahl's work, it is puzzling that his tentative theory of democratization, which actually constitutes the bulk of his seminal 1971 volume, is much less often referred to. I am surprised by that even today, since his list of key explanatory variables includes so many of what the literature still holds as important factors. The level of socioeconomic development is one of those factors, of course; anticipating the findings of Przeworski and his colleagues (2000), Dahl wrote that the level of socioeconomic development mattered not so much for transition to democracy as for "the chance that a country will be governed at the national level for *any considerable period of time* by . . . a polyarchy" (Dahl 1971, 202; emphasis added). Thus, while a significant number of us spent another 30 years debating the causal role of socioeconomic development in transitions to democracy, Dahl spoke about what "makes democracies endure" once a transition has been made, to use the phraseology of Przeworski et al. (1996).

Historical sequence, or path dependency, is another well-known factor Dahl discussed at some length, as was the influence of foreign powers and domination so much on the agenda of studies today, from the role of the European Union in Eastern Europe to the role of international peace-keeping and conflict-prevention missions, electoral missions and monitoring, international donors and international financial institutions and their conditionalities, and illicit and aversive influences through oil and other precious commodities interests. Dahl labeled another key factor "subcultural pluralism"; today we study these under the label of ethnic, religious, and other plural divisions, generally acknowledged to be a special problem for both state-building and democratization. He gave due attention to "stateness," a variable later emphasized by (among others) Linz and Stepan (1996); and finally, he put significant emphasis on elites and "political activists" and their beliefs, levels of trust, and willingness to compromise, as well as their coherence and interaction, thus predicting the role of pacts later developed in detail by O'Donnell and Schmitter. While Dahl explicitly acknowledged the tentative nature of his conclusions and the lack of adequate data to test the theory at the time, it is remarkable how well they have stood up to the test of time. The intriguing relevance of these predictions, which were clearly empirically premature at the time, should perhaps lead us to pay closer attention to the fundamentals of the approach.

Modes of Transitions Reconceptualized

The present volume is dedicated to an inquiry into to the logic of "polyarchialization" as discussed by Dahl. Yet, we also believe that we have identified a blind spot in his reasoning. Not only are electoral rights and processes indicators of polyarchy, but they can also contribute to changing the costs of both oppression and toleration, thus serving as causal factors in both democratization and its reverse: autocratization.

How can we make sense of them and build a useful theory of elections as a mode of transition? The answer lies in a combination of insights and development from Dahl (1971, 1989), the work of O'Donnell and Schmitter (1986), the theory of nested games developed by Tsebelis (1990), Schedler's (2002b) extension of Tsebelis's work in the area of "democratization by elections," and Schedler's model as elaborated in the previous chapter. Elections and electoral practices are political institutions in the traditional sense defined succinctly by Levi (1990, 405) as "formal arrangements for aggregating individuals and regulating their behavior through use of explicit rules and decision processes enforced by an actor or a set of actors formally recognized as possessing such power." More recently, understanding the outcome of games or processes, given a certain set of institutions, has been developed by scholars such as Neumann and Morgenstern (1994), North (1990) and March and Olsen (1989) (cf. Munck 2001a). While actors can be thought of as self-reflexive individuals in a social context with abilities to discern and decide on their own preferred actions, choice is always conditioned. From deductive models and games such as the famous "Prisoners' Dilemma" (invented by Flood 1952; cf. Tsebelis 1990, 61–62), to empirical process tracing and historical analyses, researchers have shown how institutions in important ways constrain actors' capabilities and choices (e.g., Bates 1989; Moe 1990). There is thus a long tradition in comparative politics of studying the role of institutions in coordinating behavior that in turn generates patterns of self-reinforcing political behavior (cf. Carey 2000, 736–39). These and other studies in the genre also show how key political institutions contribute to constituting actors and to structuring their incentives, beliefs, and expectations.

For the study of effects of electoral processes on democratization, it seems particularly relevant to focus on both constraining and enabling incentives for actors' calculations of choice in terms of their behavior.[3] This structuring of choice is done both by *defining* and *constituting* actors (e.g., as MPs, voters, or independent news media) and by *providing incentives* for some actions rather than others (e.g., to contest elections rather than to pick up an AK-47), exemplifying both the constitutive and regulatory aspects of institutions.[4] When the number of individuals is large and relations are impersonal, "players" must rely more on institutional rules for predicting the behavior of others than on knowledge about these actors as such; thus, institutions play a greater role in structuring and making such expectations plausible. Elections are such institutions *par excellance,* which can structure expectations and choices for entire nations of eligible citizens—whether in the form of expectations of behavior that furthers democratization, autocratization, or regime reproduction.

In developing a multilevel model of transitions, the most help comes from institutionalist game-theoretical insights, particularly as developed by Tsebelis (1990) followed by Schedler (2002b, and Chapter 12 in this volume). This is where we find the basis for a theory of elections as a mode of transition. The *metagame* is about the question of regime change, meaning changing the rules of how political power is distributed and exercised. We saw in Figure I.1 in the Introduction that both democratization and autocratization imply moves *toward* either end of the scale of democracy—autocracy not necessarily making it all the way. Further, the implication that there are many potential types, or several steps, of transitions was illustrated in Figure I.2. These are important notions to keep in mind as the discussion progresses below.

What characterizes democratization by elections as a mode of transition (leaving autocratization aside for a moment) is that multiparty, *de jure* competitive, elections are introduced *before* much in terms of real democratization has taken place. For whatever reason, some closed authoritarian regimes introduce multiparty elections and some minimal measure of political and civil liberties. Each election then becomes a *subgame* that is not only, sometimes not even mainly, about winning seats in the legislature or winning votes in presidential contests but about stretching, redefining, and changing the parameters of the costs and benefits of the metagame. A process of autocratization by elections implies a reverse process, whereas regime reproduction by elections denotes the use of electoral process to reproduce an equilibrium.

We are now in a position to form a first sketch of a theory of democratization by elections as a mode of transition. Let me emphasize the word "sketch." I do not believe that we are at a stage of theoretical development and empirical knowledge to be able to formulate a more definitive version. Yet, we are also not as handicapped in these regards that we cannot take the first steps. And in another way, we can go further than we had perhaps hoped when we started this project. By virtue of the richness of the previous chapters, we are in a position to broaden our theory beyond democratization to include autocratization and reproduction, thus making it a comprehensive theory (if a sketch still) that is perhaps best labeled "a theory of regime transition and reproduction by elections" even if the following spells out the part about democratization in more detail. In the interest of making the following as useful as possible for future refinements and revisions, therefore, this sketch is consciously simplified, thus violating the nuance and empirical richness of the preceding chapters, as well as parts of the literature to which the reasoning refers.

The Metagame of Regime Transitions

The processes of democratization and autocratization are both characterized by a struggle between defenders of the status quo (the ruling elite) and anti-regime reformers; hence, regime transition is a "game" between two main camps of actors. This is also how much of the literature on democratic transitions since O'Donnell and Schmitter's "tentative conclusions" in 1986 can be read (cf. Schedler 1999, 336). In the case of democratization, an authoritarian ruling elite can reasonably be assumed to see their interests as opposite to democracy. The proof is in the counterfactual. If this is not the case, why are they holding onto authoritarianism when democracy would serve their interests and goals better? They are in office and have regulatory and coercive powers on their side. So at least in the limited sense of joint interest, the members of the incumbent government are unified in viewing their objective interests as being threatened by democratic reforms and as being served by regime reproduction or even autocratization. The reformers may often be democratic; however, they can also be a mixture of (un)holy alliances and strange bedfellows who are sometimes crooks rather than democrats. It is therefore harder to deduce a single interest unifying them other than the wish to change the existing regime and unseat the incumbent ruling elite. That is more than good enough for now, however. The crucial point is that when the reformers *speak and act* in such a way as to strive for democracy, the struggle in effect becomes one of democratization, at least for the moment.

We may thus fruitfully return to Dahl's basic clear and parsimonious proposition (1971, 14–16): Any move toward polyarchy *by definition* threatens the interests, and sometimes lives, of the incumbents in the authoritarian ruling government. And they know it, of course. When pressures for reform mount, such a government will have to confront two interrelated issues. First, to what extent, or at what point, are the potential costs of reforms leading to increasing competition and inclusion that are intolerable in terms of losing power, wealth, status, protection, and so on? Second, given that all reforms are associated with some form of cost to the ruling autocrats, what do they regard as the level of acceptable costs (in terms of deaths, economic loss, loss of things like legitimacy and donor assistance, intra-elite splits, defections, and so on) of using oppression in suppressing reform? In an elegant summation of the argument, Dahl posited (1971, 15) that "the more the cost of suppression exceeds the costs of toleration, the greater the chance for a competitive regime." Oppression and toleration are thus the two main strategies available for the incumbent rulers. Both have costs and benefits attached to them. Figure 13.1 illustrates the two key analytic aspects of the metagame of regime democratization, autocratization, and reproduction.

As the costs of repression increase along the vertical axis beyond the point deemed acceptable to the incumbent autocrats, one expects liberalization in the form of increased competition to occur; and as the costs of toleration along the horizontal axis decrease to become acceptable to the ruling elite, one expect participation to be allowed to expand and become more fair. A few remarks are necessary to clarify the assumptions of the following reasoning and the depiction in Figure 13.1. The first is that costs are to some extent "real" and objective but, perhaps more importantly, also subjective in the perceptions of the rulers. What counts as "acceptable costs" to one may be unacceptable to another and has little if anything to do with our perception as observers of what is acceptable. For rulers with extreme ideological or sultanistic orientations, for example, incredible costs from human suffering and economic despair can be seen as acceptable in order to prevent reforms that would undermine a "higher" goal, as examples in Ukraine and Zimbabwe illustrate. Hence, the demarcation in Figure 13.1 of costs not as high or low, but as acceptable and unacceptable. "Unacceptable" implies "high," of course, but captures better the subjective nature of costs that are intolerable to the ruling elite.

The second assumption is that some measure of change in both dimensions, just like Dahl's dimensions of contestation and inclusion, are probably necessary to some degree for regime change to occur, although not in exactly equal measures. For example, it seems that incumbents facing increasing costs of repression *should* liberalize, but they are unlikely to do so if the costs of toleration are still extremely high (for example, if it would lead to

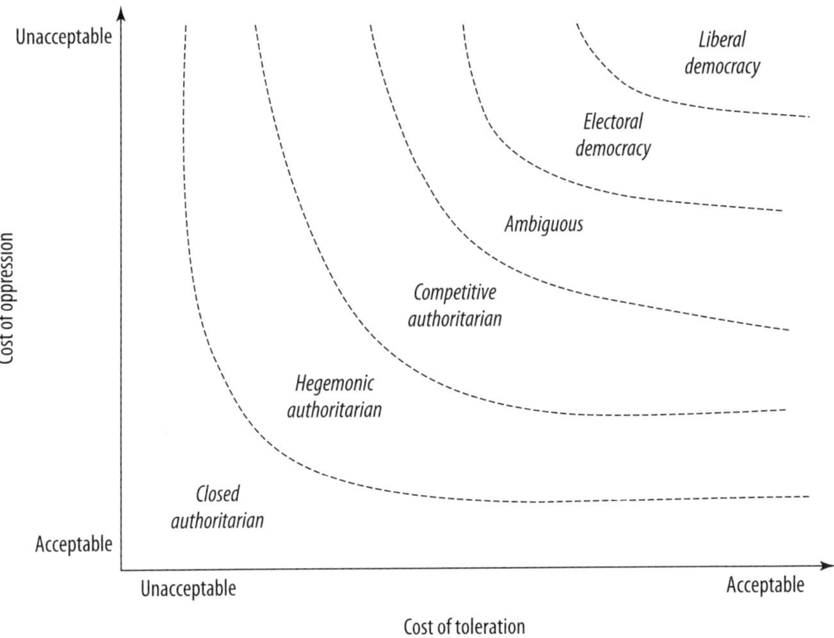

Figure 13.1. The two dimensions of the metagame of democratization, autocratization, and regime reproduction

the death of the dictator, his family, and his cronies, to give one possibility). Conversely, if the costs of toleration go down, rulers in an authoritarian regime *should* be able to afford to expand participation in open and fair processes, but they would probably feel little need to do so as long as the cost of repression is acceptably low. The sensitivity of the regime should increase, however, with changes along one of the dimensions, so that if the cost of repression has gone up significantly, a smaller decrease in the costs of toleration should be enough to induce regime change. Again, the converse should be true when only the costs of toleration have decreased. This is the logic behind the curved lines of rough demarcation indicating when various regime types are more likely to emerge.

So far, this reasoning follows Dahl as we read him, focusing on the cost of oppression and toleration from the perspective of the incumbent authoritarian rulers (who in our cases hold elections, a practice not so common in Dahl's time). Yet, in the following pages we will enrich the analysis by integrating the other side of the coin: How can opposition groups increase the cost of oppression and decrease the cost of toleration so as to enhance the prospects of democratization? And eventually and more specifically, how can the iteration of elections in autocratic regimes affect the costs in the metagame of transition?

The metagame of regime change can thus be fruitfully thought of as structured along the two dimensions depicted in Figure 13.1, with two principal actors: the rulers and the reformers. What differentiates our approach is the emphasis on processual and institutional incentives facing both actors, rather than the highly actor-centered approach of pacting. Personality and idiosyncratic processes are always important, but what conditions make varying actors make similar decisions? This is what we have tried to answer in this volume and what the present chapter seeks to theorize about.

The second level of the metagame of regime transitions concerns the internal composition and source of support of the two main actors. At least since the *Transitions* project and O'Donnell and Schmitter's emphasis on a split in the authoritarian elite as an "almost necessary" condition for a democratic transition, we have known that these are not unitary actors. An authoritarian ruling elite can have varying combinations of hard- and soft-liners or other factions. If this internal subgame leads to changes in strategies or configurations so as to change the outcome, it can affect the transition game. That was indeed one of the key insights of the *Transitions* project; a split and conflict between hard-liners and soft-liners leading to a consolidation of power with the hard-liners would stall or even reverse the liberalization process, whereas the dominance of soft-liners opened up the possibility for a negotiated pact with the reformers, guaranteeing (more or less) success for liberalization. One can think of other ways in which changes in strategies or configurations of the incumbent coalition change the end game, such as the judiciary deciding for the first time to exercise independence from the incumbent government and shifting the balance of power, and the payoffs of strategies in the transition game indicated in Moraski's contribution in this volume. Part of the story Bunce and Wolchik tell is how military, security, and other domestic actors who were once part of the incumbent governing elite defect, or at least become neutral, and in so doing shift the payoffs for reformers' strategies such as protest and legal challenges. When security agencies decide that they will no longer blindly abide by the ruler's directives, repression becomes much harder for the incumbent to even exercise, making it far less costly for the opposition to revolt.

Yet, the other principal actor, the reform bloc, in many countries is a conglomerate and usually consists of a series of domestic and international groupings unified by one common interest—to unseat the incumbent. Some among the opposition may be crooks and thieves who just want their opportunity to rip off state wealth; others may be genuine democrats. If and when important segments of the reformers defect to join the incumbents, the parameters of the struggle change in the other direction. Reformers are weakened, as the defectors provide information to the incumbents about the opposition's action strategies, bring their supporters over to the incumbent bloc, frequently enhance the ruling elite's legitimacy, and by simply reducing the combined forces of the reform bloc decrease the cost of oppression for the ruling autocrats.

If reformers can coalesce and pursue coordinated strategies, however, the cost of oppression goes up. The cost of toleration can also be more easily brought down in this situation, since rulers are more likely to be ready to negotiate with a credible and cohesive coalition of reformers and because rulers are more likely to trust promises from a united, coherent group of opponents. In a situation with various competing reformist groups, it is harder for the rulers to anticipate which group will eventually assume positions of power; making pacts with groups that later lose out poses a greater risk. The rulers may find themselves in a situation where the reform group that gains power that does not feel bound by a pact made with other groups. Tsebelis's work on nested games accommodates this notion well.[5] Borrowing from his figures (e.g., 1990, 59), Figure 13.2 depicts a simplified version of the nested metagame of transitions. Denoting the two factions in the incumbent ruling elite as hard-liners and soft-liners, and the groups within reformers as crooks and democrats, is for illustrative purposes only. In any empirical case of regime transition, the appropriate labels of various groups are contextual.

In this schematic version democratization and autocratization form a "game" consisting of two players whose principal interests are contradictory with regard to political reform. They will choose the most rational strategy based on the costs and benefits attached to oppression and toleration, respectively. This scenario is complicated by the fact that each "actor" in reality often consists of two or more factions and groups. These "subactors" engage in internal "games," thus making a nested, two-level game in Tsebelis's sense. While very useful as a general theoretical model, this is still too generic for the analysis of regime transitions, and elections as a mode of transition.

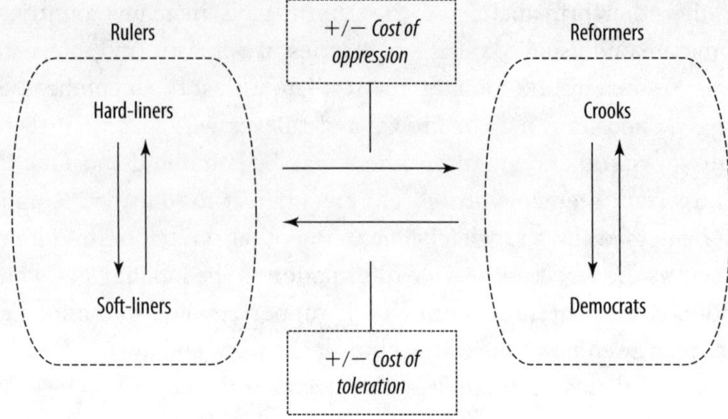

Figure 13.2. Schematic view of the metagame of transition

The first problem is that the payoffs of the strategies vary according to the context. Much of the democratization literature seeks to address that variation in terms of identifying factors that increase the costs of repression (or, alternatively, decrease the benefits of repression) and decrease the costs of toleration (or increase the benefits of toleration). For example, a strong middle class with economic assets and independence from the state, large urban populations, a split and defections in the authoritarian regime, well-organized civil society, and opposition parties, as well as international attention and sanctions, are factors that increase the cost of repression. Successful pacts between incumbents and reformers, guarantees of pardon for past human rights abuses, moderate opposition groups and leaders, and institutional and electoral rules that give the incumbent a better chance of staying in or coming back to power are factors that decrease the cost of toleration. On the opposite side, we typically find that rent incomes from oil or other extractive industries, a revolutionary ideology, dispersed rural populations, strategic superpower involvement, large-scale domestic economic ownership and investments by rulers and their cronies, and other factors make toleration more costly and repression more acceptable for ruling elites.

The second problem is that we have to recognize that costs and benefits are subjective, as discussed briefly above. The extremes of acceptable costs of staying in power—such as number of individuals beaten up, tortured, or killed; destroyed state institutions; the spread of corruption; and the like—are, as shown by many leaders across the globe, inherently in “the eyes of the beholder." Thirdly, we also have to recognize that regime reproduction, partial reform, and democratization can have unforeseen costs and benefits uncovered only as the process moves along. These are not "one-shot" games but a series of iterated interactions where one stage leads to another and where the possible outcomes, accepted costs and benefits, and available options (payoffs) vary with the results of previous actions. For example, choosing to engage in serious repression at some point means that a number of individuals in the incumbent ruling elite now have blood on their hands and will therefore be less likely to concede to liberalization if it means that they will be prosecuted. This increases the cost of toleration. On the other hand, once rulers have agreed to substantial liberalization and allowed reformers to organize opposition parties, mobilizing significant domestic and international support, the cost of oppression goes up.

Fourthly, actors miscalculate on the basis of limited or distorted information. This is perhaps particularly likely in more personalistic systems, where messengers of unwelcome news are often punished and subordinates therefore filter information sent upwards. With these caveats in mind, it becomes untenable to use the above model for prediction of behavior in a strict game-theoretical sense. The two-level nature of the game makes the costs and benefits of alternative strategies, and therefore the outcomes in the regime game, vary with the strategies and outcomes in the incumbent- and reform-subgroup games. What, then, is the logic of "democratization by elections"? Our answer is that iterative, multiparty elections change the costs of both oppression and toleration and thus are key events that affect the cost-benefit analysis for the incumbent as well as for reformers. Autocratization and regime reproduction by elections are in many ways the negative reflection of this but also have their own specific characteristics.

The Subgame of Elections

In Figure 13.3, the subgame of iterative multiparty elections has been added to the metagame of regime transitions. In an established liberal democracy, the subgame of elections is not about changing the regime; it is about keeping or changing the political leadership and party or parties in power. In a nondemocratic regime, elections can be about changing the nature of the political regime itself *as well as* changing the government. Multiparty elections can lead to uncertainty about outcomes and thus to uncertainty about who will be in power after the polls. This is the main source of the *direct* impact of the electoral process on the game of regime reproduction and transition. It mainly affects the nature of the regime indirectly, however, through changing the costs of repression and the benefits of toleration in the metagame of regime transition.

The subgame of multiparty elections, and their iterations, provide a set of institutions and processes for a structured interaction between the two main actors: government and the opposition. This game has a third principal actor, however, and that is the collective of voters. Their choices have impacts on the costs and benefits of various strategies for the ruling incumbent and the opposition elite. If large numbers of the electorate turn out for elections and vote for the opposition, the cost of electoral manipulation and intimidation goes up. A more massive scheme of fraud and use of force needs to be put in place and shielded from outsiders, the risk of adverse reactions from the international community increases, the risk of postelectoral protest and violence goes up, and so on. At the same time, the benefits for the opposition elites of daring to mobilize citizens for protest increase. If the electorate chooses to support the incumbent or exit from the process, or if the incumbent can use the electoral process to divide and co-opt the opposition, things are reversed in terms of the payoffs for alternative strategies the incumbent and opposition may chose. What happens in one game affects the viability of alternative strategies in the other games. At our present stage of theoretical development we cannot solve this complex of multiple games in the sense of standard game theory. That is also not the point here. The main function of this display is to provide a theoretical model around which the analysis of elections as a mode of transition can be understood and structured. From that analysis we can compare the main theoretical conclusions about the factors that cause elections to be a mode of regime reproduction, autocratization, or democratization, across the chapters in this volume.

So far, we have looked at the *direct* impact of iterative electoral processes on the metagame of regime transition. Why should we expect the subgame of elections to also have significant *indirect* and hence more subtle effects? The key to this question lies in the logic of elections as a struggle for political power.

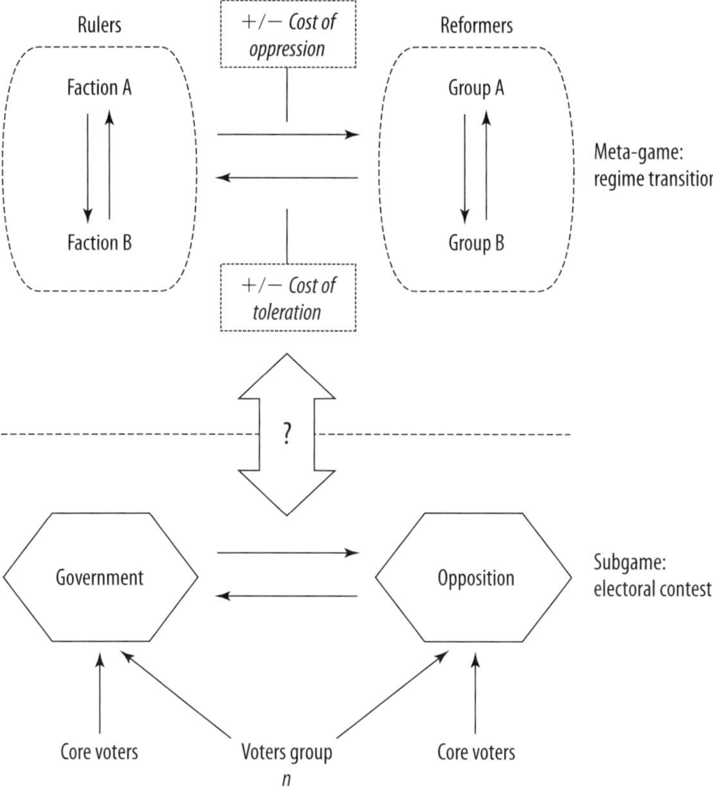

Figure 13.3. Iterative electoral subgame and the metagame of transition

Elections as a Mode of Transition

There are potentially a large number of factors that can influence the regime transition and reproduction metagame that results in various modes of transition. It is during election campaigns and their immediate aftermath that most individuals, political parties, and civil organizations peak in activism, and it is consequently when pressures are highest. Being the largest peacetime mobilization of political activism, elections provide a time for change and challenges. Second, the logic of competition for executive and legislative power in and around elections provides the means for citizens and organizations to demand and get concessions from politicians and state authorities more often than in times of non-election. To the extent that the electoral race has some degree of competitiveness, the logic of throwing out the rascals also creates pressure on incumbents to be responsive. Election time is also typically when a newly democratizing regime is under the scrutiny of the international community and of the international news media. Watchdog organizations such as Election Watch, Amnesty International, and Human Rights Watch capitalize on these occasions, lending weight to the pressures for reforms. That said, the link between elections and democratization is not theoretically tied to freedom and fairness of elections. Disappointments during a particularly bad experience with electoral practices—inflated voters' registries, political violence during the campaign and on polling day, outright fraudulent voting and collation of votes, and intimidation of voters and political opponents—naturally may stimulate activism in society even more than free elections do. In an effort to add to the existing literature, the focus in the following is not on all those *per se* but on how the subgame of repetitive multiparty elections constrains and enables strategies for actors in the transition game, affecting the two principal areas of costs of oppression and toleration so as to alter outcomes.

Table 13.1 presents a schematic overview, based on the findings in this book, of the mechanisms that make elections either a mode of autocratization or democratization. I will discuss these in turn, starting with the two sides of autocratization—decreasing costs of oppression and the Janus-faced costs of toleration—and then the two mirroring aspects of democratization: increasing costs of oppression and decreasing costs of toleration.

Autocratization: Decreasing Costs of Oppression

At the outset, it is important to point to Roessler and Howard's finding that the conditions of democratization by elections changed around the end of the cold war. This is also reflected in McCoy and Hartlyn's findings that most Latin American countries—where liberalization occurred earlier—could hold long series of elections under autocratic rule without much change at all. Indeed, McCoy and Hartlyn argue that elections in Latin America's authoritarian regimes in many cases served an important function in reproducing these regimes. Similarly, elections changed function and significance dramatically in post-Communist countries and in Africa in the period after 1989. These patterns point to the overall importance of strategic interests and the relative "comfort" autocrats could find in the incapacity of international actors to support reform and in their sometimes active support for nondemocratic regimes. These reflections are not new, only put in a slightly

Table 13.1 Mechanisms of electional impact on the metagame of regime change

	Autocratization	Democratization
Cost of repression	*Factors decreasing costs:* • Competitive clientelism • Competition for economic opportunities concentrated in the state • Effective media and information control • Strategic importance of country • Collective action failures among opposition • Geographically concentrated and disunited opposition groups	*Factors increasing costs:* • Voters becoming citizens and mobilizing for mass protest • Increased size and complexity of regime challengers • Organizations and institutions vested in prodemocratic action • Self-fulfilling prophecies: spread of democratic ideals and expectations • Diffusion of methods to use elections to achieve regime change • Increased media freedom that redefines the possible • International attention and pressures • Blatant, failed manipulation of election outcomes • Increased institutional complexity and avenues for contestation • Defections from incumbent regime
Cost of toleration	*Factors increasing costs:* • Legalization of opposition and political associations • Winner-take-all institutions • Electoral corruption, manipulation, fraud	*Factors decreasing costs:* • Incentives for elite actors and state institutions to promote democratic institutions and get "locked-in" • Gradual transition: one or two terms in office for authoritarian ruler • Allowing transformation from autocrats to democrats • Moderation of opposition • Cooptation of opposition • Skilful manipulation of elections outcomes

different theoretical framework. When strategic interests are prevalent, the costs of oppression, in the form of possible weakening of support from allies, condemnation by international NGOs, sanctions, diplomatic activities, and international support for domestic reformers, decrease significantly and therefore make autocratization more likely. Today the former Soviet republics with closer ties to Russia again face fewer restrictions on their use of oppression, while the post-Communist countries who have sought closer ties with the European Union, and in many cases membership, face a different set of incentives.

Brownlee give us further evidence that the hegemonic electoral authoritarian regimes are not only more stable but are also the type of autocratic regimes that defy democratization after a breakdown and more often turn into another nondemocratic regime. These are the regimes that have managed to decrease the cost of oppression to long-term, sustainable levels (for the incumbent government). Schedler's findings attest to how ruling autocrats that manage to censor the media effectively reduce the cost of oppression and how this can preclude regime-changing impacts of the electoral subgame on the metagame. This may also be lurking behind his surprising finding that manipulation is unrelated to the success of regime reproduction by electoral authoritarian regimes. Hegemonic regimes provide more effective means to guarantee the government in power and are thus less in need of blatant manipulation of elections. Instead of being a mode of transition, elections become a mode of regime reproduction. Although not analyzed directly, the orchestration and reproduction of the kind of competitive clientelism Lust-Okar describes can be enhanced by media collaboration. The use of the media is also a probable factor behind the many stable hegemonic regimes described by Roessler and Howard, as well as the years of stable electoral dictatorships in many Latin American countries before the third wave, as discussed by McCoy and Hartlyn.

The natural-resource-rich countries in the Middle East and Africa have lower costs of oppression for two principal reasons. One is the strategic interest of other nations. China's interest in and support for the regime in Sudan, for example, based primarily on its investment in the oil sector, has made it possible for that hegemonic electoral authoritarian regime to avoid much in the way of costs for the genocide in Darfur, let alone for holding elections void of any democratic qualities. China is not alone, however; Western countries' strategic interests have helped decrease the cost of oppression in countries like the Republic of Congo, Equatorial Guinea, and Cameroon. Resource-rich countries can also invest riches in more efficient and loyal security apparatuses. As illustrated by the study by Lust-Okar in this volume, elections do not always become a subgame that changes the costs and benefits for the actors in the metagame of transition.

This reasoning supports Bunce and Wolchik's point about regime strength.

Elections typically become a mode of regime reproduction or even autocratization in strong authoritarian regimes: A country that is economically secure or at least relatively stable, where the authoritarian regime is organized and institutionalized to avoid defections and internal splits, and in which the government has support from international actors who do not see democratization as a key priority is a stronger regime that has lower costs of repression, or just a higher threshold of what constitutes acceptable costs of repression. The incumbents in an electoral authoritarian regime must be careful in increasing the level of oppression, however; as noted by Schedler they face a dilemma in this regard. This is evident in Bunce and Wolchik's analysis as well as in the chapter by Rakner and van de Walle. The use of violence, exclusionary tactics, and obviously flawed electoral processes can lead to higher, not lower, costs of oppression. Indeed, particularly negative experiences with elections have in many cases stimulated increased vigilance and unity among reformers, as well as increased determination by international actors to have an impact on the nature of the regime. The finding that even flawed elections in Africa have on average had positive effects on democratization in the longer term, as shown in the first chapter, strengthens this conclusion. When the repetition of the electoral game leads to increasing costs for regime reproduction, it is difficult for the ruling elites to bring these costs down again.

Rakner and van de Walle provide evidence of another variant of how incumbent governments can reduce the cost of oppression for the ruling elite in the regime metagame. By continuing to make sure that the lion's share of economic resources, international aid contracts, local development projects, and economic opportunities are directly or indirectly controlled by the sitting president and his government, the ruling elite make it more advantageous for other politicians to be co-opted. For an ambitious young person, politics remains the most beneficial route to wealth and status in such a context. Thus, the electoral game can be turned into a competition for legislative or party office that can be traded for a more prestigious position as minister or for lucrative contracts and other economic opportunities, or both. The incentives for individual actors thus stack up against opposition cohesion and collective action along the lines discussed by Lust-Okar, which would work in favor of more dramatic democratization. As Rakner and van de Walle report, the continuation of such patterns has also contributed to the relatively low legitimacy of political parties in Africa. Strong support for the opposition parties is, of course, imperative if elections are to become a mode of transition to democracy, whether in the form of the post-Communist "electoral model" or some other variant. When opposition parties have low standing among the population, the cost of oppression is decreased, since the potential for mass mobilization is relatively low. Electoral authoritarianism can then be reproduced at acceptable levels of cost to the ruling elites.

Autocratization: Janus-Faced Costs of Toleration

The issue of the costs of toleration in autocratization is Janus-faced. On the one hand, when the costs of toleration go up for the rulers, they have more to lose and are less likely to concede to regime-changing measures. On the other hand, rulers can also actively minimize the costs of toleration and, when in control, can tolerate more opposition since it poses little threat. Rulers' ability to minimize the actual costs of toleration is a dimension not discussed by Dahl but one that emerges prominently in several chapters in this volume. An important part of the constitutive rights and regulations of a de jure multiparty electoral regime is the legalization of opposition parties and the rules regarding their participation in politics. Implicit in Brownlee's, Teorell and Hadenius's, and Schedler's findings is the crucial role these rules play. But these analyses also testify that the very existence of opposition can be managed and that the power of opposition groups to use elections to effectuate regime change can be undermined. This is a principal lesson in Rakner and van de Walle's contribution to this volume. Despite several electoral cycles and formal rules guaranteeing competition, autocrats in many countries have been skillful in handling the strategic interaction in the electoral arena so as to prevent opposition parties from changing the fundamental parameters of the regime-game. Successful management of opposition parties' successes and failures through a mixture of legitimate and illegitimate strategies is a way for authoritarian governments to handle the increasing costs of toleration. This has to do with how incumbents and the opposition, respectively, use the electoral subgame—for regime reproduction or regime change.

The coordination game facing the (often) large number of opposition parties is a difficult collective action problem that has proven a hard nut to crack in many African and post-Communist countries. The problem is particularly hard to solve when three factors combine: a hegemonic or competitive electoral authoritarian regime; voting that is geographically concentrated; and a government that controls significant patronage powers and wealth. Because the regime is still authoritarian, the incumbent can penalize geographical areas and political parties who are and stay in the opposition. Each faction or local leader is then better off, regardless of what the others do, if he or she forms a small party with strong local support. Regardless of who emerges as the presidential winner, the local party leader can always sell his or her legislative support to a president and his or her party in exchange for patronage and development projects in the local area, which in turn strengthens the rule of the local patron. By managing the electoral process, rewards, and incentives so as to sustain splits among opposition parties and lure adherents with the cooptation of key leaders and their followers, the regime significantly reduces the cost of tolerating the remaining opposition groups. Such regimes can even benefit from tolerating more participation from various groups as long as the incumbent government can make sure these groups do not find incentives for collective action and become a cohesive actor.

Norris's analysis provides one institutional explanation for this. She shows how electoral institutions—crucially, majoritarian electoral systems—have an autocratic-reproductive, or even autocratization, effect over the longer run. Winner-take-all systems, especially if combined with presidentialism, increase the cost of toleration significantly. When you lose, you lose everything, and the new government will have all the power resources and patronage powers at its disposal. This is an important part of the answer as to why we see so many political parties even in first-past-the-post, single-member-district systems that according to Duverger's (1954) law should lead to two-party systems. In Kenya, for example, the two dozen or so opposition parties needed two electoral cycles to solve their collective action problem, only to fail again shortly after their victory in the third election in 2002; just recently the outcome was severe violence and disruption after the 2007 elections. Most countries in Africa have various forms of majoritarian systems, whereas the successful democratizers in post-Communist and Latin American countries more often use proportional representation. Constitutive institutions matter. In particular, when the incumbent ruling elite is authoritarian and has engaged in various forms of oppression and perhaps corruption for which they can be held legally accountable, losing elections in a majoritarian system increases the costs of losing compared to more power-sharing approaches.

When opposition parties are successfully weakened and presidential power is particularly strong, defections from the opposition to the incumbent are more likely. This tendency is perhaps particularly strengthened in Africa by the extension of pervasive state resources as patronage to those who do not oppose the government, in a context where independent financial resources are few. When more of the elites are aligned with the incumbent government, there is a decrease in the number of powerful individuals who could pose a threat along with a decrease in the total cost of toleration, but at the same time regime change is made less likely. This is part of the Janus-faced costs of toleration in processes of autocratization and the reproduction of electoral authoritarian regimes.

But there is another strategy available to rulers faced with potentially increasing costs of toleration that are pushing them toward autocratization. They can lower the costs of toleration by preemptive mobilization to solidify their dominance. Brownlee's analysis in Chapter 5 brings this out very clearly, and it is implicit in several other chapters as well. By gradually allowing the elections to become more competitive and using this new context to build up a strong party organization as well as improve their image and legitimacy, governing parties can, if successful, lower both the cost of toleration (by winning more votes by legitimate means) and the need for costly oppression (since there will be less to object to).

Democratization: Increasing Costs of Oppression

The subgame of elections acquires another meaning when the metagame shifts and the existing authoritarian regime breaks down, as Brownlee notes in Chapter 5. After a series of more competitive elections the subsequent regime is much more likely to be an electoral democracy. In game-theoretic terms à la Tsebelis (1990), the strategies chosen by the players in the subgame change the payoff structure of the metagame, which in turn affects the parameters of the next iteration of the subgame.

A multiparty constitution typically also gives several state institutions new rights and responsibilities. We focus here in particular on the judicial system. With the establishment of electoral rules and regulations, law adjudication and enforcement authorities are given a formal role in the protection of political rights. It becomes possible for military, police, and security agencies as well as courts to advance their status, individual careers, and prominence through pro-democratic actions.[6] There is then a payoff structure with costs and benefits where being anti-democratic is no longer necessarily the default option. Allowing and defending the democratic rights of the people to participate in political processes by means other than voting, such as demonstrating, petitioning authorities, filing complaints, and calling on the police for protection during electoral practices, is then a possibility. When courts decide to insist on their autonomy and rule against autocratic incumbents in election-related disputes, the parallel struggle over the nature of the regime is directly affected, as evidenced most clearly in this volume by the contributions of Bunce and Wolchik, and Moraski.

Moraski describes a new but also intuitive finding that a more complex legal structure makes it harder for the incumbent to control the legal system and defeat reformers' efforts. Having to fight a multitude of legal battles naturally increases the cost of oppression that works through influencing the courts, even if factors like a parochial political culture, the degree of political corruption in the system, and beliefs of hierarchies are likely to condition these effects. When successful, a strategy of using a complex judicial structure to challenge autocrats on many fronts and levels in the postelectoral disputes game can have very strong indirect impacts on the metagame of regime transition. Moraski's contribution highlights the positive and negative roles courts can play in either supporting or negating such indirect impacts, as well as the importance of the institutional setup in determining which strategies the opposition parties can pursue—that is, how the institutional structure constrains or enables actors' behavior.

The role of self-fulfilling expectations, sometimes referred to as "discounts of the future," is also evident in the findings of several of the preceding chapters. At a certain point, pro-democratic behavior is likely to be exhibited not only by entrepreneurs, altruistic believers in democracy, and those with vested interests because of their organizational ties or other affiliations, but also by leaders and citizens from a wider segment of society. When a critical mass of individual citizens have reason to believe that other citizens and the most important elites expect democratic rules to stay in place for the foreseeable future and electoral politics to prevail, their perceptions are likely to work as a self-fulfilling prophecy. In a manner similar to Coleman's (1990) and Elster's (1982) arguments about how other social phenomena work, elections can spread democratic qualities to society when citizens believe that crucial elites, from the military to political leaders, and a majority of fellow citizens will accept and play by the new rules. At some point, even risk-aversive and perhaps even nondemocratic citizens are likely to climb on the bandwagon to demand and enact democratic principles in society. Several chapters have highlighted institutional provisions that can facilitate the creation of such expectations in the electoral game, thus increasing the costs of repression in the transition metagame.

A key to such an institutional provision is term limits. When two terms in presidential office are the end of the road for a particular individual and these term limits are adhered to, the expectation of change is built into the institution, even if the elections change only the individual in power and not the party for some time. For such self-fulfilling prophecies to be created, and especially to enhance the prospect of real alternation in power, thus changing the parameters of the regime and the transition path, coordination between opposition parties is absolutely vital. Opposition groups must solve their internal game—their collective action problem—to avoid the costs of decreasing legitimacy as a result of failed protests and challenges. When the opposition is facing a governing party in an electoral authoritarian regime, unity seems close to being an absolute necessity. When opposition parties unify, they are in a much better position to insist on other measures that drive up the cost of oppression for the incumbent, such as effective election monitoring and parallel vote counts, ambitious voter registration campaigns, and credible promises to various incumbent government and state actors to lessen their fears of losing.

Thus, opposition strategies in electoral processes play a crucial role in creating self-fulfilling expectations and lock-in mechanisms. For example, through good organization and the adoption of the "electoral model" in the electoral subgame, the opposition can increase the incumbent's costs of repression in the metagame of regime reproduction or change, as illustrated by Bunce and Wolchik's analysis in this volume. Schedler's framework in Chapter 12 is a direct extension of such reasoning, and his analysis in Chapter 7 is a powerful testimony to the importance of opposition strategies. Successful mobilization and protest by the opposition can have "magical" effects on the cost of repression for the incumbent and affect the metagame of regime transition. Ghana's evolution to democracy is an illustration of this process. The subgame of Ghana's first elections in 1992 empowered the reformers to renegotiate the parameters of the metagame, changing the rules of the game to those of a competitive electoral authoritarian regime, which in turn placed the opposition parties in a better position to challenge the governing NDC party in the 1996 elections. Opposition parties won one-third of the legislative seats and used the process to push for further changes in the regime before the 2000 election that enabled them to win a fair contest and take over power, an event that definitely pushed Ghana over the fence to at least an electoral democratic regime. Naturally, the cost of oppression is much higher if an incumbent is facing well-organized mass protests than if he is facing sporadic outbursts from what can be conceived of as extremist elements. Protests come in many forms, of course, and can include demonstrations coupled with use of media and the courts, as well as international mobilization of supporters through diplomatic and financial incentives.

Bunce and Wolchik's analysis of the post-Communist electoral revolutions provides an extra dimension to what we have seen above. Opposition strategies that can change the payoffs in favor of regime change are not simply domestic and not only a question of internal coordination. Incumbent governments may perceive increased costs of oppression as they witness what is happening in neighboring countries. Opposition parties often use the lessons learned from successful experiences in other countries in their own country, something ruling elites are quick to realize. Thus both domestically and through international diffusion, actors participating as election observers, for example, or in voters' education campaigns learn about electoral rules and procedures, issues of transparency, eligibility criteria, detecting and mitigating fraud, political rights and civil liberties, procedures for complaint and adjudication, and so on. It seems plausible that such organizations learn about and build civic capacities and organizational experience during the massive mobilization and excitement typically surrounding elections in transitional regimes.

The media are also given new rights and responsibilities that carry the potential of being a force for democratization in the metagame. The rights of voice and opinion, and freedom of information and association, constitute the media as an independent actor to the extent that these rights are realized in practice. The media also act as one of the main channels of pressure on elected politicians and candidates to improve the rights and liberties of the people. The more that media can become the transmitter for the pro-democratic calls and complaints of individuals, organizations, think tanks, state actors, and other bodies, the more they affect the regime. But why around elections? Elections are the time when media entrepreneurs are likely to test, stretch, and redefine the boundaries of both political rights and civil liberties, and by doing so tilt the metagame of transition. For example, the more that the media express popular pressures for more democracy, publicize clues about possible splits in the ruling elite, provide information on the international costs of nonreform, and contribute to a sense that the ruling elite is vulnerable, the more the cost of oppression goes up. If, however, an autocratic ruler retains a tight grip on the finances of the country and succeeds in holding onto a great degree of centralized authority, the media can be used to increase monitoring of the citizenry and reduce the flow of information to the public.

Over three decades ago, Dahl (1971) suggested that the level of political competition to a large degree determines how democratic a regime is. Our study has reaffirmed that the role of opposition parties is crucial. Even flawed elections can further the long-term goal of democracy if opposition parties are willing to retreat and fight another day. This finding clearly calls for more involvement by both domestic and international actors in policing the rules of the game.

Democratization: Decreasing Costs of Toleration

When decreasing costs of toleration are not the result of the incumbent's having a system to split and disarm the opposition but are, rather, the effect of changing and more pro-democratic strategies by the incumbent and other actors, democratization becomes more likely. A de jure multiparty electoral regime has a series of rights and rules with the potential for affecting the metagame of transition. Consider first the voter as citizen. The fundamental features of equal sovereignty in elections—one person, one vote; the right to chose between candidates and parties; the freedom of opinion and voice; and the right to form and lead associations—are all rules of the electoral regime that also constitute the citizen as such. Many citizens are likely to be targeted by voter education campaigns and messages conveyed by officials, activists, radio, newspapers and, in urban areas at least, TV. These activities are part of constituting the citizen as an equal sovereign *in principle*, endowed with rights to participate and chose between alternatives under legitimate procedures. Once the election is over, the citizen does not necessarily lose the recognition and understanding acquired. The cognitive and experiential steps taken cannot be undone. Experiential learning and socialization of citizens can build up expectations that increase the cost of oppression in the transition game. But perhaps more important are the ways in which these can decrease the cost of toleration for incumbent autocratic rulers. Constituting and safeguarding the rights of citizens are the official duties of the state and its institutions. An incumbent regime that decides to pursue a cooperative strategy and head such efforts is likely to gain in legitimacy and popular support and is more likely to be forgiven for past deeds. Any such gains work to increase the chances that the government party will win elections and will use a lot less manipulation and media control in order to do so. The level of necessary oppression goes down along with these decreases in the costs of toleration, and with a gradual transformation of the old autocratic party to an organization associated with a more democratic dispensation, the cost of toleration is drastically decreased. The decision by Jerry J. Rawlings' Provincial National Defense Council (PDNC) to move relatively quickly to a fairly liberal order, hold multiparty elections in Ghana in 1992, and win in the guise of the National Democratic Congress (NDC) party is an example of this. Although the 1992 elections were not generally viewed as free and fair, the 1996 elections were, and the NDC and Rawlings won again with almost exactly the same figures as in 1992, indicating that the democratization strategy has reduced the level of oppression and fraud significantly along the lines of the reasoning above.

A cooperative strategy does not have to involve the entire autocratic government and the state institutions it commands. While an autocratic government, as long as it is united, may feel "safe in the saddle," factions of the government can defect, especially if they feel that the cost of repression has increased beyond an acceptable level and that the new institutional electoral configuration provides avenues to lower their costs of toleration. For example, police and security forces commanders lower their own costs of toleration (which may incidentally increase both the cost of toleration and oppression for the ruler) by giving better protection to the opposition and, as in Madagascar in 2001 and in several of the post-Communist cases, by refusing to use stark violence against opposition parties during election campaigns.

Another and very important way for leaders of the ruling government to lower their costs of toleration is to defect and join forces with some opposition groups. The similarity between O'Donnell and Schmitter's findings in the *Transitions* project and our collaborative one is here striking. Splits in the authoritarian regime seem to be universally a very important factor in democratization, whether by elections or not. In the original formulation, splits and defections occurred before the holding of "founding" elections and the introduction of democracy. In processes where elections are the mode of transition, defections by individuals from the incumbent regime typically occur in conjunction with elections, prompted by the mobilization around them. What counts as acceptable costs of repression obviously can differ among participants of an authoritarian government and so can their perceptions of the likelihood that a regime change is inevitable. Those who make the calculation that costs are running too high, and that the electoral game is likely to have an impact on the regime, find themselves in a situation where the best option is to lower their costs of toleration. The most effective strategy of doing so, short of fleeing into exile, is to join the opposition. The electoral game of defection thus can have an impact indirectly but significantly on the strengths of the two sides in the transition metagame. The more defections, the higher the costs of repression are going to be for those who stay, and hence, the more likely it is that they will also defect or give up the game and accept changes in the nature of the regime.

Perhaps this is another reason behind Norris's finding that power-sharing institutions beget democratization more than winner-take-all configurations. Proportional representation and other consociational institutions offer a larger number of possible coalitions. Factions within the incumbent elite have more "ways out" in terms of various possibilities of defecting and still being important players in new governing coalitions. They can even—as literally hundreds of African defectors have chosen to do—start their own opposition party and claim their own little niche. This may even be a superior strategy, especially in more personalistic- and clientelistic-driven systems. A winner of a presidential contest will often be in need of supporting parties and defectors can, should the winds change, ally themselves with the old ruling party again in a coalition.

Concluding Remarks

We set out in this collaborative effort to inquire into the role of elections in democratization, as a new mode of transition supplementing and providing new perspectives on the transition paths elucidated by O'Donnell and Schmitter (1986) and their colleagues that gave rise to a whole new literature. Our efforts in many ways set out to test the claim by Rustow (1970) that we do not need convinced democrats to create a democracy—we need democratic institutions that can foster democrats—and that it is possible to trick, lure, and cajole leaders into behaving in democratic ways, instilling democratic beliefs. This suggests a very different pathway to democracy than many of the main works in the "transition paradigm" suggested—not only the work of O'Donnell and Schmitter but also the works of scholars such as Diamond, Linz, and Lipset (1990), Huntington (1991), Karl (1990), Linz and Stepan (1996), and Przeworski (1991). Taking seriously Dahl's (1971) proposition that the cost of oppression and the cost of toleration are the two key dimensions structuring the choice of autocratic incumbents, we have conducted an investigation into how the repetition of elections in less-than-democratic regimes of various types can affect the "metagame" of regime reproduction and change.

Primarily since the end of the cold war, holding elections in what have become known as electoral authoritarian regimes has emerged as an important mode of transition. These processes are distinct from the paths depicted in the "old" transition literature and therefore in need of a supplementary theory. This chapter has attempted to lay the foundation for such a theory by bringing in insights from the literature on parallel, multilevel games in different arenas and on different levels along with the wealth of findings presented for the first time in the preceding chapters. Elections are normally not regime-changing processes. In "normal" democratic times they are about temporary allocation of executive and legislative power. In our present period and for some time to come, however, it seems that in many countries across the globe, elections are "nested"—to use Tsebelis's (1990) excellent expression—in a larger picture of struggle between ruling elites and reformers. Repetitive electoral processes are used by both sides to influence the outcomes of the regime struggle. Several aspects of the electoral "game" have both direct and indirect effects on the pathway of the regime. Through our concerted effort of comparative case studies and regional and global studies using a variety of empirical approaches, we have been able to see a general pattern of when and how elections are successful means of autocratization and democratization, respectively. We are looking forward to further refinements and contributions, for we strongly believe that the struggle over regime change and stability is going to be played out to a significant degree through electoral processes for the foreseeable future.

Notes

Foreword

1. All of this amounts to a broad and, it would seem, coordinated authoritarian backlash against civic pluralism and democracy assistance. See Gershman and Allen (2006); National Endowment for Democracy (2006).

2. The leading advocate of a structural conditions–based approach to explaining this variation is Lucan Way, in "The Real Causes of the Color Revolution" (Way 2008). See also the debate over his essay in the January 2009 *Journal of Democracy*. For arguments emphasizing the role of indigenous organizations and tactics and/or international diffusion and assistance, see McFaul (2005); several of the other works cited by Way; the above-cited exchange in the 2009 *Journal of Democracy*; and Ackerman (2007).

INTRODUCTION: Democratization by Elections

1. Students of democratic consolidation have now improved their knowledge about the different routes that "slow deaths" of democracies might take. For example, the reassertion of military supremacy may lead to a progressive diminution of existing spaces for civilian control; state weakness may subvert the rule of law; the rise of hegemonic parties may suffocate electoral competition; the decay of electoral institutions may affect the fairness of voting; incumbents' use of state resource and media may violate civil and political rights; the introduction of exclusionary citizenship laws may circumvent democratic inclusion (Schedler 1998, 98).

2. Schedler provides an excellent overview and analysis of the manifold meanings of democratic consolidation, depending on the empirical contexts and normative goals. I think we both subscribe to Sartori's claim that collective semantic confusion among scholars should be avoided. Phenomena that are different in kind ought to be identified by different terms (Sartori 1984; 1991, 243–57).

3. Causality, as it were, is always an analytical construction and cannot be evidenced as such regardless of whether it is referred to as causal chain, link, or mechanism. It is not an empirical observation but an argument that should be guided by logical consistency and empirical reference.

4. Needless to say, this is a conceptual point and should not be mistaken for a tautological empirical theory.

5. Even if a political system were to reach the theoretical maximum on all specified indicators of democratic attributes, it would not make democracy the object. Objectification is a matter of conceptual analysis, not empirical conclusion. If we study water and its qualities, for example, finding it to be yellowish or pure does not render the color yellow or purity our object of study.

6. It is quite possible, and I would argue, preferable, to work with a graded measure of democracy and use that graduation to establish and argue for a particular cut-off point between two or more regime types. When the distribution of cases along such a continuum is known, the sensitivity to errors by certain cut-off points can be assessed. If one starts out with only a dichotomy there is no way such a test can be performed, and we will never know how great a role the classification criteria played in producing the results. In addition, scholars can certainly agree on basic defining characteristics of democracy, excluding purely authoritarian systems without necessarily agreeing on the theoretically or empirically valid cut-off points.

7. I thank Jason Brownlee for providing the inspiration to use the term *autocratization*.

8. Building on the typology developed by Diamond (2002), which has also been used in different versions throughout this book, Fig. 13.1 displays the range of regimes, the two general directions of transitions, and the spectrum where elections as a mode of transition is a possibility.

9. The story of Justice D. F. Annan and his role in modern Ghanaian politics is untold but fascinating. In brief, Jerry J. Rawlings grew up without his father (a Scottish man who never lived in Ghana), and as a young man tried to court one of Justice D. F. Annan's daughters. Annan did not allow the courtship but took in Rawlings as a son. More than 15 years later when Amarkai Amartefio managed to recruit Annan to the PNDC regime in 1984, Annan came in as Rawlings' father figure whom he could not speak up to in just any way. Annan was a liberal and was the person who managed to gradually convince Rawlings that he had to allow the expansion of political freedoms and civil liberties and move ahead with local elections in the late 1980s, then allow multiparty national elections in 1992. Annan headed that process as chairman of PNDC's National Commission for Democracy and later became the first speaker of Parliament from 1993 to 2000.

CHAPTER ONE: The Power of Elections in Africa Revisited

I would like to thank the participants in seminars at Cornell University, Yale University, the University of Kansas, Miami University, and the University of Texas, Austin, for their valuable comments on earlier versions of this chapter. Thanks also go in particular to Leonard Wantchekon, Gerardo Munch, Goran Hyden, Larry Diamond, Winifred Pankani, and Andreas Schedler for their insightful critiques. The usual caveats apply.

1. Free and fair denominations are coded in four categories: "No, not at all" when elections were wholly unfair and obviously a charade; "No, not really" when there

were numerous irregularities that affected the results; "Yes, somewhat" when there were deficiencies but they did not affect the outcome of the election; and "Yes, entirely" when elections were free and fair although there might have been some human error and logistical restrictions on operations. When distinguishing between flawed processes and essentially acceptable ones in a binominal fashion, the first two categories are collapsed into "flawed" while the later two indicate "free and fair."

2. For details about the three dimensions and the various indicators, see Lindberg (2004c, 2006a, and 2006c).

CHAPTER TWO: The Relative Powerlessness of Elections in Latin America

1. The more fully developed argument (Lindberg 2006a) does not make as broad an electoralist argument as this suggests; however, we explore it as well, since simplistic or reductionist readings of the argument often pursue this logic. For Lindberg, the units of analysis are what he terms de jure elections, which are participatory, contested, legitimate, and periodic. Elections in which most or all of the opposition choose to boycott are included (and are treated as a measure of how democratic an election is); the process of counting elections to determine a potential mode of transition through repeated elections begins anew following a coup or constitutional suspension.

2. Freedom House data, used by Lindberg and many others, distinguish between political rights and civil liberties, but in fact, there is a great deal of overlap between the two, adding empirical measurement problems to the conceptual difficulty. According to Freedom House, "Political rights enable people to participate freely in the political process, including the right to vote freely for distinct alternatives in legitimate elections, compete for public office, join political parties and organizations, and elect representatives who have a decisive impact on public policies and are accountable to the electorate. Civil liberties allow for the freedoms of expression and belief, associational and organizational rights, rule of law, and personal autonomy without interference from the state" (www.freedomhouse.org).

3. Here, we rely on what might be termed an expanded procedural definition of political democracy and the trichotomous country classifications generated by Mainwaring, Brinks, and Pérez-Liñán (2001). They categorize countries as democratic if they have open and competitive elections; a universal franchise in a historical context rather than as an absolute value; the protection of political rights and civil liberties; and elected authorities with real governing power. Semi-democracies have open and competitive elections but fail on one or more of the other criteria.

4. If we were to include information for Colombia, Costa Rica, and Venezuela through 1990, there would still be no statistically significant relationship, though the correlation is now slightly positive (0.13).

5. Not surprisingly, there is also a high correlation between a country's democracy score and the number of its elections that are competitive by the measures chosen here (e.g., r = .71 for elections in which incumbents receive less than 60% of the

vote). Yet, this is not by itself evidence for the electoralist argument; rather, it confirms that competitive elections are a constitutive element of democracy (see n. 3).

6. In the spirit of the electoralism argument we have defined transition here as movement from authoritarian to *either* semi-democratic or democratic status, based on codings by Mainwaring, Brinks, and Liñán.

7. Although Panama has a moderate democratic history, higher than some of the restorational cases, we place it in the gradual transition category because of its passage through a semi-democratic status in the Noriega years.

8. In order to test a broader range of rights and because of the cold war bias of the Freedom House scores, we incorporated alternative measures to Freedom House's Civil Liberties scale. We used the Political Terror Scale by Gibney and Dalton, which separately codes the annual State Department human rights reports and the Amnesty International reports for state-sponsored terrorism, from 1 to 5 (with 5 being worst), on detentions, human rights abuses, disappearances, torture, and political murders. In grievous cases, this scale also includes nonstate-actor-sponsored terrorism, such as insurgency movements. The CIRI Human Rights Data Set provides two separate indexes that we use—physical integrity and empowerment. Again using the State Department's human rights reports and Amnesty International reports (but privileging AI where there is a discrepancy between the two), the Physical Integrity Index measures government (only) human rights practices (torture, political imprisonment, disappearances, extrajudicial killings). We constructed a modified Empowerment Index to remove the political participation score, since it is directly related to the electoral process, and included only other civil rights of speech, movement, association, workers rights, and religious freedom.

9. We examine civil rights as measured by Freedom House civil liberties scores and the modified CIRI Empowerment Index (see n. 8), and human rights through the CIRI Physical Integrity Index. Freedom House's civil liberties scores include the measures in the CIRI empowerment index (freedoms of association, movement, expression, work, and religion) as well as physical integrity (freedom from torture, etc.), while also including questions about economic opportunity and private property rights and rule of law. Adding CIRI indices to our analysis allows us to disaggregate these concepts, while also providing a check to Freedom House's methodology and noted cold war bias. Because of the similarity between the CIRI human rights data and the Political Terror Scales, we report here only on CIRI.

CHAPTER THREE: Elections as Levers of Democratization

Previous versions of this chapter were presented at the Annual Meeting of the American Political Science Association, August 30–September 2, 2007, and at the workshop "Democratization by Elections?" at the University of Florida, Gainesville, November 30–December 2, 2007. We would like to thank the participants of these conferences for valuable suggestions, and Michael Wahman for excellent research assistance.

1. We have imputed missing values for 749 country year observations by regressing the average Freedom House/Polity index on the Freedom House scores, which have better country coverage than Polity.

2. Golder's (2005) data, recording both presidential and parliamentary elections in 1946–2000, were used for robustness tests in preliminary data analysis, without leading to any conclusions substantially different from the ones reported in this chapter.

3. Lindberg (2006a) stresses the importance of a *consecutive* series of nominally competitive elections. To capture this concept, we also computed a version of the cumulative stock variable that was set to zero if a period of noncompetitive elections (or an absence of elections) followed a period of competitive elections (that is, if Vanhanen's indicator of competitiveness turned zero after a period of positive values). This version, however, performed less well in our tests than the historical stock variable that disregards breaks in a consecutive series.

4. As a robustness test, we also computed the effective number of cumulative democratic elections using the Polity data as our measure of democracy in election years. Results obtained were no different (although from a more limited sample of countries).

5. We have followed this procedure for the following countries: all the former member states of the USSR and the People's Republic of Yugoslavia (until 1991), the Czech and Slovak Republics (until 1992), Timor-Leste (a part of Indonesia until 2002), Bangladesh (a part of Pakistan until 1971), Eritrea (a part of Ethiopia until 1993), Iceland (a part of Denmark until 1944), Ireland (a part of the UK until 1921), Yemen (a continuation of North and South Yemen from 1991), South Yemen (a part of Yemen until 1966), and East Germany (a part of Germany until 1948). We treat West Germany as a continuation of interwar Germany, reunified Germany as a continuation of West Germany, Vietnam as a continuation of North Vietnam, and Ethiopia after the secession of Eritrea, Pakistan after the secession of Bangladesh and North Yemen after the secession of South Yemen, as a continuation of themselves, which means that no data needs to be filled in for these countries.

6. We include the election variables both at time t and at time $t - 1$ in order to take into account the fact that elections are unlikely to occur on two consecutive years (only 10% of all elections are held the year after another election), which makes the election variable negatively autocorrelated temporally ($r = -.15$). As a result of this negative correlation, the one-year lagged effect of holding an election is negative (albeit not significant) if entered alone into the model.

7. However, this impact again hinges on two relatively extreme outliers: Panama in 1989 and Zambia in 1991. With these two cases excluded, the election effect is rendered completely insignificant (coef = .049; se = .042; $p = .244$).

8. These outliers are again Panama in 1989 and Zambia 1991, but now also Bangladesh in 1991. With these three cases excluded, the election effect remains significant at the 5% level (coef = .114; se = .045; $p = .011$).

9. These outliers are Panama in 1990 and Uruguay in 1989. When they are ex-

cluded, the election effect is completely insignificant (coef = .048; se = .036; p = .183).

10. If Panama is also excluded, the remaining effect is insignificant (coef = .064; se = .039; p = .103).

11. These outliers are Kuwait in 1990, Angola in 1991, Thailand in 1976, and the Slovak Republic in 1998. Without them, the cumulative election effect remains significant at the 5% level (coef = .124; se = .052; p = .018).

12. To arrive at this conclusion, we have followed the approach developed in Teorell and Hadenius (2007), where separate models are run for all observations with positive change in the democracy variable (upturns) as well as for those with negative change (downturns). The result is that most of the effects reported in Tables 3.5 and 3.6 appear when downturns are used as the dependent variable.

CHAPTER FOUR: Post–Cold War Political Regimes

1. This includes the Middle East: Polity IV changed its coding of Lebanon in 2005 from "foreign-occupied" (−66) to "above the democratic threshold" (7) after the so-called Cedar Revolution, Syria's withdrawal from the country, and the holding of post-occupation parliamentary elections.

2. To ensure a similar-case comparison, this sample includes only regimes that became hegemonic authoritarian after 1987, and thus excludes preexisting hegemonic regimes such as in Malaysia, Singapore, Mexico, and Senegal, which had held consecutive elections for some time prior to the end of the cold war. The data do not suggest, however, that these latter cases are any more liberal than their post–cold war counterparts, despite a much longer experience with electoral politics. Their mean Freedom House civil liberties score for 1987 is 5.18, which is similar to the mean civil liberties score (5.08) for the post–cold war hegemonic regimes after one or more consecutive elections.

3. Perceiving that there is no chance of a fair contest and not wishing to legitimize the electoral victory of the incumbent or the ruling party, opposition candidates and parties in hegemonic regimes sometimes boycott the elections out of protest.

4. In this sense, we are answering the important challenge laid out by Munck and Snyder (2004, 1), who write: "Methodologically, research on hybrid regimes has failed adequately to address a number of central issues involved in measurement. Most critically, this research has not provided systematic, clear procedures for developing measures that successfully handle intermediate categories and cases."

5. For a critical evaluation of both Polity and Freedom House, see Munck and Verkuilen (2002). Despite their criticisms of these and other indices of democracy for having problems with conceptualization, measurement, and aggregation, there are as yet no better alternatives that cover countries around the world annually. By drawing from *both* Freedom House and Polity, we can ensure that there is a much wider degree of consensus than might otherwise be the case if we used only one index exclusively.

6. We exclude regimes in which civil war, state collapse, foreign occupation, or other types of instability—rather than the power of the incumbent—account for the absence of national elections (or make them meaningless). These regimes are coded as "collapsed/other." See Snyder 2006 for the distinction between "closed" and "collapsed" regimes.

7. Theoretically, institutions other than national elections could allow contestation and participation in the selection of government, and thus be the basis for democracy, but in practice none exist.

8. For example, Egypt was a closed authoritarian regime between 1987 and 2004 because only one candidate (whomever the national assembly selected) was legally allowed to contest the national elections for president. In essence, the election was a referendum on the incumbent, Hosni Mubarak. But in May 2005 the constitution was amended, and in September multicandidate presidential elections were held, leading to a reclassification of the country's regime type according to the electoral process.

9. These scores correspond to the standard thresholds for classifying a country as "free" or "democratic" in each respective index (although some scholars average the Freedom House scores on political rights and civil liberties, and consider a 2.5 average as the threshold for "free").

10. We also considered Freedom House's electoral democracy index as an alternative measure for distinguishing electoral democracies from autocracies but found it to be quite lenient in its evaluation as to whether elections are "free and fair" or not. For example, this index deemed as free and fair such cases as Croatia after the 1992 election, Georgia after the 2000 election, and the Central African Republic after the 2005 election. In each of these elections, independent election monitoring groups or the press questioned the relative freedom and fairness of the elections; on the 1992 Croatia election see IRI 1992; on Georgia in 2000 see OSCE 2000; on the Central African Republic in 2005 see *Economist* 2005. Overall we found our coding scores to be very similar to Freedom House's electoral democracy designations, differing in less than 5% of the cases of potential electoral democracies, but in almost every case the discrepancy is due to Freedom House coding of the country-year as an electoral democracy and our coding rules classifying it as a competitive authoritarian, hegemonic authoritarian, or collapsed regime.

11. Information on election results derives from several sources, including the Election Results Archive (www.binghamton.edu/cdp/era/index.html), the IFES Election Guide (www.electionguide.org/index.php), the African Elections Database (http://africanelections.tripod.com), Electionworld.org, which is now hosted by Wikipedia (http://en.wikipedia.org/wiki/Elections_by_country),and newspaper and magazine articles from Lexis Nexis.

12. The 70% threshold, while admittedly arbitrary, has been used by other scholars to determine whether an election was competitive (see Levitsky and Way 2002b; Wantchekon 2003).

13. The mean and median vote and seat percentages in hegemonic authoritarian

regimes are significantly above the 70% threshold. In presidential systems, the mean vote percentage is 84% (the median is 85%). In parliamentary systems, the mean seat percentage is 87% (the median is 88%).

14. An example may be useful for understanding our coding rules for different types of authoritarian governments. We code Ethiopia as closed authoritarian between 1987 and 1994; during this period the country was ruled by executives who came to power using force and did not permit elections (Mengistu Haile Mariam between 1977 and 1991 and Meles Zenawi after the overthrow of Mengistu in 1991). In 1995 the post-Mengistu interim administration came to an end with the holding of multiparty elections, which Zenawi's party, the Ethiopian People's Revolutionary Democratic Front, won overwhelmingly (gaining 88% of the seats in parliament) due to an opposition boycott. Based on the election result and the country's Freedom House and Polity scores in 1995, which fall below the democratic threshold (4 and 1, respectively), we score it as hegemonic authoritarian beginning in 1995. Between 1996 and 2000, the Freedom House and Polity scores remain below the democratic threshold, and we maintain the hegemonic authoritarian score. In 2000 a second election was held, with similar results, again due to an opposition boycott. The Freedom House and Polity scores remain below the democratic threshold for 2000–2005, and we maintain the hegemonic authoritarian score. In 2005 a third election was held; this time the key opposition parties participated in the election, leading to a more competitive but not free and fair election (see European Union 2005). The EPRDF's share of seats fell to 60%, giving the opposition a sizable minority in parliament. Because of the fraudulent nature of the electoral process and the ensuing state violence, Freedom House and Polity maintain their low scores on the country (5 and 1, respectively, for 2005). In 2005, however, we change our categorization of Ethiopia from hegemonic to competitive, reflecting the greater contestation in the electoral process (based on the EPRDF's share of seats falling below 70%). With no changes in the Freedom House and Polity scores in 2006, we maintain the competitive authoritarian ranking for that year.

15. This point is consistent with the data that Lindberg (2006a) collected for the African cases. In elections in authoritarian regimes (countries with a Freedom House score of 3 or greater in the year before the election) between 1989 and 2003 in Africa, the mean vote percentage of the winner varies according to the degree to which the "real opposition" chooses to participate. If none of the "real opposition" groups participate, the incumbent, on average, receives 95% of the votes; if "some but not all of the main players" participate, the incumbent receives 72% of the vote; and, finally, if all of the main actors in the opposition participate, the winner's total is only 60%.

16. While other benefits might be gained from participating in elections in which the opposition has no possibility to win, such as building up electoral experience or, for a marginal political player, communicating to the incumbent and other opposition actors his or her credibility, there are also considerable costs—namely, legitimizing the incumbent's fraudulent victory.

17. Two hegemonic authoritarian regimes did collapse as a result of civil war: Liberia in 2003 and Haiti in 2004. Also, a coup d'état in Ivory Coast in 1999 overthrew a hegemonic authoritarian regime, leading temporarily to closed authoritarianism and eventually to civil war. But no stable hegemonic authoritarian regime has abandoned the procedure of multiparty elections once initiated, though contestation has remained tightly circumscribed.

18. While competitive authoritarian regimes, electoral democracies, and liberal democracies average one election every four years, in hegemonic authoritarian regimes the average is closer to one every five years.

19. Although an 84% probability may seem rather high, it is important to remember that this is the likelihood of regime continuity for the *following* year. The continuity rate is therefore much lower when 84% is multiplied by itself over the course of, say, five years (yielding less than a 50% chance of continuity).

20. Because closed authoritarian regimes, by definition, do not have national elections for the executive, there are no data for these regimes.

21. In Belarus, in contrast to the other cases, the founding election was not won by the incumbent but by an independent candidate, Alexander Lukashenko. Nonetheless, Lukashenko adopted autocratic tendencies throughout his tenure and in the second election achieved an easy victory.

22. We are grateful to Valerie Bunce, Sharon Wolchik, and Ellen Lust-Okar for encouraging us to consider this point.

23. GDP per capita data are from the World Bank (2007) and are calculated on the basis of constant 2000 dollars. These results should only be seen as suggestive, however, because missing data from a number of country-years may bias the means.

24. Note that while we use these indices to determine the overall fairness of the electoral process, and thereby to establish the threshold between authoritarianism and democracy, we do not use them as a measure to distinguish between the three types of authoritarian regimes.

25. These data exclude five cases (Azerbaijan, 1992; Bangladesh, 1991; Georgia, 2004; Indonesia, 1999; and Kyrgyzstan, 2005) in which incumbents in hegemonic authoritarian regimes were forced out of power as a result of political protest and the interim governments held fresh elections that the opposition won. These cases suggest that while hegemonic authoritarian incumbents are not vulnerable to losing power in elections in which they participate, civilian uprisings, often triggered by the massive fraud required to guarantee electoral success, are a risk to their political survival. For an analysis of the Georgia and Kyrgyzstan cases, see Bunce and Wolchik in this volume.

CHAPTER FIVE: Harbinger of Democracy

1. Geddes places a few especially resilient regimes (Egypt, Suharto's Indonesia, Stroessner's Paraguay) in "a doubly hybrid Personal/Military/Single-Party category" (1999b, 22).

2. A secondary problem involves Hadenius and Teorell's measure of democracy based on a regime's average numerical score from the Freedom House and Polity data (Hadenius and Teorell 2006). That measurement may miss the discrete shift from autocracy to democracy that accompanies many transitions. To give two examples, Hadenius and Teorell's Polity / Freedom House threshold records Nicaragua and Romania becoming democracies in 1995, whereas observers conventionally date Nicaragua's transition to 1990 and Romania's to 1992 or earlier.

3. One could add further that the actual numbers reported are heavily disputed, another reason to seek a less controversial dichotomous measure. For the debate over democracy datasets see Coppedge 2002; Marshall et al. 2002; Munck and Verkuilen 2002; Ward 2002.

4. Lindberg (2006a), and Howard and Roessler (2006) also use numerical measures for their dependent variables.

5. The theoretical justification for a Middle East regional variable comes from the field's renewed consideration of Middle East exceptionalism (see, e.g., Herb 2005; Posusney 2004; Ross 2001). As it happens, the Middle East variable remained significant across all of the models. Running the models with the other regional dummy variables did not alter the findings.

6. Thanks to Steve Levitsky and Staffan I. Lindberg for spurring me to consider these underlying dynamics.

CHAPTER SEVEN: Sources of Competition under Electoral Authoritarianism

Work on this chapter was made possible by research grant 36970-D from the Mexican National Council for Science and Technology (Conacyt). I thank Staffan I. Lindberg, Gerardo Munck, and Ellen Lust-Okar for their extensive comments on previous versions, and Monica Caudillo for research assistance. The usual disclaimers apply.

1. As a matter of fact, a good part of the comparative literature treats the latter as a valid indicator of the former. See, most prominently, Przeworski (1991, 10, 95) and Przeworski et al. (2000, 14–28).

2. On the distinction between *x*-centered and *y*-centered analyses, see Gerring (2001, 137).

3. For more extensive treatments of authoritarian elections as "nested games," see Schedler (2002a, 2006).

4. In his *Indeterminacy and Society*, Russell Hardin examines the strategic and normative implications of this simple and compelling, yet often overlooked, insight: "In strategic interaction I choose a strategy, not an outcome" (Hardin 2003, ix).

5. The term "agency losses" originated in economic literature on "principals" (the bosses) and "agents" (their employees). Essentially, agency losses are the difference between what the boss wants and what he gets.

6. I treat opposition protest as an alternative explanation whose isolated impact on electoral outcomes is to be examined. Yet opposition mobilization may well be

endogenous to authoritarian manipulation. According to my own data, however, the empirical association between levels of manipulation and levels of opposition protest is rather weak. Bivariate correlation coefficients (not reported here) are low and almost without exception insignificant. The lack of systematic linear relations need not speak of a complete dissociation, though. Manipulation and repression may still be related in either nonlinear, linear, or contradictory ways.

7. See also Bunce and Wolchik, Chapter 10 in this volume.

8. In empirical terms, the generic rejection of authoritarian governances seems to be fairly universal, while the awareness of nondemocratic rules seems to be more precarious. On worldwide citizen support of democracy, see Inglehart (2003). For more recent regional overviews, see the clusters of articles entitled "The Democracy Barometers" in the *Journal of Democracy* 18, no. 3 (July 2007) and 19, no. 1 (January 2008). For a critical review of conventional measures of democratic support, see Schedler and Sarsfield (2007).

9. Notable exceptions in the study of Mexican hegemonic party rule are Greene (2007), Langston and Morgenstern (2007), and Magaloni (2006).

10. With respect to violations of physical integrity and media restrictions, I measure changes from the previous election to the year previous to the current election.

11. The larger mean margins of victory Table 7.4 reports for my lagged measures seem to indicate that levels of competitiveness decrease from election to election. This is an illusion. The subset of elections for which I have data on previous elections (and thus lagged measures of competitiveness) is much smaller than my overall basket of cases—little more than half the size of the full set of legislative elections and less than half that of presidential elections. Within that smaller set of cases, average changes in margins of victory between elections (not reported here) do bear negative signs. They are not, however, significantly different from zero (bilateral *t*-tests). The stability of electoral results confirm the idea that the mere mechanical power of elections is not enough for opposition parties to gain strength and for authoritarian rulers to lose ground.

12. I settled on the simple procedure of stepwise elimination after much experimentation with correlation analysis, bivariate regressions (linear and nonlinear), and uncountable alternative multivariate regression models. Despite the low degrees of freedom at initial rounds of intervariable competition, backward elimination led to substantive results that are fundamentally consistent with the core findings produced by alternative procedures.

13. In fact, the emerging literature on electoral authoritarian regimes is giving more and more systematic attention to opposition politics. Recent examples are Aspinall (2005), Beaulieu (2006), Howard and Roessler (2006), Lindberg (2006a), Lust-Okar (2005a and 2005b), Posusney (2005), and van de Walle (2006).

CHAPTER EIGHT: Opposition Parties and Incumbent Presidents

1. The dataset of legislative and presidential elections used for this essay is available from Nicholas van de Walle. The data extend to the end of 2007. Botswana and Mauritius elections are not included.

2. The small number of cases in the later elections means that the corresponding numbers in Table 8.1 should be treated with caution.

3. The numbers are reported at http://africanelections.tripod.com. For a recent account of democratic developments in Madagascar, see Marcus and Ratsimbaharison (2005).

4. Most of the independents elected in 2004 had previously been in the United Democratic Front (UDF) but had defected during the nomination process for various reasons. After the election, most of them rejoined the UDF parliamentary group.

5. We thank Devra Moehler for this insight.

CHAPTER NINE: Legislative Elections in Hegemonic Authoritarian Regimes

Parts of this chapter draw directly from Ellen Lust-Okar, "Elections in Authoritarian Regimes: Catalysts for, or Obstacles to, Reform?" in *Democracy and Globalization,* ed. Anthony Langlois and Karol Soltan (New York: Routledge, 2008). I gratefully acknowledge the support of the United States Institute of Peace (Grant 182-05) and the Whitney and Betty MacMillan Center for International and Area Studies, which made this project possible.

1. Similarly, Gandhi and Vreeland (2004) find that parliamentary authoritarian regimes are less likely to experience civil conflict than their counterparts without parliaments.

2. Geddes (2005) makes this argument, although she does not distinguish between presidential and parliamentary elections on this count.

3. For a more complete discussion of the differences in election types, see Gandhi and Lust-Okar (forthcoming 2009).

4. Respondents were asked, "To what extent do you believe that the party is able to influence the government on the matters that pertain to its goals?" Of those who answered, 7.34% believed it played a large role, 23.25% that it had some effect, 23.61% that it played a small role, and 28.29% that it played no role in policymaking; 16.99% did not know, and 0.5% refused to answer or did not understand the question. CSS, University of Jordan, 2004 Democracy Survey, question 305.

5. This is demonstrated in daily conversations, shown in polls by the Center for Strategic Studies at the University of Jordan, and evident in Egypt in a survey entitled "Civilian Attitudes toward Important Political and Economic Problems" by al-Ahram Center. In the Egyptian survey, 71.5% of the respondents believed that either unemployment, high prices, or low income were the most important problem facing Egypt today.

6. The poll was conducted among 320 politically active elites, including doctors, journalists, lawyers, and politicians office, with 45.83% responding that they would seek *wasta* before beginning their task, and 19.16% looking for it after beginning (Kilani and Sakijha 2002, 126). Similarly, a 2005 German Development Institute survey in Jordan found that of 58 business elites interviewed, 86% believed that *wasta* was important for doing business with public institutions, and 56% of the respondents admitted to using *wasta* themselves. More than three-quarters of 180 low- and middle-rank civil servants surveyed believed that *wasta* was either very important (51%) or somewhat important (25%) in order to gain employment in their department (Loewe et al. 2006, 32, 34–35).

7. Based on my own fieldwork in Morocco, the Palestinian Authority and Syria, and on discussions with Egyptians, Iraqis, and Lebanese.

8. Article 99 of the Egyptian constitution states that "no member of the People's Assembly shall be subject to a criminal prosecution without the permission of the Assembly except in cases of flagrante delicto." In theory of, of course, this article is included in the constitution in order to provide greater guarantees for the independence and freedom of parliamentarians to question government, criticize policies, and otherwise perform their job uninhibited by the possibility of politically motivated prosecution. In practice, however, the immunity provided to MPs is a tremendous perk of office, commonly thought to be used unethically by parliamentarians for personal gain.

9. The infamous case of the "loan MPs" is only one example. During the two previous parliamentary sessions a number of MPs were stripped of their immunity and prosecuted for taking advantage of their parliamentary status to obtain millions of pounds in unsecured loans. Much of the money was never paid back. This case was covered in several articles by Gamal Essam El-Din in *Al-Ahram Weekly.* In "Corrupt MPs Suffer Court Fury," June 29–July 5, 2000, Essam El-Din noted that "politically, it is expected that the harsh verdicts will thrust under sharp public scrutiny the increasing use of parliamentary immunity and political clout to make illegal profits." See also his "Corruption Shockwaves," August 8–14, 2002: "Because the defendants included five former members of parliament (MPs) from the ruling National Democratic Party (NDP), the rulings reignited the debate on MPs' abuse of parliamentary immunity to secure ill-gotten gains." Also see his "Corruption Stigma Haunts NDP," July 6–12, 2000.

10. For similar discussions, see Shehata (2008) and Tuasted (2008).

11. Al-Ahram survey in Egypt, as well as discussions in Jordan and Syria.

12. Of the remainder, 3.1% of respondents named the IAF, 8.7% did not know, and 1.9% did not understand the question.

13. Over 88% were not members, and 9.43% did not understand the question. CSS 2004, question 302.

CHAPTER TEN: Oppositions versus Dictators

We thank Melissa Aten, Aida Badalova, Igor Logvinenko, Vladimir Micic, Keti Nozadze, Tsveta Petrova, Aghasi Harutyunyan, and Sara Rzayeva for their assistance with this project. In addition, we thank Marc Howard and Staffan Lindberg, as well as other participants, for their comments on an earlier draft of this paper presented at the Workshop on Democratization by Elections, organized by Staffan I. Lindberg, at the University of Florida, November 30–December 2, 2007. Finally, we thank the Smith Richardson Foundation, the Einaudi Center for International Studies and the Institute for the Social Sciences at Cornell University, and the Institute for European, Eurasian, and Russian Studies at George Washington University for their support of our research. We are also grateful to the Rockefeller Foundation for allowing us a month of uninterrupted work on the project at Villa Serbelloni in Bellagio in 2007.

1. The analysis in this chapter is based not just on studies of these elections, but also on over 200 interviews conducted with both domestic and international participants in these events. The interviews were conducted from 2005 to 2008 in the United States (Washington, DC, New York, Philadelphia, Charlottesville, and Palo Alto); Germany and Great Britain; and Armenia, Azerbaijan, Croatia, Georgia, Serbia, Slovakia, and Ukraine.

2. For detailed discussions of these cases, see Bunce and Wolchik 2008a, chaps. 5–6; also see Åslund and McFaul 2006; Kandelaki 2006; Kandelaki and Meladze 2007; Kuzio 2005a, 2005b; Marples 1999; Radnitz 2006; Silitski 2005; Tavernise 2008; Way 2005a, 2005b; and Whitmore 2007.

3. See, for example, Howard and Roessler 2006; van de Walle 2006, 2007; but see Bunce and Wolchik 2008a, chaps. 2 and 4, on the considerable difficulties involved in forging a united opposition.

4. See, especially, van de Walle 2007 on this point.

5. In other work, we have addressed the important questions of how the electoral model developed, its diffusion from one country to another, and the role of demonstration effects, similar conditions (objective and subjective), and, finally, transnational democracy promotion networks composed of American democracy promoters, local political activists, and regional activists who, following successful implementation in their own countries, shared their strategies with oppositions in neighboring countries who sought similar electoral breakthroughs (see Bunce and Wolchik 2006b, 2007a, 2007b, 2008). The existence of diffusion effects, however, does not invalidate the arguments presented in this paper because diffusion in this case, as in all cases, was uneven across time and space as a result of variations in local conditions supporting emulation. It is precisely these variations that we highlight in this chapter. On diffusion effects, see, for example, Bockman and Eyal 2002; Brinks and Coppedge 2006; Elkins and Simmons 2005; Strang and Soule 1998; and Tarrow 2005.

6. For a further assessment of the role of the international community in influencing both the survival of regimes and electoral change, see Bunce and Wolchik 2007b, 2008a, chaps. 3, 5, and 6.

7. See, for example, the suggestive data reported by Aliyev et al. 2006; but note, as well, the demonstrations involving more than 10,000 people that erupted in Armenia following the 2008 presidential election.

8. Croatia was an exception here, largely because the death of the dictator, Franjo Tudjman, in 1999 had led to the rapid disintegration of his political party, the Croatian Democratic Union. Consequently, despite an authoritarian political context, there was no organized force defending the regime.

CHAPTER ELEVEN: Judicial Complexity Empowering Opposition?

For their comments and suggestions, I would like to thank Patricia Woods as well as participants in the University of Florida workshop "Democratization by Elections?" convened by Staffan I. Lindberg. I am also grateful to many scholars and experts in Armenia and Georgia for their insight and assistance, with special thanks to Karen Andreasyan, Carolyn Campbell, Lancelot Fletcher, Irina Lortkipanidze, Heghine Manasyan, Alexander Markarov, and Gevorg Ter Gabrielyan. Research for this chapter benefited from a 2007 University of Florida College of Liberal Arts and Sciences Humanities Grant as well as from a 2008 grant from the International Research and Exchanges Board with funds provided by the U.S. Department of State through the Title VIII Program. None of these organizations are responsible for the views expressed herein.

1. O'Donnell and Schmitter (1986, 8), for example, note that administrative accountability and judicial review might be viewed as "as experimental extensions of the citizenship principle in more advanced, more 'complete' democracies" and thus less essential to democracy.

2. The term "electoral revolutions" refers to a recent wave of post-Communist transitions, which have involved the conscious deployment of an electoral model of democratization along with an upsurge in street-level, mass participation and ultimately have resulted in governmental turnover (Bunce and Wolchik 2006a, 5).

3. As the American judge Learned Hand observed, "Liberty lies in the hearts of men and women; when it dies there, no constitution, no law, no court can save it" (quoted in Schwartz 2000, 248).

4. According to Larkins (1996, 606), "despite an almost universal consensus as to its normative value, judicial independence may be one of the least understood concepts in the fields of political science and law." Russell (2001b, 1) concurs: "There is little agreement on what this condition of judicial independence is, or on what kind or how much judicial independence is required for a liberal democratic regime, or on the societal conditions on which judicial independence depends."

5. Foglesong (2001, 68–69) promotes a "quadrangulation" of judicial independence, one that considers "legalist," "behavioralist," "culturalist," and "careerist" understandings. Yet he concedes that formidable challenges inhibit such an approach, including limited access to the necessary data and information, particularly in emerging democracies and other transitional settings, like Russia.

6. In some instances, popular upsurges remove the high levels of uncertainty commonly associated with political transitions (see Bunce 2003).

7. Epp (1998, 202) chooses to focus on common law countries precisely because he expects the relationship between support structures and legal mobilization to be higher there than in other states, thanks to the ability of rights-advocacy lawyers to cultivate precedents and to build upon them. Still, many larger Romano-Germanic democracies, such as France, Germany, and Italy, have witnessed an expansion of judicial power (Tate and Vallinder 1995b, 518–23). As a result, the traditions of civil code and common law have converged of late: "Common law judges have become somewhat more active although not yet equaling their civil code peers; civil code lawyers have become more aggressive although not yet matching their common law counterparts" (Jacob 1996, 5).

8. The population of Georgia is a little less than 5 million people, while Armenia's is over 3.3 million (Anderson and Stuart 2004).

9. The NGO Sustainability Index is assembled and published by the U.S. Agency for International Development. It consists of seven dimensions: (1) legal environment, (2) organizational capacity, (3) financial viability, (4) advocacy, (5) service provision, (6) NGO infrastructure, and (7) public image (Anderson and Stuart 2004, 1).

10. Smithey and Ishiyama (2000) measure judicial power along six dimensions to examine judicial design in post-Communist states: (1) Can judicial decisions handed down by the constitutional court be overturned? (2) Does the constitution grant the court a priori review? (3) How does the length of the judges' terms compare to the term length of those political actors responsible for appointing them? (4) How many actors are responsible for appointing justices to the constitutional court? (5) Who determines the court's procedures—the court or another political actor? And, finally, (6) how difficult is it to remove constitutional court justices from office?

11. The countries that were assessed using the JRI include Albania (2001, 2004, 2006), Armenia (2002, 2004), Bosnia-Herzegovina (2001), Bulgaria (2002, 2004, 2006), Croatia (2002), Georgia (2005), Kazakhstan (2004), Macedonia (2002, 2003), Moldova (2002), Romania (2002), Slovakia (2002), Ukraine (2002, 2006), and Uzbekistan (2002). The judicial systems in Kosovo (2002, 2004), Montenegro (2002), and Serbia (2002, 2003, 2005) also were evaluated.

12. A potential problem with using the ABA/CEELI's JRI for the question at hand is that, whereas the first assessment of Armenia's judiciary preceded its 2003 election, the assessment of Georgia's judiciary occurred in 2005. Thus, the evaluations for Georgia could be misleading since they were made after the 2003 Rose Revolution. Fortunately, the ABA/CEELI provides qualitative narratives along with the JRI summary scores. These narratives trace recent political and legal developments, allowing scholars the opportunity to adjust for recent changes. In 2005, for example, respondents were provided with the following statement: "Judicial salaries are generally sufficient to attract and retain qualified judges, enabling them to support their families and live in a reasonably secure environment, without having to have re-

course to other sources of income." This statement is intended to estimate the degree to which judicial salaries promote or inhibit the quality and independence of judges. In 2005, the correspondence between this statement and the adequacy of judicial salaries in Georgia was "positive." However, as the Georgian JRI notes, this positive assessment occurred largely as a result of a recent salary increase instituted by the 2005 Law on Remuneration of Common Court Judges of Georgia and the 2005 Law on the Remuneration of Members of the Constitutional Court. Before the passage of these laws, judges' salaries were fixed by presidential decree and the interviewees "generally agreed that prior to this increase, judicial salaries were inadequate" (ABA/CEELI 2005, 26). Therefore, the relationship between judicial salaries and judicial independence at the time of the Rose Revolution should be viewed as negative rather than positive.

13. Individual access to constitutional courts varies considerably across the region. Bulgaria and Romania, for example, allow individuals access to their constitutional courts, but only indirectly—that is, through referrals from the regular court system (Schwartz 2000, 35). Other countries allow private individuals direct access, but access is context-dependent. Some allow individuals direct access only for cases that allege that a law violates the individual's constitutional rights. Others allow complaints by individuals when a government official unconstitutionally applies a valid law. In most cases, the person who brings suit must also be the aggrieved party. Only in Hungary can someone not personally affected challenge the constitutionality of a law (34–35).

14. The government is permitted to request that the Constitutional Court determine the capacity of the president to perform his duties (Armenian constitution, art. 59).

15. Recent amendments approved in a November 2005 referendum have changed this situation, however. Standing before the Constitutional Court has been greatly expanded and today includes the national ombudsman, local governments, judges and prosecutors, and ordinary citizens who have exhausted all other avenues of appeal. The amendments also reduced the number of deputies in the National Assembly required to bring suit from one-third to one-fifth (Khachatrian 2006).

16. While the Court lacked the constitutional authority to call or schedule a referendum, its members defended the ruling as "an effective means for overcoming the deep-seated public standoff" that the election had produced (Khachatrian 2003). Kocharian, on the other hand, warned that such a referendum could cause a "schism in society."

17. Schedler (2004, 245–46) depicts such conflicts as "dialogues of the deaf," in which internal critics question whether legal decisions are right or wrong based on the merits of the case while external critics become concerned with whether decisions reflect a systematic bias in favor of one party or the other in a conflict In this case, the court's political loyalties are not so self-evident. Unlike judges in other courts throughout Armenia, justices on the Constitutional Court—including its chairman, Gagik Haroutiunian—were appointed in 1996 by Kocharian's predeces-

sor, Levon Ter-Petrosian. And, while President Ter-Petrosian had appointed Kocharian prime minister in 1997, Kocharian was instrumental in Ter-Petrosian's political demise (Goble 1998).

18. Georgia's Supreme Court had lobbied to get constitutional review powers for itself but failed (Schwartz 2000, 24).

19. According to Fairbanks (2004, 116), the size of the crowds approached 100,000 by the time the CEC announced the final, falsified results.

20. As Zullo (2003) points out, "It is no accident that Georgian opposition leaders, most of whom are lawyers by training, understood the importance of lending legitimacy to their actions by working within the guidelines of law."

21. Even the role of the mass media, which was substantial (see, especially, Anable 2006), benefited from legal intervention. As Mitchell (2004, 345) notes, the scale of the celebration following the Rose Revolution could lead the outside observer to forget that the event became a mass movement only on November 22: "During most of the vigil, crowds were considerably less than 5,000 people." With such relatively small crowds, the opposition's rhetoric could have seemed out of place to anybody simply passing by. But most Georgians were not passing by the demonstrations; rather, they were watching them on television. The independent television channel Rustavi-2, in particular, provided almost nonstop coverage, including interviews and roundtables with opposition leaders. On November 13 the CEC withdrew the channel's accreditation, purportedly for failing to report on times and rates for preelection political ads. Rustavi-2 reacted by bringing suit in a district court. As civil society activist and member of the Georgian Young Lawyers' Association Tinatin Khidasheli observed "If the report [had] not been submitted in time, CEC should have reacted during the pre-election campaign and not twelve days after elections. Moreover, legally, withdrawal of accreditation is within the competence of a court, and not of the Central Electoral Commission" (Rennau 2003).

22. When asked whether he or other members of the opposition considered contesting the irregularities that occurred during the election in courts other than the Constitutional Court, Stepan Demirchyan replied resolutely, "No, there were no other places to go" (interview with the author, June 2, 2008).

CHAPTER TWELVE: The Contingent Power of Authoritarian Elections

I thank Staffan I. Lindberg and the anonymous reviewers of the book for most helpful comments on earlier versions of this chapter.

1. The notion of contingency here denotes the conditional quality of electoral effects, their dependence on intervening causal factors. Since the presence of these factors is indeterminate, the language of contingency here also points to the indeterminacy of electoral democratization. For a conceptual survey of political contingency, see Schedler (2007).

2. See, for instance, Norris, McCoy and Hartlyn, and Rakner and van de Walle in this volume.

3. For a more general conception of stable authoritarian regimes as self-enforcing equilibria that reward supporters, punish defectors, and deter challengers, see Pepinsky (2007).

4. Many authors take Samuel Huntington's much-cited dictum as either the punch line or the punching bag of their empirical inquiries: "Liberalized authoritarianism is not a stable equilibrium; the halfway house does not stand" (1991, 137).

5. On political parties and the longevity of nondemocratic regimes, see Brownlee (2007a) and Smith (2005); on authoritarian legislatures, see Gandhi and Przeworski (2006, 2007).

6. Notable exceptions are Wintrobe (1998) and Acemoglu and Robinson (2006).

7. Suspicions of endogeneity are never entirely dispelled, though. The creation of formal institutions may be an effect of durable regimes, rather than an independent cause of regime duration (see Pepinsky 2007).

8. Cox constructed his data from one primary source, the "Archigos Database on Political Leaders, 1875–2004" by Hein Goemans, Kristian Skrede Gleditsch, and Giacomo Chiozza (http://mail.rochester.edu/~hgoemans/data.htm). When classifying political regimes, he chose labels that differ slightly from mine: no-party autocracies, one-party autocracies, multiparty autocracies, and democracies.

9. Note that a complete general taxonomy of threats to regime survival would also have to include external threats, peaceful as well as violent.

10. See, for example, Anderson et al. (2005), Huntington (1991: 266–267), Przeworski (2003), Rapoport and Weinberg (2001), and Whitehead (2007).

11. "Whenever a ruling party eventually suffered an electoral defeat and allowed the opposition to assume office, the regime is classified as democratic for the entire period this party was in power under the same rules" (Przeworski et al. 2000, 24).

12. In a recent essay, Valerie Bunce asks (citing Leonardo Morlino): "Are elections [causally] important in themselves, or are they merely visible and efficient summaries of more long-term and complex developments on the ground?" (2008, 2). With respect to alternation in power, the response would be split: electoral revelations are *mirrors* of preceding democratic progress, electoral revolutions *motors* of democratic advance.

13. Naturally, if we apply the "alternation rule" to cases of democratizing or transitional alternation, we misclassify the electoral autocracies which these instances of alternation bring to an end as having been democratic all along. For a critique of the retrospective coding of political regimes, see also Brownlee (2008).

14. Note that I will discuss sources of electoral transitions only, leaving aside electoral spillovers into extra-electoral arenas. On plausible causal links through which regular elections translate into the deepening of civil liberties, see Lindberg (2006a, 111–16).

15. See Bunce and Wolchik as well as Schedler, Chapter 7, in this volume. For readings of authoritarian elections through the lenses of social movement studies, see Pop-Eleches and Robertson (2008), Thompson and Kuntz (2004), and Tucker (2007).

16. The notion of "theoretical stretching" is analogous to Giovanni Sartori's idea of "conceptual stretching" that designates the application of a concept to cases that violate its conditions of validity (Sartori 1970, 1984).

17. For recent discussions, see the debates in the *Journal of Democracy* entitled "Building Democracy after Conflict" (January 2005) and the exchange on "Sequencing" (July 2007), in response to Carothers (2007).

18. The authors' terminology differs somewhat from mine. They refer to hegemonic electoral authoritarianism as "dominant-party multiparty regimes," and to competitive electoral authoritarianism as "limited multiparty regimes."

CHAPTER THIRTEEN: A Theory of Elections as a Mode of Transition

1. Colombia, Costa Rica, and Venezuela did not succumb to authoritarian rule in the 1960s and 1970s and thus were not initially part of the third wave.

2. I know from personal experience that in such countries even an imperfect and halfway "transition" away from authoritarian rule is widely appreciated. This does not mean that people in countries that are less than democracies are satisfied with their current political system, as evidenced by various barometers (Euro-, Latino-, and Afrobarometers), but neither are citizens of the established, relatively well-governed democracies. Popular satisfaction with "democracy" is higher in Ghana and Mali than in France and the United Kingdom. It is clearly one thing for us as scholars to judge whether a country's regime is democratic "enough" to be called a democracy or not, and something else as to whether people appreciate the improvements in choice and freedom they have compared to what they used to enjoy. Nevertheless, when comparing trajectories in different countries, we need standards to facilitate fair judgment and causal inference.

3. This study, like many in the rational choice vein, does not explain why and how institutions emerge. This setback should be insignificant, since the study is not concerned with how or why states institute elections, but with what happens with their introduction. Yet, some rational-actor theorists would certainly object to being labeled institutionalists on the claim that they work from methodological individualism. I cannot see, however, how the game theoretical approach can be conceived of other than as an institutional framework where the incentives in the form of rules to a large extent produce the outcome. For a good discussion of explanations of how and why institutions emerge, see, for example, Pierson (2000).

4. This is not to suggest a return to crude functionalism in the sense of Ridley's (1975) suggestion that designing a house must involve determining who will inhabit that house and what they might do in there. But there is certainly a lot of suggestive evidence in the institutionalist literature that the initial conditions, in terms of constitutive and regulative rules envisaged by institutions, constrain and enable the choice of behavior among particular individuals.

5. Contemporary institutionalism in comparative politics underpinned by a rational-actor perspective can be traced back to a few seminal works. Early studies by

Arrow (1951) and Downs (1957) contributed by explicating assumptions as structuring individual choice that can be thought of in terms of institutions and by provoking a critique that spurred further work on the importance of the institutional context. The influential study by Olsen (1965) on the problems of collective action in face of a constant tendency for individuals to become free riders directly pointed to the need for institutions. With the right incentives provided by rules and regulations that shape expectations among individuals with regard to one other's behavior, preferred collective outcomes can be achieved.

6. This point has already been substantiated empirically by Bratton and van de Walle (1997). In their study, they found that the military in Africa intervened on behalf of sustaining or reinstating democratic processes more often than in order to subvert it.

References

ABA/CEELI. 2002. *Judicial Reform Index for Armenia*. Washington, DC: American Bar Association's Central and East European Law Initiative. Available at www.abanet.org/rol/publications/judicial_reform_index.shtml. Accessed May 21, 2007.

———. 2005. *Judicial Reform Index for Georgia*. Washington, DC: American Bar Association's Central and East European Law Initiative. Available at www.abanet.org/rol/publications/judicial_reform_index.shtml. Accessed May 21, 2007.

Acemoglu, Daron, and James A. Robinson. 2006. *Economic Origins of Dictatorship and Democracy*. Cambridge: Cambridge University Press.

Ackerman, Peter, and Jack Duvall. 2000. *A Force More Powerful: A Century of Nonviolent Conflict*. New York: Palgrave.

———. 2004. "The Secret to Success in Ukraine." *International Herald Tribune*, December 28.

———. 2007. "Skill or Conditions: What Key Factors Shape the Success or Failure of Civil Resistance?" Paper presented to the Conference on Civil Resistance and Power Politics, St. Antony's College, Oxford University, March 15–18.

Ackerman, Peter, and Adrian Karatnycky. 2005. *How Freedom Is Won: From Civic Resistance to Durable Democracy*. New York: Freedom House.

Adcock, Robert, and David Collier. 2001. "Measurement Validity: A Shared Standard for Qualitative and Quantitative Research." *American Political Science Review* 95 (3): 529–46.

Afrobarometer (Afrobarometer Network). 2004. "Afrobarometer Round 2: Compendium of Results from a 15-Country Survey." Afrobarometer Working Paper No. 34. East Lansing, MI: Michigan State University.

Ake, Claude. 2000. *The Feasibility of Democracy in Africa*. Dakar: Codresia.

Al-Ahram Center. 2000a. Survey on Civil Participation in the 2000 Egyptian Parliamentary Elections (data).

———. 2000b. Survey on Important Political and Economic Issues (data).

Alesina, Alberto, Arnaud Devleeschauwer, William Easterly, Sergio Kurlat, and Romain Wacziarg. 2003. "Fractionalization." *Journal of Economic Growth* 8:155–94.

Aliyev, Bursel, Anar Ahmadov, Aaron Erlich, and Hans Gutbroad. 2006. "2006 Data Initiative Survey for Azerbaijan and the South Caucasus: Introduction, Results and Application." Caucasian Research Resource Center, November.

Altman, David, and Anibal Pérez-Linán. 2002. "Assessing the Quality of Democracy:

Freedom, Competitiveness, and Participation in Eighteen Latin American Countries." *Democratization* 9 (2): 85–100.

Alvarez, Mike, José A. Cheibub, Fernando Limongi, and Adam Przeworski. 1996. "Classifying Political Regimes." *Studies in International Comparative Development* 31 (2): 3–36.

Amoretti, Ugo M., and Nancy Bermeo, eds. 2004. *Federalism and Territorial Cleavages*. Baltimore: Johns Hopkins University Press.

Anable, David. 2006. "The Role of Georgia's Media—and Western Aid—in the Rose Revolution." *Press/Politics* 11 (3): 7–43.

Anderson, Christopher J., André Blais, Shaun Bowler, Todd Donovan, and Ola Listhaug. 2005. *Losers' Consent: Elections and Democratic Legitimacy.* Oxford: Oxford University Press.

Anderson, Leslie, and Lawrence Dodd. 2005. *Learning Democracy*. Chicago: University of Chicago Press.

Anderson, Todd, and Jennifer Stuart. 2004. *The 2003 NGO Sustainability Index for Central and Eastern Europe and Eurasia.* Washington, DC: U.S. Agency for International Development. Available at www.usaid.gov/locations/europe_eurasia/dem_gov/ngoindex/2003.

ARKA News Agency. 2003a. "March 14, Constitutional Court Will Discuss Artashes Geghamian's Statement." *Hayastani Hanrapetutiun,* March 12. Available from ISI Emerging Markets Database at www.securities.com. Accessed June 21, 2007.

———. 2003b. "All CC Demands Are Facts." *Novoye Vremya,* March 20. Available from ISI Emerging Markets Database at www.securities.com. Accessed June 21, 2007.

———. 2003c. "Geghamian's Suit Declined." *Novoye Vremya,* March 25. Available from ISI Emerging Markets Database at www.securities.com. Accessed June 21, 2007.

Armony, A. C., and H. E. Schamis. 2005. "Babel in Democratization Studies." *Journal of Democracy* 16 (4): 113–28.

Arrow, Kenneth. 1951. *Social Choice and Individual Values.* New York: John Wiley and Sons.

Åslund, Anders, and Michael McFaul. 2006. *Revolution in Orange: The Origins of Ukraine's Democratic Breakthrough.* Washington, DC: Carnegie Endowment for International Peace.

Aspinwall, Edward. 2005. *Opposing Suharto: Compromise, Resistance, and Regime Change in Indonesia*. Stanford, CA: Stanford University Press.

Ayers, Alison J. 2006. "Demystifying Democratization: The Global Constitution of (Neo)Liberal Polities in Africa." *Third World Quarterly* 27 (2): 321–38.

Ayittey, George. 1992. *Africa Betrayed.* New York: St. Martin's Press.

Banks, Arthur S. 2000. "Protracted Transitions among Africa's New Democracies." *Democratization* 7 (3): 227–43.

———. 2002. *Cross-National Time Series Data Archive*. New York: Databanks International.

———. 2005. *Cross-National Time-Series (CNTS) Dataset, 1815–2003*. SUNY Binghamton / Databanks International. Available at www.databanks.sitehosting.net.

———. 2008. "Legislatures on the Rise?" *Journal of Democracy* 19 (2): 124–37.

Barkan, Joel D., and John J. Okumu. 1974. "Comparing Politics and Public Policy in Kenya and Tanzania." In *Politics and Public Policy in Kenya and Tanzania*, ed. Joel D. Barkan and John J. Okumu, 3–40. New York: Praeger.

———. 1979. "'Semi-Competitive' Election, Clientelism, and Political Recruitment in a No-Party State: The Kenyan Experience." In *Elections without Choice*, ed. Guy Hermet, Richard Rose, and Alain Rouquié, 88–107. New York: John Wiley & Sons.

Basedau, Matthias, Gero Erdmann, and Andres Mehler, eds. 2007. *Votes, Money, and Violence: Political Parties and Elections in Sub-Saharan Africa*. Scottsville, South Africa: University of Kwazulu-Natal Press.

Bates, Robert H. 1989. *Beyond the Miracle and the Market: The Political Economy of Agrarian Development in Kenya*. Cambridge: Cambridge University Press.

Bauer, Gretchen, and Hannah E. Britton, eds. 2006. *Women in African Parliaments*. Boulder, CO: Lynne Rienner.

Bauer, Gretchen, and Scott D. Taylor. 2005. *Politics in Southern Africa: State and Society in Transition*. Boulder, CO: Lynne Rienner.

Bayart, Jean-François. 1978. "Clientelism, Elections, and Systems of Inequality and Domination in Cameroun." In *Elections without Choice*, ed. Guy Hermet, Richard Rose, and Alain Rouquié, 66–87. New York: John Wiley & Sons.

Beaulieu, Emily. 2006. "Protesting the Contest: Election Boycotts around the World, 1990–2002." Ph.D. diss., University of California, San Diego.

Beaulieu, Emily, and Susan D. Hyde. Forthcoming. "In the Shadow of Democracy Promotion: Strategic Manipulation, International Observers, and Election Boycotts." *Comparative Political Studies*.

Beck, Nathaniel, and Jonathan Katz. 1995. "What To Do (and Not To Do) with Time-Series Cross-Section Data." *American Political Science Review* 89 (3): 634–47.

———. 1996. "Nuisance vs. Substance: Specifying and Estimating Time-Series Cross-Section Models." *Political Analysis* 6 (1): 1–36.

Beck, Thorsten, George Clarke, Alberto Groff, Philip Keefer, and Patrick Walsh. 2001. "New Tools in Comparative Political Economy: The Database of Political Institutions." *World Bank Economic Review* 15 (1): 165–76.

Beissinger, Mark R. 2002. *Nationalist Mobilization and the Collapse of the Soviet State*. Cambridge Studies in Comparative Politics. Cambridge: Cambridge University Press.

———. 2007. "Structure and Example in Modular Political Phenomena: The Diffusion of Bulldozer/Rose/Orange/Tulip Revolutions." *Perspectives on Politics* 5 (2): 259–76.

Benstead, L., and E. Lust-Okar. 2006. National Survey on Algerian Attitudes toward Parliament and Representation (data).

Bernhard, Michael. 1993. "Civil Society and Democratic Transition in East Central Europe." *Political Science Quarterly* 108 (2): 307–26.

Bienen, Henry, and Nicolas van de Walle. 1991. *Of Time and Power: Leadership Duration in the Modern World*. Stanford, CA: Stanford University Press.

Bierschenk, Thomas. 2006. "The Local Appropriation of Democracy: An Analysis of the Municipal Elections in Parakou, Republic of Benin, 2002-03." *Journal of Modern African Studies* 44:543–71.

Blake, Charles H., and Christopher G. Martin. 2006. "The Dynamics of Political Corruption: Re-Examining the Influence of Democracy." *Democratization* 13 (6): 1–14.

Bockman, Johanna, and Gil Eyal. 2002. "Eastern Europe as a Laboratory for Economic Knowledge: The Transnational Roots of Neoliberalism." *American Journal of Sociology* 108 (September): 310–52.

Bogaards, Matthijs. 2000. "Crafting Competitive Party Systems: Electoral Laws and the Opposition in Africa." *Democratization* 7 (4): 163–90.

———. 2004. "Counting Parties and Identifying Dominant Party Systems in Africa." *European Journal of Political Research* 43:173–97.

Boix, Carles, and Susan C. Stokes. 2003. "Endogenous Democratization." *World Politics* 55 (4): 517–49.

Bollen, Kenneth, and R. W. Jackman. 1989. "Democracy, Stability, and Dichotomies." *American Sociological Review* 54:612–21.

Booth, John A. 1995. "Introduction: Elections and Democracy in Central America: A Framework for Analysis." In *Elections and Democracy in Central America Revisited*, ed. Mitchell A. Seligson and John A. Booth. Chapel Hill: University of North Carolina Press.

Bowler, Shaun, Elisabeth Carter, and David M. Farrell. 2003. "Changing Party Access to Elections." In *Democracy Transformed?* ed. Bruce Cain, Russell Dalton, and Susan Scarrow. Oxford: Oxford University Press.

Bowler, Shaun, and Bernard Grofman, eds. 2000. *Elections in Australia, Ireland, and Malta under the Single Transferable Vote: Reflections on an Embedded Institution*. Ann Arbor: University of Michigan Press.

Bratton, Michael. 2007. "Formal versus Informal Institutions in Africa." *Journal of Democracy* 18 (3): 96–110.

———. 2008. "Formal versus Informal Institutions in Africa." In *How People View Democracy*, ed. Larry Diamond and Marc F. Plattner, 102–16. Baltimore: Johns Hopkins University Press.

Bratton, Michael, and Wonbin Cho. 2006. "Where Is Africa Going? Views from Below." Afrobarometer Working Paper No. 60, Lansing, MI: Department of Political Science, Michigan State University.

Bratton, Michael, and Nicolas van de Walle. 1997. *Democratic Experiments in Africa: Regime Transitions in Comparative Perspective*. New York: Cambridge University Press.

Brinks, Daniel, and Michael Coppedge. 2006. "Diffusion Is No Illusion: Neighbor

Emulation in the Third Wave of Democracy." *Comparative Political Studies* 39 (May): 463–89.

Brownlee, Jason. 2002. "The Decline of Pluralism in Mubarak's Egypt." *Journal of Democracy* 13 (October): 6–14.

———. 2007a. *Authoritarianism in an Age of Democratization*. Cambridge: Cambridge University Press.

———. 2007b. "A New Generation of Autocracy in Egypt." *Brown Journal of World Affairs* 14 (1): 73–85.

———. 2008. "Ruling against Type: Regimes in the Twenty-First Century." Paper presented at 104th Annual Meeting, American Political Science Association, Boston, August 28–31, 2008.

Brumberg, Daniel. 2003. "The Trap of Liberalized Autocracy." In *Islam and Democracy in the Middle East*, ed. Larry Diamond, Marc F. Plattner, and Daniel Brumberg, 35–47. Baltimore: Johns Hopkins University Press.

Buckhart, Ross, and Michael Lewis-Beck. 1994. "Comparative Democracy: The Economic Development Thesis." *American Political Science Review* 88 (4): 903–10.

Bunce, Valerie J. 1994. "Sequencing of Political and Economic Reforms." In *East-Central European Economies in Transition*, ed. John Hardt and Richard Kaufman, 49–63. Washington, DC: U.S. Congress, Joint Economic Committee.

———. 1999. *Subversive Institutions: The Design and the Destruction of Socialism and the State*. Cambridge Studies in Comparative Politics. Cambridge: Cambridge University Press.

———. 2001. "Democratization and Economic Reform." *Annual Review of Political Science* 4:43–65.

———. 2003. "Rethinking Recent Democratization: Lessons from the Post-Communist Experience." *World Politics* 55 (2): 167–92.

———. 2007. "The Tasks of Transition and Their Transferability." Paper presented at the Project on Democratic Transitions, Seminar II: "Lessons Learned and Testing their Applicability." Foreign Policy Research Institute, Philadelphia, February 22–24.

———. 2008. "Reflections on Elections." *APSA-CP Newsletter* 19 (2): 1–5.

Bunce, Valerie J., and Sharon L. Wolchik. 2006a. "Favorable Conditions and Electoral Revolutions." *Journal of Democracy* 17 (4): 5–18.

———. 2006b. "International Diffusion and Postcommunist Electoral Revolutions." *Communist and Post-Communist Studies* 39 (3): 283–304.

———. 2007a. "Democratizing Elections in the Postcommunist World: Definitions, Dynamics, and Diffusion." *St. Antony's International Review* 2 (2): 64–79.

———. 2007b. "The Impact of International Democracy Assistance on the Transition to Democracy in Azerbaijan: A Failed Case." Paper presented at Workshop on International Democracy Assistance and the Transition to Democracy, Stanford University, Palo Alto, CA, October.

———. 2007c. "Youth and Postcommunist Electoral Revolutions: Never Trust Anyone over 30?" In *Reclaiming Democracy: Civil Society and Electoral Change in Cen-*

tral and Eastern Europe, ed. Joerg Forbrig and Pavol Demes. Bratislava: German Marshall Fund.

———. 2008a. "American Democracy Promotion and Electoral Change in Postcommunist Europe and Eurasia." Unpublished book manuscript.

———. 2008b. "Azerbaijan's 2005 Parliamentary Elections: A Failed Attempt at Transition." Paper prepared for CDDRL Workshop on External Influences on Democratic Transitions, Stanford University, Stanford, CA, October.

Burgess, Stephen F. 2004. "The Impact of Structural Adjustment and Economic Reform on the Transition Process in East Africa." In *Democratic Transitions in East Africa: A Comparative and Regional Perspective,* Paul J. Kaiser and F. Wafula Okumu, 120–41. London: Ashgate Publishers.

Burnell, Peter. 2001. "The Party System and Party Politics in Zambia: Continuities Past, Present and Future." *African Affairs* 100:239–63.

Cardoso, Fernando Henrique, with Brian Winter. 2006. *The Accidental President of Brazil: A Memoir.* New York: Public Affairs.

Carey, John M. 2000. "Parchment, Equilibria, and Institutions." *Comparative Political Studies* 33 (6/7): 735–61.

Carothers, Thomas. 1991. *In the Name of Democracy: U.S. Policy toward Latin America in the Reagan Years.* Berkeley: University of California Press.

———. 1997. "Democracy without Illusions." *Foreign Affairs* 76: 85–99.

———. 2002a. "A Reply to My Critics." *Journal of Democracy* 13 (3): 33–38.

———. 2002b. "The End of the Transition Paradigm." *Journal of Democracy* 13 (1): 5–21.

———. 2006. *Confronting the Weakest Link: Aiding Political Parties in New Democracies.* Washington, DC: Carnegie Endowment for International Peace.

———. 2007. "How Democracies Emerge: The 'Sequencing' Fallacy." *Journal of Democracy* 18 (1): 12–27.

Carter Center. 1990. "Observing Nicaragua's Elections, 1989–1990." Available at www.cartercenter.org/documents/1153.pdf.

Case, William F. 2006. "Manipulative Skills: How Do Rulers Control the Electoral Arena?" In *Electoral Authoritarianism: The Dynamics of Unfree Competition*, ed. Andreas Schedler, 95–112. Boulder, CO: Lynne Rienner.

Chabal, Patrick. 1998. "A Few Considerations on Democracy in Africa." *International Affairs* 74 (2): 289–303.

Chandra, Kanchan. 2001. "Ethnic Bargains, Group Instability, and Social Choice Theory." *Politics & Society* 29 (3): 337–62.

———. 2004. *Why Ethnic Parties Succeed: Patronage and Ethnic Headcounts in India.* Cambridge: Cambridge University Press.

Chehabi, H. E., and Juan J. Linz. 1998. "A Theory of Sultanism, 1." In *Sultanistic Regimes,* ed. H. E. Chehabi and Juan J. Linz, 3–25. Baltimore: Johns Hopkins University Press.

Cheibub, José A., Adam Przeworski, Fernando N. Limongi, and Michael M. Alvarez. 1996. "What Makes Democracies Endure?" *Journal of Democracy* 7 (1): 39–55.

Chikhladze, Giga. 2003. "EurasiaNet Q&A—Labor Party Leader: Georgia Faces 'Real Threat' of Civil War." *Eurasianet.org*, December 3. Available at www.eurasianet.org/departments/recaps/articles/eav120303.shtml.

Clark, Elisabeth S. 2000. "Why Elections Matter." *Washington Quarterly* 23 (3): 27–40.

Clark, John F. 2006. "Armed Arbiters: When Does the Military Step into the Electoral Arena?" In *Electoral Authoritarianism: The Dynamics of Unfree Competition*, ed. Andreas Schedler, 129–48. Boulder, CO: Lynne Rienner.

Coleman, James. 1990. *Foundations of Social Theory*. Cambridge: Harvard University Press.

Collier, David, and Robert Adcock. 1999. "Democracy and Dichotomies: A Pragmatic Approach to Choices about Concepts," *Annual Review of Political Science* 2: 537–65.

Collier, David, and Steven Levitsky. 1997. "Democracy with Adjectives: Conceptual Innovation in Comparative Research." *World Politics* 49:430–51.

Collier, David, and James E. Mahon, Jr., 1993. "Conceptual 'Stretching' Revisited: Adapting Categories in Comparative Analysis." *American Political Science Review* 84 (4): 845–55.

Collier, Paul, and Nicholas Sambanis, eds. 2005. *Understanding Civil War: Evidence and Analysis*. Vol. 1. Washington, DC: The World Bank.

Colomer, Joseph M. 2004. *Handbook of Electoral System Choice*. New York: Palgrave Macmillan.

Conaghan, Catherine M. 2005. *Fujimori's Peru: Deception in the Public Sphere*. Pittsburgh: University of Pittsburgh Press.

Constitution of the Republic of Armenia. July 5, 1995. Available in English via the Council of Europe's Venice Commission at www.venice.coe.int. Accessed June 18, 2007.

Constitution of the Republic of Georgia. July 5, 1995. Available in English via the Council of Europe's Venice Commission at www.venice.coe.int. Accessed June 18, 2007.

Coppedge, Michael. 1994. *Strong Parties and Lame Ducks: Presidential Partyarchy and Factionalism in Venezuela*. Stanford, CA: Stanford University Press.

———. 2002. "Democracy and Dimensions: Comments on Munck and Verkuilen." *Comparative Political Studies* 35 (1): 35–39.

———. 2005. "Thickening Thin Concepts: Issues in Large-*N* Data Generation." In *Regimes and Democracy in Latin America*, Vol. 2, *Methods and Data*, ed. Gerardo Munck. Oxford: Oxford University Press.

Coppedge, Michael, A. Alvarez, and C. Maldonado. 2008. "Two Persistent Dimensions of Democracy: Contestation and Inclusiveness." *Journal of Politics* 70 (3): 632–47.

Coppedge, Michael, and Wolfgang H. Reinicke. 1990. "Measuring Polyarchy." *Studies in Comparative International Development* 25 (1): 51–73.

Cox, Gary W. 1997. *Making Votes Count: Strategic Coordination in the World's Electoral Systems*. Cambridge: Cambridge University Press.

———. 1999. "Electoral Rules and Electoral Coordination." *Annual Review of Political Science* 2:145–61.

———. 2007. "Authoritarian Elections and Leadership Succession, 1975–2000." Unpublished typescript. Department of Political Science, University of California, San Diego.

CSS (Center for Strategic Studies). 1993, 1995–2004. University of Jordan, Jordanian Democracy Polls (data).

———. 1998. Istatla'a al-Ra'i Hawl al-Dimuqratiyya fi-l-Urdunn, 1998 [Opinion Polls on Democracy in Jordan, 1998]. Markaz al-Dirasat al-Istratajiyya, al-Jami'at al-Urdun.

Dahl, Robert A. 1971. *Polyarchy: Participation and Opposition*. New Haven: Yale University Press.

———. 1989. *Democracy and Its Critics*. New Haven: Yale University Press.

Dalton, Russell J., Doh L. Shin, and Willy Jou. 2007. "Popular Conceptions of the Meaning of Democracy: Democratic Understanding in Unlikely Places." Center for the Study of Democracy, University of California at Irvine, Paper 07-03. Available at http://repositories.edlib.org/esd107-03.

Danielyan, Emil. 2003. "Armenia Poll Sparks Domestic Outcry, Western Criticism." *Eurasianet.org*, March 7. Available at www.eurasianet.org/departments/rights/articles/eav030703.shtml. Accessed May 25, 2007.

D'Anieri, Paul. 2006. "Explaining the Success and Failure of Post-Communist Revolutions." *Communist and Post-Communist Studies* 39:331–50.

de Mesquita, Bruce Bueno, Alastair Smith, Randolph M. Siverson, and James D. Morrow. 2003. *The Logic of Political Survival*. Boston: MIT Press.

Diamond, Larry. 1996. "Democracy in Latin America: Degrees, Illusions, and Directions for Consolidation." In *Beyond Sovereignty: Collectively Defending Democracy in the Americas*, ed. Tom J. Farer, 52–104. Baltimore: John Hopkins University Press.

———. 1997. "Prospects for Democratic Development in Africa." *Essays in Public Policy*, No. 74. Stanford, CA: Stanford University, Hoover Institution on War, Revolution and Peace.

———. 1999. *Developing Democracy: Toward Consolidation*. Baltimore: Johns Hopkins University Press.

———. 2002. "Elections without Democracy: Thinking about Hybrid Regimes." *Journal of Democracy* 13 (2): 21–35.

———. 2006. "Building Democracy after Conflict." *Taiwan Journal of Democracy* 2 (December): 93–116.

———. 2008a. "The Democratic Rollback: The Resurgence of the Predatory State." *Foreign Affairs* 87 (2): 36–48.

———. 2008b. *The Spirit of Democracy: The Struggle to Build Free Societies throughout the World*. New York: Times Books.

Diamond, Larry, Jonathan Hartlyn, and Juan J. Linz. 1999. "Introduction: Politics, Society, and Democracy in Latin America." In *Democracy in Developing Countries:*

Latin America, 2nd ed., ed. Larry Diamond, Jonathan Hartlyn, Juan J. Linz and Seymour Martin Lipset, Boulder, CO: Lynne Rienner.

Diamond, Larry Jay, Juan J. Linz, and Seymour Martin Lipset, eds. 1988. *Democracy in Developing Countries*. Boulder, CO: Lynne Rienner.

———. 1990. *Politics in Developing Countries: Comparing Experiences with Democracy.* Boulder, CO: Lynne Rienner.

Diamond, Larry, and Marc Plattner, eds. 1999. *Democratization in Africa*. Baltimore: Johns Hopkins University Press.

Di Palma, Giuseppe. 1990. *To Craft Democracies: An Essay on Democratic Transitions*. Berkeley, CA: University of California Press.

———. 1991. "Legitimation from the Top to Civil Society: Politico-Cultural Change in Eastern Europe." *World Politics* 44 (1): 49–81.

———. 1993. *To Craft Democracies: An Essay on Democratic Transitions*. Berkeley, CA: University of California Press.

Dobbins, James, Seth G. Jones, Keith Crane, and Beth Cole DeGrasse. 2007. *The Beginner's Guide to Nation-Building.* Santa Monica, CA: RAND Corporation.

Dodson, J. Michael, and Donald W. Jackson. 2001. "Judicial Independence and Instability in Central America." In *Judicial Independence in the Age of Democracy: Critical Perspectives from around the World*, ed. Peter H. Russell and David M. O'Brien, 251–72. Charlottesville: University Press of Virginia.

Downs, Anthony. 1957. *An Economic Theory of Democracy.* New York: Harper Collins.

Drake, Paul W., and Eduardo Silva. 1986. "Introduction: Elections and Democratization in Latin America, 1980–85." In *Elections and Democratization in Latin America, 1980–1985*, ed. Paul W. Drake and Eduardo Silva. La Jolla, CA: Center for Iberian and Latin American Studies, University of California at San Diego.

Dunleavy, Patrick, and Helen Margetts. 1995. "Understanding the Dynamics of Electoral Reform." *International Political Science Review* 16 (1): 9–29.

Duverger, Maurice. 1954. *Les Partis Politiques*. Paris: Colin.

Economist. 2005. "An Election in the Central African Republic." *The Economist*, March 17.

Eisenstadt, Todd A. 2004. *Courting Democracy in Mexico: Party Strategies and Electoral Institutions*. Cambridge: Cambridge University Press.

Elkins, Zachary, and Beth Simmons. 2005. "On Waves, Clusters, and Diffusion: A Conceptual Framework." *The Annals of the American Academy of Political and Social Science* 598 (1): 33–51.

Ellingsen, Tanja. 2000. "Colorful Community of Ethnic Witches' Brew? Multiethnicity and Domestic Conflict During and After the Cold War." *Journal of Conflict Resolution* 44 (2): 228–49.

Ellis, Stephen. 2006. "The Roots of African Corruption" *Current History* 105 (691): 203–8.

Elster, Jon. 1982. "The Case for Methodological Individualism." *Theory and Society* 11 (4): 453–82.

Epp, Charles. 1998. *The Rights Revolution: Lawyers, Activists, and Supreme Courts in Comparative Perspective*. Chicago: University of Chicago Press.

Epstein, David, Robert Bates, Jack Goldstone, Ida Kristensen, and Sharyn O'Halloran. 2006. "Democratic Transitions." *American Journal of Political Science* 50 (July): 551–69.

Epstein, Lee, Jack Knight, and Olga Shvetsova. 2001. "The Role of Constitutional Courts in the Establishment and Maintenance of Democratic Systems of Government." *Law & Society Review* 35 (1): 117–64.

Erdmann, Gero. 2004. "Party Research: Western European Bias and the 'African Labyrinth'" *Democratization* 11 (3): 63–87.

Erdmann, Gero, and Matthias Basedau. 2007. "Problems of Categorizing and Explaining Party Systems in Africa." GIGA Working Papers, No. 40. Leibniz: German Institute of Global and Area Studies, January.

Esfandiari, H. 2003. "Is Iran Democratizing? Observations on Election Day." in *Islam and Democracy in the Middle East*, ed. L. Diamond, M. F. Plattner, and D. Brumberg, 124–29. Baltimore: Johns Hopkins University Press.

Eurasia Insight. 2003. "Second Round of Armenia's Presidential Election Marred by Fraud." *Eurasianet.org*, March 6. Available at www.eurasianet.org/departments/insight/articles/eav030603.shtml. Accessed May 25, 2007.

European Commission. 2005. "A New Agenda for Europe and Jordan: Working Together to Strengthen Democracy and Human Rights, Promote Trade and Investment and Increase Security in the Region," June 23. Brussels. Available at http://ec.europa.eu/comm/external_relations/jordan/intro/230605.htm. Accessed June 12, 2006.

European Union. 2005. "Ethiopia, Legislative Elections, 2005: European Union Election Observation Mission; Final Report." Available at http://ec.europa.eu/external_relations/human_rights/eu_election_ass_observ/ethiopia/2005_final_report.pdf.

Fairbanks, Charles H., Jr. 2004. "Georgia's Rose Revolution." *Journal of Democracy* 15 (2): 110–24.

Fennema, Meindert. 2000. "Legal Repression of Extreme-Right Parties and Racial Discrimination." In *Challenging Immigration and Ethnic Relations Politics*, ed. Ruud Koopmans and Paul Statham. Oxford: Oxford University Press.

Filippov, Mikhail, Peter C. Ordeshook, and Olga Shvetsova. 2004. *Designing Federalism: A Theory of Self-Sustainable Federal Institutions*. New York: Cambridge University Press.

Finkel, Steven F., Anibal Perez-Linan, Mitchell A. Seligson, and Dinorah Azpuru. 2006. "Effects of U.S. Foreign Assistance on Democracy Building: Results of a Cross-National Quantitative Study." Final Report. U.S. Agency for International Development, January 12. Available at http://pdf.usaid.gov/pdf_docs/Pnade694.pdf.

Fish, M. Steven. 1998. "Democratization's Prerequisites." *Post-Soviet Affairs* 14 (July–September): 212–47.

———. 2006. "Stronger Legislatures, Stronger Democracies." *Journal of Democracy* 17 (1): 5–20.

Fish, Steven, and Mathew Kroenig. 2008. *The Handbook of National Legislatures: A Global Survey.* New York: Cambridge University Press.

Fisher, Sharon. 2006. *Political Change in Post-Communist Slovakia and Croatia: From Nationalist to Europeanist.* New York: Palgrave Macmillan.

Flood, M. M. 1952. "Some Experimental Games." Research Memorandum RW-789. Santa Monica, CA: RAND Corporation.

Foglesong, Todd. 2001. "The Dynamics of Judicial (In)dependence in Russia." In *Judicial Independence in the Age of Democracy: Critical Perspectives from around the World,* ed. Peter H. Russell and David M. O'Brien, 62–88. Charlottesville: University Press of Virginia.

Fomunyoh, Christopher. 2001. "Democratization in Fits and Starts." *Journal of Democracy* 12 (3): 37–50.

Foweraker, Joe, and Todd Landmann. 2002. "Constitutional Design and Democratic Performance." *Democratization* 9 (2): 43–66.

Francisco, Ronald. 2004. "After the Massacre: Mobilization in the Wake of Harsh Repression." *Mobilization: An International Journal* 9 (June): 107–26.

Freedom House. Various dates. "Annual Survey of Freedom Country Ratings." Available at www.freedomhouse.org.

———. 2006. *Freedom in the World, 2006.* Accessed at www.freedomhouse.org/template.cfm?page=363&year=2006.

———. 2006. *Freedom in the World Country Ratings, 1972 through 2005.* Available at www.freedomhouse.org.

Gagnon, V. P. 2004. *The Myth of Ethnic War: Serbia and Croatia in the 1990s.* Ithaca, NY: Cornell University Press.

Gallagher, Michael. 2005. "Conclusions." In *The Politics of Electoral Systems,* ed. Michael Gallagher and Paul Mitchell. Oxford: Oxford University Press.

Gandhi, Jennifer, and Ellen Lust-Okar. Forthcoming. "Elections under Authoritarianism." *Annual Review of Political Science.*

Gandhi, Jennifer, and Adam Przeworski. 2001. "Dictatorial Institutions and the Survival of Dictators." Paper presented at the Annual Meeting of the American Political Science Association, San Francisco, CA.

———. 2006. "Cooperation, Cooptation, and Rebellion under Dictatorships." *Economics and Politics* 18 (1): 1–26.

———. 2007. "Authoritarian Institutions and the Survival of Autocrats," *Comparative Political Studies* 40 (11): 1279–1301.

Gandhi, Jennifer, and James Vreeland. 2004. "Political Institutions and Civil War: Unpacking Anocracy." Unpublished paper, Yale University Center on International and Area Studies, August 30.

Ganev, Venelin I. 2007. *Preying on the State: The Transformation of Bulgaria after 1989.* Ithaca, NY: Cornell University Press.

Garber, Larry, and Glenn Cowan. 1993. "The Virtues of Parallel Vote Tabulations." *Journal of Democracy* 4 (April): 95–107.

Garretón, Manuel Antonio, Marcelo Cavarozzi, Peter Cleaves, Gary Gereffi, and Jonathan Hartlyn. 2003. *Latin America in the Twenty-First Century: Toward a New Socio-Political Matrix*. Miami: North-South Center Press and Lynne Rienner.

Gasiororwski, Mark J., and Timothy J. Power. 1998. "The Structural Determinants of Democratic Consolidation." *Comparative Political Studies* 31 (10): 740–72.

Gates, Scott, Håvard Hegre, Mark P. Jones, and Håvard Strand. 2006. "Institutional Inconsistency and Political Instability: Polity Duration, 1800–2000." *American Journal of Political Science* 50 (4): 893–908.

Gazibo, Mamoudou. 2005. "Foreign Aid and Democratization: Benin and Niger Compared." *African Studies Review* 48 (3): 47–67.

Geddes, Barbara. 1999a. "Authoritarian Breakdown: Empirical Test of a Game Theoretic Argument." Paper presented at the annual meeting of the American Political Science Association, Atlanta, GA.

———. 1999b. "What Do We Know about Democratization after Twenty Years?" *Annual Review of Political Science* 2:115–44.

———. 2003. *Paradigms and Sand Castles: Theory Building and Research Design in Comparative Politics*. Ann Arbor: University of Michigan Press.

———. 2005. "Why Parties and Elections in Authoritarian Regimes?" Paper presented at the 101st Annual Meeting, American Political Science Association, Washington, DC.

Geertz, Clifford. 1983. *Local Knowledge*. New York: Basic Books.

Gerring, John. 2001. *Social Science Methodology: A Criterial Framework*. Cambridge: Cambridge University Press.

Gerring, John, Strom C. Thacker, and Rodrigo Alfaro. 2005. "Democracy and Human Development." Paper presented at the Annual Meeting of the American Political Science Association, Washington, DC.

Gershman, Carl, and Michael Allen. 2006. "The Assault on Democracy Assistance." *Journal of Democracy* 17 (April): 36–51.

Gibson, Clark C. 2002. "Of Waves and Ripples: Democracy and Political Change in Africa in the 1990s." *Annual Review of Political Science* 5:201–21.

Gill, M. S. 1998. "India: Running the World's Biggest Election." *Journal of Democracy* 9 (1): 164–68.

Gillespie, Charles G. 1986. "Uruguay's Transition from Collegial Military-Technocratic Rule." In *Transitions from Authoritarian Rule*, Vol. 2: *Latin America*, ed. Guillermo O'Donnell, Philippe C. Schmitter, and Laurence Whitehead. Baltimore: Johns Hopkins University Press.

Gillespie, Charles G., and Luis Eduardo Gonzalez. 1989. "Uruguay: The Survival of Old and Autonomous Institutions." In *Democracy in Developing Countries: Latin America*, ed. Larry Diamond, Juan J. Linz, and Seymour Martin Lipset. Boulder, CO: Lynne Rienner.

Ginsburg, Tom. 2003. *Judicial Review in New Democracies: Constitutional Courts in Asian Cases.* New York: Cambridge University Press.

Gloppen, S., L. Rakner, and L. Svåsand. 2007. "Political Paralysis in Malawi: Repercussions of Party Splits in a Weakly Institutionalized Democracy." Paper presented at the ECPR General Conference, Pisa, September 5–8.

Goble, Paul. 1998. "Why Ter-Petrosyan Fell." *Radio Free Europe / Radio Liberty Newsline,* February 6. Available at www.rferl.org/newsline/1998/02/060298.asp. Accessed July 31, 2007.

Golder, Matt. 2005. "Democratic Electoral Systems around the World." *Electoral Studies* 24:103–21.

Goldsmith, Arthur A. 2000. "Sizing up the African State." *Journal of Modern African Studies* 38 (1): 1–20.

Gould, Andrew C. 1999. "Conflicting Imperatives and Concept Formation." *Review of Politics* 61 (3): 439–63.

Green, Elliott. 2006. "Ethnicity and the Politics of Land Tenure Reform in Central Uganda." *Commonwealth and Comparative Politics* 44 (3): 370–88.

Greene, Kenneth F. 2007. *Why Dominant Parties Lose: Mexico's Democratization in Comparative Perspective*. Cambridge: Cambridge University Press.

Günther, Richard, Nikiforos P. Diamandouros, and Hans-Jürgen Puhle. 1995. *The Politics of Democratic Consolidation: Southern Europe in a Comparative Perspective.* Baltimore: Johns Hopkins University Press.

Hadenius, Axel. 1992. *Democracy and Development.* Cambridge: Cambridge University Press.

———. 2001. *Institutions and Democratic Citizenship*. Oxford: Oxford University Press.

Hadenius, Axel, and Jan Teorell. 2005a. "Assessing Alternative Indices of Democracy." Concepts and Methods Working Paper Series, 6, International Political Science Association (IPSA). Available at www.concepts-methods.org/working_papers/20050812_16_PC%206%20Hadenius%20&%20Teorell.pdf.

———. 2005b. "Authoritarian Regimes, 1972–2003: Patterns of Stability and Change." Paper presented at Conference on Authoritarian Regimes: Conditions of Stability and Change, Istanbul, Turkey, May 29–31.

———. 2006. "Authoritarian Regimes: Stability, Change, and Pathways to Democracy, 1972–2003." Kellogg Institute Working Paper no. 331, University of Notre Dame, Notre Dame, IN.

———. 2007. "Pathways from Authoritarianism." *Journal of Democracy* 18 (1): 143–56.

Haggard, Stephan, and Robert R. Kaufman. 1995. *The Political Economy of Democratic Transitions*. Princeton, NJ: Princeton University Press.

Hagmann, Tobias. 2006. "Ethiopian Political Culture Strikes Back: A Rejoinder to J. Abbink." *African Affairs* 105 (421).

Haidar, Khatoun. 2005. "Both Lebanese Election Laws Were Unfair." *The Daily Star* (Beirut), May 25.

Hakobyan, Anna. 2003. "Armenia: Kocharian Retains Presidency." *Transitions Online*, March 10. Available at www.ceeol.com/aspx/issuedetails.aspx?issueid=be14f105-53d2-11d7-91f3-0000b4a60532. Accessed July 27, 2007.

Hale, Henry. 2004. "Divided We Stand." *World Politics* 56 (January): 165–73.

———. 2005. "Regime Cycles, Democracy, Autocracy, and Revolution in Post-Soviet Eurasia." *World Politics* 58 (October): 133–65.

———. 2006. "Democracy or Autocracy on the March? The Colored Revolutions as Normal Dynamics of Patronal Presidentialism." *Communist and Postcommunist Studies* 39 (September): 305–29.

Hamzawy, A., and N. J. Brown. 2005. "Can Egypt's Troubled Elections Produce a More Democratic Future?" *Carnegie Endowment for International Peace*. Available at www.carnegieendowment.org/publications/index.cfm?fa=view&id=17807&prog=zgp&proj=zdrl,zme.

Hardin, Russell. 2003. *Indeterminacy and Society*. Princeton: Princeton University Press.

Hartlyn, Jonathan. 1998. *The Struggle for Democratic Politics in the Dominican Republic*. Chapel Hill: University of North Carolina Press.

Hartlyn, Jonathan, and Jennifer McCoy. 2006. "Observer Paradoxes: How to Assess Electoral Manipulation." In *Electoral Authoritarianism: The Dynamics of Unfree Competition*, ed. Andreas Schedler, 41–54. Boulder, CO: Lynne Rienner.

Hartlyn, Jonathan, and Arturo Valenzuela. 1994. "Democracy in Latin America since 1930." In *Cambridge History of Latin America*, ed. Leslie Bethell, vol. 6, pt. 2: *1930 to the Present*, 99–162. Cambridge: Cambridge University Press.

Hassim, Shireen. 2006. *Women's Organizations and Democracy in South Africa: Contesting Authority*. Madison: University of Wisconsin Press.

Hazaymah, M. 2005. "Awad al-, 'Idrak al-Nakhabin al-Urdunniyin lil-'awamal alati tahadud taswitihim." *Majalat al-'Aloum al-Ijtima'i* 33 (3): 675–709.

Helmke, Gretchen. 2002. "The Logic of Strategic Defection: Court-Executive Relations in Argentina under Democracy and Dictatorship." *American Political Science Review* 96 (2): 305–20.

———. 2005. *Courts under Constraints: Judges, Generals, and Presidents in Argentina*. Cambridge: Cambridge University Press.

Helmke, Gretchen, and Stephen Levitsky, eds. 2006. *Informal Institutions and Democracy. Lessons from Latin America*. Baltimore: Johns Hopkins University Press.

Herb, Michael. 2005. "No Representation without Taxation? Rents, Development and Democracy." *Comparative Politics* 37 (3): 297–316.

Herbst, Jeffrey. 2001. "Political Liberalization after Ten Years." *Comparative Politics* 34:357–75.

Herman, Edward S., and Frank Brodhead. 1984. *Demonstration Elections: U.S.-Staged Elections in the Dominican Republic, Vietnam, and El Salvador*. Boston: South End Press.

Hermet, Guy. 1974. *Communists in Spain*. Dartmouth, UK: Dartmouth Publishing Co.

———. 1978. "State-Controlled Elections: A Framework." In *Elections without Choice*, ed. Guy Hermet, Richard Rose, and Alain Rouquié, 1–18. New York: Wiley.

Hermet, Guy, Richard Rose, and Alain Rouquié. 1978. *Elections without Choice*. New York: Wiley.

Herron, Erik S., and Kirk A. Randazzo. 2003. "The Relationship between Independence and Judicial Review in Post-Communist Courts." *Journal of Politics* 65 (2): 422–38.

Horowitz, Donald L. 1985. *Ethnic Groups in Conflict*. Berkeley: University of California Press.

———. 1991. *A Democratic South Africa? Constitutional Engineering in a Divided Society*. Berkeley: University of California Press.

Hourani, H., et al. 1998. *Who's Who in the Jordanian Parliament: 1993–1997*. Amman, Jordan: Sindbad Publishing.

———. 2004. *Who's Who in the Jordanian Parliament: 2003–2007*. Amman, Jordan: Sindbad Publishing.

Howard, Marc M., and P. G. Roessler. 2006. "Liberalizing Electoral Outcomes in Competitive Authoritarian Regimes." *American Journal of Political Science* 50 (2): 365–81.

Huntington, Samuel P. 1991. *The Third Wave: Democratization in the Late Twentieth Century*. Norman: University of Oklahoma Press.

Hyden, Goran. 2005. "Barriers to Party Systems in Africa: The Movement Legacy." Paper presented at the 48th Annual Conference of the African Studies Association, Washington, DC, November 17–20.

Hyden, Goran, and Michael Bratton, eds. 1992. *Governance and Politics in Africa*. Boulder, CO: Lynne Rienner.

Hyden, Goran, and Colin T. Leys. 1972. "Elections and Politics in Single-Party Systems: The Case of Kenya and Tanzania." *British Journal of Political Science* 2 (4): 389–420.

Inglehart, Ronald. 2003. "How Solid Is Mass Support for Democracy—And How Can We Measure It?" *PS: Political Science & Politics* 36 (1): 51–57.

International IDEA. 2003. *Funding of Political Parties and Election Campaigns*. Stockholm: International Institute for Democracy and Electoral Assistance.

———. 2009. *Parliamentary Elections*. Available at www. idea.int/vt/parl.cfm. Accessed January 14, 2009.

IRI (International Republican Institute). 1992. "Elections in the Republic of Croatia." Available at www.iri.org/eoreports.asp.

———. 2006. "Armenia Voter Study: Armenia National Voter Study." November. Available at www.iri.org/eurasia/armenia/pdfs/2006-11-06-Armenia-poll.pdf. Accessed January 10, 2009.

Ishiyama, John, and John Quinn. 2006. "African Phoenix? Explaining the Electoral Performance of the Formerly Dominant Parties in Africa." *Party Politics*. 12 (3): 317–40.

Jacob, Herbert. 1996. "Introduction." In *Courts, Law, and Politics in Comparative Per-*

spective, ed. Herbert Jacob, Erhard Blamkemburg, Herbert M. Kritzer, Doris Marie Provine and Joseph Sanders. 1–15. New Haven: Yale University Press.

Jarstad, Anna. 2001. *Changing the Game: Consociational Theory and Ethnic Quotas in Cyprus and New Zealand.* Uppsala, Sweden: Department of Peace and Conflict, Uppsala University.

Javeline, Debra. 2003. "The Role of Blame in Collective Action: Evidence from Russia." *American Political Science Review* 97 (1): 107–21.

Jones-Luong, Pauline. 2002. *Institutional Change and Political Continuity in Post-Soviet Central Asia: Power, Perceptions, and Pacts*. Cambridge Studies in Comparative Politics. Cambridge: Cambridge University Press.

Joseph, Richard. 1997. "Democratization in Africa after 1989: Comparative and Theoretical Perspectives." *Comparative Politics* 29 (2): 363–82.

———. 1998. "Africa, 1990–1997: From Abertura to Closure." *Journal of Democracy* 9 (2): 3–17.

Kagwanja, Peter Mwangi. 2006. "Power to Uhuru: Youth Identity and Generational Politics in Kenya's 2002 Elections." *African Affairs* 105 (418).

Kandelaki, Giorgi. 2006. *Georgia's Rose Revolution: A Participant's Perspective.* Special Report. Washington, DC: United States Institute of Peace.

Kandelaki, Giorgi, and Giorgi Meladze. 2007. "Enough! Kmara and the Rose Revolution." In *Reclaiming Democracy: Civil Society and Electoral Change in Central and Eastern Europe*, ed. Joerg Forbrig and Pavol Demes. Bratislava: German Marshall Fund of the United States.

Karl, Terry. 1986. "Imposing Consent: Electoralism and Democratization in El Salvador." In *Elections and Democratization in Latin America, 1980–1985*, ed. Paul W. Drake and Eduardo Silva. La Jolla, CA: Center for Iberian and Latin American Studies, University of California at San Diego.

———. 1990. "Dilemmas of Democratization in Latin America." *Comparative Politics* 3 (October).

———. 1995. "The Hybrid Regimes of Central America." *Journal of Democracy* 6 (3): 72–87.

———. 2000. "Electoralism: Why Elections Are Not Democracy." In *The International Encyclopedia of Elections*, ed. Richard Rose. Washington, DC: Congressional Quarterly Books.

Keefer, Philip. 2002. *Database of Political Institutions: Changes and Variable Definitions*. New York: World Bank.

———. 2005. "DPI2004 Database of Political Institutions: Changes and Variable Definitions." Mimeo. New York: World Bank Development Research Group.

———. 2007. "DPI2006 Database of Political Institutions." New York: World Bank. Available at http://info.worldbank.org/governance/wgi2007.

Khachatrian, Haroutiun. 2003. "Constitutional Court Stirs Armenian Political Controversy." *Eurasianet.org*, April 23. Available at www.eurasianet.org/departments/rights/articles/eav042303.shtml. Accessed May 25, 2007.

———. 2006. "Armenia's Constitutional Court Takes on New Political Weight." *Eur-*

asianet.org, October 26. Available at www.eurasianet.org/departments/insights/articles/eav102606a.shtml. Accessed 25 May 2007.

Kiiza, J., S. Makara, and L. Rakner, eds. 2008. *Electoral Democracy in Uganda: Understanding the Institutional Dynamics, Processes, and Outcomes of the 2006 Multiparty Elections.* Kampala: Fountain Publishers

Kilani, S., and B. Sakijha. 2002. *Wasta: The Declared Secret*. Amman: Jordan Press Foundation.

Kinne, Brandon J. 2005. "Decision Making in Autocratic Regimes: A Poliheuristic Perspective." *International Studies Perspectives* 6 (1): 114–28.

Koelble, Thomas A., and Edward LiPuma 2006. "The Effects of Circulatory Capitalism on Democratization: Observations from South Africa and Brazil." *Democratization* 13 (4).

Konings, Piet. 2004. "Opposition and Social Democratic Change in Africa: The Social Democratic Front in Cameroon." *Commonwealth and Comparative Politics* 42 (3): 289–311.

Krutz, Jeffrey. 2006. "African Cities and Incumbent Hostility: Explaining Opposition Success in Urban Areas." Paper presented at the African Studies Association Meeting, November, San Francisco.

Kubicek, Paul. 1999. "Organized Labor in Postcommunist States: Will the Western Sun Set on It, Too?" *Comparative Politics* 32 (1): 83–102.

Kuenzi, Michelle, and Gina Lambright. 2001. "Party System Institutionalization in 30 African Countries." *Party Politics* 7 (4): 437–68.

———. 2005. "Party Systems and Democratic Consolidation in Africa's Electoral Regimes." *Party Politics* 11 (4): 423–46.

Kurzman, Charles. 2004. *The Unthinkable Revolution in Iran.* Cambridge: Harvard University Press.

Kuzio, Taras. 2005a. "From Kuchma to Yushchenko: Ukraine's 2004 Presidential Elections and the Orange Revolution." *Problems of Post-Communism* 52 (March/April).

———. 2005b. "Ukraine's Orange Revolution: The Opposition's Road to Success." *Journal of Democracy* 16 (2): 117–30.

———. 2006. "Ukraine Is Not Russia: Comparing Youth Political Activism." *SAIS Review* 26 (Summer).

Lambright, Gina. 2007. "Elections, Accountability, and Government Performance in Uganda." Unpublished paper, George Washington University.

Lamounier, Bolivar. 1989. "*Authoritarian Brazil* Revisited: The Impact of Elections on the *Abertura*." In *Democratizing Brazil: Problems of Transition and Consolidation,* ed. Alfred Stepan, 43–79. Oxford: Oxford University Press.

Langston, Joy. 2006. "Elite Ruptures: When Do Ruling Parties Split?" In *Electoral Authoritarianism: The Dynamics of Unfree Competition*, ed. Andreas Schedler, 57–75. Boulder, CO: Lynne Rienner.

Langston, Joy, and Scott Morgenstern. 2007. "Campaigning in an Electoral Authoritarian Regime: The Case of Mexico." Unpublished paper, CIDE, Mexico City, and University of Pittsburgh, Pittsburgh, PA.

Larkins, Christopher M. 1996. "Judicial Independence and Democratization: A Theoretical and Conceptual Analysis." *American Journal of Comparative Law* 44: 605–26.

Law on the Constitutional Court of Armenia. 30 December 1997. Available in English at the International Constitutional Law Project at www.servat.unibe.ch/law/icl/info.html. Accessed 2 August 2007. (See also Council of Europe's Venice Commission at www.venice.coe.int.)

Law on the Constitutional Court of the Republic of Georgia. 7 July 1995. Available in English from the Council of Europe's Venice Commission, www.venice.coe.int. Accessed 18 June 2007.

LCPS (Lebanese Center for Policy Studies). 2003. "Decentralization, Democratization, and Local Governance in the Arab Region." Lebanese Center for Policy Studies, Beirut, November.

LeBas, Adrienne. 2006. "Polarization as Craft: Party Formation and State Violence in Zimbabwe." *Comparative Politics* 38 (4).

Lehoucq, F. 2003. "Electoral Fraud: Causes, Types, and Consequences." *Annual Review of Political Science* 6:233.

Lemarchand, Rene. 2007. "Consociationalism and Power Sharing in Africa: Rwanda, Burundi, and the Democratic Republic of the Congo." *African Affairs* 106 (422).

Levi, Margareth. 1990. "A Logic of Institutional Change." In *The Limits of Rationality*, ed. Karen Schweers Cook and Margareth Levi. Chicago: University of Chicago Press.

Levitsky, Stephen. 2003. "Autocracy by Democratic Rules: The Dynamics of Competitive Authoritarianism in the Post–Cold War Era." Paper prepared for the conference, "Mapping the Great Zone: Clientelism and the Boundary between Democratic and Democratizing," Columbia University, New York, April 4–5.

Levitsky, Stephen, and Lucan Way. 2002a. "Autocracy by Democratic Rules: The Dynamics of Competitive Authoritarianism in the Post–Cold War Era." Revised version of paper prepared for Annual Meeting of the American Political Science Association Meeting, Boston, August 28–31. Available at http://astro.temple.edu/~lway/autdem. Accessed August 10, 2005.

———. 2002b. "Elections without Democracy: The Rise of Competitive Authoritarianism." *Journal of Democracy* 13 (2): 51–65.

———. 2005. "International Linkage and Democratization." *Journal of Democracy* 16 (3): 20–34.

———. 2006. "Linkage and Leverage: How Do International Factors Change Domestic Balances of Power?" In *Electoral Authoritarianism: The Dynamics of Unfree Competition*, ed. Andreas Schedler. Boulder, CO: Lynne Rienner.

———. 2007. "Competitive Authoritarian Regimes: The Evolution of Post-Soviet Competitive Authoritarianism, 1992–2005." Paper presented at the conference "Why Communism Didn't Collapse: Understanding Regime Resilience in China, Vietnam, Laos, North Korea and Cuba," Dartmouth College, Hanover, NH, May 25–26.

Li, Quan, and Rafael Reuveny. 2003. "Economic Globalization and Democracy: An Empirical Analysis." *British Journal of Political Science* 33:29–54.

Lichbach, Mark Irving. 1998. "Contending Theories of Contentious Politics and the Structure-Action Problem of Social Order." *Annual Review of Political Science* 1:401–24.

Lijphart, Arend. 1986. "Proportionality by Non-PR Methods: Ethnic Representation in Belgium, Cyprus, Lebanon, New Zealand, West Germany, and Zimbabwe." In *Electoral Laws and Their Political Consequences,* ed. Bernard Grofman and Arend Lijphart. New York: Agathon Press.

———. 1994. *Electoral Systems and Party Systems: A Study of Twenty-seven Democracies, 1945–1990.* Cambridge: Cambridge University Press.

———. 1997. "Unequal Participation: Democracies' Unresolved Dilemma." *American Political Science Review* 91:1–14.

———. 1999. *Patterns of Democracy: Government Forms and Performance in 36 Countries.* New Haven: Yale University Press.

———. 2004. "Constitutional Design for Divided Societies." *Journal of Democracy* 15 (2): 96–109.

Lindberg, Staffan I. 2002. "Problems of Measuring Democracy: Illustrations from Africa." In *Development and Democracy: What Have We Learned and How?* ed. Goran Hyden and Ole Elgstrom. London: Routledge.

———. 2004a. "Democratization and Women's Empowerment: The Effects of Electoral Systems, Participation, and Repetition in Africa." *Studies in Comparative International Development* 38 (1): 28–53.

———. 2004b. "When Do Opposition Parties Boycott Elections?" Paper prepared for the international conference "Democratization by Elections? The Dynamics of Electoral Authoritarianism," CIDE, Mexico City, April 2–3. Available at www.svet.lu.se/Staff/Personal_pages/Staffan_lindberg/When_Do_Opposition5.pdf. Accessed August 10, 2005.

———. 2004c. "The Democratic Qualities of Multiparty Elections: Participation, Competition, and Legitimacy in Africa." *Journal of Commonwealth and Comparative Politics* 42 (1): 61–105.

———. 2005. "Consequences of Electoral Systems in Africa: A Preliminary Inquiry." *Electoral Studies* 24 (1): 41–64.

———. 2006a. *Democracy and Elections in Africa.* Baltimore: Johns Hopkins University Press.

———. 2006b. "Opposition Parties and Democratization in Sub-Saharan Africa." *Journal of Contemporary African Studies* 24 (1): 123–38.

———. 2006c. "The Surprising Significance of African Elections." *Journal of Democracy* 17 (1): 139–51.

———. 2007. "Institutionalization of Party Systems? Stability and Fluidity among Legislative Parties in Africa's Democracies." *Government and Opposition* 42 (2): 215–41.

Lindberg, Staffan I., and Minion K. C. Morrison. 2005. "Exploring Voter Alignments in Africa: Core and Swing Voters in Ghana." *Journal of Modern African Studies* 43 (4): 1–22.

———. 2008. "Are African Voters Really Ethnic or Clientelistic? Survey Evidence from Ghana." *Political Science Quarterly* 123 (1): 95–122.

Linz, Juan J. 1973. "The Future of an Authoritarian Situation or the Institutionalization of an Authoritarian Regime: The Case of Brazil." In *Authoritarian Brazil: Origins, Policies, and Future*, ed. Alfred Stepan, 233–54. New Haven: Yale University Press.

———. 1975. "Totalitarian and Authoritarian Regimes." In *Handbook of Political Science 3*, ed. F. I. Greenstein and N.W. Polsby. Reading, MA: Addison-Wesley.

———. 1978. "Non-Competitive Elections in Europe." In *Elections without Choice,* ed. Guy Hermet, Richard Rose, and Alain Rouquié, 36–65. New York: John Wiley & Sons.

———. 1990. "The Perils of Presidentialism." *Journal of Democracy* 1 (1): 51–69.

Linz, Juan J., and Alfred Stepan. 1978. *The Breakdown of Democratic Regimes.* Baltimore: Johns Hopkins University Press.

———. 1996. *Problems of Democratic Transition and Consolidation: Southern Europe, South America, and Post-Communist Europe*. Baltimore: Johns Hopkins University Press.

Lipset, Seymour Martin. 1959. "Some Social Requisites of Democracy: Economic Development and Political Legitimacy." *American Political Science Review* 53 (1): 69–105.

———. 1994. "The Social Requisites of Democracy Revisited." *American Sociological Review* 59 (February): 1–22.

Loewe, M., et al. 2006. *The Impact of Favoritism on the Business Climate: A Study on Wasta in Jordan.* Bonn: German Development Institute.

Londregan, John B., and Keith. T. Poole. 1996. "Does High Income Promote Democracy?" *World Politics* 49 (1): 56–91.

Lust-Okar, Ellen. 2001. "The Decline of Jordanian Political Parties: Myth or Reality?" *International Journal of Middle East Studies* 33 (4): 545–70.

———. 2004. "Divided They Rule: The Management and Manipulation of Political Opposition." *Comparative Politics* 1 (January): 159–79.

———. 2005a. "Democracy in Jordan: Opportunities Lost." USIP workshop entitled "Beyond Liberalized Autocracy? New Options for Promoting Democracy in the Arab World," Washington, DC, July 18–19.

———. 2005b. "Opposition and Economic Crises in Jordan and Morocco." In *Authoritarianism in the Middle East: Regimes and Resistance*, ed. Marsha Pripstein Posusney and Michelle Penner Angriste. Boulder, CO: Lynne Rienner.

———. 2006a. "Elections under Authoritarianism: Preliminary Lessons from Jordan." *Democratization* 13 (3): 456–71.

———. 2006b. *Structuring Conflict in the Arab World: Incumbents, Opponents, and Institutions.* Cambridge: Cambridge University Press.

———. 2008. “The Politics of Jordanian Elections: Competitive Clientalism.” In *Political Participation in the Middle East and North Africa,* ed. Ellen Lust-Okar and S. Zerhouni. Boulder, CO: Lynne Reinner.

———. Forthcoming. “Reinforcing Informal Institutions through Authoritarian Elections: Insights from Jordan.” *Middle East Law and Governance: An Interdisciplinary Journal.*

Lust-Okar, Ellen, and A. Jamal. 2002. “Rulers and Rules: Reassessing Electoral Laws and Political Liberalization in the Middle East.” *Comparative Political Studies* 35 (3): 337–70.

Lust-Okar, Ellen, and T. Masoud. In progress. “Competitive Clientalism in Egypt: Candidates and Voters in Egypt’s Parliamentary Elections.”

Lyons, Terrence. 2005. *Demilitarizing Politics: Elections on the Uncertain Road to Peace.* Boulder, CO: Lynne Rienner.

Magaloni, Beatriz. 2006. *Voting for Autocracy: Hegemonic Party Survival and Its Demise in Mexico.* New York: Cambridge University Press.

———. 2008. “Credible Power-Sharing and the Longevity of Authoritarian Rule.” *Comparative Political Studies* 41 (4–5): 715–41.

Mainwaring, Scott. 1993. “Presidentialism, Multipartism, and Democracy: The Difficult Combination.” *Comparative Political Studies* 26 (2): 198–228.

Mainwaring, Scott, Daniel Brinks, and Aníbal Pérez-Liñán. 2002. “Classifying Political Regimes in Latin America, 1945–1999.” *Studies in Comparative International Development* 36 (1): 37–65.

Mainwaring, Scott, and Aníbal Pérez-Liñán. 2005. “Latin American Democratization since 1978: Democratic Transitions, Breakdowns, and Erosions.” In *The Third Wave of Democratization in Latin America: Advances and Setbacks*, ed. Frances Hagopian and Scott Mainwaring. Cambridge: Cambridge University Press.

Maltz, Gideon. 2007. “The Case for Presidential Term Limits.” *Journal of Democracy* 18 (2): 128–42.

Manning, Carrie. 2005. “Assessing African Party System Consolidation: Ideology Versus Institutions.” *Party Politics* 11 (6): 707–27.

March, James G., and Johan P. Olsen. 1989. *Rediscovering Institutions.* New York: Free Press.

Marcus, Richard R., and Adrien M. Ratsimbaharison. 2005. “Political Parties in Madagascar: Neopatrimonial Tools or Democratic Instruments?” *Party Politics* 11 (4): 495–512.

Marples, David R. 1999. *Belarus: A Denationalized Nation: Postcommunist States and Nations* Amsterdam: Harwood Academic.

Marshall, Monty G., Ted Robert Gurr, Christian Davenport, and Keith Jaggers. 2002. “Polity IV, 1800–1999: Comments on Munck and Verkuilen.” *Comparative Political Studies* 35 (1): 40–45.

Marshall, Monty, and Keith Jaggers. 2003. *Polity IV Project: Political Regime Characteristics and Transitions, 1800–2003.* Available at www.cidcm.umd.edu/inscr/polity.

———. 2005. "Political Regime Characteristics and Transitions, 1800–2004: Dataset Users' Manual." Polity IV Project, University of Maryland. Available at www.cidcm.umd.edu/polity.

Massicotte, Louise, and Andre Blais. 1999. "Mixed Electoral Systems: A Conceptual and Empirical Survey." *Electoral Studies* 18 (3): 341–66.

Mayrargue, Cedric. 2006. "Yayi Boni, Un President Inattendu? Construction de la Figure du Candidat et Dynamiques Electorales au Benin." *Politique Africaine* 102:155–72.

McCann, Michael W. 1994. *Rights at Work: Pay Equity Reform and the Politics of Legal Mobilization.* Chicago: University of Chicago Press.

McFaul, Michael. 2005. "Transitions from Post-Communism." *Journal of Democracy* 16 (3): 5–19.

Miles, William F., ed. 2007. *Political Islam in West Africa.* Boulder, CO: Lynne Rienner.

Mitchell, Lincoln. 2004. "Georgia's Rose Revolution." *Current History* 103 (675): 342–48.

Moe, Ronald C. 1990. "Traditional Organizational Principles and the Managerial Presidency: From Phoenix to Ashes." *Public Administration Review* 50 (2): 129–40.

Moehler, Devra C. 2006. "Public Participation and Support for the Constitution in Uganda." *Journal of Modern African Studies* 44 (2).

Moehler, Devra C., and Staffan I. Lindberg. 2007. "Narrowing the Legitimacy Gap: The Role of Turnovers in Africa's Emerging Democracies." Afrobarometer Working Paper no. 88. East Lansing, MI: Michigan State University.

———. 2009. "Electoral Institutions and Political Shepherds: Effects on Citizens' Attitudes to Democracy in Africa." *Journal of Politics* 71 (4).

Monga, Célestin. 1997. "Eight Problems with African Politics." *Journal of Democracy* 8 (3): 156–79.

Montgomery, Tommie Sue. 1995. *Revolution in El Salvador: From Civil Strife to Civil Peace.* Boulder, CO: Westview Press.

Morlino, Leonardo. 2004. "What Is a Good Democracy?" *Democratization* 11 (5): 10–32.

Morrison, Minion K. C. 2004. "Political Parties in Ghana through Four Republics." *Comparative Politics* 36:421–42.

———. 2006. "Ghana's Political Parties: How Ethno/Regional Variations Sustain the National Two-Party System." *Journal of Modern African Studies* 44 (4).

Mozaffar, Shaheen, and James R. Scarritt. 2005. "The Puzzle of African Party Systems." *Party Politics* 11 (4): 399–421.

Mozaffar, Shaheen, James R. Scarritt, and Glen Galaich. 2003. "Electoral Institutions, Ethno-political Cleavages, and Party Systems in Africa's Emerging Democracies." *American Political Science Review* 97 (3): 379–90.

Mozaffar, Shaheen, and Andreas Schedler. 2002. "The Comparative Study of Electoral Governance." *International Political Science Review* 23 (1): 5–27.

Munck, Gerardo L. 2001a. "Game Theory and Comparative Politics: New Perspectives and Old Concerns." *World Politics* 53 (January): 173–204.

———. 2001b. "The Regime Question: Theory Building in Democracy Studies." *World Politics* 54: 119–44.

———. 2006. "Drawing Boundaries: How to Craft Intermediate Regime Categories." In *Electoral Authoritarianism: The Dynamics of Unfree Competition*, ed. Andreas Schedler. Boulder, CO: Lynne Rienner.

Munck, Gerardo L., and Richard Snyder. 2004. "Mapping Political Regimes: How the Concepts We Use and the Way We Measure Them Shape the World We See." Paper presented at the 2004 Annual Meeting of the American Political Science Association.

Munck, Gerardo L., and Jay Verkuilen. 2002. "Conceptualizing and Measuring Democracy: Evaluating Alternative Indices." *Comparative Political Studies* 35 (1): 5–34.

National Endowment for Democracy. 2006. *The Backlash against Democracy Assistance*. Report prepared by the NED for Senator Richard G. Lugar, Chairman, Committee on Foreign Relations, U.S. Senate, June 8.

Neumann, John von, and Oskar Morgenstern. 1994. *Theory of Games and Economic Behavior*. Princeton: Princeton University Press.

Nohlen, Dieter. 2005. *Elections in the Americas: A Data Handbook*. Vols. 1–2. Oxford: Oxford University Press.

Norris, Pippa. 2004. *Electoral Engineering*. New York: Cambridge University Press.

———. 2005. *Radical Right*. New York: Cambridge University Press.

———. 2008. *Driving Democracy*. New York: Cambridge University Press.

North, Douglass C. 1990. *Institutions, Institutional Change, and Development*. Cambridge: Cambridge University Press.

Nugent, Paul. 2001. "Winners, Losers, and Also Rans: Money, Moral Authority, and Voting Patterns in the Ghana 2000 Elections." *African Affairs* 100:405–28.

O'Donnell, Guillermo. 1992. "Transitions, Continuities, and Paradoxes." In *Issues in Democratic Consolidation: The New South American Democracies in Comparative Perspective*, ed. Scott Mainwaring, Guillermo O'Donnell, and J. Samuel Valenzuela. Notre Dame, IN: University of Notre Dame Press.

———. 1994. "Delegative Democracy." *Journal of Democracy* 5 (1): 55–69.

———. 2004. "Why the Rule of Law Matters." *Journal of Democracy* 15 (4): 32–46.

O'Donnell, Guillermo, and Phillippe C. Schmitter. 1986. *Transitions from Authoritarian Rule*, Vol. 4: *Tentative Conclusions about Uncertain Democracies*. Baltimore: Johns Hopkins University Press.

O'Donnell, Guillermo A., Jorge Vargas Cullell, and Osvaldo Iazzetta. 2004. *The Quality of Democracy*. Notre Dame, IN: University of Notre Dame Press.

O'Leary, Brendan, and John McGarry. 2004. *The Northern Ireland Conflict: Consociational Engagements*. Oxford: Oxford University Press.

———. 2006 "Consociational Theory, Northern Ireland's Conflict, and Its Agreement, 1: What Consociationalists Can Learn from Northern Ireland." *Government & Opposition* 41 (1): 43–63.

Olsen, Mancur. 1965. *The Logic of Collective Action*. Cambridge: Harvard University Press.

Olukoshi, Adebayo, ed. 1998. "The Senegalese Opposition and Its Quest for Power." In *The Politics of Opposition in Contemporary Africa*, ed. A. Olukoshi. Stockholm: Nordic Africa Institute.

OSCE (Organization for Security and Co-operation in Europe). 2000. "Republic of Georgia Presidential Election, 9 April 2000, Final Report." Warsaw: OSCE Office for Democratic Institutions and Human Rights, June 9. Available at www.osce.org/documents/html/pdftohtml/1356_en.pdf.html.

———. 2007. *Election Observation Handbook*. 5th ed. Warsaw: Organization for Security and Co-operation in Europe. Available at www.osce.org/publications/odihr/2005/04/14004_240_en.pdf.

Paden, John N. 2005. *Muslim Civic Cultures and Conflict Resolution: The Challenge of Democratic Federalism in Nigeria*. Washington, DC: Brookings Institution.

Peceny, Mark, Caroline C. Beer, and Shannon Sanchez-Terry. 2002. "Dictatorial Peace?" *American Political Science Review* 96 (1): 15–26.

Pepinsky, Thomas B. 2007. "Durable Authoritarianism as Self-Enforcing Coalition." Unpublished typescript. University of Colorado, Boulder, Department of Political Science.

Pérez, Orlando. 1995. "Elections under Crisis: Background to Panama in the 1980s." In *Elections and Democracy in Central America, Revisited*, ed. Mitchell A. Seligson and John A. Booth. Chapel Hill: University of North Carolina Press.

Persson, Torsten, and Guido Tabellini. 2007. "Democratic Capital: The Nexus of Political and Economic Change." Unpublished manuscript. Stockholm University, Stockholm, and University of Bocconi, Milan.

Petrova, Tsveta. 2007. "A Postcommunist Transition in Two Acts: The 1996–1997 Anti-Government Struggle in Bulgaria as a Bridge between the First and Second Waves of Transition in Eastern Europe." In "Waves and Troughs of Post-Communist Reform," ed. Valerie J. Bunce, Michael McFaul, and Kathryn Stoner-Weiss. Unpublished book manuscript.

Pierson, Paul. 2000. "Increasing Returns, Path Dependence, and the Study of Politics." *American Political Science Review* 84 (2): 251–67.

Pitcher, Anne. 2006. "Forgetting from Above and Memory from Below: Strategies of Legitimation and Struggle in Postsocialist Mozambique." *Africa* 76:1.

Polity. Various years. Available at www.systemicpeace.org/polity/polity4.htm.

Pop-Eleches, Grigore, and Graeme B. Robertson. 2008. "Elections and Liberalization in the Post–Cold War Era." Unpublished typescript. Princeton University and University of North Carolina at Chapel Hill.

Posner, Daniel. 2004. "Measuring Ethnic Fractionalization in Africa." *American Journal of Political Science* 48 (4): 849–64.

———. 2005. *Institutions and Ethnic Politics in Africa*. Cambridge: Cambridge University Press.

Posner, Daniel, and Daniel Young. 2007. "The Institutionalization of Political Power in Africa." *Journal of Democracy* 18 (3): 126–40.

Posusney, Marsha Pripstein. 2004. "Enduring Authoritarianism: Middle East Lessons for Comparative Theory." *Comparative Politics* 36 (2).

———. 2005. "Multiparty Elections in the Arab World: Election Rules and Opposition Responses." In *Authoritarianism in the Middle East: Regimes and Resistance*, ed. Marsha Pripstein Posusney and Michele Penner Angrist, 91–118. Boulder, CO: Lynne Rienner.

Posusney, Marsha Pripstein, and Michele Penner Angrist, eds. 2005. *Authoritarianism in the Middle East: Regimes and Resistance*. Boulder, CO: Lynne Rienner.

Powell, Bingham G. 1982. *Contemporary Democracies: Participation, Stability, and Violence*. Cambridge: Harvard University Press.

———. 2000. *Elections as Instruments of Democracy*. London: Yale University Press.

———. 2004. "The Chain of Responsiveness." *Journal of Democracy* 15 (4): 91–105.

Powers, Nancy. 1992. "The Transition to Democracy in Paraguay: Problems and Prospects." Kellogg Institute Working Paper no. 171, University of Notre Dame, Notre Dame, IN.

Prempeh, H. Kwasi. 2008. "Presidents Untamed." *Journal of Democracy* 19 (2): 109–23.

Przeworski, Adam. 1986. "Some Problems in the Study of the Transition to Democracy." In *Transitions from Authoritarian Rule*, Vol. 3: *Comparative Perspectives*, ed. Guillermo O'Donnell, Philippe C. Schmitter, and Laurence Whitehead, 47–63. Baltimore: Johns Hopkins University Press.

———. 1991. *Democracy and the Market: Political and Economic Reforms in Eastern Europe and Latin America*. Cambridge: Cambridge University Press.

———. 2003. "Why Do Political Parties Obey Results of Elections?" In *Democracy and the Rule of Law*, ed. José María Maravall and Adam Przeworski, 114–44. Cambridge: Cambridge University Press.

Przeworksi, Adam, Michael Alvarez, José A. Cheibub and Fernando Limongi. 1996. "What Makes Democracies Endure?" *Journal of Democracy* 7 (1): 39–55.

———. 2000. *Democracy and Development: Political Institutions and Well-Being in the World, 1950–1990*. Cambridge: Cambridge University Press.

Puddington, Arch. 2007. *Freedom in the World: Freedom Stagnation amid Pushback against Democracy*. Washington, DC: Freedom House.

———. 2008. "The 2007 Freedom House Survey: Is the Tide Turning?" *Journal of Democracy* 19 (April): 61–73.

Radio Free Europe. 2003a. "Georgian Elections Results Invalidated in Kutaisi." *Radio Free Europe / Radio Liberty Newsline*, November 14. Available at www.rferl.org/content/Article/1143042.html. Accessed June 21, 2007.

Radio Free Europe. 2003b. "Supreme Court Partially Annuls Georgian Election Results." *Radio Free Europe / Radio Liberty Newsline*, November 25. Available at www.rferl.org/content/Article/1143048.html. Accessed June 21, 2007.

Radnitz, Scott. 2006. "What Really Happened in Kyrgyzstan?" *Journal of Democracy* 17 (April).

Rae, Douglas W. 1967. *The Political Consequences of Electoral Laws*. New Haven: Yale University Press.

Rakner, Lise, Lars Svåsand, and Nixon Khembo. 2007. "Fissions and Fusions, Foes and Friends: Party System Restructuring in the 2004 Elections in Malawi." *Comparative Political Studies* 40 (9): 1112–37.

Ramírez, Sergio. 1999. *Adiós Muchachos: Una Memoria de la Revolución Sandinista*. México DF: Aguilar.

Randall, Vicky, and Lars Svåsand, eds. 2002. *Parties, Party Systems and Democratic Consolidation in the Third World*. Special Issue. *Democratization* 9 (3).

Rapoport, David C., and Leonard Weinberg. 2001. "Elections and Violence." In *The Democratic Experience and Political Violence*, ed. David C. Rapoport and Leonard Weinberg, 15–50. London: Frank Cass.

Reilly, Benjamin. 2001. *Democracy in Divided Societies: Electoral Engineering for Conflict Management*. New York: Cambridge University Press.

———. 2002. "Electoral Systems for Divided Societies." *Journal of Democracy* 13 (2): 156–70.

Remmer, Karen. 1999. "Regime Sustainability in the Latin Caribbean, 1944–1994." *Journal of Developing Areas* 33 (Spring): 331–54.

Rennau, Marina. 2003. "Georgia in Pivotal Standoff with Independent Media." *Eurasianet.org*, November 17. Available at www.eurasianet.org/departments/recaps/articles/eav120303.shtml. Accessed August 10, 2007.

Reynolds, Andrew. 1999. *Electoral Systems and Democratization in Southern Africa*. New York: Oxford University Press.

———. 2005. "Reserved Seats in National Legislatures." *Legislative Studies Quarterly* 30 (2): 301–10.

———. 2006. *Electoral Systems and the Protection and Participation of Minorities*. London: Minority Rights Group International.

———. 2007. "Minority MPs in National Legislatures: Existing Research and Data Gaps." London: Minority Rights Group International / UNDP.

Reynolds, Andrew, Ben Reilly, and Andrew Ellis. 2005. *International IDEA Handbook of Electoral System Design*. 2nd ed. Stockholm: International IDEA. Available at www.idea.int/esd/index.cfm.

Ridley, Fredrick F. 1975. *The Study of Government*. London: Allen and Unwin.

Riker, William H. 1986. *The Art of Political Manipulation*. New Haven: Yale University Press.

Roeder, Philip G., and Donald Rothchild, eds. 2005. *Sustainable Peace: Power and Democracy after Civil Wars*. Ithaca, NY: Cornell University Press.

Rose, Richard. 2001. *International Encyclopedia of Elections*. Washington, DC: CQ Press.

Ross, Michael. 2001. "Does Oil Hinder Democracy?" *World Politics* 53 (3): 325–61.

Rothschild, Donald. 2002. "Settlement Terms and Post-Agreement Stability." In *Ending Civil Wars*, ed. Stephen Stedman, Donald Rothchild, and Elizabeth Cousens. Boulder, CO: Lynne Reinner.

Russell, Peter H. 2001a. "Conclusion: Judicial Independence in Comparative Perspective." In *Judicial Independence in the Age of Democracy: Critical Perspectives from around the World*, ed. Peter H. Russell and David M. O'Brien, 301–7. Charlottesville: University Press of Virginia.

———. 2001b. "Toward a General Theory of Judicial Independence." In *Judicial Independence in the Age of Democracy: Critical Perspectives from around the World*, ed. Peter H. Russell and David M. O'Brien, 1–24. Charlottesville: University Press of Virginia.

Rustow, Dankwart A. 1970. "Transitions to Democracy: Toward a Dynamic Model." *Comparative Politics* 2 (3): 337–63.

Salih, M. A. Mohamed. 2003. "Conclusions." In *African Political Parties*, ed. M. A. Mohamed Salih, 348–57. London: Pluto Press.

SANA (Syrian Arab News Agency). 2007. "President al-Assad gets 97.62 Percent in the Referendum on a New Constitutional Term." May 29. Available at www.sana.sy/eng/141/2007/05/29/120564.htm. Accessed June 16, 2008.

Sandbakken, Camilla. 2006. "The Limits to Democracy Posed by Oil Rentier States: The Cases of Algeria, Nigeria, and Libya." *Democratization* 13 (6).

Sandbrook, Richard. 2005. "Origins of the Democratic Developmental State." *Canadian Journal of African Studies* 39 (3): 549–81.

Sari, Helmi. 2002. "Tahlil Mahtawi al-Baramij al-Intikhabiyyah li-marashahi al-Intikhabat li'aam 1997 fil-Urdunn." In *Dirasat fi al-Intikhabat al-Niyabiyyah al-Urduniyyah 1997*, ed. Hani Hourani et al. Amman: Sindbad Publishing House.

Sartori, Giovanni. 1970. "Concept Misformation in Comparative Politics." *American Political Science Review* 64 (4): 1033–46.

———. 1984. "Guidelines for Conceptual Analysis." In *Social Science Concepts: A Systematic Analysis*, ed. Giovanni Sartori. Beverly Hills: Sage Publications.

———. 1987. *The Theory of Democracy Revisited.* Chatham, NJ: Chatham House.

———. 1991. "Comparing and Miscomparing." *Journal of Theoretical Politics* 3 (3): 243–57.

———. 1994. *Comparative Constitutional Engineering: An Inquiry into Structures, Incentives, and Outcomes.* New York: Columbia University Press.

Scarritt, James, and Shaheen Mozaffar. 1999. "The Specification of Ethnic Cleavages and Ethnopolitical Groups for the Analysis of Democratic Competition in Contemporary Africa." *Nationalism and Ethnic Politics* 5 (1): 82–117.

Schedler, Andreas. 1998. "What Is Democratic Consolidation?" *Journal of Democracy* 9 (2): 91–107.

———. 1999. "Conceptualizing Accountability." In *The Self-Restraining State: Power and Accountability in New Democracies*, ed. Andreas Schedler, Larry Diamond, and Marc F. Plattner. Boulder, CO: Lynne Rienner.

———. 2000. "Mexico's Victory: The Democratic Revelation." *Journal of Democracy* 11 (4): 5–19.

———. 2001. "Measuring Democratic Consolidation." *Studies in Comparative International Development* 36 (1): 66–92.

———. 2002a. "Elections without Democracy: The Menu of Manipulation." *Journal of Democracy* 13 (2): 36–50.

———. 2002b. "The Nested Game of Democratization by Elections." *International Political Science Review* 23 (1): 103–22.

———. 2004. "Arguing and Observing: Internal and External Critiques of Judicial Impartiality." *Journal of Political Philosophy* 12 (3): 245–65.

———, ed. 2006a. *Electoral Authoritarianism: The Dynamics of Unfree Competition*. Boulder, CO: Lynne Rienner.

———. 2006b. "Patterns of Repression and Manipulation: Towards a Topography of Authoritarian Elections." Paper presented at the 20th World Congress of the International Political Science Association, Fukuoka, Japan.

———. 2006c. "When Do Losers Protest? Opposition Strategies under Electoral Authoritarianism." Paper presented at the 102nd Annual Meeting of the American Political Science Association, Philadelphia.

———. 2007. "Mapping Contingency." In *Political Contingency: Studying the Unexpected, the Accidental, and the Unforeseen*, ed. Ian Shapiro and Sonu Bedi, 54–78. New York: New York University Press.

Schedler, Andreas, and Rodolfo Sarsfield. 2007. "Democrats with Adjectives: Linking Direct and Indirect Measures of Democratic Support." *European Journal of Political Research* 46 (5): 637–59.

Schlumberger, Oliver, ed. 2007. *Debating Arab Authoritarianism: Dynamics and Durability in Nondemocratic Regimes*. Palo Alto, CA: Stanford University Press.

Schmitter, Philippe. 1978. "The Impact and Meaning of 'Non-Competitive, Non-Free and Insignificant' Elections in Authoritarian Portugal, 1933–74." In *Elections without Choice*, ed. Guy Hermet, Richard Rose, and Alain Rouquié, 145–68. New York: Wiley.

Schmitter, Philippe, and Terry Lynn Karl. 1991. "What Democracy Is . . . And Is Not." *Journal of Democracy* 2 (3): 75–88.

Schumpeter, Joseph. 1942. *Capitalism, Socialism, and Democracy*. New York: Harper & Row.

———. 1947. *Capitalism, Socialism, and Democracy*. 2nd ed. New York: Harper Press.

———. 1950. *Capitalism, Socialism, and Democracy*. 3rd ed. New York: Harper and Brothers.

Schwartz, Herman. 2000. *The Struggle for Constitutional Justice in Post-Communist Europe*. Chicago: University of Chicago Press.

Scranton, Margaret. 1998. "Electoral Observation and Panama's Democratic Transition." In *Electoral Observation and Democratic Transitions in Latin America*, ed. Kevin J. Middelbrook. La Jolla, CA: Center for Iberian and Latin American Studies, University of California at San Diego.

Seligson, Mitchell A., and John A. Booth. 1995. *Elections and Democracy in Central America, Revisited*. Chapel Hill: University of North Carolina Press.

Shapiro, Martin, and Alec Stone Sweet. 2002. *On Law, Politics, and Judicialization*. New York: Oxford University Press.

Shefter, Martin. 1994. *Political Parties and the State: The American Historical Experience.* Princeton: Princeton University Press.

Shehata, S. 2008. "Egyptian Parliamentary Campaigns." In *Political Participation in the Middle East and North Africa,* ed. Ellen Lust-Okar and S. Zerhouni. Boulder, CO: Lynne Reinner.

Shephard, Robin. 2007. "The Economy and Democratic Change: The Missing Link?" In *Reclaiming Democracy: Civil Society and Electoral Change in Central and Eastern Europe,* ed. Joerg Forbrig and Pavol Demes. Bratislava: German Marshall Fund.

Shugart, Matthew Soberg, and Martin P. Wattenberg, eds. 2001. *Mixed-Member Electoral Systems: The Best of Both Worlds?* New York: Oxford University Press.

Silitski, Vitali. 2005. "The Long Road from Tyranny: Post-Communist Authoritarianism and Struggle for Democracy in Serbia and Belarus." Unpublished book manuscript.

Skaaning, Svend-Erik. 2006. "Democracy beside Elections: An Inquiry into the (Dis) Respect for Civil Liberty in Latin America and Post-Communist Countries after the Third Wave." Ph.D. diss., University of Aarhus, Aarhus, Denmark.

Skilling, H. Gordon. 1983. "Interest Groups and Communist Politics Revisited." *World Politics* 36 (1): 1–27.

Smith, Benjamin B. 2005. "Life of the Party: The Origins of Regime Breakdown and Persistence under Single-Party Rule." *World Politics* 57 (3): 421–51.

Smith, Peter H. 2005. *Democracy in Latin America.* Oxford: Oxford University Press.

Smithey, Shannon Ishiyama, and John Ishiyama. 2000. "Judicious Choices: Designing Courts in Post-Communist Politics." *Communist and Post-Communist Studies* 33:163–82.

Smulovitz, Catalina, and Enrique Peruzzotti. 2000. "Societal Accountability in Latin America." *Journal of Democracy* 11 (4): 147–58.

Snyder, Jack. 2000. *From Voting to Violence: Democratization and Nationalist Conflict.* New York: Norton.

Snyder, Richard. 2006. "Beyond Electoral Authoritarianism: The Spectrum of Non-democratic Regimes." In *Electoral Authoritarianism: The Dynamics of Unfree Competition,* ed. Andreas Schedler. Boulder, CO: Lynne Rienner.

Snyder, Richard, and James Mahoney. 1999. "The Missing Variable: Institutions and the Study of Regime Change." *Comparative Politics* 32 (1): 103–22.

Soares, Benjamin F. 2006. "Islam in Mali in the Neoliberal Era." *African Affairs* 105 (418).

Soares, Glaucio Ary Dillon. 1986. "Elections and the Redemocratization of Brazil." In *Elections and Democratization in Latin America, 1980–1985,* ed. Paul W. Drake and Eduardo Silva. La Jolla, CA: Center for Iberian and Latin American Studies, University of California at San Diego.

Staton, Jeffrey K. 2006. "Constitutional Review and the Selective Promotion of Case Results." *American Journal of Political Science* 50 (1): 98–112.

Strang, David, and Sarah Soule. 1998. "Diffusion in Organizations and Social Movements: From Hybrid Corn to Poison Pills." *Annual Review of Sociology* 24:265–90.

Taagepera, Rein, and Matthew Soberg Shugart. 1989. *Seats and Votes: The Effects and Determinants of Electoral Systems*. New Haven: Yale University Press.

Tarrow, Sidney G. 2005. *The New Transnational Activism*. Cambridge Studies in Contentious Politics. Cambridge: Cambridge University Press.

Tate, C. Neal, and Torbjörn Vallinder. 1995a. "The Global Expansion of Judicial Power: The Judicialization of Politics." In *The Global Expansion of Judicial Power*, ed. C. Neal Tate and Torbjörn Vallinder, 1–10. New York: New York University Press.

———. 1995b. "Judicialization and the Future of Politics and Policy." In *The Global Expansion of Judicial Power*, ed. C. Neal Tate and Torbjörn Vallinder, 515–28. New York: New York University Press.

Tavernise, Sabrina. 2008. "Protesters and Policy Clash as Armenia Unrest Grows." *New York Times*, March 2.

Taylor, Scott D. 2006. "Divergent Politico-Legal Responses to Past Presidential Corruption in Zambia and Kenya: Catching the 'Big Fish,' or Letting Him off the Hook?" *Third World Quarterly* 27 (2): 281–301.

Teorell, Jan, and Axel Hadenius. 2007. "Determinants of Democratization: Taking Stock of the Large-*N* Evidence." In *Democratization: The State of the Art*, ed. D. Berg-Schlosser. Opladen, Germany: Barbara Budrich Publishers.

Tezcur, G. M. 2008. "Intra-Elite Struggles and Iranian Elections." In *Political Participation in the Middle East and North Africa*, ed. Ellen Lust-Okar and S. Zerhouni. Boulder, CO: Lynne Reinner.

Thompson, Mark R. 2004. *Democratic Revolutions: Asia and Eastern Europe*. London: Routledge.

Thompson, Mark R., and Philipp Kuntz. 2004. "Stolen Elections: The Case of the Serbian October." *Journal of Democracy* 15 (4): 159–72.

———. 2006. "After Defeat: When Do Rulers Steal Elections?" In *Electoral Authoritarianism: The Dynamics of Unfree Competition*, ed. Andreas Schedler, 113–28. Boulder, CO: Lynne Rienner.

Toulabor, Comi. 2005. "CAR, CDAP et UFC: Le Difficile Implantation Territoriale du Multipartisme au Togo." In *Gouverner les Sociétés Africaines*, ed. Patrick Quantin, 113–32. Paris: Karthala.

Trejo, Guillermo. 2004. "The Political Foundations of Ethnic Mobilization and Territorial Conflict in Mexico, 1975–2000." In *Federalism and Territorial Cleavages*, ed. Ugo Amoretti and Nancy Bermeo. Baltimore: Johns Hopkins University Press.

Tripp, Ali M. 2000. *Women and Politics in Uganda*. Madison: University of Wisconsin Press.

Tsebelis, George. 1990. *Nested Games: Rational Choice in Comparative Politics*. Berkeley: University of California Press.

Tuastad, D. 2008. "The 2005 Local Elections in Gaza: Authoritarianism and Fragmentation in Palestinian Politics." In *Political Participation in the Middle East and North Africa*, ed. Ellen Lust-Okar and S. Zerhouni. Boulder, CO: Lynne Reinner.

Tucker, Alan. 1950. "A Two-Person Dilemma." Mimeo. Stanford University, Palo Alto, CA.

Tucker, Joshua. 2007. "Enough! Electoral Fraud, Collective Action Problems, and Post-Communist Colored Revolutions." *Perspectives on Politics* 5 (3): 535–51.

Turkish Daily News. 2003. "Shevardnadze and Opposition Leaders Chart Strategies." *Turkish Daily News*, November 17. Available from ISI Emerging Markets Database at www.securities.com. Accessed June 21, 2007.

UNDP (United Nations Development Program). 2004. *Democracy in Latin America: Towards a Citizen's Democracy*. New York: United Nations.

Vachudova, Milada Anna. 2005. *Europe Undivided: Democracy, Leverage, and Integration after Communism*. Oxford: Oxford University Press.

Valenzuela, Samuel J. 1992. "Democratic Consolidation in Post-Transitional Settings: Notion, Process, and Facilitating Conditions." In *Issues in Democratic Consolidation: The New South American Democracies in Comparative Perspective*, ed. Scott Mainwaring, Guillermo O'Donnell, and Samuel J. Valenzuela. Notre Dame, IN: University of Notre Dame Press.

van de Walle, Nicholas. 2001. *African Economies and the Politics of Permanent Crisis, 1979–1999*. Cambridge: Cambridge University Press.

———. 2002. "Elections without Democracy: Africa's Range of Regimes." *Journal of Democracy* 13 (2): 66–80.

———. 2003. "Presidentialism and Clientelism in Africa's Emerging Party Systems." *Journal of Modern African Studies* 41 (2).

———. 2006. "Tipping Games: When Do Opposition Parties Coalesce?" In *Electoral Authoritarianism: The Dynamics of Unfree Competition*, ed. Andreas Schedler, 77–94. Boulder, CO: Lynne Rienner.

———. 2007. "Meet the New Boss: Same as the Old Boss; The Evolution of Political Clientelism in Africa." In *Patrons, Clients, and Policies: Patterns of Democratic Accountability and Political Competition*, ed. Herbert Kitschelt and Steven I. Wilkinson. Cambridge: Cambridge University Press.

Vanhanen, Tatu. 1997. *Prospects of Democracy: A Study of 172 Countries*. London: Routledge.

———. 2005. *Measures of Democracy, 1810–2004*. Computer file. FSD1289, version 2.0 (2005-08-17). Tampere: Finnish Social Science Data Archive [distributor].

Villalón, Leonardo A., and A. Idrissa. 2005. "The Tribulations of a Successful Transition: Institutional Dynamics and Elite Rivalry in Mali." In *The Fate of Africa's Democratic Experiments: Elites and Institutions*, ed. Leonardo A. Villalón and Peter Von Doepp, 49–74. Bloomington: Indiana University Press.

Villalón, Leonardo A., and Peter Von Doepp. 2005. *The Fate of Africa's Democratic Experiments: Elites and Institutions*. Bloomington: Indiana University Press.

Von Doepp, Peter. 2006. "Politics and Judicial Assertiveness in Emerging Democracies: High Court Behavior in Malawi and Zambia." *Political Research Quarterly* 59 (3): 389–99.

Wantchekon, Leonard. 2003. "Clientelism and Voting Behavior: Evidence from a Field Experiment in Benin." *World Politics* 55 (3): 399–422.

Ward, Michael D. 2002. "Green Binders in Cyberspace: A Modest Proposal." *Comparative Political Studies* 35(1): 46–51.

Way, Lucan A. 2005a. "Authoritarian State Building and the Sources of Regime Competitiveness in the Fourth Wave: The Cases of Belarus, Moldova, Russia, and Ukraine." *World Politics* 57 (January).

———. 2005b. "Ukraine's Orange Revolution: Kuchma's Failed Authoritarianism." *Journal of Democracy* 16 (2): 131–45.

———. 2006. "Authoritarian Failure: How Does State Weakness Strengthen Electoral Competition?" In *Electoral Authoritarianism: The Dynamics of Unfree Competition*, ed. Andreas Schedler, 167–81. Boulder, CO: Lynne Rienner.

———. 2008. "The Real Causes of the Color Revolutions." *Journal of Democracy* 19 (3): 55–69.

Weber, Max. 1988. "Politik als Beruf." In *Gesammelte Politische Schriften*, ed. Johannes Winckelmann, 505–60. Tübingen: J. C. B. Mohr (orig. 1919).

Wedeen, Lisa. 1999. *Ambiguities of Domination: Politics, Rhetoric, and Symbols in Contemporary Syria*. Chicago: University of Chicago Press.

Whitehead, Laurence. 2007. "The Challenge of Closely Fought Elections." *Journal of Democracy* 18 (2): 14–28.

Whitmore, Brian. 2007. "Armenia: Parliamentary Vote Sets Scene for 2008 Presidential Race." *Radio Free Europe / Radio Liberty*, May 11.

Wiatr, Jerzy J. 1962. "Elections and Voting Behaviour." Paper No. 8. London: London School of Economics.

Wintrobe, Ronald. 1998. *The Political Economy of Dictatorship*. Cambridge: Cambridge University Press.

Woods, Patricia. 2008. *Judicial Power and National Politics: Courts and Gender in the Religious-Secular Conflict in Israel*. Albany: State University of New York Press.

World Bank. 2007. *World Development Indicators*. Available at www.worldbank.org.

Yoon, Mi Yung, and Sheila Bunwaree. 2006. "Women's Legislative Representation in Mauritius: 'A Grave Democratic Deficit.'" *Journal of Contemporary African Studies* 24 (2): 229–47.

Zakaria, Fareed. 1997. "The Rise of Illiberal Democracy." *Foreign Affairs* 76 (6): 22–41.

———. 2007. *The Future of Freedom: Illiberal Democracy at Home and Abroad*. Rev. ed. New York: Norton.

Zullo, Claude. 2003. "Georgia's Rose Revolution Rooted in Law." *Central Asia-Caucasus Institute Analyst*, December 3. Available at www.cacianalyst.org/newsite. Accessed June 7, 2007.

Contributors

Jason Brownlee is an assistant professor of government at the University of Texas at Austin. He is the author of *Authoritarianism in an Age of Democratization* (2007) and has published articles in the *Journal of Democracy* and *World Politics,* among other journals. Professor Brownlee researches and writes on the politics of hereditary succession and the history of American nation-building attempts.

Valerie J. Bunce is professor of government and the Aaron Binenkorb Chair of International Studies at Cornell University. Since the collapse of Communism, her research has focused primarily on nationalism, state-building, and state dissolution; democratic transitions; and peace-making after internal wars. She is coauthor of a book with Sharon Wolchik on American democracy promotion and electoral change in post-Communist Europe and Eurasia.

Larry Diamond is a senior fellow at the Hoover Institution, co-editor of the *Journal of Democracy,* and co-director of the International Forum for Democratic Studies of the National Endowment for Democracy. He is also professor of political science and sociology (by courtesy) and coordinator of the Democracy Program of the Center on Democracy, Development, and the Rule of Law at Stanford University. He is the author of *The Spirit of Democracy: The Struggle to Build Free Societies throughout the World* (2008), *Squandered Victory: The American Occupation and the Bungled Effort to Bring Democracy to Iraq* (2005), and *Developing Democracy: Toward Consolidation* (1999). In addition, he has edited or co-edited more than 30 books on democratic development around the world, including studies of Nigeria, Korea, Greater China, and the Middle East, and has advised many governmental and nongovernmental organizations. During the first three months of 2004, he served as a senior advisor to the Coalition Provisional Authority in Iraq.

Axel Hadenius is professor of political science at Lund University, Sweden. His main research interests are international democratization and state administrative capacity. He is the author of *Democracy and Development* (1992) and *Institutions and Democratic Citizenship* (2001).

Jonathan Hartlyn is professor of political science at the University of North Carolina at Chapel Hill, where he has served as department chair and director of the Institute of Latin American Studies. He is the coauthor of *Latin America in the Twenty-First Century: Toward a New Socio-Political Matrix* (2003), and author of *The Struggle for Democratic Politics in the Dominican Republic* (1998) and *The Politics of Coalition Rule in Colombia* (1988). He is also the coauthor of "Democracy in Latin America since 1930" (with Arturo Valenzuela) in *The Cambridge History of Latin America*, Vol. 6, Part 2 (1994).

Marc M. Howard is associate professor of government at Georgetown University. His research focuses on a variety of topics related to democracy and democratization, including civil society, citizenship, hybrid regimes, right-wing extremism, and public opinion. In addition to numerous journal articles, he is the author of *The Weakness of Civil Society in Post-Communist Europe* (2003) and *Varieties of Citizenship in the European Union* (forthcoming).

Staffan I. Lindberg is assistant professor of political science and African studies at the University of Florida. His dissertation won APSA's Juan Linz Award for the best dissertation in 2005. He is the author of *Democracy and Elections in Africa* (2006), and his articles on women's representation, political clientelism, voting behavior, party and electoral systems, and the legislature and executive-legislative relationships have appeared in the *Journal of Politics, Political Science Quarterly, Electoral Studies, Studies in International Comparative Development, Journal of Democracy, Government and Opposition, Journal of Modern African Studies,* and *Democratization*. He is the co-principal investigator for a five-year consortium research program, "The State, Politics and Power in Africa," which involves six other institutions from Europe and Africa.

Ellen Lust-Okar is associate professor of political science and chair of the Council on Middle East Studies, Yale University. Her research examines authoritarian politics, with an emphasis on the Arab world. She is the author of *Structuring Conflict in the Arab World* (2005) and co-editor of *Political Participation in the Middle East and North Africa* (forthcoming), as well as various journal articles and book chapters. Her current work focuses on the politics of elections in the Arab world.

Jennifer L. McCoy is professor of political science at Georgia State University and director of the Americas Program at the Carter Center in Atlanta. From 1988 to 1998, she also served as a consultant and senior associate of the Carter Center and from 1994 as senior associate of the Policy Research Center at Georgia State University. Her areas of expertise include democratization in Latin America, the role of international actors in mediating processes of democratization, and the emergence of global electoral rights and anti-corruption norms. She is editor of and contributor to *The Unraveling of Representative Democracy in Venezuela* (with David Myers; 2004) and author of *Political Learning and Redemocratization in Latin America: Do Politicians Learn from Political Crises?* (2000) and *Venezuelan Democracy under Stress* (1995). Her articles have appeared in journals such as *World Politics, International Politics, Latin American Research Review, Journal of Inter-American Studies and World Affairs, Journal of Developing Societies, Journal of Democracy, North-South, Hemisphere*, and *Current History.*

Bryon Moraski is associate professor of political science at the University of Florida. He is the author of *Elections by Design: Parties and Patronage in Russia's Regions* (2006) and has published articles in *American Journal of Political Science, Democratization, Europe-Asia Studies, Government and Opposition, Journal of Communist Studies and Transition Politics, Journal of Elections, Public Opinion and Parties, Journal of Politics*, and *Slavic Review*. His research focuses on the relationship between political institutions and political behavior, primarily in Russia and Eastern Europe. It includes relations among branches of government, the politics of institutional choice, and the influence of short-term electoral incentives on the prospects for democratic consolidation.

Pippa Norris is the McGuire Lecturer in Comparative Politics at the John F. Kennedy School of Government, Harvard University. Her work compares democracy, elections and public opinion, political communications, and gender politics in many countries worldwide. Her books include *A Virtuous Circle* (2000), *Digital Divide* (2001), *Democratic Phoenix* (2002), *Rising Tide* (with Ronald Inglehart; 2003), *Electoral Engineering* (2004), *Sacred and Secular* (with Ronald Inglehart; 2004, winner of the Virginia Hodgkinson prize), and *Radical Right* (2005). Her most recent books are *Driving Democracy: Do*

Power-Sharing Institutions Work? (2008) and an edited volume, *Making Democracy Deliver: Governance for Human Development.*

Lise Rakner is a senior research fellow and political scientist at Bergen University in Norway. She researches and analyzes policy related to Southern and Eastern Africa. Thematically, her work has focused on the issues of democratization and human rights, economic reform, taxation, institutional change, and international aid. Her current research concerns electoral administration and party developments in sub-Saharan Africa and more generally the relationship between political and economic processes of reform, accountability, and the development of political institutions. She has consulted for NORAD, SIDA, DFID, the World Bank, and the Norwegian Ministry of Foreign Affairs.

Philip G. Roessler is the Andrew Mellon Post-Doctoral Fellow in Comparative Government at the University of Oxford. His research centers on democratization and hybrid regimes, civil war, and African politics. He has published articles in the *American Journal of Political Science* and *Comparative Politics.* He writes on strategies of regime control and civil war onset in Africa based on extensive field research in Darfur, Sudan, and systematic analysis of other conflicts in the region.

Andreas Schedler is professor of political science at Centro de Investigación y Docencia Económicas (CIDE) in Mexico City. He is editor of *The Dynamics of Unfree Competition* (2006) and co-editor with Larry Diamond and Marc F. Plattner of *The Self-Restraining State: Power and Accountability in New Democracies* (1999). He has conducted research on democratization and electoral governance.

Jan Teorell is associate professor of political science at Lund University. He has been a visiting scholar at the Center for Basic Research in the Social Sciences, Harvard University, and at the Contemporary Europe Research Center, Melbourne University, Australia. In 2004–2006, he served as project coordinator at the Quality of Government Institute, Göteborg University. His current research interests include political methodology and comparative politics, particularly political participation, public opinion, corruption, and comparative democratization.

Nicolas van de Walle is the Jack S. Knight Professor of International Studies, associate dean for International Studies in the College of Arts and Sciences, and director of the Mario Einaudi Center for International Studies, all at Cornell University. He is also a nonresident fellow at the Center for Global Development in Washington, DC. He has published widely on democratization issues as well as on the politics of economic reform in Africa and on the effectiveness of foreign aid. His most recent book is *Overcoming Stagnation in Aid-Dependent Countries* (2005).

Sharon L. Wolchik is professor of political science and international affairs at George Washington University. She is the author of *Czechoslovakia in Transition: Politics, Economics, and Society* (1991) and co-editor of *Ukraine: The Search for a National Identity* (1999); *Women and Democracy: Latin America and Central and Eastern Europe* (1998); *The Social Legacy of Communism* (1994); *Women, State and Party in Eastern Europe* (1985); and *Foreign and Domestic Policy in Eastern Europe in the 1980s* (1983). She is currently researching the role of women in the transition to post-Communist rule in Central and Eastern Europe, as well as on ethnic issues in post-Communist societies, and the development of party systems and other aspects of politics in the Czech and Slovak Republics.

Index